W0114396

RETRIBUTION

ALSO BY JONATHAN KARL

Tired of Winning

Betrayal

Front Row at the Trump Show

The Right to Bear Arms

RETRIBUTION

DONALD TRUMP AND THE CAMPAIGN THAT CHANGED AMERICA

JONATHAN KARL

DUTTON

DUTTON

An imprint of Penguin Random House LLC
1745 Broadway, New York, NY 10019
penguinrandomhouse.com

Library of Congress Cataloging-in-Publication Data has been applied for.

ISBN 9798217047000 (hardcover)
ISBN 9798217047017 (ebook)

Printed in the United States of America
2nd Printing

The authorized representative in the EU for product safety and compliance is Penguin Random House Ireland, Morrison Chambers, 32 Nassau Street, Dublin D02 YH68, Ireland, https://eu-contact.penguin.ie.

For Maria

CONTENTS

RETRIBUTION

INTRODUCTION

Dead tired and losing my voice, I decided to make a quick call before lying down for the first time in more than twenty-four hours.

The phone rang once, and then it rang a second time. I expected it would go to voicemail.

It was 7:30 a.m. on November 6, 2024, the morning after the election. I had been up all night tracking the results live for ABC News and had just gotten back to my hotel room after discussing Donald Trump's victory on *Good Morning America.* A historic victory, and one I had not seen coming. I had spent much of the previous four years reporting on Trump's efforts to overturn the last election, his lonely exit from the White House, his legal travails, and the dire warnings from so many people who had been close to him about what would happen if he ever returned to power.

And now, despite it all, Trump had won—and won big. By any objective measure, his victory was stunning. He swept all seven battleground states. He made inroads into some of the most reliably Democratic cities in the country—San Francisco, Chicago, New

York—and performed better with nonwhite voters than any Republican presidential candidate in decades. It wasn't a landslide. His margin of victory in the Electoral College ranked forty-fourth out of sixty total US presidential elections, well behind Ronald Reagan's in 1980 and 1984 and Barack Obama's in 2008. But he had achieved something no Republican presidential nominee had in two decades: He won the popular vote.

With Trump now heading back to the White House, I figured I would call him and leave a voicemail message acknowledging his win and congratulating him on his victory. Thanks to American democracy, the man I had described as a threat to American democracy would soon be the forty-seventh president of the United States.

The phone rang a third time.

I've covered every presidential election since 1992, and never before had it occurred to me to call a president-elect hours after the votes were tallied. But Trump and I had been talking quite regularly during the final months of the campaign. In fact, we had talked the previous afternoon, on Election Day. The ever-confident Trump had seemed uncharacteristically unsure about the outcome.

"I don't know. I can't read it," he told me a few hours after he'd voted and before the first votes were counted. "We have a lot of enthusiasm, but I cannot read it, and I don't think anybody can read it."

I had made my first call to Trump's cell phone in July, the morning after a would-be assassin had tried to kill him in Butler, Pennsylvania. By the time the fall campaign was underway, I was talking to him every few days. Our relationship had grown contentious in recent years—he'd labeled me "a third-rate reporter," called me "a real scumbag," and declared "you will never make it"—but as Election Day approached, he almost always answered my calls, especially early in the morning or late at night. If he didn't pick up, I'd leave a message, and occasionally he'd call back.

I had also spoken to Hunter Biden on Election Day. "The stakes are so incredibly high," he told me.

The stakes were high for the country, of course, but also for Hunter himself. He had already been convicted on gun charges and pleaded guilty to tax evasion; he would likely be sentenced to prison before the end of the year. A Trump victory could very well unleash on his family a Justice Department hell-bent on retribution—and annihilate his father's legacy.

Joe Biden launched his successful campaign for president in 2019 to fight for the "soul of this nation." While Biden was no longer on the ballot, a Trump return to the White House would mean that Biden had fully lost that fight—and lost it badly. The eighty-one-year-old man's decision to run for reelection in the first place was already considered a catastrophic error by Democrats across the country.

Even so, I told Hunter I thought the stakes were higher for Trump. If he won the election, he would become one of the most powerful presidents in American history and set the direction of the Republican Party—and possibly the country—for a generation. If he lost, he could spend the rest of his life trying to stay out of prison.

"I sure hope it's the latter," Hunter said with a nervous laugh.

The phone rang a fourth time.

"Hello."

Trump's voice was hoarse. It sounded like I had just woken him up.

"Mr. President-Elect, it's Jonathan Karl," I said. "I just wanted to call to say congratulations."

"On what, Jonathan?"

The exhausted president-elect wanted to hear more. A simple

"congratulations" would not suffice; he needed to hear me describe out loud what he had accomplished. The exchange reminded me of a scene from the television series *Breaking Bad*, in which the main character, a drug dealer played by Bryan Cranston, annihilates his enemies, consolidates his power, and makes a demand of another dealer: "Say. My. Name."

"On what, Jonathan?" Trump asked a second time.

The man had survived two assassination attempts. He had survived the impeachments, the indictments, and the convictions. He had survived his 2020 election defeat, and he had survived his own disgraceful attempts to overturn it. Those indictments would quickly evaporate, and thanks to a recent Supreme Court decision outlining the broad scope of presidential immunity, he'd have wide latitude to operate as president without fear of future legal troubles. The very elites who had mocked him, snubbed him, and tried to ostracize him would soon be making pilgrimages to see him at Mar-a-Lago. He wasn't just coming back; he was coming back stronger than ever. He was coming back with a vengeance.

"You tell me what," Trump demanded.

During the closing weeks of his campaign, Trump had vowed retribution against his domestic enemies and America's allies around the world. He had promised mass deportations of millions of undocumented immigrants. He had pledged to impose global tariffs that economists warned would tank the economy. He had mused about shooting journalists. His former chief of staff had called him a fascist. Our world was about to change. But at this moment, there was only one answer to Trump's question:

"On the greatest comeback victory in the history of American politics."

CHAPTER ONE

FELON AND FRONT-RUNNER

The day after Donald Trump won the Iowa caucuses in January 2024, the insurance company Allianz published a so-called Risk Barometer that warned of growing political unrest around the globe. "We have an increasing detachment of the political elite from the working class and the people that actually go to work every day," said Oliver Bäte, the company's CEO. "And that, I see as the number one risk for our societies."[1]

The Risk Barometer didn't get much attention outside the business world, but it described precisely the conditions—*the detachment of the political elite from the people who actually go to work every day*—that made Donald Trump's improbable return to power possible.

After his lonely departure from the White House in 2021, Trump was detested by elites of all kinds—in the world of politics, yes, but also in business, law, academia, and media. Large corporations had refused to donate to candidates who had supported him. Major law firms had refused to represent him. Big tech companies had banned him from their social media platforms. Many of the people who served in his own administration had abandoned him, some darkly warning that he must never be allowed to return to power.

Hatred of those elites quickly became the driving force of Trump's 2024 campaign. He told his supporters that their problems and frustrations were caused by those same elites who had denounced him, had investigated him, and were now prosecuting him. The more he was attacked—by powerful figures in law, politics, and the media—the stronger his connection with the people who felt let down by those powerful figures grew. If voters returned him to power, he promised he would root out not just his own enemies but the enemies of ordinary, working-class Americans as well.

"For those who have been wronged and betrayed," he declared at a March 2023 rally in Waco, Texas, "I am your retribution."[2]

By mid-April 2024, Trump had vanquished all his rivals in what had become one of the most lopsided, contested presidential primaries in American political history. More than thirty states had voted, and Trump had won all but one of them: Vermont, arguably the most liberal state in the country, had gone for former South Carolina Governor Nikki Haley. His opponents had high profiles, and several of them were very well funded, but they had all dropped out by the first week of March. And unlike in 2016 and 2020, Trump also consistently led his likely Democratic opponent in the polls—and he had for months.

Politically, he had never been stronger.

Nevertheless, Trump was angry when he stood before the cameras on April 18, 2024—because he was not a free man. For the third day that week, he had been ordered to sit in a New York courtroom where he would have to relive an embarrassing and decades-old chapter of his life that had come back to haunt him. The jury his lawyers had worked to select that week would decide the fate of the first former president of the United States in history to be charged with a felony—or thirty-four felonies, to be precise.

On the days the court was in session, Trump wasn't allowed to travel around the country to campaign. He couldn't play golf. He couldn't even leave the confines of the New York courthouse at 100 Centre Street in lower Manhattan. Aides and Secret Service agents would make a daily lunch delivery to his grimy holding room, giving him some fast food to eat during the court's brief midday break.

To make matters worse, the decrepit old courthouse had a notoriously bad heating and air-conditioning system. The place was frigid. Shortly after the court reconvened for the third day of jury selection, Judge Juan Merchan issued an apology from the bench. "First, jurors, I want to apologize that it's chilly in here," he said. "We're doing what we can to control the temperature, but it seems like it's one extreme or the other. So, bear with us as we try to work that out."

Once the day's proceedings ended, Trump exited the courtroom and turned left down a dark hallway. With his entourage of lawyers and advisors lingering near the entrance to the courtroom, he walked along the worn tile floor and stopped to speak to a small group of reporters and a single television camera shared by the networks on the other side of a security barrier. The reporters were far enough away that he had to raise his voice, almost to the point of shouting, to be heard, his words echoing along the courthouse's marble walls.

"I'm sitting here for days now, from morning till night, in that freezing room," Trump complained.[3] Looking directly into the camera, he said he should be out campaigning, not forced to defend himself against charges brought by Manhattan's Democratic district attorney.

"I'm supposed to be in Georgia," he said, his voice straining to reach the microphone on the other side of the metal bike-rack barricade. "I'm supposed to be in North Carolina, South Carolina. I'm supposed to be in a lot of different places campaigning, but I've been here all day on a trial that really is a very unfair trial."

In reality, though, Trump hadn't campaigned much in the weeks before the trial began. With his Republican rivals vanquished, the presumptive GOP nominee was spending as much time selling Trump-branded products as he was campaigning. A few weeks after winning the New Hampshire primary, for example, he helped launch a line of Trump "Never Surrender" sneakers—bright gold and just $399 a pair![4] And not long after Nikki Haley, his last remaining rival for the Republican nomination, dropped out, he kicked off a joint venture with country music singer Lee Greenwood selling "God Bless the USA Bibles" for $59.99 the week before Easter. It was, according to the marketing materials, "the only Bible endorsed by President Trump!"[5]*

The leading candidate for president of the United States hawking his wares like this was certainly a spectacle, but Trump was facing a serious cash crunch. He had been ordered to pay a $454 million judg-

*The Associated Press uncovered evidence these "God Bless the USA Bibles" were actually made in China. In October 2024, AP reported that 120,000 copies of the Trump-endorsed bibles had been shipped to the United States from the city of Hangzhou in eastern China. The estimated value of these made-in-China bibles was less than $3 a piece, a far cry from the $59.99 Trump was encouraging his supporters to pay for them. In a 2025 financial disclosure, the White House revealed that Trump made $1.3 million off sales of these bibles in 2024.

ment after losing a civil fraud case earlier that year, and he had been hit with a separate $88 million bill after being found liable for sexually abusing and damaging the reputation of a woman named E. Jean Carroll.

Now Trump had no choice but to spend four days a week (the court was not in session on Wednesdays) in a New York courtroom for the duration of his criminal trial, which was expected to last about two months. Over the course of the first three days, 190 potential jurors had been questioned, but a complete jury—including six alternates—had still not been chosen.

Although the trial hadn't really started, the once-and-future president had already endured multiple indignities. The seventeen-story courthouse was not only cold; it was constantly under construction, with scaffolding surrounding its exterior for the entire trial. At the same time, the building seemingly hadn't been renovated since it opened in 1941. The place was filthy, and parts of the courtroom were held together with duct tape. "DANGER" signs in the hallways warned that asbestos removal was underway. There was a plastic device filled with bait and poison just outside the main entrance: a trap to capture and kill rats.

The court proceedings themselves would bring a series of embarrassments to Trump. Stormy Daniels, the porn actress at the center of the case, testified, in rather graphic detail, that she'd had sex with Trump just four months after his wife, Melania, had given birth to their son, Barron. She would also testify, in Trump's presence, that he had encouraged her to spank him with a rolled-up magazine that featured an article praising him as a business genius. Her deposition led Trump to audibly curse from his seat at the defense table, prompting Judge Merchan to call Trump's lead counsel, Todd Blanche, to the bench for an admonishment. Blanche needed to keep his client under control.

Even the mundane process of selecting the jury included its share of humiliation. As prospective jurors were questioned, Trump's lawyers highlighted the harsh things some of them had posted about him on social media. One juror apologized after the former president's counsel read an old social media post of hers aloud: "I wouldn't believe Trump if his tongue were notarized."

As both prosecutors and defense lawyers know, an entire case can be won or lost during the jury selection process, a reality Trump seemed keenly aware of as he sized up each person who could potentially control his fate.

On the final day of jury selection, a prospective juror asked to skip her questioning, telling the lawyers she was "sure" she'd be disqualified. Before she was asked any questions, she told the court to look at page 3 of the written questionnaire she, like all prospective jurors, had been asked to fill out. "I served time in Massachusetts," she said. "I wrote down all my crimes—and I am about to cry, sorry. It was over ten years ago, and you guys keep calling me back for jury [duty]. I am pretty sure I shouldn't be here."

Wiping away tears, she told the court her story of being arrested and convicted on drug-related charges while working as a dental hygienist. She served her time, and although she couldn't return to her previous job because of her criminal record, she found work managing a gym and began to rebuild her life. But she lost friends. And she stopped staying in touch with two cousins who worked for the federal government—keeping their calls "short and sweet," she said—

because she worried that their jobs meant they couldn't be associated with a felon.

Donald Trump, seated just ten feet away from the woman, watched intently as she spoke.

"I am a firm believer that when people do something, they should be accountable for their actions, and it is probably because of what I went through," the woman said. "I believe in the Constitution, so yes, I believe in all of this and I will be impartial to everything."

But the former dental hygienist wouldn't be serving on this jury. She was dismissed after Judge Merchan ruled that paperwork issues related to her decade-old felony conviction rendered her ineligible. As she left the courtroom, she turned to Trump and his lawyers and said, "Good luck."

This little, long-forgotten episode at the outset of Trump's criminal trial served as a vivid reminder that, for most Americans, a felony conviction is something that turns your life upside down. Even after you serve your punishment, being a convict can cost you your job, your friends, and, in some circumstances, even your ability to serve on a jury.

Manhattan District Attorney Alvin Bragg's case was the first—and, as it turned out, only—criminal case against Donald Trump to go to trial. But for Trump's opponents who were hoping to see the former president be held accountable for his actions, Bragg's was the last case they wanted to go forward. On the long list of Trump's alleged misdeeds, the allegations underlying the Manhattan case seemed downright trivial.

Consider the facts: Trump's one-time lawyer and fixer Michael

Cohen paid $130,000 to Stormy Daniels shortly before the 2016 election to keep her from speaking publicly about a sexual encounter she claimed she had with Trump years earlier. But Trump wasn't charged for paying the hush money itself; he was charged over how he'd accounted for it. Prosecutors alleged Trump had concealed the payments, falsely labeling them in his business records as legal expenses rather than reimbursements to his lawyer for the nondisclosure agreement.

As Trump put it, he was stuck in a Manhattan courtroom for two months over bookkeeping. "A legal expense is a legal expense. It's marked down in the book, quote—'legal expense,'" Trump said. "It's perfectly marked down."

Bragg and his team relied on an unorthodox legal theory, indicting the former president on felony charges—not misdemeanors—by arguing the alleged falsification of business records was in service of another crime.[6] That second crime, according to Bragg, was the violation of a rarely used state election law that prohibits politicians from using "unlawful means" to influence an election. Trump bought Stormy Daniels's silence, Bragg argued, to protect himself from another embarrassing story in the wake of the leaked *Access Hollywood* tape in 2016, in which he was heard boasting that he could get his way with beautiful women because he is famous. "When you're a star, they let you do it. You can do anything," he said to Billy Bush in the recording that threatened to destroy his 2016 campaign. "Grab 'em by the pussy. You can do anything."

So . . . the guy who had been indicted in two separate federal cases for allegedly pilfering America's most sensitive national security secrets and unleashing a mob on the US Capitol building in an effort to overturn an election was on trial for mislabeling hush-money payments to a porn star. He had been indicted for far more serious federal crimes by special counsel Jack Smith and District Attorney Fani Willis in Fulton County, Georgia, but Trump's legal team had successfully delayed those proceedings, making it unlikely they would go to trial anytime soon.

The allegations in the New York case may have been true—and the jury ultimately found them to be—but the relatively trivial and convoluted charges made it easy for Trump to portray himself as the victim of a political prosecution. Unable to join the fawning crowds of his supporters at rallies, Trump made the "witch hunt" against him the central message of his campaign while the trial was underway.

For those weeks in April and May 2024, Trump brought the campaign to the criminal court building at 100 Centre Street in Manhattan. The dark hallway outside his courtroom became his rally stage.

A steady stream of Republican politicians made the pilgrimage to New York to prove their loyalty to Trump by denouncing the trial. They would come in and sit on the uncomfortable wooden benches beside the defense table, awkwardly scrolling on their phones once the testimony began. Doug Burgum and Vivek Ramaswamy, two of Trump's former rivals for the Republican nomination, attended, as did several senators, including his future vice president, JD Vance. Kash Patel, his future choice to run the FBI; Pam Bondi, his future attorney general; and Susie Wiles, his future chief of staff, also made the trek.

Senator Ted Cruz was one of the few high-profile Trump allies who didn't show up at the courthouse, but his name was invoked during testimony by Trump's former aide and spokesperson Hope Hicks. Hicks recounted conversations Trump had with David Pecker, the owner of the *National Enquirer*, after the tabloid had published a series of laughably unserious and false articles targeting Trump's Republican rivals in the 2016 presidential primary, including a story claiming that Cruz's father was involved in the assassination of President John F. Kennedy.

"Mr. Trump was just congratulating him on the great reporting," Hicks recalled. She said Trump told Pecker, "This is Pulitzer-worthy!"

The Republicans who did attend the proceedings soon began to follow the same routine. They would sit quietly on the benches behind the defense table, making sure Trump saw them as he walked into the court. And after the proceedings ended, they would rush to the cameras outside to denounce the prosecutors, the judge, and the witnesses—saying all the things Trump himself could not due to the limited gag order Judge Merchan had imposed on him.

Then-Senator JD Vance described his experience in a post on X. "We started in Trump Tower with a beautiful view of Central Park," he wrote. "Then you come to a dingy courthouse with people like Alvin Bragg. They prevent his supporters from getting too close to the court house, and they prevent his friends from standing too close to him. The president is expected to sit here for six weeks to listen to the Michael Cohens of the world."

He added, "I'm now convinced the main goal of this trial is psychological torture."[7]

The trial had already been underway for about a month when I made the journey to the courthouse on May 14 to witness the spectacle for myself. Some thirty years earlier, I had been dispatched there by an editor when I was a young reporter for the *New York Post.* It was hard to believe that Donald Trump was now stuck in the same place. I had covered him in all his glory over the years: at Trump Tower, at his campaign rallies, and in the White House. I simply couldn't imagine him sitting in that dingy criminal court building. I needed to see it in person.

After making my way past the barricades surrounding the courthouse and through the security checkpoints outside the building and in the lobby, I rode a creaky elevator up to the fifteenth floor, where I went through one more round of security and walked down the hall into a large, wood-paneled courtroom with harsh fluorescent lights. Once inside, I took my seat as one of the sixty-two members of the press allowed to observe the day's proceedings.

Reporters, legal analysts, and several cable news anchors filled five rows of uncomfortable wooden benches; along with the four sketch artists, the journalists were the first people to enter the room. The prosecutors eventually walked in through a side entrance and took their places, followed by the court stenographers. Finally, it was Trump's turn.

Preceded by two Secret Service agents, Trump walked in through the doors in the rear of the courtroom. Like everyone else in attendance, I watched intently as he strolled down the center aisle, turning his head slightly from side to side, surveying the members of the news media who would be witnessing the proceedings that day and making eye contact with those he recognized. As Trump walked down the aisle, he appeared to be making a mental note of who was there. With no television cameras allowed, his only audience for the next few hours would be those of us in the courtroom and another group of reporters sitting in an overflow room watching a closed-circuit video feed of the proceedings. When Trump spotted me in the third row, he smirked and shook his head, seemingly saying, "Oh great, you're here, too."

Trump usually made that entrance into the courtroom a few times a day: once in the morning, once after the lunch break, and once after the afternoon break. He was most animated during those walks down the aisle, when all eyes were on him. He usually had a large entourage of lawyers and guests following behind him. On this day, it included his son Eric and Eric's wife, Lara; former rivals Ramaswamy and Burgum; legal advisors Boris Epshteyn and Alina Habba; and several members of Congress. House Speaker Mike Johnson had kicked off the day with a press conference outside the courthouse, denouncing what he called "a sham of a trial."

When Judge Merchan walked in—"All rise!"—Trump had to stand just like the rest of us. The judge then summoned the members of the jury, who walked right in front of Trump and the defense table on their way to the jury box. Like several other reporters in the room, I had brought a small pair of binoculars, allowing me to get a closer look at the expressions of the jurors and of Trump. The former president's back was to those of us in the gallery, but there was a screen in the front of the courtroom streaming a live, closed-circuit video feed of the defense table.

My first day in the courtroom featured the testimony of the prosecution's star witness, Trump's one-time fixer Michael Cohen.

Cohen had been the ultimate Trump loyalist, defending him no matter the cost and bullying anybody who would question his boss.

In fact, when I had interviewed Trump a decade earlier—more than a year before he launched his first presidential bid—Cohen had threatened my young producer, Jordyn Phelps, promising to knock over our camera if I asked any questions Cohen didn't like. Cohen had once famously said that he would do anything for Trump, even take a bullet for him.[8] But those days were long gone. Now he was a Trump turncoat, witness for the prosecution.

As far as I could tell, Trump didn't make eye contact with Cohen once during his former fixer's two full days on the witness stand. In fact, Trump's eyes were closed for long periods of time. He seemed intent on sending Cohen a message: He didn't care what he had to say, and didn't want to acknowledge his presence.

"Is he sleeping?" I wrote in my notes as Cohen testified. "Or is he just sending a message to Cohen that his testimony isn't worth opening his eyes for?"

Cohen had practically worshipped Trump throughout the ten years he worked for him. His entire sense of self-worth seemed to be tied to his close proximity to the business mogul. He had craved his approval. Since turning on Trump, Cohen was still every bit as obsessed with him, maybe even more so, but the nature of the relationship had changed. Cohen was constantly attacking Trump on social media and on a podcast he had started, branding him a "dictator douchebag" and a "Cheeto-dusted cartoon villain," who should be in prison. He even sold anti-Trump merchandise, including a T-shirt depicting the former president in an orange jumpsuit behind bars.

The insults were so persistent and over-the-top, in fact, that Cohen now appeared to be craving something deeper than Trump's approval. He hungered for evidence that he was hurting Trump as much as he believed Trump had hurt him. And now, during Cohen's big moment of defiance, Trump was pretending he didn't even know who Cohen was.

Trump wasn't so passive outside the courtroom. In the days and weeks leading up to the trial, he used his social media platform to attack Cohen, the prosecutors, the judge, and even the judge's daughter. "JUDGE JUAN MERCHAN IS TOTALLY COMPROMISED, AND SHOULD BE REMOVED FROM THIS TRUMP NON-CASE IMMEDIATELY," he posted on Truth Social in late March. "HIS DAUGHTER, LOREN, IS A RABID TRUMP HATER, WHO HAS ADMITTED TO HAVING CONVERSATIONS WITH HER FATHER ABOUT ME."[9]

Concerned about threats against the court and his family—as well as witness intimidation—Judge Merchan imposed that limited gag order on the former president. He could still criticize the judge and Alvin Bragg, but other members of the court, prosecution team, and potential witnesses were off-limits. But the $1,000 fine imposed for each violation of the gag order was hardly enough to change Trump's behavior. Eventually, the exasperated judge said he would be forced to put Trump in a jail cell if he continued to disobey the court's directives.

"Mr. Trump, it's important to understand that the last thing I want to do is put you in jail. You are the former president of the United States, and possibly the next president as well," Judge Merchan said as Trump sat at the defense table flanked by his lawyers. "As much as I do not want to impose a jail sanction . . . I will, if necessary and appropriate."

When he came over to the camera in the hall outside the courtroom, Trump complained bitterly about the gag order and said he was willing to be locked up to speak out. "Frankly, you know what, our Constitution is much more important than jail," Trump said. "It's not even close. I'll do that sacrifice any day."

Judge Merchan's threat was taken seriously by Trump's legal

team—and the Secret Service, which held meetings to plan for how agents would handle Trump being sent to short-term confinement. Never before had the Secret Service had to consider how it would protect somebody in jail.

"We had serious conversations about it, and I at one point told him, he and I might be—getting a lot closer," Sean Curran, the lead agent on Trump's security detail, later recalled. "Look, if it came to it, I'd be sitting right next to him. That's how much I care for him. That's how much I felt that he deserved the level of protection that any of our protectees should get. There's nothing I would have not done for him."

The Secret Service also had to consider the possibility that Trump would serve a long-term prison sentence if he had been convicted in either of the federal cases.

"We would have had to probably own a certain portion of that facility," Curran later said. "It's still a law, you know, whether someone is in prison or not. The law still dictates that we have to protect them."[10]

Trump's reaction to Merchan's threat to impose "a jail sanction" if he violated the gag order again was to outsource his attacks on witnesses and other court personnel to the parade of guests who accompanied him to the trial every day. Several of them, including Vance, made the attacks on social media and at press conferences outside the courthouse. Unlike Trump, his supporters were not bound by a gag order.

But on the morning before Stormy Daniels took the stand, Trump couldn't hold back. At about 7:30 a.m., he posted a tirade on Truth Social expressing his outrage about the upcoming witness without mentioning her by name. He called Judge Merchan "CROOKED &

HIGHLY CONFLICTED," adding, "No Judge has ever run a trial in such a biased and partisan way."[11]

As Trump's motorcade was preparing to make its way from Trump Tower to the courthouse, the former president's top lawyer, Todd Blanche, placed an urgent call to Dan Scavino, the only person other than Trump who had direct access to Trump's social media accounts. Blanche told him he had just seen the Truth Social post complaining about the next witness and that it must be taken down immediately. Scavino balked, saying he didn't want to delete it before talking to Trump, who was currently tied up doing a radio interview. But Blanche insisted the post needed to be deleted immediately—and that if it wasn't, Trump was at risk of being sent to jail by Judge Merchan. Scavino relented and deleted it—something that almost never happened with Trump's social media posts, no matter how controversial.

When Blanche saw Trump a short while later, he told him about forcing Scavino to delete the Truth Social post and explained that, whether or not Trump's words were actual witness tampering, they came right up to the line. Judge Merchan would almost certainly see Trump's words as another violation of the gag order, Blanche said, adding that the post wasn't worth the risk of getting sent to jail. Trump reluctantly agreed.

On May 21, the twentieth day of the trial, Trump was meeting with his legal team in his apartment on the sixty-sixth floor of Trump Tower when one of his Secret Service agents said that the former president would not be able to take the elevator down to the lobby. The problem: One of the elevators that went up to his apartment was out of service, leaving only one other elevator available. Putting the former president on the only working elevator, the Secret Service believed, represented a security threat. He would need to walk down instead.

So Trump—along with his personal assistant Walt Nauta, his legal team, and his top advisors—headed toward the stairwell. And the man who dislikes walking so much that he has been known to drive a golf cart onto the putting green trekked all the way down to the lobby from the third-highest floor in Trump Tower.* At one point, Nauta asked Trump if he wanted to take a break. After all, it was probably the longest walk Trump had taken for years. But no, Trump didn't want to take a break. In fact, he reached the lobby before his lawyers did.

Trump's team was rather amazed by the seventy-seven-year-old man's long journey down the stairwell. Someone suggested he tell reporters about the feat before entering the courtroom that day. He could point to the effort as an example of his own physical fitness relative to Joe Biden's. *Could you imagine Biden walking down all those stairs?* Trump, however, curtly dismissed the suggestion. Don't talk about this with anybody, he admonished. He didn't want the world to know that an elevator at Trump Tower had been out of service. And so Trump's remarkable journey down the stairwell was never mentioned again.

Well, it wasn't mentioned directly.

At the end of that day's proceedings, Trump went to his usual

*Fortunately for Trump, he had to walk down only fifty-six flights of stairs, because Trump Tower isn't actually as tall as the numbers on its floors suggest. When Trump built the place, he skipped ten numbers to make the upper residential floors seem higher than they really are.

position in front of the hallway camera to address the small group of reporters assembled there. "We appreciate you suffering with us. You've been with us for five weeks," Trump told the journalists. "We'll be resting pretty quickly, meaning resting the case. I won't be resting. I don't rest. I'd like to rest sometimes, but I don't get to rest."

I'd like to rest sometimes, but I don't get to rest.

Trump's words were entirely truthful—and literal. He really didn't get any rest that day. In fact, he'd hiked down more than fifty flights of stairs without stopping and then had to go right into court.

On May 28, Todd Blanche summed up the Trump team's defense. Although Trump had suggested he wanted to testify, the defense didn't call a single witness, focusing its argument primarily on the questionable credibility of the prosecution's witnesses. After all, this was a case that depended largely on the testimony of a porn actress, the owner of a supermarket tabloid newspaper, and Michael Cohen, who himself had been convicted for lying to Congress in another case.[12]

"Michael Cohen. He is the human embodiment of reasonable doubt," Blanche told the jury, noting that Cohen had lied to both houses of Congress, judges, federal investigators, and his own family. "He is literally like an MVP of liars. He lies constantly."

"Michael Cohen is the GLOAT," Blanche added. "He is literally the greatest liar of all time."

Once Blanche had finished, Judge Merchan announced jury deliberations would begin the following day. Trump would be required to show up as normal in the morning and remain at the courthouse while the jury deliberated. When he arrived the next day, he stopped at his familiar spot by the camera outside the courtroom and complained that the case was rigged. "Mother Teresa could not beat these charges," Trump said. "We'll see how we do. It's a very disgraceful situation."

Now, it's rather unlikely Mother Teresa would have ever found herself accused of falsifying records to conceal hush-money payments to a porn star, but Trump had some legitimate complaints about the case and about the motivation of the prosecutor, an elected Democrat. The jury was also drawn from a population that had voted against him in the last presidential election by overwhelming margins.

The second day of deliberations drew to a close around 4:15 p.m., and Trump and his lawyers returned to the courtroom expecting the jury and the defendant to be dismissed for the day. "At this time, I am going to excuse the jury at around 4:30," Judge Merchan announced.

As everyone in the courtroom waited for the fifteen minutes to pass before being sent home, Trump seemed to be in an uncharacteristically great mood. His three lawyers were chatting and smiling at the defense table. In the gallery, Trump legal advisors Boris Epshteyn and Alina Habba had an animated conversation with Eric Trump.

There was a reason for the good cheer coming from the Trump side. If the jury had not reached a verdict after two full days of deliberations, they believed the odds were in Trump's favor. The longer the jury deliberated, they thought, the more likely they would be unable to agree on a verdict. And a hung jury would mean no conviction.

As he waited at the defense table, Trump appeared happier than he had during the entire trial. ABC's Peter Charalambous was in the courtroom and watched Trump and Blanche lean toward each other, their shoulders touching, and laugh out loud. "Blanche is struggling to contain his laughter, leaning forward onto the table and covering his mouth," Peter wrote.

At 4:37 p.m., however, Judge Merchan shocked the court by saying he had just received a note from the jury asking for an extra thirty minutes to complete its paperwork. A verdict had been reached. "Please let there be no outbursts, no reactions of any kind when we take the verdict," Merchan told the court.

Suddenly, the laughter stopped. The mood at the defense table darkened.

The notes from Peter and Josh Einiger, a reporter with ABC's New York affiliate, captured the scene: "The sound of muted whispering in the room, reporters typing, the occasional cough. Thick, thick tension."

"It's dead quiet at this point," their notes continued. "We are just waiting. Even the sound of typing has slowed."

Trump and Blanche continued to speak intermittently as they awaited the jury's verdict, but the topic of the conversation had changed. There was no more laughter. The other two lawyers sitting with Trump at the defense table, Susan Necheles and Emil Bove, sat silently, staring straight ahead.

Shortly after 5 p.m., the six alternate jurors entered the courtroom and sat in the first row of the gallery. Then the twelve jurors walked in, passing right in front of Trump and the defense table, making no eye contact with the most famous defendant in the world. Once they took their seats in the juror box, Judge Merchan directed a question at juror 1, who was acting as the jury foreperson.

"Without telling me the verdict, has the jury, in fact, reached a verdict?" he asked.

"Yes, they have," the juror responded.

And with that, Merchan directed the court clerk to take the verdict from the jury foreperson.

"How say you to the first count of the indictment, charging Donald J. Trump with the crime of falsifying business records in the first degree, guilty or not guilty?"

"Guilty."

"How say you to count two?"

"Guilty."

And so it went for all thirty-four counts, as the muffled sound of cheers outside made its way into the courtroom. After the first few answers of "guilty," Trump started slowly shaking his head, staring forward. He didn't turn to look at the jury, and he said nothing as the guilty verdicts continued to roll in. But his anger was obvious when he stepped out into the hallway and walked up to the camera there for the very last time.

"The real verdict is going to be November 5th, by the people, and they know what happened here, and everybody knows what happened here," Trump said. "This was a rigged, disgraceful trial."

"I'm a very innocent man."

Many of Trump's critics had predicted that his electoral prospects would plummet if a jury found him guilty of a felony. That analysis turned out to be wildly wrong.

The conviction didn't change a thing in terms of Trump's standing with voters—other than maybe garnering him some additional sympathy. The politics surrounding the New York case may have also raised doubts in Americans' minds about the legitimacy of the far more serious federal cases involving Trump's handling of classified documents and his role in the January 6 assault on the US Capitol. Regardless, those cases were clearly not going to go to trial before the election.

But the guilty verdict in New York did clarify Trump's personal stakes in the election. He would either lose and spend the rest of his life trying to stay out of prison. Or he would win and return to the White House, vindicated, triumphant and ready to get retribution.

CHAPTER TWO

THE BRIDGE TO NOWHERE

From a cold, damp concrete prison cell deep inside Russia in late 2023, Alexei Navalny was paying close attention to political developments in America—and was disturbed by what he saw.

"Trump's agenda and plans look truly scary," the Russian opposition leader wrote to his friend, photographer Evgeny Feldman, on December 3, 2023. "And it's clear that if during the course of the campaign Biden's health fails, he can forget something etc, then Trump will become president. Surely that obvious thing must worry the Democrats?"[1]

Navalny's already lengthy sentence had recently been extended by nearly two decades. Prosecutors had hit him with a long list of charges—fraud, embezzlement, contempt of court, violation of parole—but the real reason he was being punished was that he was trying to build a democratic opposition movement in Russia. Russian President Vladimir Putin had banned Navalny's political party and, a few years earlier, allegedly ordered Russian security agents to poison him.

Now Navalny was locked up in Corrective Colony No. 6, or IK-6, a notorious prison camp on the outskirts of the Russian town of Melekhovo. The abuse he endured there was both physical and mental. Much of his time was spent in solitary confinement as punishment for violating trivial rules, such as improperly buttoning his uniform or washing his face at the wrong time.[2] When he was moved around the prison, an alarm would sound signaling the other prisoners to step back and turn away. Navalny was not allowed to speak to, or even make eye contact with, the other prisoners. Navalny himself described his captors' icy soullessness in a letter to a friend in Berlin months earlier. "If they're told to feed you caviar tomorrow, they'll feed you caviar," he wrote. "If they're told to strangle you in your cell, they'll strangle you."[3]

On Christmas Day 2023, the Russian government announced Navalny had been moved to an even more grueling penal colony: IK-3, also known as "Polar Wolf," in Siberia. According to former inmates, the prison was "devised to break the human spirit, by making survival depend on total and unconditional obedience to the will of guards."[4] Navalny was found dead under suspicious circumstances on February 16, 2024.

Shortly after Navalny's death, progressive *New York Times* political columnist Ezra Klein published an audio essay raising many of the same concerns as Navalny had.[5]

"I have this nightmare that Trump wins in 2024," he said, expressing doubts about Joe Biden's age and ability to defeat Donald Trump a second time. "And then in 2025 and 2026, out come the campaign tell-all books, and they're full of emails and WhatsApp messages between Biden staffers and Democratic leaders, where they're all saying to each other, 'This is a disaster, he's not going to win this, I can't bear to watch this speech, we're going to lose.' But they didn't say any of it publicly, they didn't do anything, because it was too dangerous for their careers, or too uncomfortable given their loyalty to Biden."

Klein—and Navalny—were right to express their concerns about Biden's age, and they were right that plenty of Democrats were terrified about the president's reelection prospects. In a February 2024 ABC News/Ipsos poll, a staggering 86 percent of respondents believed Biden was too old to serve another term—including 73 percent of *Democrats* surveyed.[6] The risks of nominating Biden again were seemingly obvious—to everyone except the president's inner circle and Biden himself.

"Folks, this is a big deal, this election," Biden told donors at a fundraiser in Massachusetts just two days after Navalny wrote his letter outlining concerns about the president. "If Trump wasn't running, I'm not sure I'd be running. But we cannot let him win, for the sake of the country."[7]

When he returned to Washington that night, Biden faced a group of reporters as he got off Air Force One. "Would you still be running for reelection if Trump wasn't running?" one shouted at him.

"I expect so," Biden replied. "But he is running. *I have to run*."

When Michigan Governor Gretchen Whitmer heard about what Biden said, she told people privately that his comments had saddened her. Biden, who often pointed out he was the only person who had defeated Trump in an election, seemed to be saying he was also the only who could beat him in 2024.

I have to run.

Whitmer believed Democrats had a deep bench of young leaders who could step up if Biden bowed out of the race, and who would have a better chance of winning. A recent poll had found her to be 10 points more popular than Biden in Michigan, a state Democrats would likely need to win to keep Trump out of the White House.[8]

In early 2024, an exasperated Whitmer wondered why Biden was running at all. She had been onstage with him four years earlier—right before he won Michigan's Democratic primary and sewed up his party's nomination—when he stood with some of the party's rising stars (in addition to Whitmer, Senators Cory Booker and Kamala Harris were onstage with Biden that night) and made what Whitmer believed was a promise to serve one term and then pass the torch to a new generation of Democrats.

"Look, I view myself as a bridge, not as anything else," Biden told the crowd. "There's an entire generation of leaders you saw stand behind me. They are the future of this country."[9]

They are the future of this country.

Biden had never explicitly promised to serve a single term, but many Democrats believed he had implied that was his plan. And now four years later, Biden seemed to be echoing Trump's words at the 2016 Republican convention, when he declared in his acceptance speech, "I alone can fix it." Several younger, popular Democratic leaders could have jumped into the race if Biden decided to pass the baton. Not just Whitmer but also Pennsylvania Governor Josh Shapiro, California Governor Gavin Newsom, Illinois Governor JB Pritzker, Kentucky Governor Andy Beshear, and Vice President Harris to name a few.

But none of them even hinted they would challenge Biden for the Democratic nomination, and several would-be primary opponents even joined his reelection bid as campaign chairs. Representative Dean Phillips of Minnesota, a relatively unknown but rising Democratic congressman with grave concerns about Biden's age and political prospects, tried to get ahold of Whitmer and Pritzker to see if they had any interest in mounting a campaign, and they wouldn't even take his calls.

As long as Biden decided to run, then the nomination was his. Any effort to take him on was understood to be a political suicide mission.

"It was a culture of fear," Phillips later told me. "[There was] a group that made it pretty clear what the consequences would be for anybody who would step out of line."

Failing to recruit a more high-profile Democrat to run, Phillips eventually launched a longshot bid of his own. So did Robert F. Kennedy Jr., who had a famous name but had become a political pariah to many Democrats, including many in his own family. Neither of them had a chance: The Democratic National Committee, at Biden's direction, rearranged the primary calendar to be maximally favorable to the president, and made clear that there would be no debates. Major donors were warned that supporting any Democratic challenger to Biden would result in being cut off not just from the White House but also from the party's congressional leadership. As the DNC's executive director declared in August 2022, months before the president even announced he was running for reelection: "We're with Biden. Period."[10]

Biden didn't announce his decision to run for a second term—arguably the most consequential decision of his presidency—until April 2023. And in my conversations with his inner circle, no one was able to recall a specific meeting or conversation among Biden's senior advisors when there was a serious discussion of whether or not he should run again.

"We never had a meeting on it," Bruce Reed, one of Biden's closest advisors in the White House, told me. "I think all of us always viewed that as up to him, and his main concern going into '24—as it was in 2020—was, What's the best way to stop Trump? That's what got him off the sidelines the first time. That's what kept him in the game the second time. And so, it had to be a personal decision, a family decision."

"My understanding is it was sort of a foregone conclusion," another senior official in Biden's inner circle later told me of Biden's reelection bid. "He was doing really well, the Democratic Party was totally behind him, and he was up for it and felt like he needed to finish the job."

Biden's advisors downplayed the obvious warning signs. His approval rating cratered as the country watched his administration botch the US military's withdrawal from Afghanistan in August 2021—resulting in thirteen dead service members and another forty-five wounded—and it never fully recovered. The rate of inflation eventually came down, but prices were on the whole 20 percent higher on Election Day 2024 than they were when Biden first took office. Even Democratic senators would privately admit to reporters after the election that the administration "utterly mismanaged" the southern border.[11]

But in the spring of 2023, Democrats were coming off a surprisingly successful showing in the 2022 midterms, polls showed more Americans viewing Biden favorably, and he had just delivered an energetic State of the Union address that had, for the moment, quelled intraparty concerns about his age.

And Biden had real legislative accomplishments, signing into law more sweeping—and expensive—pieces of legislation than any president since Lyndon Baines Johnson. The investments were staggering, especially a $1 trillion bipartisan infrastructure bill, the most ambitious such investment since the creation of the interstate highway system under President Dwight D. Eisenhower.

The way Biden's top advisors saw it, he'd had a great first two years and was at the top of his game. Perhaps most importantly, the family was behind him.

I had been speaking regularly with the president's son Hunter since the summer of 2023, trying to set up a television interview where he could respond to the serious legal charges he was facing and the allegations of wrongdoing being levied against him. And there was a lot to respond to.

House Republicans had made Hunter a central figure in their effort to impeach the president, focusing on allegations that he'd leveraged access to his father in overseas business deals for monetary gain. The lawmakers were never able to uncover a smoking gun directly tying Joe Biden to Hunter's work for energy companies in Ukraine and China, but former associates told the House Oversight Committee that Hunter was known to sell "an illusion of access" to his father.[12]

The discovery of Hunter's laptop computer just weeks before the 2020 election had also provided Republicans ample material to demonize both the younger and elder Biden. Hunter had been a crack addict, and the ugly details of his dependence were documented in the photographs and videos on the computer's hard drive of him posing provocatively in nothing but his underwear and a scarf, lying shirtless in bed with unknown women, sleeping with a crack pipe in his mouth.

Hunter described his addiction in brutal detail in his memoir, *Beautiful Things*, published shortly after his father became president. He outlined his shockingly self-destructive behavior, troubled personal life, and insatiable crack habit. For five months in 2016, his homeless drug dealer had moved into his apartment in Washington, just blocks from the White House, while his father was still serving as vice president. During another stretch of time two years later, a drugged-out Hunter lived in a short-term rental at the Chateau Marmont in West Hollywood, where John Belushi had died from a drug overdose in 1982.

After reading about Hunter's life running around Washington and California on a seemingly never-ending crack cocaine binge, I found it hard to believe he was still alive.

At one point in early 2019—shortly before his father announced his presidential bid—Hunter's family attempted to conduct an intervention. His stepmother, Jill, invited him to the Biden family's house in Wilmington, Delaware, for dinner. When he arrived, he was greeted by his father, all three of his children (two of whom had flown in from college), and two counselors from a rehab center in Pennsylvania where he had previously received treatment for his addiction.

"Not a chance," he said to his father, getting angry as soon as he saw the counselors.

The attempted intervention immediately went off the rails, and Hunter later recalled his father looking terrified. Hunter described the painful details in *Beautiful Things*.

"I don't know what else to do," Joe Biden cried out to his son. "I'm so scared. Tell me what to do."

"Not fucking this," Hunter replied, refusing to sit down with either the counselors or his father. "Don't ever ambush me like this again."

Hunter then ran out of the house. His father chased him down the driveway. "He grabbed me, swung me around, and hugged me," Hunter remembered. "He held me tight in the dark and cried for the longest time. Everybody was outside now. When I tried to get in my car, one of my girls took the keys and screamed, 'Dad you can't go!' I shouted back, 'You're not doing this!'"[13]

Joe Biden was just months from launching his presidential campaign, which he would call a "battle for the soul of this nation," and he had lost control of his son.

In many ways, the elder Biden's life has been defined by tragedy. He'd lost his other son, Beau, to brain cancer four years before that failed intervention. His first wife and baby daughter were killed in a car crash in 1972, shortly after Biden was first elected to the Senate. Hunter and Beau were badly hurt in that crash as well, and Biden was sworn into office from the hospital room in Delaware where his young sons were being treated. Beau, just weeks before his fourth birthday, was still lying in bed with a broken leg when it was time for his father to take his oath. Senator-elect Biden didn't want to leave his sons' side, so Senate leaders offered to conduct the ceremony from the hospital. It was an intensely emotional scene that played out in front of the television cameras.

As Joe Biden stood up next to Beau's bed to make some remarks, he held Hunter, who had not yet turned two, in his arms.

"As you can see, my one son Hunter is alive and well and kicking and raising hell and in good shape," he said. "And my other son, Beau, who is in traction here, is in good shape and good spirits and is a good little guy."

With Beau's death four decades later, Joe Biden had endured the loss of a wife, a daughter, and his eldest son. As he was preparing to launch his campaign in 2019, he seemed to have two goals: Get elected president, and keep Hunter alive. As he told a colleague of mine who knows Hunter well, "I'll be damned if I am going to lose another one."

When Joe Biden officially announced he was running for president on April 25, 2019, Hunter was living in California, still using crack and drinking heavily. His life remained a mess, but he had lied to his family, telling them he was doing well and getting treatment. As badly as Joe Biden wanted to run for president, he was worried all the attention and pressure of the campaign would hurt his fragile, drug-addicted son. Then again, the excitement of the campaign could be a way to bring his son closer, maybe even to give him a larger cause to live for and to shock him into sobriety.

I later asked Hunter how his drug problems factored into his father's decision, and he told me his father had repeatedly said to him that he would not run if it would make life harder for his son. Hunter said he responded with a flash of anger.

"If you don't fucking run for president because of me, that will kill me," Hunter told me he'd said to his father. "That will be the thing that kills me. I won't ever be able to live with myself if you don't do this."[14]

As it turned out, the campaign put Hunter's misdeeds and personal life under a harsh, glaring spotlight. Trump and his allies used Hunter's business dealings to attack Joe Biden, and Trump supporters would even carry signs to rallies reading, "Where's Hunter?" He literally couldn't hide.

"Whenever I apologized to [my father] for bringing so much heat onto his campaign, he responded by saying how sorry he was for putting me on the spot, for bringing so much heat onto me, especially at a time when I was so determined to get well," Hunter wrote in his memoir. "That's the biggest political debate my dad and I had for months: Who should apologize to whom?"

When I first met Hunter, in July 2023, he was in the process of defending himself against criminal charges brought by David Weiss, a Trump-appointed US attorney for Delaware who would later be elevated to special counsel by his father's attorney general, Merrick Garland. Hunter tentatively agreed to do an interview as soon as the court proceedings were over, which he believed would be relatively soon. His legal team was preparing to enter into a complicated plea agreement that summer, whereby he would plead guilty to two misdemeanors related to his failure to pay more than $100,000 in income taxes in 2017 and 2018* and agree to abide by a series of steps, including regular drug testing, that would have erased another charge related to his purchase of a handgun while addicted to drugs. In addition to the guilty plea, Hunter had prepared a heartfelt statement accepting responsibility and apologizing for what he had done.

The agreement fell apart, however, when it was presented to a federal judge in Delaware and the defense and prosecution realized they disagreed on a key facet of the deal: whether it precluded the prosecution from bringing additional, unrelated charges against the younger Biden. Without a plea agreement, Hunter's legal troubles weren't ending; they were only beginning. He would now be facing two

---

*Hunter Biden did eventually pay off his tax liabilities—plus interest and penalties—with the help of Kevin Morris, a wealthy entertainment lawyer who later told the House Oversight Committee he was motivated to help the president's son financially because of Hunter's very public struggles with addiction. "He was getting—in my opinion, getting the shit beat out of him by the world," Morris testified. "I believe, and still believe today, he's a very good person and a great guy. And, you know, that's why I decided to step in."

separate federal trials—one on the tax charges and the other on the gun charge. My interview with him was postponed indefinitely.

But I kept in touch with Hunter and got to know him in the process. He had been sober for a little over four years, had remarried, and had a young son named after his late brother, Beau. He was trying to put his life back together and was working to establish some kind of a relationship with the daughter he'd had with a dancer at a Washington, DC, strip club—while litigating a child support case against her mother.[15] He was subject to nonstop personal and political attacks and death threats, making it difficult for him to go out in public and prompting the Secret Service to increase the 24/7 protective detail assigned to him. He spent much of his time in the garage of the house he was renting in California, making paintings on large canvases. And all the while, he continued to talk to his father every day.

Although my television interview with Hunter never came together, I traveled back to California after his father dropped out of the 2024 election and spoke to him for several hours. As was the case in all my conversations with him, Hunter seemed straightforward and candid, and, as you'll see over the course of this book, was willing to answer just about any question I asked. He spoke like a man with nothing to hide, which is perhaps not surprising given that the world had already seen the deepest, darkest secrets he had, thanks to his infamous laptop.

"In a perfect world, I think that we always thought that one term was for him truly to be the bridge kind of candidate, not just because of his age but because that felt like the right thing," he told me in October 2024, explaining his father's thought process. "At least to me, it felt like the right thing. To be the guy that saved democracy by defeating Donald Trump and restoring some faith in our institutions and showing the government could actually work for you."

Indeed, reporting from *Politico* in December 2019 indicated Joe Biden himself had conveyed the same thing to his aides. "According to four people who regularly talk to Biden," Ryan Lizza wrote, "it is virtually inconceivable that he will run for reelection in 2024, when he would be the first octogenarian president."[16]

What changed? "No one anticipated Donald Trump coming back," Hunter told me. "And basically within at least, if not nine months, the first year, it became obvious that Donald Trump was not going anywhere. And so it was a permanent campaign."[17]

Although Biden had been elected in 2020 with a relatively narrow mandate—lead the country out of the COVID-19 pandemic and return a sense of normalcy to public life after the chaos of the Trump era—his party surprisingly won control of both the House and the Senate, which made it possible for him to think bigger. In March 2021—just two months after he was sworn into office—Biden invited a group of historians to the White House. During the conversation, there were references to Franklin Delano Roosevelt and LBJ—larger-than-life Democratic presidents who fundamentally redefined the relationship between government and the public. The implications were clear: Biden had the chance to do the same.[18]

Such expansive goals could not be accomplished in his first one hundred days alone. And "if he was going to make the decision not to run, he would have had to have made it far, far sooner than any other president has had to make that choice," Hunter told me. "If you make it clear that you're a lame duck from the summer of 2022, you're dead in the water in terms of your ability to actually impact the things that you ran for president for in the first place."

Those calculations were likely on Biden's mind when he held his first news conference as president, just days after his meeting with the historians. A reporter asked him if he planned to run for reelection. No decision had been made, no paperwork filed, but Biden blurted out an answer: "That's my expectation."

When I asked Hunter about when his father chose to run again, he gave me essentially the same answer as everyone else in Biden's inner circle. "The truth of the matter is," he said, "it just went. The machinery just went."

There were those who tried to gum up the works. Dean Phillips, the congressman from Minnesota, recalled being alarmed after Biden visited House Democrats at the Capitol in fall 2021 to talk about a key legislative priority, the bipartisan infrastructure package, and wasn't able to articulate the points he was trying to get across. "It was such a fiasco that he had to come back, probably three weeks later," Phillips said. "[Then-Speaker Nancy] Pelosi invited him back to the caucus—so twice in three weeks—to try again. And it was the same poorly presented, disjointed, rambling kind of spiel that never got to the point."

"That's, for me, the first time I thought, 'Holy shit! This is a problem.'"

Phillips went public with his concerns about a year later, telling a local Minnesota radio host in July 2022 that he hoped Biden would not run for reelection—and that "most of" his colleagues felt the same way. "I think the country would be well served by a new generation of compelling, well-prepared, dynamic Democrats to step up," he said.[19]

But none of those Democrats stepped up, and on April 25, 2023, Biden made his reelection bid official with a three-minute video announcement that focused on the importance of protecting democratic norms and institutions from "MAGA extremists" as images from the January 6 attack on the US Capitol flashed across the screen. "Let's finish this job," Biden said. "I know we can. Because this is the United States of America." Within days, his campaign had announced that a number of potential Democratic primary opponents—Whitmer, Shapiro, Newsom, Pritzker—would serve as either campaign co-chairs or members of a "national advisory board." The race was over before it could even begin.

But serious questions about Biden's political prospects remained, and *Washington Post* columnist David Ignatius gave voice to them in a September 2023 op-ed calling for Biden to step aside. "If he and Harris campaign together in 2024, I think Biden risks undoing his greatest achievement—which was stopping Trump," Ignatius wrote. "Time is running out. In a month or so, this decision will be cast in stone. It will be too late for other Democrats, including Harris, to test themselves in primaries and see whether they have the stuff of presidential leadership."[20]

A month after that article was published, Biden was sitting for an interview with Robert Hur, the special counsel appointed by Attorney General Garland to investigate Biden's mishandling of classified material in the years after he served as vice president. It did not go well, with the president forgetting—or failing to articulate—when Trump was first elected, when he launched his own presidential bid, and when he left office as vice president. "If it was 2013—when did I stop being vice president?" Biden asked at one point, according to a transcript of the interview. "2017," a lawyer from the White House counsel's office responded.[21]

Hur released his final report in February 2024 and declined to bring charges against Biden, but his findings were nonetheless damning for the president. "Our investigation uncovered evidence that President Biden willfully retained and disclosed classified materials after his vice presidency when he was a private citizen," Hur wrote.

But the prosecutor didn't believe charges were warranted, in part because he didn't believe he'd be able to secure a conviction at trial. Why? "Mr. Biden would likely present himself to a jury, as he did during our interview of him, as a sympathetic, well-meaning, elderly man with a poor memory." Hur also noted a particularly personal example of Biden's poor memory: "He did not remember, even within several years, when his son Beau died."[22]

At a time when Biden's age was already at the forefront of voters' minds, the line shot through Washington like lightning. "It's clear [Biden] does not have the cognitive ability to be president," House Majority Whip Tom Emmer tweeted.[23] A senior House Democrat, granted anonymity, told *Axios* the report was "obviously concerning."[24]

The White House was quick to point out that the special counsel had decided not to bring charges against him—and that, in stark contrast to Donald Trump, Biden had fully cooperated with the investigation. But Biden's team was well aware of how politically damaging the report was—and went into overdrive attacking Hur and his credibility. "The report uses highly prejudicial language to describe a commonplace occurrence among witnesses: a lack of recall of years-old events," the president's lawyers wrote in a letter. "This language is not supported by the facts, nor is it appropriately used by a federal prosecutor in this context."

White House aides and Democrats would quickly grow even harsher in their criticism, portraying Hur—a registered Republican—

as essentially a political hack who was trying to hurt the president for partisan reasons.

At 7:22 p.m. the night Hur's report was released, reporters received a notice from the White House that Biden would be delivering previously unscheduled remarks at 7:45 p.m., just twenty minutes later. The president finally arrived at the lectern at 8:30 p.m., looking and sounding angry. "I know there's some attention paid to some language in the report about my recollection of events," he said. "There's even a reference that I don't remember when my son died. How in the hell dare he raise that? Frankly, when I was asked the question, I thought to myself, wasn't any of their damn business."*

If the press conference ended there, the fiery response may have helped blunt the political damage Hur had inflicted earlier that day. But Biden decided to take a handful of questions from assembled reporters, including one on the state of hostage and ceasefire negotiations between Israel and Hamas.

"As you know, initially, the president of Mexico, Sisi, did not want to open up the gate to allow humanitarian material to get in," Biden said, intending to refer to the president of *Egypt*, Abdel Fattah el-Sisi. "I talked to him. I convinced him to open the gate."

It may have been an innocent mistake—who among us hasn't misspoken in a similar manner—but it was a gaffe Biden could not afford. And it wouldn't be the last.

The Biden Justice Department didn't publicly defend the integrity of its special counsel. But senior DOJ officials close to Attorney

*As the transcript—and later the audio recording of the interview, which was released in May 2025—revealed, it was Biden, not the special counsel, who brought up Beau Biden's death.

General Garland who I spoke to believed Hur's report was accurate and—if anything—generous to Biden.

"The only reason it was a big deal is that it was true and the White House knew it was true," a senior Biden Justice Department official later told me. The official added that Hur's report should have been "an early warning" for Democrats that Biden was too old to run for president again. In the view of this official, a senior Biden appointee, the failure of the White House to heed the warning presented in Hur's report proved to be disastrous.

CHAPTER THREE

FREE ON WEDNESDAYS

Maybe Donald Trump was operating under some hidden strategy. Maybe he was just getting a little bored as his New York criminal trial dragged on. But leaving the courthouse on Friday, April 26, 2024, the former president made a move that would change the course of the 2024 campaign.

"I just want to say that I've invited Biden to debate," Trump announced to the camera in the dark hallway outside the courtroom where he had been spending the bulk of his time since the start of his trial nearly three weeks earlier. "He can do it anytime he wants, including tonight. . . . I'm here; I'm ready, willing, and able. And if he wants, I'll do it on Monday night, Tuesday night, or Wednesday night."

Earlier that day, President Biden had been asked in an interview with Howard Stern if he would be willing to debate Trump as he had in 2020. Yes, Biden said in response, but he left the timing vague: "I don't know when, but I am happy to debate him."

Trump's request for an early debate was an unusual one. Presidential general election debates have always taken place in the fall, after the political parties hold their conventions and formally nominate the candidates. In 2020, Trump and Biden faced off against each other on September 29 and October 22. The earliest a general election presidential debate had ever been held, in fact, was September 21, 1980, when Ronald Reagan debated independent candidate John Anderson at the Baltimore Convention Center.*

Trump had floated the idea of an early debate with Biden a handful of times in recent months. In February, he told right-wing pundit Dan Bongino, who would later be named Trump's second-term deputy FBI director, that the two should debate "immediately" for the "good of the country."[1] In early March, he put out a statement on Truth Social claiming he would agree to a face-off with Biden even if the debate was hosted by the Democratic National Committee: "I am calling for Debates, ANYTIME, ANYWHERE, ANYPLACE!"[2] In April, Trump's top campaign advisors, Susie Wiles and Chris LaCivita, urged the Commission on Presidential Debates to schedule an early contest, citing the growing percentage of Americans who vote well before Election Day.[3]

But the former president's comments outside the courtroom represented an urgent and direct challenge intended to get Biden's attention and force him to respond.

Trump had no way of knowing it, but the Biden team was angling for an early debate as well. On the same day Trump's trial began in

*Then-President Jimmy Carter was invited to participate in the debate, but he refused, citing the presence of Anderson. "Once you start opening up the system, it is hard to say where you draw the line," White House press secretary Jody Powell said, explaining Carter's rationale.

New York, President Biden's top political advisors sent him a six-page memo outlining a plan for two debates with Trump—and suggesting the first should be held on June 26 or 27.

"The first debate would be in the spring, before YOUR Democratic Convention in August, and the second debate would be in the early part of September, after Labor Day," read the memo, which was signed "Senior Advisors" and written by his former chief of staff Ron Klain, then a key campaign advisor, and senior White House officials Bruce Reed and Anita Dunn. The memo suggested Biden "move quickly to set timing and a plan for debates so YOU enter the debate process from a position of strength."*

Biden's advisors, in their memo to the president, made a similar case as Trump's advisors: With so many states offering early voting, reaching voters before the fall was more important than ever. But the real reason Klain, Reed, and Dunn were pushing for an early debate—a reason they omitted from their memo to the president—was simple: They feared Biden was losing.

The polling had been consistently grim for Biden since he'd launched his reelection bid in April 2023. By January 2024, just 36 percent of Americans approved of the job he was doing as president while 56 percent disapproved, according to the average of national polls compiled by ABC's *FiveThirtyEight*. Trump was unpopular, too, but no matter how dire his legal troubles became, polls suggested he was viewed more favorably than his Democratic opponent.

Biden's State of the Union address in March had presented him with a golden opportunity to get back on track. His campaign team

*The peculiar capitalization of "YOUR" and "YOU" was repeated throughout this four-page memo to President Biden. It seems odd, but it was apparently standard practice in memos written by the staff to the president in the Biden White House.

knew he needed a huge moment, and not just because his polling numbers were lagging behind Trump's. His fundraising had slumped, Democrats were divided over the administration's approach to Israel's war against Hamas in Gaza, and, as ever, Americans had serious concerns about the president's age.

With so much at stake, Biden spent four full days at Camp David preparing for the speech—and he was joined by more than just his typical circle of political advisors. Historian Jon Meacham was there, and Hollywood legend Steven Spielberg—winner of three Academy Awards—joined the team via Zoom. Biden delivered his address four times from start to finish at Camp David, reading it off teleprompters each night at 9 p.m.—the same time the actual speech was set to kick off on March 7.

Spielberg—a master storyteller who is widely considered one of the greatest directors in American history—watched Biden's practice speeches and offered advice on his delivery. "Steven always added value," one of Biden's senior political advisors told me when asked about the director's role. "For State of the Union, he basically directed the president. I mean, he went through page by page [and asked], 'What do you want to say here? What do you really want to mean here?'"

"It was great," the advisor added. "Like a master class."

Biden's inner circle was tight-lipped about his Hollywood help. The fact that the director of such Hollywood blockbusters as *Raiders of the Lost Ark* and *Saving Private Ryan* was helping the president prepare for the State of the Union address was not something they announced publicly.

The preparation seemed to pay off. Political pundits generally considered Biden's speech a success—and it was without question one of his most energetic public appearances as president. He touted his legislative accomplishments, firing up Democrats so much that, at one point, they broke out into a chant: "Four more years!" Toward the end of his sixty-seven-minute speech, Biden addressed his age directly. "I know I may not look like it, but I've been around a while," he joked. "When you get to be my age, certain things become clearer than ever."

He continued: "My fellow Americans, the issue facing our nation isn't how old we are, it's how old are our ideas. Hate, anger, revenge, retribution are the oldest of ideas. But you can't lead America with ancient ideas that only take us back. To lead America, the land of possibilities, you need a vision for the future and what can and should be done."

Biden didn't say Trump's name—referring to him as "my predecessor" thirteen times over the course of the speech—but he drew a stark contrast with his GOP opponent. And when he was predictably heckled by Republicans—including Representative Marjorie Taylor Greene, the die-hard Trump loyalist—he hit right back, just as he had practiced at Camp David, turning the rudeness of his audience into an opportunity to further make his case.

As Biden addressed border security, for example, some Republicans began chanting "Build the wall! Build the wall!" He answered by challenging GOP lawmakers to vote for a bipartisan border security bill that had been languishing in Congress ever since Trump came out against it. "I would respectfully suggest, my Republican friends owe it to the American people: Get this bill done," he said. "If my predecessor is watching, instead of playing politics and pressuring members of Congress to block the bill, join me in telling the Congress to pass it."

Several sections of the speech likely would have been more appropriate at a campaign rally than in the House chamber, but that passion was exactly what Biden needed. "This was not Old Man Joe," Peter Baker wrote in *The New York Times*. "This was Forceful Joe. This was Angry Joe. This was Loud Joe. This was Game-On Joe."[4]

And the speech caught Donald Trump's attention. "That may be the Angriest, Least Compassionate, and Worst State of the Union Speech ever made," the former president posted on Truth Social that night. "It was an Embarrassment to our Country!"[5]

The performance helped rejuvenate Biden's grassroots support and fundraising for the campaign surged in the following days. But Biden's standing in the polls didn't change. Ultimately, the reality of the race was unchanged: Biden was unpopular, and he was losing to Trump.

And that's why Biden's senior advisors had pushed for an early debate. By getting onstage with Trump, they believed, Biden would remind voters that the election wasn't simply a *referendum* on his performance as president but rather a *choice* between him and Trump. As Biden himself often said, "Don't compare me to the Almighty. Compare me to the alternative."

The way Anita Dunn and Biden's other senior advisors saw it, a debate could help shift the focus away from what voters didn't like about Biden to what they didn't like about Trump. "We needed America to be reminded why they had voted against him to begin with," Dunn later told me.

When Biden accepted Trump's challenge, he did so with Trumpian flair.

"Donald Trump lost two debates to me in 2020. Since then, he hasn't shown up for a debate," Biden said in a video posted on social media on May 15, referencing Trump's decision to skip the Republican primary contests. "Now he's acting like he wants to debate me again. Well, make my day, pal. I'll even do it twice."[6]

Biden closed the video with a not-so-subtle reminder of his opponent's grueling trial schedule, which forced Trump to be in court nearly every day of the week: "I hear you're free on Wednesdays."*

The bipartisan Commission on Presidential Debates (CPD) had already announced plans to hold four contests—three presidential and one vice presidential—starting on September 16 at Texas State University, but both the Trump and Biden campaigns were eager to ditch the organization. The CPD had sponsored all general election presidential debates since 1988, but both campaigns found its leaders to be arrogant and presumptuous. The commission had announced the dates and locations of its planned debates without consulting either campaign, and curtly rebuffed the Trump team's request to start the process earlier.

Within minutes of Biden's accepting Trump's challenge, representatives from the two campaigns started fielding proposals directly from the television networks that were hoping to host debates. And within just a couple of hours, the two contests were set: one hosted by CNN on June 27, and one hosted by ABC News on September 10. "I am Ready and Willing to Debate Crooked Joe at the two proposed times in June and September," Trump posted on Truth Social. "I

*Within minutes of Biden's post, his campaign's website featured T-shirts with the same jab—"Free on Wednesdays"—on sale for $32 apiece. The president had until that point generally avoided commenting on his rival's legal woes directly, but his campaign clearly made a decision to draw attention to the proceedings.

would strongly recommend more than two debates and, for excitement purposes, a very large venue, although Biden is supposedly afraid of crowds—That's only because he doesn't get them."

"Crooked Joe Biden is the WORST debater I have ever faced—He can't put two sentences together!" the former president added. "Let's get ready to Rumble!!!"[7]

Trump wanted live audiences, but because he was so eager to debate, he and his team essentially let the Biden campaign dictate the dates and the rules. The first debate would be a ninety-minute contest, held in an empty CNN studio in Atlanta. Both men would be given a pen, a pad of paper, and a bottle of water—and at the Biden team's insistence, their microphones would be muted unless it was their turn to speak, so as to avoid a repeat of the chaotic first debate between them in 2020.

The Biden campaign believed they had already scored a big win. The debate would be on friendlier ground—CNN, not Fox News—and the rules were exactly as they demanded. What could possibly go wrong?

At least one of Trump's closest allies believed goading Biden into a debate was a terrible idea.

"This is a huge mistake. You got to call off this Biden thing," Steve Bannon, Trump's former chief strategist, told the former president after the dates were set. "The debate, it's ridiculous."

"Biden's not your opponent right now," Bannon explained.

"What are you talking about?" Trump said.

"Well, he's not the nominee."

"Well, that's all just a—"

"No, no," Bannon said, interrupting him. "The only guy who's your opponent is the name that's on the ballot that gets mailed. Up until that time, they can change out anybody."

The way Bannon saw it, Trump was already beating Biden. A debate, in his mind, presented the former president with a no-win situation. A strong performance from Biden would provide his campaign with a badly needed boost. And if Biden bombed, Democrats would have time to replace him with a new nominee who would be harder to beat.

"You either crush him and he's gone, or he fights you to a draw—he can't beat you, but he fights you to a draw—and then you've reinnervated [his campaign]," Bannon recalled telling Trump. "They'll throw another three billion dollars into it, and you've made it a race."

And not everybody in Biden's inner circle was in favor of an early debate. Steve Ricchetti, another senior Biden advisor, expressed doubts about debating Trump at all, arguing that it would just give Trump a massive audience to spread lies—about Biden, about the 2020 election, and about January 6.

Hunter Biden also advised his father against debating Trump. "Why would you honor this guy that is a—forget the convicted-criminal bullshit—that is a traitor to this country, [with] a place on a stage with the president of the fucking United States?" he asked. "He tried to overthrow our democracy! Like, why? Why are we paying him any respect whatsoever? And who needed that debate the most? Not us. *He* did."

Former House Speaker Nancy Pelosi was a little more delicate with her language, but she saw things the same way. "I said, like five months before all this was agreed to, 'Don't be onstage with him—ever,'" she later told me. "Why would you be on the stage with somebody who has no connection to truth whatsoever—[who] just makes a joke of the whole thing?"

The reality of the situation, though, was that Biden *did* need to get on that stage with Trump—and not just because Trump was leading in the polling. Biden needed to prove to American voters that he wasn't too old for the job.

"We had to debate," Anita Dunn told me. "There was not an option not to debate, because of the age issue for Biden. He was eighty-one years old, and there were questions about him."

According to trusted Biden advisor Bruce Reed, it wasn't that Biden *wanted* to debate his opponent. "Not because he couldn't take it, but just because a debate with Trump is not on the level," Reed said. "He's going to lie, he's not going to get fact-checked. . . . And so I think if there had been a way to not do any [debates] at all, we would have taken that. But we didn't have any choice."

CHAPTER FOUR

A TALE OF TWO JUNES

On June 15, 2024, Air Force One touched down in Los Angeles ahead of an event designed to provide the Biden campaign with a jolt of energy—and money. The fundraiser for the president's reelection bid would be hosted by two of the biggest names in Hollywood—George Clooney and Julia Roberts—and it was expected to bring in a record haul.

Several other stars were on the program as well—including Barbra Streisand, Jack Black, and Jason Bateman—but the main attraction would be a conversation onstage at the Peacock Theater between President Joe Biden and former President Barack Obama, moderated by late-night TV host Jimmy Kimmel.

The timing of the gala was not ideal for Biden, who would need to traverse nine time zones to get to Los Angeles after wrapping up his second trip to Europe in as many weeks. He spent most of the day before in Fasano, Italy, meeting one-on-one with Italian Prime Minister Giorgia Meloni and Pope Francis before participating in the closing session of the G7 Summit, a gathering of leaders from seven major industrial countries. By the time Biden boarded Air Force One for the return trip to the United States, it was 11:06 p.m. local time. He wouldn't arrive in Los Angeles for fifteen hours, with the plane stopping at Joint Base Andrews outside Washington, DC, to refuel on the way.

At least one of Biden's top aides was furious with the schedule. The date of the fundraiser was dictated not by the White House or the president's campaign, but by Clooney and Roberts, as both actors were in the middle of shooting movies. "The only day George Clooney and Julia Roberts can do it is that day," the Biden advisor told me. "Which means you're going to fly an eighty-one-year-old man, who has already done transatlantic travel twice, from Italy to California and expect him to perform that afternoon. I will tell you what: Barack fucking Obama could not have done that."

The president's schedule is always packed, but Biden's first two weeks of June were truly grueling—in part because various aides with different priorities were not coordinating with one another. "Everybody was kind of in their own lanes, doing their own thing about June," another top Biden advisor recalled. "Unfortunately, nobody—none of us—put the big picture together, which was the travel."

"The travel," in this instance, referred to two flights to Europe and back—one to France for a commemoration of the eightieth anniversary of D-Day, one to Italy for the G7 Summit—followed immediately by the whirlwind trip from DC to California for the fundraiser.

The D-Day commemoration and G-7 meetings were fairly nonnegotiable. Meloni had announced months earlier that the G7 Summit would be held from June 13 to 15 at the Borgo Egnazia hotel in Puglia, and there was no changing the anniversary of the day that tens of thousands of Allied troops heroically landed on the beaches of Normandy. And when Clooney and Roberts let Biden's team know about their limited availability, that was that. The campaign needed the money.

This meant Biden would host the annual White House congressional picnic on June 4, depart for France that night, spend five days traveling around the country and meeting with world leaders like French President Emmanuel Macron and Ukrainian President Volodymyr Zelensky, fly back to Delaware on June 9, travel to Washington to host a concert commemorating Juneteenth on June 10, deliver a speech about gun control on June 11, fly to Italy on June 12, participate in the G7 Summit for the next two days, meet with Pope Francis, fly back to Washington on June 14, and immediately continue on to Los Angeles the morning of June 15 to participate in the fundraiser that night.

There's no question Biden was jet-lagged when he arrived in Los Angeles. Before appearing onstage with Obama and Kimmel, the president posed for individual pictures with hundreds of donors who had bought premium tickets, some of whom had spent as much as $500,000 to attend.[1] Some of those same donors would later say Biden appeared frail, his voice so weak it was hard to hear him. "It felt like he was still the smart, witty guy we've all followed for many years," one supporter who gave $100,000 said. "But the volume and speed are turned way down—to an alarming level."[2]

According to a guest at the fundraiser, a White House aide brought Biden over to see Clooney, who had known the president for a long time and done many fundraisers with him over the years.

"Mr. President, you remember George," the aide said to Biden, according to the guest.

"Oh yeah, George, how are you doing?" Biden said, apparently not recognizing who he was talking to.

"George *Clooney*," the aide said to Biden.

When it came time for the main event, which was not televised, Biden and Obama took good-natured questions from Kimmel that were designed to draw a few laughs and giving both presidents a chance to make the case for reelecting Biden—in front of a crowd full of people who had spent thousands of dollars to be there. This was not exactly a hard-hitting interview, and it lasted just thirty-six minutes.

"Is this country suffering from what they call Trump amnesia? I mean, why do so many Americans seem to remember the Trump administration the same way we do a colonoscopy?" Kimmel joked.

"All they got to do is remember what it was like. You know, what he did with—remember the pandemic?" Biden said. "He said, 'Don't—don't worry, just inject a little bleach in your body.'"

Biden's responses were not sharp, particularly when contrasted with those of Obama, who effortlessly hit each softball question Kimmel threw his way. And as Biden mumbled his way through various answers, Obama would occasionally jump in to help him get to the point.

"He was exhausted. I mean, he was truly exhausted," Hunter Biden later told me, recalling his reaction as he watched his father speak. "I remember him up on that stage and just going, like, 'Get this fuckin' thing over with.'"

Jon Favreau, a former speechwriter for Obama, was sitting near the front of the theater and later recalled Biden speaking in a slow, halting manner that was difficult to follow. "I said to my wife, either he'll do great at the debate, and we'll realize he was just tired tonight, or he'll perform like this and then the whole country will be talking about it," Favreau said.[3]

But the evening came and went with no attendees saying anything negative about Biden's performance—at least publicly. A small group of journalists was allowed into the event—the rotating members of the White House press pool that travels with the president on Air Force One—and not one reported that the president appeared exhausted and not particularly coherent at the event. The pool report, written by a reporter for Agence France-Presse, noted, "Biden was forceful when the discussion turned to abortion and the Supreme Court." Missing from that dispatch, however, was the fact that Biden apparently misremembered the number of Supreme Court justices nominated to the court by Donald Trump.

"The next president is likely to have two new Supreme Court nominees," Biden remarked before trailing off. "Two more. He's already appointed two that are—have been very negative in terms of the rights of individuals. The idea that, if he's reelected, he's going to appoint two more flying flags upside down is really—I'm—I really mean it. There's—" At that point, Kimmel jumped in to ask another question.[4]

All in all, the event accomplished its immediate goal, raising an astonishing $30 million in a single night for Biden's campaign.[5]

But just a few hours after the gala ended, a journalist for *The Hollywood Reporter* posted a shaky video clip from inside the theater that showed Biden standing onstage with Kimmel and Obama at the conclusion of their conversation and waving to the applauding crowd on one side of the auditorium before taking a few steps and looking out, with a big smile, at the crowd straight ahead of the stage.[6] As Biden stared motionless for a few seconds, Obama walked over to him, gently grabbed his hand, and led him off the stage.

The snippet immediately went viral, playing over and over again on pro-Trump news outlets and social media accounts alongside commentary implying Biden had frozen up and needed Obama's assistance to get off the stage. Hunter Biden, who was at the fundraiser, saw what happened and knew immediately that it was going to be a problem.

"I almost jumped up on the stage and said, 'Don't ever fucking do that to the president of the United States again—ever,'" Hunter told me, insisting his father was simply taking some time to acknowledge the crowd. "I literally watched it happen, and I knew that that was going to be a meme. How [Obama] couldn't fucking understand that in that moment . . ."

In Hunter's mind, Obama was simply in a rush to leave—but knew he couldn't before Biden did. "Barack Obama wanted to be off that stage," Hunter told me months later, still clearly angry about what had happened. "He wanted to be out of there. That really, really, really, really pissed me off."

And for good reason. Biden's last, best chance to turn the race around—his debate with Donald Trump—was coming up, and his campaign was, yet again, having to spend much of its time fending off questions about his age and mental fitness.

Less than two weeks earlier, *The Wall Street Journal* published a bombshell report that finally put in print what many Democrats had been saying privately for months: "Behind Closed Doors, Biden Shows Signs of Slipping."[7]

The story, written by the *Journal*'s Annie Linskey and Siobhan Hughes, described several Oval Office meetings Biden had hosted with congressional leaders in recent months, during which Biden "read from notes to make obvious points, paused for extended periods and sometimes closed his eyes for so long that some in the room wondered whether he had tuned out."

"I used to meet with him when he was vice president," former House Speaker Kevin McCarthy told the newspaper. "He's not the same person."

Most of the article's more explosive on-the-record claims came from Republicans, but the *Journal* said that its reporters had spoken to more than forty-five people who either participated in meetings with Biden or were briefed on them—and that many Democrats also expressed concerns about how the president seemed.

The blowback from the White House and its allies was fierce, and it was quick. "Congressional Republicans, foreign leaders and non-partisan national-security experts have made clear in their own words that President Biden is a savvy and effective leader who has a deep record of legislative accomplishment," White House spokesman Andrew Bates told the *Journal*.

Ben LaBolt, the White House communications director, called the article a "complete and utter editorial fail" by *The Wall Street Journal*. "Makes you wonder who they're taking orders from . . ." he added, alluding to conservative billionaire Rupert Murdoch's ownership of the paper.[8]

Former Speaker Nancy Pelosi was still furious about the story when I met with her in her office at the Capitol nearly four months later—*after* Biden had dropped out of the race. "They *completely* misrepresented the facts in that article," she told me, her voice rising. "I remember they sat here, and I said, 'Never let them in the office again.'" According to Pelosi, when the *Journal* reporters interviewed her for the story, she told them about her "firsthand experiences" with Biden's "wisdom, experience, strength, and strategic thinking"—and the quotes didn't make it into the final article.[9]

But all the sniping at *The Wall Street Journal* couldn't erase a central reality of the 2024 campaign: The vast majority of voters already agreed with the article's premise long before it was ever published. Few people needed to read a deeply reported story about the president's fitness or hear from anonymous Democrats; they had concerns about Biden's age and mental acuity because of what they had seen and heard with their own eyes and ears. In fact, the ABC News/Ipsos poll I mentioned earlier that found a whopping 86 percent of Americans—*including 73 percent of Democrats*—believed the president was too old to serve another term was conducted nearly four months before *The Wall Street Journal* piece was published.[10]

Biden had been in the public eye for more than half a century at this point, and the Biden of 2024 had clearly lost a step. Even Hunter would later acknowledge as much. "He *does* speak slower," he told me in October 2024. "He *does* walk slower. His voice *is* lower. He *will* forget a name. But I can tell you with one hundred percent certainty, my dad's all there. He's completely, absolutely capable of taking the call at three o'clock in the morning when the phone rings."

Biden's senior advisors inside the White House seemed to truly believe that as well. Perhaps they saw only what they wanted to see, but most aides that I talked to who witnessed Biden operating behind the scenes insisted he was still fully in command. That said, one senior member of the administration told me in early 2024 that, while Biden was still fully capable of serving as commander in chief, he believed the president would be best off avoiding significant events after 4:30 p.m. He was sharp during the day, this aide said, but less so as the evening approached.

In the months after Biden ended his reelection campaign, a number of Republican officials and conservative pundits accused the White House—and many of the media outlets that covered it—of perpetrating a massive conspiracy to hide Biden's diminished faculties from the American people.

Individual reporters would at times downplay legitimate questions about the president, of course—and White House aides would occasionally make outlandish comments about his fitness*—but there was no secret cabal shielding the true Biden from the public. Americans saw the most damning evidence of his mental decline on their cell phones and TV screens. And a handful of viral videos—coming less than a week after the *Journal* story was published—didn't do anything to alleviate those concerns.

The first such video, recorded at the White House's Juneteenth concert on June 10, showed Biden standing frozen, arms at his side, with a vacant stare and an unmoving grin on his face for nearly half a minute as Kirk Franklin performed the song "Love Theory" onstage. The entire crowd around him was dancing or swaying to the music—including Vice President Kamala Harris immediately to his right—but Biden stood stiff as a board until another attendee put his arm around him and gave him a fist bump.

The next video came days later, from the G7 Summit in Italy, and appeared to show Biden wandering aimlessly away from other world leaders, only for Italian Prime Minister Giorgia Meloni to tap him on the arm and gently guide him back to the group. The cover of the *New York Post* the following morning captured the moment in a series of pictures under the headline "Meander in Chief: Biden Embarrasses US with Confused Wanderings at World Conference."[11]

*In August 2023, White House press secretary Karine Jean-Pierre responded to questions about voters' concerns about Biden's age by claiming, "It is hard for us to keep up with this president." A few months later, she told reporters she would put Biden's stamina up "against anyone . . . on any day of the week."

Defenders of the president could easily point out that these moments were taken out of context or overblown—and they did. The Juneteenth concert was held just hours after Biden landed back in Washington after his first nearly weeklong trip to France that month, and he was understandably tired. And the G7 video truly was unfair, with right-wing social media influencers cropping out the wider angle of the shot. If they hadn't, viewers would have seen that Biden wasn't walking off confusedly; he was going to greet a paratrooper who had just landed nearby as part of a ceremony.

"Beware cheap fakes . . . and all the bad faith actors who post them," LaBolt tweeted, using a term the White House had adopted to dismiss unflattering videos of the president.[12]

"The strategy is obvious," Nick Catoggio wrote for *The Dispatch*, a conservative media outlet. "Influential liberals hope to convince voters that any footage of Joe Biden seeming feeble henceforth should be presumed to be deceptive enemy propaganda and dismissed out of hand."[13]

The problem with that strategy, though, was that the clips kept coming. Some of them were doctored, but others were entirely real. And soon, Biden would have his most damaging flub of all—in front of a live audience of more than 50 million viewers.[14]

Even as Biden crisscrossed the Atlantic and the country in the weeks before his debate with Trump—meeting with world leaders, A-list celebrities, even the pope—his mind was much closer to home, in Wilmington, Delaware.

On June 3, the day before Biden left for France, Hunter was set to go on trial for charges related to his purchase of a handgun in 2018 while he was addicted to crack. As I've noted earlier in the book, the president was incredibly close to and constantly worried about his only living son. Hunter's personal struggles—and subsequent legal troubles—affected him profoundly.

"I am the President, but I am also a Dad," Biden said in a statement as the trial began. "As the President, I don't and won't comment on pending federal cases, but as a Dad, I have boundless love for my son, confidence in him, and respect for his strength. Our family has been through a lot together, and Jill and I are going to continue to be there for Hunter and our family with our love and support."[15]

First Lady Jill Biden made the journey to the Delaware courthouse to be there with her stepson, sitting in the courtroom, just behind the defense table, as the trial got underway. Her presence came as a surprise to several of Biden's top advisors, most of whom didn't find out she was going to attend the trial until they received a news alert on their phones.

The Biden family had spent time together at their home in Rehoboth Beach the weekend before the trial began, with the president departing for the White House before Hunter's proceedings kicked off on Monday morning. The First Lady, however, stuck around, making a point to be in the courtroom at the J. Caleb Boggs Federal Building as much as she could. For the first several days of the trial, she sat with Hunter's wife, Melissa, and half sister, Ashley, in the front row of the gallery, departing only to meet her husband in Normandy for the D-Day commemoration ceremonies. Hours later, however, she was on a plane back to Delaware so she could be seated in her usual spot behind Hunter for the fifth day of the trial.[16] From

Europe, President Biden closely followed the trial, asking deputy chief of staff Annie Tomasini for updates during breaks between his meetings with foreign leaders and at the end of each day.

Back in Wilmington, the witness testimony and presentation of evidence were difficult for the First Lady to sit through. Prosecutors led everyone in attendance through some of the darkest days of Hunter's life: excerpts from his 2021 memoir discussing the depths of his crack addiction, bank records showing his withdrawal of $150,000 in cash, testimony from a woman he met at a strip club, old text messages between Hunter and Hallie Biden—the widow of his brother, Beau, with whom Hunter later had a romantic relationship. At one point during the trial, Lucien Bruggeman, my ABC News colleague in the courtroom, noticed the first lady and her daughter, Ashley, fighting off tears as they had their arms around each other.[17]

As the proceedings dragged on, more and more Biden family members began to show up, including Hunter's daughter Naomi and his uncle, James. During closing arguments, lawyer for the prosecution, Leo Wise, pointed out the large Biden contingent to members of the jury, reminding them that no one is above the law. "You may recognize them from the news, from the community," Wise said, gesturing toward the three rows of Bidens. "None of that matters."[18]

After three hours of deliberation—spread over two days—the jury reached its verdict: Hunter was found guilty of all three counts against him. He looked stunned and patted his lawyer Abbe Lowell on the back before turning to his family in the gallery and hugging his wife, Melissa. Minutes later, he was photographed leaving the building holding hands with both Melissa and Jill. As soon as he got to the car, Hunter called his father.

"Dad, I'm okay," he told his father. "I'm surrounded by people who love me. I have never felt more support than I've had this whole week."

The president was at the White House when the verdict was reached, according to his schedule, and was about to have lunch with Vice President Harris. "Jill and I love our son, and we are so proud of the man he is today," he said in a statement. "I will accept the outcome of this case and will continue to respect the judicial process as Hunter considers an appeal. Jill and I will always be there for Hunter and the rest of our family with our love and support. Nothing will ever change that."

President Biden was, ironically enough, set to deliver a speech that afternoon at the Washington Hilton on the need for additional gun laws—and he did. But just before he went onstage, White House reporters received an email that his schedule had been updated to include a last-minute trip to Wilmington immediately after the address. My ABC News colleague Molly Nagle was present at Delaware Air National Guard Base when Biden landed and wrote that the president "hugged his son and spent several minutes with him on the tarmac."

He spent the night in Wilmington but left for Italy the following morning at 7:42 a.m.

The weeks leading up to the debate were far less eventful for Donald Trump. He was convicted on thirty-four counts in Manhattan at the end of May, of course, but kept a relatively low profile during the month of June. He joined TikTok, turned seventy-eight years old, and traveled around the country, holding several closed-door fundraisers in California and a smattering of rallies in Nevada, Michigan, Wisconsin, and Pennsylvania. But by his standards, he was remarkably quiet. "Suddenly Trump's Got Nothing to Say About Hunter Biden," read the headline of a June 5 *Politico* story that highlighted the lack of jabs from the former president as the trial of his rival's son got underway.[19]

Presidential candidates clearing their public schedule in the days and weeks leading up to a debate is not atypical, as they huddle with advisors to hash out strategy, memorize talking points, and engage in mock debates. That wasn't exactly what Trump was up to, but he was getting ready for the debate in his own way.

Trump himself never had much patience for formal debate prep, although he would occasionally go through the motions during his first two White House bids. "You can go too much in that stuff," he told reporters before his first face-off with Biden in September 2020.[20] Nearly four years later, with two such debates against Biden already under his belt, Trump couldn't have been more confident. "President Trump takes on numerous tough interviews every single week and delivers lengthy rally speeches while standing, demonstrating elite stamina," Trump aide Jason Miller reporters in mid-June.[21]

Instead of conducting mock debates, Trump held what his campaign billed as a series of "informal policy discussions" with top Republican officials and policymakers, including former acting director of Immigration and Customs Enforcement Tom Homan (his future border czar), longtime aide Stephen Miller (his future deputy chief of staff), Senator Marco Rubio (his future secretary of state), and his soon-to-be vice presidential pick, Senator JD Vance. The various pairings chatted about immigration, crime, inflation, abortion, and foreign policy—but also about more Trump-specific questions, like how to frame the four indictments he was currently under and how to respond to Biden's inevitable January 6–related barbs.

At least a handful of those "informal policy discussions" took place with Rubio and GOP Senator Eric Schmitt of Missouri at the headquarters of the Republican National Committee in Washington, DC, on June 13.[22] The trip represented Trump's first return to Capitol Hill since supporters stormed the building more than three years prior, and the former president met separately with the House and Senate Republican conferences.* His campaign suggested the visit was scheduled so that he could "express his campaign priorities and policies" to members of Congress[23]—and he saw a handful of potential vice presidential picks while in town—but ultimately, the summit served as an opportunity for the presumptive nominee to assert his dominance over congressional leaders and cement his place atop the Republican Party once again.

"This is an outstanding group of people," Trump told reporters after meeting with GOP senators at the National Republican Senatorial Committee headquarters. "I'm with them 1,000 percent, they're with me 1,000 percent. We agree on just about everything, and if [we don't], we work it out." The president, whose birthday was the following day, received a cake from lawmakers with two sets of candles[24]—"45" and "47"—and members of the House presented Trump with a baseball and bat from the recently played Congressional Baseball Game, in which the Republicans had trounced the Democrats by a score of 31–11.[25]

Even Senator Mitch McConnell, who had all but written Trump off following the events of January 6, sounded optimistic after

*Democratic Representative Bennie Thompson, chair of the House Select Committee to Investigate the January 6th Attack, issued a statement upon learning of Trump's visit: "After inciting a deadly insurrection that defiled the halls of Congress, how dare Trump show his face on these grounds? Congressional Republicans allow him to waltz in here when it's known he has no regard for democracy."

catching up with the former president. “He and I got a chance to talk a little bit, we shook hands a few times,” he said. “He got a lot of standing ovations. It was an entirely positive meeting.”[26]

Republican Congressman Matt Gaetz, talking to reporters as he left the event, put it best: “It was a pep rally for President Trump.”[27]

President Biden didn’t have much time for debate prep earlier in the month given his hectic schedule, but his team had carved out almost a full week for him at Camp David—the presidential retreat in Frederick County, Maryland—to focus on his upcoming matchup with Trump. And given how Biden preferred to prepare for such events, he’d need every minute.

“He wanted to know everything about everything,” recalled one of his top advisors. “Majoring in the minor, crazy amounts of information.” Several of the president’s top aides—including former chief of staff Ron Klain and top advisor Bruce Reed—oversaw the compilation of enormous binders of background material for the president to sift through.[28]

Campaign aides had set up two podiums in the retreat’s small theater for the president to face off against Bob Bauer—his personal lawyer who was reprising his role from 2020 as a stand-in for Donald Trump—and had a true-to-form replica of the CNN set constructed inside the Hackberry Hangar at Camp David. Strategist Anita Dunn, Bauer’s wife, played the role of moderator Dana Bash, and communications director Ben LaBolt played Jake Tapper. More than a dozen close advisors were present to offer counsel, and Steven Spielberg, reprising the role he had played in the prep sessions for Biden’s State of the Union address, joined via Zoom to offer advice as well.

The problem, though, was that Biden's whirlwind first few weeks of June had taken a toll: He had come down with a head cold. "You could hear it in his voice on Monday, and then on Tuesday, the cold was getting worse," Dunn later recalled. "By Wednesday, they were giving him COVID tests, which came back negative."

And so rather than spending his days sparring with Bauer onstage and practicing his retorts, Biden remained more or less holed up in his cabin, the Aspen Lodge. Klain, Reed, and senior advisor Mike Donilon devoted some time going over strategy with him there, but the real value of debate prep comes from having to think on your feet and go through the motions of responding in real-time. And they weren't doing as much of that as anyone had hoped.

"We never did a full mock," one of Biden's senior advisors told me. "The closest we got was on Monday. We did an hour and ten minutes—but we never did a full hour thirty. And frankly, compared to what we did in 2020, it was minimal."

Biden's performance in the practice sessions themselves wasn't "that bad," according to several of the people there, but there just weren't enough of them. On Tuesday, for example, one of the senior advisors told me they didn't see Biden until 4:30 or 5 p.m. in the evening. "We probably did fifty minutes of Q&A, and then we talked afterward," this person told me. "That was it."

On Thursday, the day of the debate, Biden departed Camp David shortly after 1 p.m. and, after a pit stop at Joint Base Andrews, headed to Atlanta, where he was greeted by a crowd of supporters holding campaign signs and chanting "Four more years!" and "Let's go, Joe!" As the president settled in at a hotel near the venue, the First Lady popped over to a Biden Victory Fund event. "Joe's ready to go. He's prepared. He's confident," she said. "You know what a great debater he is."

Biden had been scheduled to go over to the CNN studio as soon as he landed in Atlanta to walk through the debate set to get a feel for the lighting, the placement of the moderators, and the lectern behind which he would be standing. Such a walk-through is standard practice for candidates before a big debate. But Biden skipped it and asked instead to be taken directly to his hotel.

"I don't need to go to see the stage," he told his advisors shortly after landing at the airport in Atlanta. Jeffrey Katzenberg, the Hollywood mogul who had become a top Biden fundraiser and advisor, told the president it would be a mistake not to go take a look at the debate set, but Biden didn't want to talk about it. He had participated in countless debates over the years. Why would he need a walk-through?

Instead, Biden arrived on-site for the debate approximately twenty minutes before it was set to begin. His campaign team exuded confidence, even posting a picture of Biden right before he went onstage that mocked conspiracy theories being spread by right-wing influencers. "I don't know what they've got in these performance enhancers," the post from @JoeBiden read, alongside a photo of the president holding a can of "Zero Malarkey" water with his face on it. "But I'm feeling pretty jacked up."[29]

As one senior advisor told me, though, "He didn't know what he was walking in to."

CHAPTER FIVE

DEBATE DEBACLE

As Donald Trump and Joe Biden prepared to take the stage for the CNN debate in Atlanta, Vice President Kamala Harris was in a basement conference room at the Fairmont Century Plaza hotel in Los Angeles getting ready to watch along on television. Just steps down the hall, a camera crew had set up a temporary TV studio where she would do four back-to-back live interviews immediately after the debate with news anchors from ABC, CBS, CNN, and MSNBC.

Harris's husband, Second Gentleman Doug Emhoff, was also in Los Angeles, but he'd been dispatched to a star-studded debate watch party in Beverly Hills at the home of interior designer Michael Smith, whose 11,000-square-foot mansion is a frequent stop for politicos in Hollywood. Smith had hosted a Biden–Harris fundraiser the previous December, featuring a performance by Lenny Kravitz in front of an audience that included Joe and Jill Biden, California Governor Gavin Newsom, former House Speaker Nancy Pelosi, and entertainment world titans like David Geffen, Barbra Streisand, Steven Spielberg, and Shonda Rhimes.[1]

The debate provided another opportunity to raise money for the campaign by assembling some big names. On the political side, Emhoff was joined by several of the Democratic Party's rising stars, including Governors JB Pritzker, Andy Beshear, and Gretchen Whitmer. The Hollywood contingent included the actress Jane Fonda and the legendary director Rob Reiner.

Following the pre-debate cocktail party, where the group of about seventy-five people heard from the Democratic governors, the crowd divided into two groups. Some of them watched the debate from the living room, where Smith had brought in two large-screen televisions, and the others headed down the hall to watch in the family room.

Pritzker found himself in the living room, with a front-row seat next to the wall. Before Biden could even finish answering the first question, he sent a text message to another person in the back of the room: "This is a fucking disaster."

In the other room, Jane Fonda was getting emotional as Biden struggled through the first few rounds of questions, mumbling his answers while losing his train of thought and looking confused. One watch-party attendee told me they saw tears streaming down Fonda's cheeks; another disputed that but noted she was clearly very upset.

During the first commercial break, Rob Reiner leapt from his seat and started ranting loudly. "We're fucked!" he blurted out. "We are going to lose!" Reiner grew so loud and animated, in fact, that another person in the room, Democratic strategist Chad Griffin, encouraged him to go outside to get some fresh air.

On his way out, Reiner came face-to-face with Emhoff. "We cannot win with this!" Reiner shouted out. "This is malpractice! We are going to lose this!"

To some people in attendance, Reiner appeared to be in a heated argument with Emhoff, as if the vice president's husband were somehow to blame for Biden's meltdown on the debate stage—or had been complicit in hiding the extent of Biden's mental decline. Reiner later told me that wasn't the case. "People thought I was yelling at Doug Emhoff," he said. "I wasn't yelling at him. He just happened to be right there when I was yelling out to the whole room."

But there was no downplaying what everyone at that watch party had witnessed: Biden's performance was a total disaster. Emhoff left Smith's home before the debate even ended, as did most of the other VIPs. There was no point in sticking around and watching Democrats' chances of keeping Donald Trump out of the White House crumble before their eyes.

Before the moderators had asked even a single question at the debate, viewers could see that something was clearly off with Biden; his uneasiness was palpable as soon as he was introduced and shuffled across the stage. Walking stiffly toward his lectern, Biden glanced around the room, seemingly unsure of which direction to look, before offering a brief wave and finger-point to no one in particular. There was no audience in the dark, cavernous studio, but he eventually locked eyes with the CNN moderators and mumbled a barely audible, "Hey, folks. How are ya?"

He eventually made it to his lectern but was briefly cloaked in darkness due to a lighting glitch onstage. "Good to be here," he said.

Campaign operatives and political pundits have long argued—since the first televised presidential debate between Richard Nixon and John F. Kennedy in 1960—that how a candidate looks to voters matters nearly as much as, if not more than, what he or she says. And Joe Biden looked awful.

Donald Trump exhibited no such signs of confusion as he was introduced; the former reality-TV star was playing for the cameras from the moment he was called to the stage, using his walk out to send a visual message to the audience watching on television: He wasn't there to debate, but to do battle.*

Trump marched slowly and purposefully to the lectern with a scowl. He didn't offer any lame pleasantries, and he barely made eye contact with his opponent. Unlike Biden, Trump had checked out the debate stage earlier in the day. He knew exactly where the cameras were and had reviewed how he looked on a television monitor. There were no shadows when he took his place behind his lectern. And he didn't even think about shaking Biden's hand.

Jake Tapper's first question went to Biden, and it was one the president had spent ample time preparing for. After all, it was *the* central question facing his campaign: "What do you say to voters who feel they are worse off under your presidency than they were under President Trump?"

Biden appeared confused—frightened, even—with his mouth slightly agape as Tapper finished rattling off some inflation numbers. "You have to take a look at what I was left when I became president, what Mr. Trump left me," Biden responded before raising a closed fist halfway toward his mouth as he cleared his throat. He crammed sev-

---

*As anyone who has watched professional wrestling knows, a contender's entrance is a way to win over the crowd before the match even starts. And Trump isn't just a fan of professional wrestling; he's been inside the ring during WrestleMania and is a member of the World Wrestling Entertainment Hall of Fame.

eral statistics into his two-minute response—clearly trying to tick through a series of economic points he'd practiced during those few debate prep sessions at Camp David—but his voice was weak and he fumbled some of the numbers: "We created 15,000 new jobs. We brought out—in a position where we have 800,000 new manufacturing jobs."

Biden continued: "I come from a household where the kitchen table—if things weren't able to be met during the month, was a problem. Price of eggs, the price of gas, the price of housing, the price of a whole range of things. That's why I'm working so hard to make sure I deal with those problems."

As Biden stumbled through his words, a wry grin broke out on Trump's face. The debate had started less than a minute earlier, but the former president sensed weakness. He knew that it—the debate, possibly the election—was over.

"We had the greatest economy in the history of our country," Trump blurted out with his typical bravado when Tapper pressed him on the same question. "We had never done so well. Every—everybody was amazed by it. . . . Everything was rocking good."

Biden had been prepared to shoot down Trump's exaggerations and untruths, particularly regarding his economic record. He was armed with statistics about the massive tax cut Trump signed into law that disproportionately benefited the wealthy; he was ready to pounce on Trump's record-shattering deficits. But when it came time to speak, Biden made his points weakly and unconvincingly. And then, as he was supposed to be pushing back on Trump's fabrications, he dropped a whopper of his own.

"The truth is, I'm the only president this century that doesn't have any—this, this decade—doesn't have any troops dying anywhere in the world, like he did," Biden stammered. The line was poorly delivered. It also wasn't true. American troops had died on Biden's watch: Thirteen service members were killed in the terrorist attack at Abbey Gate in Kabul during his administration's disastrously abrupt and poorly executed withdrawal from Afghanistan, and three more soldiers were killed in a drone attack near the Syrian border with Jordan in January 2024.[2]

Most of the debate was broadcast as a split screen, with Biden on the right half and Trump on the left—and Trump took advantage of the setup. As Biden struggled to get his words out, Trump played to the camera, tilting his head and looking at his opponent as though to channel what tens of millions of Americans watching at home were wondering: *What is this guy talking about?*

In response to a question about the national debt, for example, Biden got lost in a tangle of numbers, conflating millions and billions and trillions and blinking repeatedly before completely losing track of what he was talking about. He looked down and grimaced as he struggled to find the words. It was almost physically painful to watch.

"Look, if—" Biden said, pausing awkwardly. "We finally beat Medicare."

Another particularly devastating moment came during an exchange about the border. Biden began by talking about increasing the number of asylum officers and noted that border crossings had begun to decline. But then he started to trail off: "I'm going to continue to move until we get the total ban on the—the total initiative relative to what we're going to do with more Border Patrol and more asylum officers."

"President Trump?" Tapper asked.

"I really don't know what he said at the end of that sentence," Trump responded. "I don't think he knows what he said, either."

Watching along from the ABC News studio in New York, I sensed I was witnessing the end of the Biden campaign. I texted several people close to Biden, and all the responses expressed some degree of dread.

"I am in a state of shock," one Democratic congressman who supported Biden texted me back. "He is diminished to an extent that has become undeniable. It is far worse than even I thought."

Democratic Senator Michael Bennet was watching at home in Colorado with his wife. Just a few minutes in, he started to get frantic text messages from his three daughters, one of whom was watching in New Delhi, India. "To summarize their reaction," Bennet said, "'You can't be serious. We're going to lose.'"

Nancy Pelosi was watching the debate alone in her Washington, DC, apartment. She later told me she was worried about Biden's health. "I was personally concerned," she said. "He was ashen-faced and so uncertain."

Hunter Biden was also watching alone—and he's glad he was. "I can't be in a room with people commenting when Dad's on the screen," he later told me. "So I was literally in my bedroom alone. And I knew it when he walked out. I mean, I literally knew when he walked out, this was not going to go well."

Vice President Harris, in the underground meeting room at the Fairmont in Los Angeles, didn't say much as she watched her running mate flounder on national television. Joined by three of her top advisors—chief of staff Sheila Nix, communications director Kirsten

Allen, and press secretary Brian Fallon—Harris sat at the end of a conference table, papers spread out in front of her. She had a pen in her hand to take notes for her scheduled post-debate interviews, and she wasn't looking at her cell phone, relying on her advisors to monitor the reaction online.

"What is happening here?" she finally asked.

Nix and Fallon said nothing. Allen, continuing to stare at the television, brought some gallows humor. "I don't think this was the plan," she said.

The debate eventually came to a merciful end, and Trump made a beeline for the exit on his right. Biden, meanwhile, hung around onstage a little longer, joined by First Lady Jill Biden. She grabbed his hand and gingerly helped him down one step, leading him to the moderators' table so he could shake Bash's and Tapper's hands.

Out at the Fairmont Hotel, Kamala Harris turned again to Kirsten Allen, the advisor she most relied on to give her the unvarnished truth. Allen had graduated from Howard University—where she was a member of the same Alpha Kappa Alpha sorority that Harris belonged to when she was a student there—and was one of the few people who worked on Harris's 2020 presidential campaign at a senior level and was still with the vice president in 2024.

"What's the overall reaction?" Harris asked her.

"People are saying he should drop out of the race," Allen answered.

The vice president didn't have much time to process the disaster that had just unfolded. She was due to speak to a group of supporters via Zoom in five minutes, and then she would need to hustle down the hall to sit for her live post-debate television interviews. It was going to be up to Harris to attempt to explain Biden's debate performance.

Moments later, the Biden campaign's senior leadership team reached out to discuss how Harris should handle her interviews. The vice president put the call on speakerphone.

"The simple truth is that he has a cold," said Jen O'Malley Dillon, Biden's campaign manager. She advised Harris to respond to questions about the debate by pointing out that Biden wasn't feeling well and then pivoting to criticism of Trump.

Harris knew how ridiculous she would sound claiming Biden's debate performance was due to a cold, but she didn't argue about it with O'Malley Dillon on the call. As soon as she hung up, however, she told her staff she was going to ignore the campaign manager's advice.

"I'm not saying that," Harris said to her advisors. "It won't be helpful to him if I have no credibility."

By the time her interviews began, she had landed on a talking point she felt comfortable with. "Well, it was a slow start, there's no question about that," she told Rachel Maddow on MSNBC. "But I thought it was a strong finish."

CNN's Anderson Cooper wasn't satisfied with that response, however, and kept peppering Harris with questions about Biden's mental state. "The man we saw on the stage tonight," Cooper asked, "is that the person you see in meetings every day?"

Harris's answer was interesting. "The person that you saw on the debate stage that has for the last three and a half years, *up until today*, performed," she said (emphasis mine), before going on to list a litany of what she considered Biden's accomplishments. "So I'm not going to spend all night with you talking about the last ninety minutes when I've been watching the last three and a half years of performance." At no point during the interview did she blame the president's collapse on how he was feeling—or say anything about him having a cold.

Although Biden didn't leave the debate venue in Atlanta until shortly after 10:45 p.m., his night wasn't over yet. He and Jill Biden stopped by a debate watch party at the nearby Hyatt Regency, and the supporters there were surprisingly energized considering what they had just witnessed. "Four more years!" they chanted as the Bidens entered the room. "Four more years!"

The First Lady grabbed the microphone first and proceeded to talk to her husband onstage almost as though he were a child. "Joe, you did such a great job!" she declared. "You answered every question, you knew all the facts!"

A great job? Answered every question? Knew all the facts?

"And what did Trump do?" she asked the crowd. "Lied!" attendees shouted back.

President Biden told a meandering story about an old John Wayne movie, and he remained in the ballroom shaking hands and posing for pictures until finally leaving just a few minutes before midnight. He still had one more stop—a Waffle House restaurant.

"How do you think you did tonight?" a reporter asked.

"I think we did well," the president responded, adding that he had a sore throat.

Reporters pressed him again. *Was he sure about that? There were already calls for him to drop out of the race.*

"No. It's hard to debate a liar," Biden said. "*The New York Times* pointed out he lied twenty-six times."

The Trump team, meanwhile, was already putting together a TV commercial featuring Biden's abysmal performance. The ad came together within hours and highlighted Biden's incoherence on the debate stage in a particularly brutal and searing way. But it also undermined the Biden campaign's spin on the debate—*Trump lied!*—by zeroing in on the biggest falsehood Biden himself peddled onstage.

The ad started with footage of Biden stammering through his words: "I'm the only president this century that doesn't have any—this, this decade—doesn't have any troops dying anywhere in the world." The words were then repeated as images of flag-draped caskets being unloaded at the military base in Dover, Delaware—the bodies of the thirteen Americans killed during the withdrawal from Afghanistan in August 2021—flashed on the screen. The commercial concluded with a photograph of Biden taken during the ceremony for the soldiers' grieving families that showed him looking down at his watch. "Biden doesn't remember the troops who died because of his mistakes?" the ad's narrator asked. "Biden lied. Soldiers died. It's not just his dementia. It's his dishonesty."

The ad was brutally effective—or, it would have been. The Trump campaign reviewed the spot as soon as it was completed the following day and decided not to air it. In the Trump team's mind, Biden had already been defeated—the objective at this point was to keep a clearly weakened opponent from dropping out of the race.

CHAPTER SIX

BIDEN DIGS IN

The day after his disastrous debate with Donald Trump, President Biden appeared at a rally in Raleigh, North Carolina, and delivered one of the more vigorous speeches of his campaign. Feeding off the energy of a crowd of about two thousand supporters—his largest crowd of the entire campaign—he landed his attacks on Trump in a way he seemed utterly incapable of doing the night before. His voice was still raspy, but he sounded stronger, almost shouting his lines.

"Did you see Trump last night? My guess is he set—and I mean this sincerely—a new record for the most lies told in a single debate," Biden said, prompting a wave of applause.

He still looked old and moved around stiffly, but the guy who had trouble stringing sentences together hours earlier appeared more like a viable candidate again. As he ran through his attacks on Trump, the crowd repeatedly interrupted with chants of "Four more years! Four more years!" and, a couple of times, "Lock him up! Lock him up!"

For a few brief moments inside that arena, Biden and his supporters could pretend that the catastrophe of the night before hadn't happened. But it had, of course—and the president's campaign was now facing an existential crisis. The question was no longer whether Biden could defeat Trump, but whether he could survive as the Democratic nominee. A drumbeat to push him out of the race had already begun, and it was starting in the pages of *The New York Times*.

"I watched the Biden-Trump debate alone in a Lisbon hotel room, and it made me weep," *New York Times* columnist Thomas L. Friedman, a man Biden had known and respected for decades, wrote the day after the debate. "I cannot remember a more heartbreaking moment in American presidential campaign politics in my lifetime, precisely because of what it revealed: Joe Biden, a good man and a good president, has no business running for re-election."[1]

Biden addressed the big issue toward the end of his remarks in North Carolina. "I know I'm not a young man, to state the obvious," he said. "Folks, I don't walk as easy as I used to. I don't speak as smoothly as I used to. I don't debate as well as I used to. But I know what I do know: I know how to tell the truth. I know—I know—I know right from wrong. And I know how to do this job."

The crowd, filled with Biden loyalists, burst into cheers.

"And I know like millions of Americans know: When you get knocked down, you get back up," he continued. "Folks, I give you my word as a Biden. I would not be running again if I didn't believe with all my heart and soul I can do this job."

The crowd loved it. His campaign advisors were relieved, believing things were back on track. But a strong speech in the middle of the day on Friday wasn't enough to erase Thursday night's trainwreck from the minds of the tens of millions of Americans who'd watched.

And the president's North Carolina appearance was hardly a heavy lift: He had a teleprompter, spoke for only twenty minutes, and was facing a friendly crowd that had just been pumped up by several musical performances and speeches from North Carolina's most popular Democrats.

One person who wasn't reassured by Biden's improved performance was David Remnick, the editor of *The New Yorker*. Remnick was a Biden supporter, but after watching the debate, he became convinced that the president's campaign was now a "national endangerment" and that Biden was unfit not only to run against Trump but to remain in office for another four years.

"He is increasingly unsteady," Remnick wrote in a *New Yorker* column. "It is not just the political class or the commentariat who were unnerved by the debate. Most people with eyes to see were unnerved. At this point, for the Bidens to insist on defying biology, to think that a decent performance at one rally or speech can offset the indelible images of Thursday night, is folly."[2]

Two days after the debate, I reached out to Hunter Biden. He didn't pretend the debate was anything but awful. "I sat there, and it literally was the longest ninety minutes of my life," he told me. "It was worse than eight days of me being on trial."

But Hunter wasn't blaming his father for the performance; he was blaming his father's campaign team—for the intense travel schedule leading up to the debate, for how debate preparation was handled, for the decision to participate in a debate in the first place. He placed much of the blame on Biden's senior advisor Anita Dunn and her husband, Bob Bauer, who'd played the role of Donald Trump in the debate prep sessions at Camp David. "I know that I sound really angry right now, and I want you to know the reason that I sound really angry is because I'm really angry," he told me. "And I'm angry because I think that he has been incredibly mismanaged."

He was even more livid, however, at those in the Democratic Party now suggesting that his father drop out of the race. If Joe Biden stepped aside, he argued, the party would be torn apart by the battle over who would replace him. "Are people fucking out of their fucking minds?" he said, his voice rising. "We're going to give up the incumbency for there to be a fight on the floor [of the Democratic Convention] over whether we nominate AOC and Bernie Sanders? Fucking out of their minds!"

On ABC News's Sunday-morning news program, I interviewed Senator Chris Coons of Delaware, one of Biden's best friends in the Senate and a co-chair of the Biden–Harris campaign. I knew he would defend the president against the growing chorus of Democratic voices urging him to end his campaign, but I was stunned by the lengths Coons went to deny reality. He acknowledged Biden had a "weak debate performance" and "answered a few questions in ways that were not the most forceful," but he quickly pivoted to lecturing me—and in turn all those who had concerns about Biden remaining the nominee. "The only Democrat who's ever beaten Donald Trump is Joe Biden," he told me. I followed up with this:

KARL: You don't think that Joe Biden is the only Democrat that can beat Donald Trump, do you?

COONS: I think he's the only Democrat who can beat Donald Trump.

KARL: Really?

COONS: And let me tell you, he had the single-best day of grassroots fundraising after the debate. The first poll that we saw after the debate showed Joe Biden gaining ground on Donald Trump.

I'm still stunned as I reread those words. A Democratic senator with a national leadership position on the campaign was telling me that an eighty-one-year-old Joe Biden was the only Democrat in America who could defeat Donald Trump? And even more preposterously, he was telling me the debate had actually *helped* Biden?

If you were searching for evidence that Democrats tried to engage in a cover-up of Biden's deteriorating age and health, you could consider this interview. Except Coons wasn't concealing behind-the-scenes information—he was aggressively spinning what Americans across the country had seen with their own eyes. The conversation reminded me of former Iraqi President Saddam Hussein's spokesman, Mohammed Saeed al-Sahhaf (more widely known as "Baghdad Bob"), who held press conferences in 2003 declaring that victory was at hand and that the American "infidels" would soon surrender—just as US tanks began rolling into Baghdad.

A number of influential voices were calling on Biden to drop out of the race in those days immediately following the debate, but not a single Democrat in Congress or Democratic governor had publicly said Biden needed to go. Former President Barack Obama also vouched for his two-time running mate. "Bad debate nights happen," he said in a written statement. "Trust me, I know. But this election is still a choice between someone who has fought for ordinary folks his entire life and someone who only cares about himself."[3]

The day after the debate, Nancy Pelosi acknowledged Biden's

performance "wasn't great" but added that, "from a values standpoint, it far outshone the other guy." She claimed she didn't know of anybody who was pushing Biden to get out of the race: "I'm not doing it, and I don't know anyone who's doing it."[4]

Even now, I don't fully understand why Democratic officials remained silent about Biden's fate in those first few days after the debate. Many of them fully agreed—privately—with what columnists like Thomas Friedman and David Remnick had written, but they kept that to themselves. Some surely hoped Biden and his team would come to the conclusion on their own that it was time to get out of the race, but others had the opposite view, believing that, because Biden would never drop out, calls for him to do so would only weaken him further against Trump.

The Sunday after the debate, the Biden family gathered at Camp David for a decidedly apolitical reason: a photo session with acclaimed photographer Annie Leibovitz. The decision to go through with the long-planned photo shoot didn't sit well with Ron Klain, Biden's former chief of staff.

"You need to stay in Washington," Klain told Biden. "You need to have an aggressive plan to fight and to rally the troops."[5]

The coming together of the entire Biden family at such a critical moment caused widespread speculation that the "family meeting" included soul-searching about the state of the campaign and reports that the family, especially Jill and Hunter, insisted the president stay in the race and "keep fighting." But multiple people who were at Camp David tell me there was surprisingly little talk of the disastrous debate that had just occurred or the way it had transformed the campaign.

"It was like a classic Biden family afternoon. Newspapers strewn all over the place. He's got his notebooks. He's making phone calls," recalled one of the people there for the photo shoot. "Hunter's little baby Beau was swimming, the kids were trying to figure out what they're going to wear—it was like a very classic family gathering."

On Tuesday, July 2, five days after the debate, Representative Lloyd Doggett became the first elected Democrat to say publicly what so many others were saying privately. "Recognizing that, unlike Trump, President Biden's first commitment has always been to our country, not himself, I am hopeful that he will make the painful and difficult decision to withdraw," the lawmaker from Texas said in a statement. "I respectfully call on him to do so."[6]

Doggett was not a particularly influential member of the Democratic caucus, but he had given party leadership, including Pelosi and Minority Leader Hakeem Jeffries, a heads-up before making his statement—and neither of them tried to talk him out of it. Pelosi's public support for Biden had clearly softened from a few days earlier. "I think it's a legitimate question to say, 'Is this an episode, or is this a condition?'" she told Andrea Mitchell on MSNBC on July 2. "And so, when people ask that question, it's completely legitimate—of both candidates."[7]

That same day, Representative Marie Gluesenkamp Perez, a moderate Democrat from Washington state, made a blunt admission in an interview with a local ABC station—but didn't call on Biden to end his campaign. "We all saw what we saw, you can't undo that, and the truth, I think, is that Biden is going to lose to Trump," she said. "[But] a core tenet of democracy is that you accept the results of an election, and the reality is that primary voting has already happened to a degree that Biden is the nominee."[8]

One day later, Biden convened a meeting with Democratic

governors from across the country. Many made the trek to the White House to see the president themselves; others appeared virtually via Zoom. According to multiple sources who listened to or attended the meeting, no governor said—or even suggested—Biden should abandon his campaign. In a CNN interview before the meeting, Kentucky Governor Andy Beshear said he and his peers just wanted to "make sure he's doing OK."[9]

The summit itself was a mixed bag for the president. In an apparent attempt to cut the tension, Biden began the meeting with a joke. "I'm fine," he told the governors. "I don't know about my brain, though."

The joke fell flat, but Biden went on to discuss his plans for addressing the concerns raised by the debate. One of his suggestions, first reported by *The New York Times*, hit with even more of a thud than his joke: He would work fewer hours and stop scheduling events after 8 p.m. so that he could get more sleep.[10]

Sixteen years earlier, Hillary Clinton had famously run an ad during the Democratic presidential primary, noting that the commander in chief needs to be prepared whenever a crisis strikes—even if that's in the middle of the night. "It's three a.m., and your children are safe and asleep," the ad's narrator says. "But there is a phone in the White House, and it's ringing. Something is happening in the world. Your vote will decide who answers that call." Was Biden now suggesting he would no longer be answering those calls?

Governor JB Pritzker of Illinois traveled to Washington to attend the meeting in person. When it was his turn to speak, he pointed to the grim polling that showed Trump ahead in the battleground states that would decide the election, and he asked Biden a direct question: "What is the plan to turn things around?" Biden responded with words, but no real answer. It was glaringly obvious to at least some of those in the room that he didn't have a plan. As the meeting broke up, Biden–Harris campaign manager Jen O'Malley Dillon quietly went up to Pritzker and said she would get back to him soon with an answer. She never did.

Still, no governor emerged from the meeting calling on Biden to consider ending his campaign. In fact, most of them said nothing at all. Just three—Kathy Hochul of New York, Wes Moore of Maryland, and Tim Walz of Minnesota—went to the cameras assembled outside the White House to talk about their discussion with the president, and all three insisted the party was united behind him.

"Joe Biden is in it to win it," Hochul said.[11]

One of the many elected Democrats who privately believed Biden needed to step aside was Senator Mark Warner of Virginia. He had long been concerned about Biden's age—one "holy shit" moment for him came when Biden turned down the opportunity to do the typical presidential interview before the Super Bowl in 2024—but the debate spurred him into action. The following day, he began calling his Senate colleagues to share his worries that Trump would win back the White House if Biden stayed in the race.

Congress was not in session, but Warner called approximately thirty-five of his Democratic Senate colleagues over the course of the week, and just about all of them expressed serious anxiety over Biden's ability to defeat Trump. Most agreed the party would be better off if he ended his campaign, and some said he needed to do so immediately—before the July 4th holiday—to give the party time to coalesce around a new nominee.

Independence Day came and went, though, and Biden remained as committed as ever to his reelection bid. On Friday, July 5—eight days after the debate—he tried to address the concerns about his age in a prime-time interview with my ABC colleague George Stephanopoulos, which would be played in its entirety with no edits. The anticipation was intense: The interview would be the first real test of Biden's cognitive ability since the debate.

"I thought, this is basically a one-topic interview," George later told me. "If he can handle the questions, he's got a shot to remain the candidate, whether or not he hasn't got to win, and if he can't, that's probably going to be it."

At first, White House officials said they wanted the president's interview to last only ten minutes, an absurdly short amount of time given what Biden hoped to accomplish: demonstrate he had the mental acuity and stamina to continue his campaign and to serve another four years as president. George insisted it needed to be at least twenty minutes. The Biden team ultimately agreed.

The Trump campaign, of course, would be watching closely. While the ABC team was still setting up for the interview in an empty middle school classroom in Madison, Wisconsin, senior Trump advisor Jason Miller tweeted what he claimed was a big scoop: "Hearing they're re-taping the ABC interview now as Biden bombed it in the first run."[12]

It was an absurd thing to say and he knew it. The ABC interview with Biden hadn't even started yet.

A few minutes later—before the interview began—Biden sent a message intended to put an end to the nervous chatter about him among Democrats once and for all. "Let me say this as clearly as I can," he posted on X. "I'm the sitting President of the United States. I'm the nominee of the Democratic party. I'm staying in the race."[13]

When the interview finally kicked off, George got straight to the point. "Let's start with the debate," he said. "You and your team said—have said—you had a bad night. But your—"

"Sure did," Biden interrupted.

"Was this a bad episode or the sign of a more serious condition?" George asked, posing what Pelosi had days earlier described as a "legitimate question."

"It was a bad episode," Biden responded. "No indication of any serious condition. I was exhausted. I didn't listen to my instincts in terms of preparing and—and a bad night."

Biden's voice was stronger than it had been during the debate, but not by much. By the time George got to his third question, I realized the interview was not going to quell the growing doubt about Biden.

"Did you ever watch the debate afterwards?" George asked.

"I don't think I did, no," Biden said.

I remember being flummoxed by that response. Did he really not remember if he had gone back to watch his performance?

The president went into the interview with two objectives: to reassure Democrats that the debate was an aberration and to make crystal clear that he would not be ending his reelection bid. "Look, I mean, if the Lord Almighty came down and said, 'Joe, get outta the race,' I'd get outta the race," Biden said. "The Lord Almighty's not comin' down."

The interview was hardly reassuring to Democratic lawmakers who doubted Biden's ability to win and serve another four years—his voice was still weak, and some of his answers disjointed—but the president's answer to George's final question made some of them downright angry.

STEPHANOPOULOS: And if you stay in and Trump is elected and everything you're warning about comes to pass, how will you feel in January?

BIDEN: I'll feel as long as I gave it my all and I did the good [sic] as job as I know I can do, that's what this is about.

The mangled syntax was a problem given the nature of the concerns about Biden, but the sentiment behind it was even more damaging. The president would be okay with handing the White House over to Donald Trump as long as he gave it his all? The same Donald Trump he had described as an "existential threat" to the country months earlier?[14] No, the top priority of most Democrats at this point was keeping Trump as far from power as they could—and Biden's interview had provided more evidence that he wasn't up to the task.

President Biden, however, seemed to consider the interview a success. He stuck around for several minutes of small talk once it was over, telling George some old stories about Greeks in Delaware and talking about politics in Wisconsin. If Biden was concerned about the fate of his candidacy or the growing Democratic effort to oust him, he didn't show it.

On the same day Biden sat down with Stephanopoulos, *The Washington Post* published a story about Senator Warner's conversations with his fellow Senate Democrats. According to reporters Leigh Ann Caldwell and Liz Goodwin, Warner was "attempting to assemble a group of Democratic senators to ask President Biden to exit the presidential race."[15]

The story was accurate, but it actually understated just how many senators Warner had been talking to—and how long his effort had been underway. Even with Congress out of session, he had spoken with nearly all his Democratic colleagues, and according to a source familiar with Warner's efforts, at least half a dozen of them planned to publicly call for Biden to end his campaign before Congress reconvened the following week.

But as soon as Warner's effort became publicly known, the White House moved to put an end to it, with assistance from Senate Majority Leader Chuck Schumer. The Democrat from New York knew about Warner's phone calls and personally had no problem with them, but once *The Washington Post* published its story, he asked Warner and other Democratic senators considering going public with their demands of Biden to wait to give the president a chance to address their concerns and consider his options.

One senator, Michael Bennet of Colorado, had already privately concluded that Biden would lose if he stayed in the race—and issued a statement via a spokesperson that stopped just short of calling on the president to end his campaign. "Sen. Bennet believes President Biden must reassure the American people that he can run a vigorous campaign to defeat Donald Trump," it read. "As the Senate comes back into session this week, he plans to discuss with his colleagues the most viable path forward in this existential election."[16]

Bennet would later tell me that he was driven to speak out by what he was hearing from his constituents back home in Colorado. Even before the debate, he had been facing tough questions about Biden's viability—and why the president was running for reelection.

"There was a sense that, 'If you guys really think Donald Trump is such a threat to our democracy, why are you running somebody against him that doesn't seem like he's going to win?'" Bennet told me, summarizing what he had heard in his town hall meetings in late June. "This is *before* the debate."

In the days after Biden's lackluster performance in Atlanta, Bennet held a series of events in western Colorado and received even more pointed feedback. Voters were pleading with him to convince Biden that the time had come for him to move on. "'I've seen this with my mom. I've seen this with my dad,'" Bennet remembered voters telling him. "'You've got to talk to the president. . . . This isn't going to get better.'"

The Senate reconvened on Tuesday, and Democrats in the chamber got together for their weekly lunch meeting. Twelve days had passed since Biden's disastrous debate, but this was the first time the entire Democratic caucus had gathered in one place to discuss what had happened. During the private meeting, Bennet, Senator Sherrod Brown of Ohio, and Senator Jon Tester of Montana made the case that if the party didn't change course, Democrats would lose the presidency—and likely control of Congress, too.

But still, not a single Democratic senator—or governor—had publicly called on Biden to drop out of the race. And Lloyd Doggett was still the only Democratic House member publicly saying Biden should step aside.

At least one prominent House Democrat, however, had reached out to Biden privately and made the case for ending his campaign. Representative Jamie Raskin of Maryland—a key figure on the January 6 Committee and in Donald Trump's second impeachment trial—wrote the president a four-page letter that was dated July 6 but wouldn't be released publicly for another two weeks. The two men had forged a bond over politics, and also their personal grief. Biden had consoled Raskin after his son, Tommy, died by suicide on December 31, 2020—one week before the January 6 attack on the Capitol.

"I write as your admirer, your supporter and your fellow politician. I write also as your friend who has treasured your compassion and wisdom," Raskin began the letter. "But I write you now, above all, as a fellow citizen who shares your mad love for American democracy and freedom. We are under siege every day by the autocrats and monarchists, from Moscow to Mar-A-Lago, and the decisions we make will be historic for the fate of our country and our freedom."[17]

The first three pages of the missive read like a political love letter. Raskin praised Biden for defeating Donald Trump in 2020 and for steadfastly defending American democracy. "I write to remind you of your true greatness as a leader," he said. "In our times, you have always been the ringing clear voice of democracy in a world being ripped apart by strongmen and dictators."

He then reminded Biden of his own words, quoting extensively from a speech Biden had delivered earlier in the year at Valley Forge, Pennsylvania, where George Washington and his Continental Army took refuge during some of the darkest days of the Revolutionary War. "There is a remarkable passage in that Valley Forge speech of yours which I cannot get out of my mind," Raskin wrote. "You observed that, 'in the rotunda of the Capitol, there's a giant painting of General George Washington—not President Washington—and he is resigning his commission as Commander-in-Chief of the Continental Army.' You say that, 'The artist that painted that portrait memorialized that moment because he said it was one of the highest moral lessons ever given to the world.'"

Raskin was reminding Biden that he himself had argued that voluntarily relinquishing power was the ultimate act of greatness. As

Biden noted in his Valley Forge speech, "When Washington got elected president, he could have stayed for two, three, four, or five terms till he died. But that wasn't the America he and the American troops at Valley Forge had fought for."

Before ending his letter, Raskin, a baseball fan, invoked the experience of the Hall of Fame pitcher Pedro Martínez in game 7 of the 2003 American League Championship Series between the Boston Red Sox and the New York Yankees. The Red Sox were ahead by three runs and just five outs away from reaching the World Series and ending one of the longest championship droughts in sports history. Pedro had pitched a great game, but he was clearly tired by the eighth inning, and Red Sox manager Grady Little wanted to take him out. Pedro insisted on staying in the game, however, and proceeded to blow the lead, setting the Yankees up to win in extra innings and denying the Red Sox a chance at their first World Series victory since 1918.

"There is no shame in taking a well-deserved bow to the overflowing appreciation of the crowd when your arm is tired out, and there is real danger for the team in ignoring the statistics," Raskin wrote. "Your situation is tricky because you are both our star pitcher and our Manager. But in democracy, as you have shown us more than any prior president, you are not a Manager acting all alone; you are the co-Manager along with our great team and our great people. Caucus with the team, Mr. President. Hear them out. You will make the right decision."

Biden would eventually reach the conclusion Raskin hoped, but not for several more weeks. In the meantime, the president tried once more to stamp out the idea that he was going anywhere with a densely written two-page letter on July 8 addressed to "Fellow Democrats" and delivered to congressional leaders.

"We had a Democratic nomination process and the voters have spoken clearly and decisively," Biden wrote. "I received over 14 million votes, 87% of the votes cast across the entire nominating process. I have nearly 3,900 delegates, making me the presumptive nominee of our party by a wide margin."

Biden's tone had markedly changed. No longer was he apologizing for or explaining his bad debate performance, and the letter sharply demanded his fellow Democrats back off: He had won the nomination fair and square, and he wasn't going to let anyone take it away from him. "This was a process open to anyone who wanted to run," the letter read. "Only three people chose to challenge me. One fared so badly that he left the primaries to run as an independent. Another attacked me for being too old and was soundly defeated. The voters of the Democratic Party have voted. They have chosen me to be the nominee of the party."

The president was clearly irritated—if not irate—with the growing drumbeat from his so-called allies. "The question of how to move forward has been well-aired for over a week now," he wrote. "And it's time for it to end."[18]

With at least one very important Democrat, Biden's letter backfired.

"The letter was, I have to say, I do not think was written by Joe Biden," Nancy Pelosi later told me, saying there was an anger to the letter that didn't sound like Biden. "It didn't even grant us any part of the success. Members were like, 'What is this letter? What is this letter?' So the letter was not helpful. I don't think he wrote it."

Biden sounded even angrier when he called into *Morning Joe*, the MSNBC show hosted by Joe Scarborough and Mika Brzezinski, later in the day. "I'm getting so frustrated by the elites—now I'm not talking about you guys—the elites in the party," Biden said in the audio-only interview. "Any of these guys that don't think I should run, run against me. Announce for president, challenge me at the convention."

It was a friendly interview. The hosts had been defending Biden against post-debate criticism.* But when Brzezinski prefaced a question by calling Biden "the presumptive nominee," Biden shot back: "I'm more than the presumptive, I'm going to be the Democratic nominee."[19]

The following day, Pelosi placed a call to Biden's closest aide, deputy chief of staff Annie Tomasini, to arrange a visit to the White House for a private conversation with the president. She had asked Biden for a meeting a couple of days earlier, and he told her to set up the particulars with Tomasini. This was the first time the former Speaker of the House had ever called Tomasini. Normally, Pelosi would set up her visits through the president's political advisors or his chief of staff and meet with Biden in the West Wing. But Tomasini could set up the meeting quietly, arranging for Pelosi to go directly to the White House living quarters—avoiding the West Wing, where she would likely be seen by a lot of people. Tomasini was more like a member of the Biden family than a political operative. Without telling anybody else in the White House, she made arrangements for Pelosi to see the president at 10 a.m. the next day.

---

*Just a few months earlier, Scarborough had viciously attacked those with concerns about Biden's cognitive ability. "Eff you if you can't handle the truth," he said, straight to the camera. "This version of Biden—intellectually, analytically—is the best Biden ever. Not a close second."

When the morning came, Pelosi made a quick stop before heading to the White House: MSNBC's studios on Capitol Hill. She was set to appear on *Morning Joe*, the very show where Biden had days earlier attacked the "elites" in the party and insisted he wasn't getting out of the race. "It's up to the president to decide if he is going to run," she told cohost Jonathan Lemire. "We're all encouraging him to make that decision, because time is running short."

But wait a minute. Hadn't Biden already declared—clearly and definitively—that he had made his decision? That he wasn't going anywhere? Lemire pointed that out, and asked Pelosi whether *she* wanted him to run. "I want him to do whatever he decides to do," she replied. "And that's the way it is."[20]

Pelosi's comments were devastating to Biden. She was no longer Speaker of the House, but there were few people more admired and respected among Democrats than her—and she was making it clear she did not accept the decision Biden had already made.

Pelosi's interview took place at 7:40 a.m. She arrived at the White House about two hours later, using a private entrance on the South Lawn, out of sight from those working in the West Wing. Tomasini led her to an elevator that took her up to the private White House residence.

Pelosi and Biden met alone in a room on the second floor of the White House called the Yellow Oval, a beautiful and ornate living area with sweeping views of the South Lawn. For Pelosi, it was a rare visit to the living quarters of the White House. She had been to the West Wing countless times, but during her nearly forty years in Congress she had been upstairs in the residence only about a half-dozen times. As they sat alone together, Pelosi expressed her concerns about the state of the race. The polls were bad, not just for Biden but for

Democrats in key congressional races. She told Biden that he had been a great president with a towering legacy of legislative accomplishment, but she said a Republican victory in November—a Trump victory—would destroy everything he had built. If Trump won, there would be no Biden legacy. She did not directly tell him she believed he should drop out. Echoing what she had said on *Morning Joe*, she told him he had a hugely consequential decision to make.

To answer Pelosi's concerns about the polls, Biden placed a call to his senior political advisor, Mike Donilon, and put him on speakerphone, asking him to share his assessment of the race with the former speaker. Donilon later told me he had no idea Biden was meeting with Pelosi and was surprised to get the call, but he said the polls had not changed much since the debate. Trump had a slight lead, he acknowledged, but it was within the margin of error and, he insisted, Biden could still win.

Pelosi curtly dismissed Donilon's comments. "What about the battleground states?" she said. Donilon insisted Biden was still statistically tied with Trump in the battleground states too. Again, Pelosi was entirely unconvinced and made it clear she had come to talk to the president, not to debate his political advisor. Biden ended the call and resumed his one-on-one talk with Pelosi.

At the end of the meeting, Pelosi suggested to Biden that they pray together. In her hand, the former Speaker held a pocket rosary coin—a medallion about the size of a quarter, with beads and a crucifix. Biden took out a similar coin he had in his pocket. And with that, the two Catholics shared a moment of prayer.

It was the last real conversation Pelosi ever had with Joe Biden. In fact, for the next several months, the president would not say a single word to her.

Whether he realized it or not, Biden's defiant letter to Democrats had done nothing to slow the momentum of the campaign against him within the party—the walls were closing in. Just moments after Pelosi left the White House—where she conveyed the sentiments of congressional Democrats—*The New York Times* published an op-ed making clear that Biden was bleeding support from the Democratic donor community. "I Love Joe Biden," read the title of the piece by actor George Clooney. "But We Need a New Nominee."

Clooney was arguably the party's most influential figure in Hollywood, a prolific Democratic fundraiser, and a spokesman for progressive causes. As I noted in chapter 4, he had headlined the Biden campaign's biggest fundraiser just a few weeks earlier. His words were not merely the flippant musings of an actor—they represented the serious doubts about Biden held by Democratic elites across the country.

"It's devastating to say it, but the Joe Biden I was with three weeks ago at the fund raiser was not the Joe 'big F-ing deal' Biden of 2010," Clooney began. "He wasn't even the Joe Biden of 2020. He was the same man we all witnessed at the debate."

"We are not going to win in November with this president," Clooney continued. "On top of that, we won't win the House, and we're going to lose the Senate. This isn't only my opinion; this is the opinion of every senator and Congress member and governor who I've spoken with in private. Every single one, irrespective of what he or she is saying publicly."[21]

Before publishing his article, Clooney had sent it to Jeffrey Katzenberg, a co-chair of the Biden–Harris campaign and a major figure in

Hollywood whom Clooney knew well. He'd also sent it to Biden's senior advisor Steve Ricchetti, who tried to talk Clooney out of publishing it. "Give us a week or two" to work things out, Ricchetti pleaded. Clooney refused and sent the article off to *The New York Times*.

Several people close to Biden believed Barack Obama was somehow behind the Clooney op-ed. The former president, after all, was close to Clooney. And while Obama hadn't said anything publicly to suggest Biden should get out of the race, several of his former White House aides were among the loudest voices urging Biden to drop out—and plenty of Biden's allies suspected Obama had coordinated with his friend Clooney. A spokesperson for Obama insists the former president did not see the article before it was published, and Clooney himself told me Obama had nothing to do with it. President Biden's son, however, doesn't buy it.

"Really? He didn't know that [Clooney] was going to [write that]?" Hunter Biden later mused to me. "I can tell you this: If Barack Obama asked him *not* to do it, he wouldn't have done it."

To the Biden family, the Clooney op-ed was just another indication that Obama wasn't standing by the man who had served as his vice president and instead was working behind the scenes to undermine him. They didn't feel betrayed by George Clooney. He was a celebrity, a donor, an activist. They had no real personal connection to him. They felt betrayed by Obama.

"I don't think that President Obama harbors ill will towards my dad, or even like an underlying kind of arrogance or jealousy that is so distinct that he wanted to push him out," Hunter Biden told me. "I just think that our ideas of loyalty are fundamentally different, just fundamentally different about what it means to be a friend."

CHAPTER SEVEN

BUTLER

When Secret Service agent Nick Menster heard the first gunshot fired at the Butler Farm Show grounds in western Pennsylvania on July 13, 2024, his thoughts immediately went to the toy firecrackers his kids had been throwing around on his driveway for the Fourth of July, just nine days earlier.

"I'm thinking is there a heckler behind me with a cap gun, with some POP-ITS, throwing them down just to make a distraction?'" he recalled. "So I'm waiting for somebody to say something over the radio, 'heckler,' something, and then I heard nothing."

When the second shot went off, Menster knew the cracks weren't coming from POP-ITS. "I just instinctively just went up there, and I yelled at the president to get down," he remembered. "I said it three times: 'Get down. Get down. Get down.'"[1]

A man with an AR-15 rifle was shooting at Donald Trump from less than two hundred yards away. And Menster, the assistant special agent in charge of Trump's security detail, did what he had spent a lifetime preparing for: He put himself between the sound of the gunfire and the man whose life he was charged with protecting.

Over the next few minutes, Menster would also find himself in a situation he had never anticipated: being tasked with protecting a man who was fighting back, resisting his Secret Service agents as they attempted to rush him to safety. The episode would be a dangerous breach of protocol and, quite possibly, Trump's finest hour.

Donald Trump began his day on Saturday, July 13, 2024, at his Mar-a-Lago resort in West Palm Beach.

The Republican National Convention was due to start in just two days, and the GOP nominee had still not selected his running mate. In fact, he had only recently begun the process of formally interviewing candidates for the job. That morning, he was conducting his first, and only, interview with JD Vance, the thirty-nine-year-old senator from Ohio. The night before, he had met with North Dakota Governor Doug Burgum and Senator Marco Rubio of Florida.

According to Vance, Trump told him he was "probably" going to choose him but wasn't ready to make the decision official yet. And then, seconds later, Trump turned to one of his aides and reversed course. "Actually, wouldn't it really set the world ablaze if we just made the decision today?" Trump asked. Looking at Vance, he added, "Why don't you come up with me and we'll make the announcement today in Butler, Pennsylvania?"[2]

Moments later, Trump changed his mind yet again, telling Vance the campaign needed more time to set up the announcement. So Vance went home to Ohio to be with his family and wait with anticipation to hear whether Trump's decision was truly final. A few hours later, Trump flew with a small group of campaign staffers to Pittsburgh, where his motorcade was ready to take him on the forty-five-minute drive to the town of Butler, Pennsylvania.

Nobody expected much news out of the rally scheduled for that evening. The Trump campaign had quietly told reporters Trump would not be announcing his running mate there, leading some reporters who regularly covered the Republican nominee to skip the rally and go straight to Milwaukee ahead of the convention. Trump's entourage was smaller than usual, too, with top campaign aides like Chris LaCivita and Jason Miller also heading to Wisconsin early to prepare for the convention.

That said, Butler, Pennsylvania, almost perfectly fit the profile of Trump Country. A place that seemed to have been left behind by just about everybody, it epitomized the land of the "forgotten men and women" that Trump promised to represent when he first ran for president.

Butler was once a thriving manufacturing town, home to a Pullman-Standard plant that made more than five hundred railroad cars every week in the early 1900s.[3] Located less than forty miles north of Pittsburgh, Butler had been a place with good, high-paying union jobs, a large Carnegie library, solid schools, and plenty of well-built middle-class homes. A minor league baseball team moved into town in the 1930s, and Whitey Ford played there on his way to Yankee Stadium and Cooperstown.[4]

Butler's population peaked at nearly twenty-five thousand in the 1940s. As the United States entered World War II, the Pullman-Standard plant quickly retooled its production to make artillery shells and aerial bombs, while thousands of Butler County's young men shipped off to Europe and the Pacific front.[5]

But a few short years after most of those men had returned home, the country and their county began to change. As the size of the federal government grew, Butler's population began to shrink. In 1951, the baseball team left town. And as air travel and interstate highways overtook the railroads, the old Pullman-Standard railcar plant shut down in 1982, spiking the countywide unemployment rate to 17.5 percent.[6] The massive, rusted-out building was finally demolished in 2005, replaced by a strip mall that, when Trump came to visit Butler, housed a Gabe's Discount Store, Family Dollar, and soon-to-be closed Joann Fabrics. Neither the promises of politicians nor the tech booms of the 1990s and 2010s did much to improve life for those who still lived there.

By the time Donald Trump came to town, Butler's population had slid to slightly more than thirteen thousand. And like so many other places in the industrial Midwest, Butler proved fertile ground for a politician looking to attack the elites in both parties and promising to make America great again. In 2016, Trump won Butler County in a landslide—with two out every three voters casting their ballots for him.

On July 6, 2024, a twenty-year-old man named Thomas Matthew Crooks registered to attend Donald Trump's rally at the Butler Farm Show grounds the following week. Trump's campaign had announced the pre-convention rally three days earlier, and Crooks conducted several internet searches the day he registered, typing the words "Where will trump speak from at butler farm show" and, ominously, "How far away was oswald from kennedy."[7]

There's no record of Crooks ever attending a Trump rally, or any other campaign event, before he registered to see Trump in Butler. He was from Bethel Park, another small western Pennsylvania town not far from Pittsburgh. A 2022 graduate of Bethel Park High School, he was a good student but didn't make much of an impression on his teachers or classmates. A school counselor described him as "your typical average kid—more on the quiet side, relatively intelligent."[8] A former classmate remembered him as "just a normal person who seemed like he didn't like talking to people."[9] After high school, Crooks enrolled in a local community college and graduated with an associate's degree in engineering science about two months before registering for the Trump rally. He planned to attend classes at Robert Morris University—a small private college outside Pittsburgh—in the fall.

Crooks had no record of any behavioral issues or brushes with the law. Law enforcement officials later described him as a strikingly intelligent student, scoring high enough on his SAT to go to an Ivy League school. But they also noted he might have struggled for years with an undiagnosed disorder.[10] He registered to vote as a Republican after turning eighteen, and made only one political donation in his life, giving $15 to a Democratic-aligned group in 2021.

While Crooks didn't appear to be very politically active, he did have an interest in firearms. He tried to join his high school's rifle club but, according to two classmates, was quickly rejected. "He didn't just not make the team—he was asked not to come back because of how bad of a shot he was. It was considered dangerous," his classmate Jameson Myers told my ABC News colleague Olivia Rubin. "On the first day of preseason, he basically couldn't even hit the target."[11]

But on August 10, 2023, a little more than a year after graduating high school, Crooks joined the Clairton Sportsmen's Club near his hometown. Over the next eleven months, he registered to use the club's firing ranges forty-three times, spending several holidays there, including Valentine's Day, Halloween, and Christmas. His last visit was on July 12, 2024, the day before the rally in Butler.[12]

When the Secret Service senior special agent assigned to cover the rally arrived at 8 a.m. that morning, he noticed a long line of Trump supporters waiting to get in, five hours before the fairgrounds would be open to the public and ten hours before Trump was set to take the stage. The line still stretched around the fairgrounds when my colleague Lalee Ibssa arrived at the rally two hours later, a phenomenon she was used to after covering more than two hundred Trump events. Just twenty-five years old, Lalee worked harder than just about anybody on the campaign beat, going almost anywhere Trump went as ABC's "embed" on the Republican's campaign.

Lalee didn't think much of it at the time, but the first thing she noticed as she walked into the rally venue was how lax the security seemed to be. She had to go through metal detectors, of course, and put her bags through an X-ray machine. But she didn't have to open her equipment up for Secret Service agents and turn it on like she usually did, and the typical bomb-detecting dogs were nowhere to be found. A fellow embed from CNN who entered the rally with Lalee noticed the same thing.

"I remember looking at her and saying, 'Oh my God, security was so chill today,'" Lalee later recalled. "And she said, 'That's the quickest we've ever gotten in.'"

Corey Comperatore was already waiting in line to get into the rally when Lalee arrived. A fifty-year-old former volunteer fire chief from nearby Buffalo Township, Corey had registered to attend the event as soon as it was announced and had told his wife and two daughters they needed to get there early to ensure they could get seats up front. "I have to make sure I sit nice and close, because Trump's gonna call me up on that stage," Corey joked with his wife and daughters. "He's gonna go, 'Corey. Where's Corey? I can't do this without Corey up here. Oh, there he is. Come on up here.'"[13]

I never had the chance to meet Corey Comperatore, but I've since learned he had a lot in common with my father. Like my dad, Corey had been a volunteer firefighter his entire adult life. My dad served in the Navy Reserves, while Corey was a ten-year veteran of the Army Reserves. Both men loved cars and were meticulous in caring for their own vehicles. Corey was known as someone quick to help out people in need, never expecting anything in return—exactly what brought my father to the fire department. And both Corey and my father were big fans of Donald Trump.

Like everyone else registered for the rally, Corey had been receiving text messages from the campaign since signing up, telling him where to show up, when the gates would open, and what he was allowed to bring. "Really, though, he's been texting me all week," Corey joked as his daughters laughed at the idea Trump would call him up to the stage. "Every day, I've been getting a text from him."[14]

At about 11 a.m., Thomas Matthew Crooks arrived outside the Butler Farm Show grounds, taking a drive around the area before returning home. Earlier that morning, he'd stopped by a local hardware store to buy a ladder—the final piece of equipment he'd need to orchestrate his plan.[15]

The rally opened to the general public at 1 p.m., and rallygoers began shuffling through the magnetometers and sending their small bags through X-ray machines. Text messages between Secret Service agents suggested that, at this point, their biggest concern was the blistering heat: It was 95 degrees outside, and there was already a line at the medical tent.[16]

The team providing security for the area immediately surrounding the rally described a festival-like atmosphere in the hours ahead of Trump's speech, requiring agents to separate potential threats from rallygoers picnicking and drinking across the fairgrounds.[17] Security officials were also dealing with some communications glitches, including spotty cell service and interference on the Secret Service radios, caused in part by an event in Pittsburgh with another protectee: First Lady Jill Biden.

At 1:30 p.m., Crooks was back at his home in Bethel Heights. He told his father he was planning to go to the local gun range and asked to use his AR-15 rifle.[18] That wasn't an unusual request for Crooks; he had taken the rifle on his many other visits to the gun club.

After leaving the house, Crooks stopped to buy ammunition—fifty rounds of .223 Remington full metal jacket—but he didn't go to the range. Instead, he returned to Butler, arriving outside the Trump rally at 3:47 p.m. Crooks parked his car, took out a drone, and flew it over the rally site for eleven minutes, watching the video on the drone's controller. The view from the drone would have given Crooks a clear look at the stage, the lectern behind which Trump would be speaking, the buildings surrounding the fairgrounds, and the locations of Secret Service and local SWAT team snipers.

Typically, Secret Service agents would have immediately detected a drone flying around a secure site and, if necessary, neutralized it.

In fact, the Secret Service had a drone-detection system on the ground in Butler, but it had gone down that morning. Agents attempted to fix it for hours, even placing calls to a 1-800 troubleshooting number for help before eventually getting it operational again at about 4:30 p.m.—more than half an hour after Crooks had flown his drone over the area.[19]

By 5 p.m., three different local law enforcement officers began to take notice of Crooks, finding his movements and behavior suspicious. A member of the local SWAT sniper team, for example, noticed Crooks seemed intensely focused on the buildings—and the snipers—outside the rally. "It really appeared to me that he had absolutely zero interest in anything that was happening inside the fence," the officer later recalled.[20]

One of the local snipers stationed outside the security perimeter by a complex of buildings owned by an equipment company noticed Crooks appeared to have a rangefinder with him. At approximately 5:15 p.m., he snapped two photos of the twenty-year-old man with his phone and texted them to other members of the local law enforcement team with a series of three messages:

Are you watching this guy up against our building?

Long hair gray tshirt white shorts

He has a range finder.[21]

"I noticed he was on a cellphone," another member of the local sniper team who'd spotted Crooks later recalled. "And I was sitting there with binoculars. So I zoom in on his cellphone, and I could tell that he's looking at news feeds. . . . Then he takes his phone and he puts it in his pocket, and he pulls out—it's a rangefinder."[22]

The rangefinder—a device used to determine the distance between objects—raised a red flag immediately, because it can be used to help a shooter determine if he or she is close enough to hit a target. "When I noticed him looking through this rangefinder he was looking towards the stage," the sniper testified. "I was like, yeah, this is not right."

Word of Crooks's behavior began to slowly spread across the local law enforcement officials at the rally as Trump's motorcade arrived at 5:33 p.m. By this point, members of the local sniper team had lost sight of the gunman and were scrambling to find him again. Five minutes after Trump arrived, a local Butler police officer notified a Secret Service agent stationed at the entrance used by Trump's motorcade about Crooks's suspicious actions—and that they had lost sight of him.

Over the next thirteen minutes, a series of calls and messages about Crooks—including his description and movements—were shared with the Secret Service. But there is no evidence that any of that information was relayed to the agents in charge of security at the rally or to the members of President Trump's security detail positioned near the stage.

Upon arriving, Trump was led into a holding area backstage, where he met with a few VIPs, including a local mayor and Dave McCormick, the Republican US Senate candidate. Trump also spent a few minutes with a ninety-five-year-old Butler resident named Malphine Fogel, whose son Marc, a schoolteacher, had been held in a Russian prison for more than two years after being arrested with a tiny amount of medical marijuana.[23] Trump promised Malphine he'd bring her son home when he returned to the White House.*

---

*Fogel was released from Russian custody on February 11, 2025, in exchange for cybercrime kingpin Alexander Vinnik. "He promised me he would get him out—and he kept

As Trump prepared to take the stage around 6 p.m., my colleague Rachel Scott stood in front of an ABC camera at the Butler Farm Show grounds and got ready for a live report that would air on the Saturday broadcast of *World News Tonight*. Rachel and her producer Ben Siegel almost didn't go to Butler. They had considered going straight to Milwaukee for the convention like several other reporters on the Trump beat, but ABC Washington bureau chief Rick Klein insisted they attend just in case Trump made news by announcing his running mate at the rally.

At 6:04 p.m., as Rachel began her live report for ABC's *World News Saturday*, Trump emerged in the background, walking onstage as Lee Greenwood's "God Bless the USA" blasted from the speakers. The news had been fairly slow on that Saturday. Rachel's report previewed the upcoming Republican National Convention and provided an update on Trump's search for a running mate.

"With the former president just now taking the stage behind me right here in Pennsylvania, no formal offer has been extended yet, but we know that Donald Trump has narrowed it down to at least three Republicans," Rachel said as the crowd chanted "USA! USA! USA!"

"Trump has said himself that he wants to do this during the week of the convention, possibly as early as Monday. But he has also very much enjoyed this public vetting process, calling it a 'highly sophisticated version of *The Apprentice*.'"

Rachel's live report ended at 6:05 p.m. Six minutes later, as she was still standing in front of the camera, shots rang out.

---

his promise, and I can't thank him enough," Fogel's mother said after her son's release. Melania Trump invited both Fogels to attend Trump's joint address to Congress one month later, and they did, receiving a shout-out from Trump himself during the high-profile event.

Moments earlier, just outside the rally's security perimeter, local Butler police officers had been in an all-out scramble to get to Crooks. A Butler police officer had spotted the soon-to-be gunman at about 6:06 p.m., but as the officer moved toward him, Crooks picked up a backpack and sprinted off. Minutes later, bystanders spotted Crooks climbing onto the roof of a building and yelled out to the police.

Meanwhile, a few hundred yards away, Trump was inviting Republican Senate candidate Dave McCormick up on stage. "Can we bring him up for a couple of minutes later?" Trump asked. "A little bit later? All right. You get ready, McCormick. You get ready. I'll get you up here."

Back outside the security perimeter, a local detective who had been assigned to manage traffic at an intersection outside the fairgrounds' entrance spotted Crooks and jumped out of his car to pursue him, attempting to climb onto the roof where the shooter was now positioned. With a boost from another policeman, he managed to briefly get his head up high enough to see him.

"I see Crooks facing downrange towards the stage, but his eyes are back at me as I'm coming up," the officer later recalled. "His facial expressions [were] surprised. His eyes were very big, like, what are you doing up here? And from there, he just slowly turned on his waist, like—he was proned out like this, and he kind of slowly turned around. And as I came up, that's when he pointed his firearm in my face."

The detective tried to lift himself onto the roof but couldn't maintain his grip. "As I'm coming up and he's got the gun pointed at me, I don't know if I reach for my gun, if I slip," he recalled. "But all I know from that point is I'm looking at him, and all my weight is on my, like, arms, my hands, and I don't have a grip. . . . The next thing I know is, I'm smack against the ground and fall."[24]

From the ground, the detective started yelling out to the other police officers and into his radio about what he had just seen. "He's got a long gun! Male on the roof!" he repeated over and over. "He's got a gun, he's got a long gun! He's right up there!"[25]

Months of congressional and FBI investigations did not uncover any evidence that the Secret Service detail with President Trump heard any of that, but some of the agents at the perimeter of the event did, including at least one Secret Service sniper who began turning his rifle in the direction of the roof where Crooks was positioned. At that moment, 6:11 p.m., Crooks fired off eight shots.

Fifteen seconds after opening fire, Crooks was killed by the Secret Service sniper.[26] "When I fired my shot, he disappeared from my sight," the sniper later recounted to investigators. "After taking my shot, I immediately went ahead and put another live round into the weapon if I had to take a follow-up shot. And he didn't come back."[27]

If not for that Secret Service sniper, Crooks could have continued firing, possibly pulling off a shot that killed Trump. Remarkably, that rally in Butler marked the first time the Secret Service had deployed snipers to a Trump rally since he had left the White House, previously reserving those resources for events involving the sitting president. The Secret Service would later tell FBI investigators that the sniper unit was deployed due to an increasingly dangerous threat environment related to intelligence that the Iranian regime was targeting Trump, not because the Butler rally itself posed a specific threat.

In other words, if it weren't for the threat from Iran, the Secret Service would not have deployed the sniper who took out Thomas Crooks while he was attempting to assassinate Trump. As one senior Trump advisor put it to me, "Iran saved Donald Trump."

At the time Crooks fired his AR-15 rifle, Trump had turned his head to point at a chart about illegal immigration on a large screen to his right. Trump reached for his right ear as his Secret Service agents jumped into action.

"Get down! Get down! Get down!" shouted Nick Menster, the agent who first thought the shots were Pop-Its or a cap gun.

With that, Trump fell to the ground along with three agents, each of whom was attempting to put themself between Trump and whatever gunfire might come next.

"I shielded him the best I could with my entire body," Menster later recalled. He wasn't sure if Trump had been hit by a bullet, but he could see what he described as "a dark liquid pooling" in front of the former president.

"Sir, are you bleeding?" he asked.

"Yes," Trump replied. "From my right ear."

Not knowing how bad the injury was, Menster grabbed the white cloth Trump keeps with him when he speaks to wipe away sweat and applied pressure to Trump's ear as he and two other agents were lying on top of him. They remained on the ground, waiting for an indication that either the gunman had been neutralized or the path to get off the stage had been secured.

"Shooter's down!" yelled one of the agents. "Are we good to move?"

"Are we clear?" another asked.

"We're clear! We're clear!" another replied. "Let's move!"

The agents tried to bring Trump to his feet, but he told them to hold on. Being tackled to the ground had literally knocked the shoes off his feet. "Let me get my shoes," he said. "Let me get my shoes."

The thousands of supporters in attendance were anxiously looking toward the stage to see if he was okay. "Everybody in the first row, nobody went down to the ground," one attendee later told Rachel Scott. "They all stood up. They wanted to protect the president. All we were concerned about was him."

Other Trump supporters described praying to God, hoping that divine intervention might save the life of the former president. "We huddled and we started praying, and we just started praying and thanking God," one woman told Rachel.

The next sixty seconds may have been the most important of the 2024 campaign—and perhaps of Trump's life.

The iconic photograph on the cover of this book captures one of those seconds. The video of Trump raising a fist and yelling out to the crowd—"Fight! Fight! Fight!"—captures more. But the full picture, pieced together using several different camera angles and the recollections of the agents charged with protecting Trump's life, tells a remarkable story not fully appreciated at the time: Trump's iconic moment happened only because he fought back when the Secret Service attempted to move him out of harm's way. He resisted his own protectors.

In the moments after shots rang out in Butler, the agents in Trump's security detail had one job to do. While keeping their bodies between the former president and any other potential danger, they needed to rush him off the stage, into his armored vehicle, and off to the nearest hospital. But Trump had other plans.

"We were doing our best to cover him with our entire bodies and to get him off that stage as quickly as possible," Menster, the assistant to the special agent in charge, later recalled. "One thing I have never trained for is a protectee fighting back. Usually, after they experience something like this, they want to leave."[28]

But Trump, for a moment, refused.

The voice of lead agent Sean Curran could be heard on the live television feed as the agents helped Trump rise to his feet and began to guide him off the stage: "Sir, we have to move to the car."

"Wait! Wait!" Trump said, moving toward the lectern where he had just been speaking. He pushed his way forward to see his supporters. Despite the nearly a dozen bullets that had just been sprayed toward the crowd, many of the attendees stayed put, resisting the natural instinct to run for cover.

When I first saw what happened, I wondered why the agents were allowing him to be exposed again. If the crowd could see him, surely somebody out there with a gun could see him, too. At that point, no one knew whether the shooter was acting alone. The Secret Service would later acknowledge it was a breach of protocol, but Trump was in charge at this moment, not his agents—and he had something to say to his supporters, both in the crowd and watching along across the country.

Pumping his right arm in the air, Trump pushed through the agents and repeated the word that would come to define his campaign: "Fight! Fight! Fight!"

The entire sequence lasted less than a minute, and Trump was swiftly guided off the stage and stuffed into an armored SUV. Menster, Curran, and another agent straddled the former president in the back seat, trying to discern the extent of his injuries.

"Everything's stable in here," Menster radioed, hoping to "bring it down one click just so we could focus on driving and any secondary attacks that might be out there."

As the motorcade raced out of the Butler Farm Show grounds and took a hard right at the first intersection, the agents heard another terrifying sound.

Pop! Pop! Pop! Pop!

They initially believed something had exploded right under their vehicle—and the same thing happened in another car in the motorcade carrying Trump's senior aides, including his future chief of staff Susie Wiles. The former president's SUV filled with smoke, and Menster thought he smelled gunpowder.

He picked up his radio and yelled to ask what had just happened. Was this a second attack?

He quickly received an answer from a member of the Secret Service Counter Assault Team protecting the route to the hospital: A guy was setting off fireworks in his front yard—at the exact moment the motorcade taking the former president, who had just been shot, sped by his house. There was no second attack.[29]

Lead agent Sean Curran, whom the president would go on to appoint as head of the Secret Service, later recounted how the experience affected him—and his relationship with Trump—to CBS News's Jennifer Jacobs. "Part of me probably still hasn't processed it. I haven't—from that day to now—I haven't stopped," he said. "I felt like I couldn't let him out of my sight. Not to the point where I'd be overworked, but to a point where I felt like I needed to be with him to ensure that things were done the way I needed them to be done. I didn't want to leave his side. I think he probably didn't want me to leave his side, either."[30]

Days before the rally in Butler, a Secret Service advance team had visited Butler Memorial Hospital and met with medical staff to discuss where Trump would be taken in the unlikely event of an emergency. This is standard practice: For every public appearance of a president or presidential candidate with Secret Service protection, there's a plan in place about what to do in the event of an assassination attempt.

Trump's motorcade needed just eight minutes, racing through the streets of Butler, to arrive at its destination. As planned, the small community hospital was put on lockdown. While the former president was there, nobody would be allowed in or out.

Once the motorcade pulled up to the hospital entrance, the Secret Service agents rushed Trump to the doors of the emergency room. As he entered the hospital, he greeted his aides who had been in the motorcade but who had not seen or talked to Trump since the shots were fired: Dan Scavino, Susie Wiles, and Steven Cheung. The doctors hadn't examined him yet, but Trump quickly made clear that he had not changed one bit.

"How is it playing on TV?" the former president asked. "We're going to make some big news, aren't we?"

After meeting with doctors for an initial examination that lasted about fifteen minutes, Trump was brought into a hospital room to await further tests. "How is the press treating us?" Trump asked his aides. "How are the pictures?"

Cheung, a longtime Trump spokesman and media advisor, pulled out his phone to show the former president some of the pictures taken of the shooting, including the photo taken by Associated Press photographer Evan Vucci that is on the cover of this book. As a large American flag waved in the background, Trump, surrounded by his

Secret Service agents, could be seen with his arm raised and blood running down his face.*

"That's iconic," Trump said. "That's the most American photo I have ever seen."

In addition to bandaging up his ear, the medical team at the hospital gave Trump a series of tests, including a CT scan, to see if he had suffered a concussion. When the doctor came back to show Trump the results and to let him know he was fine, Trump took a look at the image. His brain was in great shape, he declared. One of the people who was there in the hospital room told me Trump asked for a copy of the scan and suggested his staff should send it out to show how much better his brain is than President Biden's.

Secret Service agent Menster wasn't sure whether the injury to Trump's ear had been caused by a bullet—as opposed to something else that had been shattered by a bullet, or by the agents falling on top of him—until he was examined by the doctors. "I think at the hospital, we were unclear. We were thinking of all the scenarios. But it was pretty quickly confirmed that he didn't bump his head," he later said. "It was pretty quickly confirmed that this was the real deal, and we just lived through it."[31]

Trump's life may have been saved because he had turned his head to look at the chart displayed on the big screen behind him—showing US–Mexico border crossings under his presidency compared to Biden's—just as the shots were fired. Trump would later say that he loved that chart "more than I even love the police" and would credit

---

*When Trump tried to ban the Associated Press from the Oval Office early in his second term—prompting a lawsuit from the wire service—Evan Vucci became the star witness to describe the impact of the ban. "I'm trying to keep my ego in check," Vucci said about the iconic image he took that was made possible by the type of access that the White House was now limiting. "It's a pretty good photo."

it with saving his life. At a town hall in Oaks, Pennsylvania, weeks before the election, he described the chart as his "favorite piece of paper anywhere in the world," adding that he kisses it and sleeps with it "every night."[32]

The Butler detective who tried to climb the roof to get to the shooter—a man who has chosen to remain anonymous as of the writing of this book—may have saved Trump's life, too. Although the officer slipped before he could reach the roof, he frightened and rushed Crooks, giving the would-be assassin less time to make his shot. It quickly became an article of faith among many of Trump's religious supporters that God had intervened to save the former president's life.

But not everyone was so blessed.

After the first shot, Corey Comperatore, who had succeeded in getting the seats close to the stage that he'd wanted so badly, lunged to protect his daughter Allyson.

"When I heard the first shot, in my mind I had thought, 'Oh my gosh, did a sniper just kill somebody?'" Allyson later recalled. "And then the next thing, as my dad was pushing me down, that's when Trump ducked behind the podium. And that's when I was like, 'Oh my god, somebody's shooting.'"

Allyson's sister Kaylee ducked into the bleachers when she heard the shots, and discovered moments later that her father had been hit. "I felt his blood completely splatter my leg, and I looked and I saw him laying face down in the bleachers," she recalled. "I started screaming, but in my head I kept saying, 'Wake up, wake up, this is a dream, wake up.' And then you realize it's not a dream, and you feel like your whole world is just over."[33]

Two other rally attendees—fifty-seven-year-old Marine veteran David Dutch and seventy-four-year-old James Copenhaver—were hit by bullets Crooks fired. They managed to survive, but both sustained life-changing injuries. "It was like getting hit with a sledgehammer in the chest," Dutch recalled. "I could feel my ribs were all busted up."[34]

President Biden was attending Mass at St. Edmond's Catholic Church in Rehoboth Beach, Delaware, when the shots rang out in Butler. The details wouldn't come out for several days, but he had just concluded a private meeting with Chuck Schumer, at which the Senate Democratic leader conveyed that many members of his caucus believed Biden should drop out of the presidential race. But Biden's own political crisis would have to take a back seat to the news he learned minutes after the church service concluded.

As soon as she saw the reports out of Butler, Biden aide Annie Tomasini placed an urgent call to the Secret Service team with Biden at church, asking them to inform the president of what had happened before he left Mass. Once outside, Biden ordered his team in Rehoboth Beach to activate the Emergency Briefing Room (EBR), a camera setup that travels just about everywhere the president does, in case he needs to make an impromptu speech to the country. Biden's aides had not yet written him a speech, but he wanted to speak immediately about what had happened.

Trump was back in his hospital room with the same small group of aides—Wiles, Cheung, and Scavino, and personal assistant Walt Nauta—when the White House announced Biden would be delivering an address to the nation. Trump wanted to watch Biden's remarks, of course, but the room didn't have a working television, so Cheung pulled up a live CNN feed on his phone.

"There's no place in America for this kind of violence," Biden said. "It's sick. It's sick. It's one of the reasons why we have to unite this country. We cannot allow for this to be happening. We cannot be like this."

As Biden wrapped up his brief remarks—about two minutes in total—Tomasini asked the president's lead Secret Service agent, Stuart Allison, to reach out directly to Sean Curran, his counterpart with the Trump detail, to "get Mogul on the phone," referring to Trump's Secret Service code name. She also asked White House chief of staff Jeffrey Zients to reach out to Susie Wiles to arrange the call. Biden wanted to speak to his opponent as soon as possible.

Trump was still with his doctors at first, but the current and former presidents connected once Trump left the hospital and was on his way to the airport in Pittsburgh. Two Biden aides who overheard the conversation told me the call lasted about three minutes in total, and that the two men repeatedly referred to each other as "Joe" and "Donald." Trump himself would later tell me it was a "very nice" conversation.

Biden expressed concern for Trump and his family, reiterating what he had said in his televised speech: Political violence has to stop. "This is tragic," he said. "I mean, this should never have happened."

"Hopefully this brings us all together," Trump told Biden, according to a Trump aide who was with him.

"I can't wait to see you," Trump said, according to both Biden and Trump aides who overheard the call. "I can't wait to shake your hand."

I can't wait to shake your hand.

"It was not the Donald Trump you see on TV," one of the Biden aides told me.

While Trump and Biden were making nice over the phone, anger over what had just happened was beginning to bubble up across the country. The ABC team covering the rally—Rachel, Lalee, Ben Siegel—experienced some of it firsthand.

They had remained at the Butler Farm Show grounds, talking to eyewitnesses and trying to gather more information about what had happened. They quickly realized that Trump's supporters were *mad*. Most of their rage was directed at the gunman, of course, but some of it was reserved for those whose rhetoric they believed had incited someone to take a shot at their president: the media. "You did this!" someone shouted at Lalee as she tried to interview attendees, adding a racial slur for good measure.

I first heard the news of the attempt on Trump's life while I was on the floor of the Fiserv Forum in Milwaukee, where the Republican National Convention was set to begin two days later. Together with the ABC team on the ground in Milwaukee, I quickly pivoted to breaking-news mode, setting up a live camera outside the arena and making calls to find out what had happened. Was it gunfire or fireworks? Had Trump been hit? How badly was he hurt? One of the first people I reached was Dave McCormick, who had been right there on stage with Trump. He told me it was definitely gunfire and that somebody sitting right behind him had been hit and hurt badly, or worse.

As I reported live on ABC for hours after the shooting, I could feel the partisan resentment building as the world waited to hear from Trump and learn more about how badly he was hurt. "While this campaign is, for the moment, in a state of shock and pause," I reported on air that evening, "it's a campaign that seems like it is very well going to come back with a vengeance."

Trump was still in the hospital when JD Vance, who would be chosen as his running mate two days later, made his first statement on the shooting. No one knew anything about the gunman or his motives, but Vance placed the blame for the assassination attempt squarely on Trump's Democratic opponents.

"Today is not just some isolated incident," Vance declared just two hours after the shots were fired. "The central premise of the Biden campaign is that President Donald Trump is an authoritarian fascist who must be stopped at all costs. That rhetoric led directly to President Trump's attempted assassination."[35]

Vance would later tell podcaster Joe Rogan that he was playing miniature golf with his children back in Cincinnati when he first heard the news about the assassination attempt. He didn't have his own Secret Service detail because he had not yet been chosen as Trump's running mate.

"I actually thought they had killed him because, when you first see the video, he grabs his ear, and then he goes down," Vance recalled. "And I'm like, 'Oh my god, they just killed him.'"

What did Vance do next? "I grab my kids up, throw them in the car, go home, and load all my guns," he said, claiming he went into "fight or flight" mode, "and basically [stood] like a sentry inside by the front door."[36]

Vance's rhetoric and actions were those of a man looking to turn the temperature of the country up rather than down, to redirect Trump supporters' outrage over the attempt to kill the former president from the man who fired the shots to Trump's (and his own) political opponents. The statement was incendiary, exactly the kind of thing that could further divide the country. Would Trump do the same?

The former president's first statement after he stuck his fist in the air and urged his supporters to "fight!" came twenty-two minutes later. In a Truth Social post, he thanked the Secret Service and local law enforcement for their quick response to the shooting, gave an update on his condition, and expressed condolences to the family of Corey Comperatore.

Trump had just been shot, but he did not lash out in anger. Unlike his future running mate, he did not try to pin the blame for what had happened on his political opponents. As it became clear that Trump himself was trying to calm things down—and that he had avoided serious injury—the tension in the air began to ease.

But the race had been transformed yet again. The photo of Trump's fist in the air was everywhere, and about thirty minutes after the shooting, Elon Musk posted a video of Trump's defiant moment on the stage and declared, "I fully endorse President Trump and hope for his rapid recovery."[37]

Musk's was easily the most important endorsement of the campaign—possibly in the history of American politics. Musk, the richest man in the world, would go on to spend nearly $290 million to help elect Trump and play an extremely prominent role in his administration.[38]

Exactly one minute after Musk's endorsement, Robert F. Kennedy Jr., who was then still running for president as an independent, posted a statement of his own. "Now is the time for every American who loves our country to step back from the division, renounce all violence, and unite in prayer for President Trump and his family," he wrote.[39]

Kennedy—whose uncle had been assassinated in 1963 and whose father had been killed in 1968—knows political violence. After reading his statement live on ABC, I called him to say I found his words powerful and reassuring—and asked him if he would be reaching out to Trump.

Kennedy told me he was planning to meet with Trump in Milwaukee the following day, the first step toward a Trump–Kennedy alliance that would've seemed unlikely, if not outlandish, before the events in Butler. Kennedy's endorsement of Trump, which would come weeks six weeks later, would prove to be the second-most important of the campaign.

The morning after Donald Trump was shot in Butler, I woke up with a sense of fear—and relief. The bullet had come frighteningly close to killing Trump, and I was relieved it missed and the assassination attempt failed. But I was worried about how the country would react, and who Trump's supporters would blame. A successful assassination would have certainly torn the country apart, but a near-miss could still do the same if Trump wanted it to.

Twelve hours in, he didn't. But how long would that last?

CHAPTER EIGHT

"I HAD GOD ON MY SIDE"

In the first few hours after the attempted assassination of Donald Trump on Saturday night, the political world seemed to grind to a halt. The Biden campaign paused all its ads and implored staffers to "refrain from issuing any comments on social media or in public."[1] The images from Butler were plastered on TV screens across the country, crowding out virtually all other news. What were previously the biggest stories of the day—President Biden's press conference at the conclusion of the NATO Summit in Washington, the continued efforts to nudge Biden off the Democratic ticket, speculation about Trump's vice presidential selection—faded into the background. There were even questions about whether the Republican National Convention—set to kick off in Milwaukee on Monday afternoon—should go on as scheduled.

Trump, however, quickly put an end to those questions, calling the convention organizers to make clear that the event would proceed apace. "The convention is going to continue—with a vengeance,"

Reince Priebus, chairman of the RNC host committee and Trump's former chief of staff, told me after he spoke with his former boss.

That was mostly right. The convention was going to go on. In fact, Trump was now set to arrive in Milwaukee earlier than previously planned.

The convention, though, wasn't exactly proceeding with "a vengeance." Retribution had been a central theme of Trump's campaign to that point, and it would eventually become one again. But for those fateful few days in July, the former president—relishing the world's sympathy and feeling unthreatened by his increasingly weak Democratic opponent—tried a new persona on for size. "Thank you to everyone for your thoughts and prayers yesterday, as it was God alone who prevented the unthinkable from happening," he posted on Truth Social early Sunday morning. "In this moment, it is more important than ever that we stand United, and show our True Character as Americans, remaining Strong and Determined, and not allowing Evil to Win. I truly love our Country, and love you all, and look forward to speaking to our Great Nation this week from Wisconsin."[2]

Trump's plane touched down at Milwaukee's Mitchell International Airport shortly before 6 p.m. local time, about twenty-four hours after the shots rang out in Butler. The public didn't get to see much of him after he landed—just eighteen seconds of grainy cell phone footage—as he walked down the stairs of the plane, paused to do three of his signature fist pumps, and was quickly whisked away in an armored SUV that would take him to the Pfister Hotel, where he was staying.

Senator Lindsey Graham of South Carolina was also on the former president's flight to Milwaukee. One of Trump's allies in the Senate and a regular golf partner, Graham had been scheduled to play a round with the former president at his club in Bedminster, New Jersey, on Sunday morning—but that didn't happen, for obvious reasons.

Graham had been finishing up eighteen holes on Saturday at the exclusive Winged Foot Golf Club in New York, where he was playing on Trump's membership, when he heard the news about the attempted assassination. He decided against reaching out to Trump immediately, assuming, correctly, that he had too much on his plate. But later that night, Graham received a phone call.

"Lindsey, I can't play golf tomorrow," Trump told him.

"Why not?" the senator replied in jest.

"Because I got shot!" Trump responded.

On Monday morning, I decided to call Trump's cell phone to leave him a voicemail message. I didn't expect he would answer or call me back; he'd just survived a near-death experience, after all, and was in the final stages of selecting his running mate. I had not spoken to him in a long time, but he had made it abundantly clear to others that he was furious about my recent book, *Tired of Winning: Donald Trump and the End of the Grand Old Party*.

Even so, I had known the man for thirty years and wanted to let him know how horrified I was by the attempt on his life—and express my relief that he survived. At the same time, I was also deeply concerned about how Trump would respond to being shot. The political climate was already heated; would his mind lead him to the same place JD Vance had gone, blaming his opponents for what happened? If it did, how would his most fervent supporters react?

To my surprise, Trump called me back a few hours later. I was sitting next to David Muir on the ABC News set inside Milwaukee's

Fiserv Forum when the name "Donald Trump" flashed on my phone's screen. The Republican National Convention was about to begin, and Vance had just been named the GOP vice presidential candidate thirty minutes earlier. I showed David who was calling and answered the phone.

"How are you feeling, sir?" I asked.

"I'm doing all right, Jonathan," he said. "I'm doing all right."

Trump marveled at how close the bullet had come to striking him in the head, referencing a remarkable picture taken by my friend Doug Mills, a photographer for *The New York Times*, that showed a bullet flying by his head as he turned to look to his right. "A half an inch, a quarter of an inch," he said, and it would have been all over.

"Did that change you, coming that close to death?" I asked. "Did it change you? How could it not?"

"I don't like to think about that," he said. "But, yes, I think it has had an impact."

Despite everything that had happened the past two days, Trump sounded more relaxed than I had ever heard him. He even seemed to genuinely appreciate the message I had left him.

"You're a good man, Jonathan," he said, before quickly adding, "You used to be a better man, but you're a good man."

He then began retelling a story he had told me dozens of times about an interview I did with him at the Old Post Office building in Washington, DC—what would later become the Trump International Hotel—a full decade earlier. As readers of *Front Row at the Trump Show* might remember, he would regularly tell this story when he saw me. Despite the assassination attempt, the new running mate, and the convention, it appeared like he just wanted to chat.

"You wouldn't believe all the people who are calling me," Trump said. "You wouldn't believe it. I've heard from everybody."

One phone call seemed to surprise him more than any other.

"Jeff Bezos called," he told me, marveling at how friendly the call from the world's second-richest man had been. While in the White House, Trump had regularly raged against Bezos over the newspaper he owned, *The Washington Post*, and accused the company he founded, Amazon, of ripping off the US Postal Service.

Bezos wasn't the only high-profile adversary to reach out to Trump after the assassination attempt. President Biden had said the night before that he'd had a "short but good conversation" with his 2024 opponent. I asked Trump how it went.

"It was very nice," he said. "He couldn't have been nicer."

Although Trump had just tapped Vance as his running mate, he didn't seem to harbor the same partisan grudges about the shooting. Where Vance claimed the Biden campaign's rhetoric had "led directly" to the assassination attempt,[3] Trump was expressing appreciation for Biden's call.

We spoke for nearly ten minutes. Before I hung up, I asked him what he planned to say in his convention speech.

"I've completely rewritten it," he said. He had originally planned a "humdinger" of an address—one filled with harsh attacks on Biden and the Democrats—but now, he insisted, "it will be more of a unity speech."[4]

Trump's speech wasn't scheduled until Thursday night, but he didn't want to wait to greet the Republican delegates in Milwaukee. So as the prime-time programming got started around 9 p.m. on Monday, country music star Lee Greenwood took to the stage to provide the live soundtrack for a "surprise" appearance by the "next president of the United States."

The delegates applauded wildly, and the cheering grew even louder as video of Trump standing in a dark hallway backstage, a bandage covering his right ear, showed up on the jumbotron. Almost instantaneously, the mood in the Fiserv Forum shifted. We were no longer at a political convention. This was a full-on religious revival.

"Prayer works," Greenwood said, as the piano riff of his hit song "God Bless the USA" began in the background. "In this nation based on faith, prayer works. Because he was sure, as Donald Trump turned his head just slightly, that the bullet missed him just enough to save his life to be the next president of the United States."

Trump began to walk through the backstage tunnels toward the floor, slowing his pace just enough to emerge from the tunnel precisely when Greenwood began to sing. He pumped his fist for the crowd, mouthed "thank you," and paused to soak in the moment. "He seems emotional in a way that I don't think I have ever seen Donald Trump," I said to David Muir on the ABC News broadcast. "It almost looks like he is choking up."

As Trump made his way to the seat in the VIP box where he would spend the remainder of the evening, he greeted the others in his box. The first hand he shook was Tucker Carlson's, before moving down the line to Florida Congressman Byron Donalds, his sons Don Jr. and Eric, JD Vance, and House Speaker Mike Johnson.

"We are here tonight with one purpose," Greenwood told the crowd after he finished his song. "And that is to elect Donald J. Trump as the next president of the United States. He is here tonight to show his courage, his defiance against somebody who tried to kill him. You will not take this man down!"

It was as dramatic a moment as I'd ever seen at a political convention.

In our phone call earlier on Monday, Trump didn't just tell me that he had rewritten his own speech—he also made clear that he expected others at the convention to do the same thing. There would be no talk of the "Biden crime family." The vicious personal attacks that had long been a staple of Trump's rallies would be toned down. Messages would be uplifting, and about the future, not the grievances of the past. Trump was winning. America was rallying behind him. There was no need to destroy an opponent who had already destroyed himself.

Most speakers got the message. "I know that many of you are angry. But now is the time for us to unite!" South Dakota Governor Kristi Noem, Trump's future secretary of Homeland Security, said. "We must work—win the hearts and minds of every American. Wake them up with truth and wisdom. *Listen* to them. You can't win people over by arguing with them."

Even Tucker Carlson, a pundit so controversial he had been fired by Fox News, praised Trump for not inflaming the situation after the assassination attempt and managed to speak for ten minutes without mentioning Biden by name once. "What's happened over the past month, since the debate, and particularly on Saturday in Butler, I think a lot of people are wondering, what is this? This doesn't look like politics. Something bigger is going on here," he said. "I think even people who don't believe in God are beginning to think, 'Well, maybe there's something to this, actually.' And I'm starting to think it's going to be okay, actually. I do think that."

At least one Republican lawmaker, however, seemed to miss the memo. "Today's Democrat agenda, their policies are a clear and present danger to America, to our institutions, our values, and our people," Senator Ron Johnson of Wisconsin bellowed in his Monday afternoon speaking slot. He continued raging against Democrats for several more minutes until his speech came to an end, making no mention of unity.

The following day, Johnson claimed that the wrong version of his speech—the one written before the events of Butler—had been loaded into the teleprompter.[5]

Johnson's flub was reminiscent of the chaos that had engulfed Trump's first Republican Convention in 2016, when some delegates had led a last-ditch effort to deny Trump the nomination. That convention felt like an awkward wedding reception bringing together two families who clearly didn't like each other.

But by 2024, Trump's takeover of the Republican Party was finally complete. He had a vision for how he wanted the week to go, and he had the team—and speakers—in place to execute it. Other than Johnson's screwup, the convention was remarkably well run.

As I reported from Milwaukee all week, what stood out to me the most was the sense of optimism and inevitability that seemed to permeate the Fiserv Forum. The delegates and other attendees were remarkably friendly to the reporters who had flocked to Milwaukee. Presidential nominating conventions are generally upbeat affairs, but this one felt different. It wasn't even August yet, but to many delegates—and key players on Trump's campaign team—the race seemed over. Donald Trump was on his way back to the White House.

Maybe it was the polling.

Trump had opened up a three-point lead over Biden nationally by the time the RNC kicked off, and his advantage was even greater in the battleground states. "We have nearly 20 paths to get to what we need to get," Chris LaCivita, who was helping run the campaign, said on the second day of the convention, referring to the Electoral College. "And [the Democrats] have one, maybe two."[6] A few days earlier, *The Atlantic* had published a lengthy article by Tim Alberta detailing the campaign's supreme confidence in November's outcome. The title? "Trump Is Planning for a Landslide Win."[7]

Maybe it was Biden's weakness.

As Republicans were gearing up to nominate Trump for a third time, Democrats were in the middle of a full-blown meltdown. Biden's debate performance had put his struggles—political and otherwise—on full display, but he and his team seemed dead set on forging ahead despite the growing chorus of Democratic leaders publicly urging him to step aside.

On Wednesday evening, ABC's *World News Tonight with David Muir* began with two devastating stories for the Democrats. My colleague Mary Bruce reported that Biden had just been diagnosed with COVID-19, forcing him to cancel campaign events in Las Vegas and rush back home to Delaware. He was so weak that he appeared to struggle to climb the short stairs to get on Air Force One. And I followed up Mary's report with an exclusive story about Senate Democratic Leader Chuck Schumer traveling to Biden's beach house in Delaware over the weekend to deliver a blunt message: He should drop out of the race. Republicans in Milwaukee knew what

Democratic officials had finally started to grapple with: Joe Biden could not win another term.

Maybe it was the aftermath of the shooting in Butler.

Trump had never shied away from embracing his most fervent supporters' portrayal of him as a divine figure. Throughout the 2024 campaign, he even shared a video that distorted Paul Harvey's famous speech "So God Made a Farmer" to declare that he himself had been sent by God to serve as a "caretaker" of God's "planned paradise."[8] After Trump escaped death—by a fraction of an inch—that sentiment only intensified. When many of Trump's supporters confidently talked about him in Milwaukee as "the next president of the United States," they genuinely believed it: God Himself was on their side.

Just about every obstacle remaining between Donald Trump and a return to the White House seemed to be collapsing all at once. On Monday, District Judge Aileen Cannon dismissed special counsel Jack Smith's classified documents case against the former president on the dubious grounds that Smith had not been lawfully appointed to his role. And on Tuesday, the last vestiges of conservative opposition to Trump evaporated as Florida Governor Ron DeSantis and former South Carolina Governor Nikki Haley—Trump's most serious opponents in the deeply unserious Republican presidential primary—sang his praises from the stage in Milwaukee.

"President Trump asked me to speak to this convention in the name of unity. It was a gracious invitation, and I was happy to accept," Haley said.

In fact, Trump hadn't extended the invitation personally; Susie Wiles, his de facto campaign manager, had. And Trump didn't speak with Haley at all in Milwaukee—not even to thank her for her speech.

Even so, Haley offered her "strong" endorsement of the man who repeatedly called her "birdbrain" and mocked her husband's military service. "You don't have to agree with Trump 100 percent of the time to vote for him. Take it from me. I haven't always agreed with President Trump, but we agree more often than we disagree."

Throughout her campaign, Haley had warned Republicans against renominating Trump in no uncertain terms. She argued that the former president she'd once served as ambassador to the United Nations lacked "moral clarity"[9] and said he had "no business being commander in chief."[10] She also refused to endorse Trump upon suspending her campaign, telling her supporters it was up to him to "earn the votes of those in our party and beyond it who did not support him."

Still, she was far from the most fervent former Trump critic who spoke at the RNC in Milwaukee.

No, that title belonged to JD Vance, the thirty-nine-year-old US senator from Ohio who Trump had chosen to serve as his running mate. A decade earlier, Vance—the author of the bestselling memoir *Hillbilly Elegy*—considered himself part of the "Never Trump" movement, writing in *The New York Times* that Trump was "unfit for our nation's highest office"[11] and voting for third-party candidate Evan McMullin in the 2016 election. He said he found Trump "reprehensible" because he made people he cared about—"immigrants, Muslims, etc."—afraid.[12] Vance described Trump as "cultural heroin"[13] and wondered if he would be "America's Hitler."[14] In the final days of the 2016 campaign, after the *Access Hollywood* tape was released, he asked, "What percentage of the American population has @realDonaldTrump sexually assaulted?"[15]

Vance was forced to grapple with those comments immediately upon launching his bid in July 2021 to replace the retiring GOP Senator Rob Portman in Ohio. "Like a lot of people, I criticized Trump back in 2016," Vance told Fox News at the time. "And I ask folks not to judge me based on what I said in 2016, because I've been very open that I did say those critical things and I regret them, and I regret being wrong about the guy."

Trump ultimately endorsed Vance for the Republican Senate nomination, at one point musing onstage at a rally that the wannabe senator was "kissing my ass" because of how much he wanted the former president's support. And by 2024, Vance's opinion on Trump had done a complete 180. "Just personally, I like him," he told the *New York Times*' Ross Douthat in a June interview. "He's much more complex than the media gives him credit for. People think that this guy is motivated entirely by personal grievance and by power, and that he just wants to become president so that he can destroy American democracy. That's not at all who he is."[16]

In one sense, Vance was right. Despite Trump's reputation for personal pettiness and holding grudges, he has historically had no problem welcoming former critics to the MAGA cause—as long as those former critics are able to prove their loyalties have shifted. He relishes the idea of winning people over, and if nothing else, he enjoys watching them grovel. Lindsey Graham, for example, once described Trump as "the most unprepared person" to be commander in chief that he'd ever met,[17] and made the case for kicking him out of the Republican Party.[18] Eight years later, he was aboard the former president's plane en route to Milwaukee for the GOP convention.

The conversation on that flight to Milwaukee went back and forth between two subjects: the shooting that had just happened the day before in Butler and Trump's decision on a vice presidential pick, which would be announced the following day.

Trump would be seventy-eight years old when sworn into office if he were to win, and barring a change to the Constitution, he would be unable to run for a third term. His choice for vice president, therefore, was a monumental one; it could crown the heir apparent to the MAGA movement and potentially define the trajectory of the Republican Party for a generation. He had narrowed a rather large pool down to three finalists by that point—Doug Burgum, Marco Rubio, and JD Vance. Would he appeal to more traditional Republican voters by choosing Burgum or Rubio, or would he decide to energize his most fervent supporters by tapping the combative, isolationist, and über-populist Vance?

Senator Graham, a staunch foreign policy hawk, spent most of the plane ride advocating against Trump choosing Vance as his running mate. The freshman senator had no governing experience, he argued, and he wouldn't bring Trump any new voters—while Rubio could help shore up support among the types of Republicans who supported Haley and DeSantis in the GOP primary and would be crucial to winning in November. It was a similar case to the one being made at the time by allies of the powerful media magnate Rupert Murdoch, who also desperately wanted to keep Vance off the ticket and had been urging Trump to pick Burgum. "Now leading in the polls, [Trump] doesn't need an attack-dog VP or someone to rally his core voters. He needs a choice who shows mature judgment and has the ability to appeal to anxious and undecided voters," read an editorial published in the Murdoch-owned *Wall Street Journal*. "The need for stability and experience should eliminate the young MAGA-in-a-hurry types like Sen. J.D. Vance."[19]

But Vance had powerful allies in his corner, including Tucker Carlson, Elon Musk, and Trump's son Don Jr. Weeks earlier, as word leaked out that Trump was cooling on the senator from Ohio, Carlson called the former president, with whom he had developed a close relationship. As *The New York Times* first reported, the former Fox News host argued that Burgum and Rubio couldn't be trusted, and outlined a conspiratorial scenario: If Trump chose a more traditional Republican as his running mate, what was to stop his opponents—the intelligence community, the "deep state"—from assassinating him and installing their preferred candidate? "When your enemies are pushing a running mate on you," Carlson told Trump, "it's a pretty good sign you should ignore them."[20]

Carlson later told me the *Times* report was accurate, that he had warned Trump he risked assassination if he chose a running mate acceptable to the Republican establishment.

The argument may have worked. As Trump neared a decision, Fox News radio host Brian Kilmeade asked him about reports he was unlikely to pick Vance because he has a beard. "No," Trump responded. "He looks like a young Abraham Lincoln." The remark prompted Vance to reach out to the campaign, asking, "Lincoln? That's a good sign, right?"

Fox News's Harris Faulkner traveled to Mar-a-Lago to interview Trump the morning of July 13, and off-camera, the president told her that Vance would likely be the pick. But by the time Trump landed in Milwaukee the night before the opening of his convention, both Carlson and Graham were convinced that Trump had changed his mind once again. Both men told me they believed that Trump had decided to pick Rubio.

Carlson told me he "forcefully" made the case to Trump once he arrived in Milwaukee to choose Vance. And if Trump *had* been leaning toward picking Rubio, he had changed his mind yet again by Monday afternoon.

"After lengthy deliberation and thought, and considering the tremendous talents of many others, I have decided that the person best suited to assume the position of Vice President of the United States is Senator J.D. Vance of the Great State of Ohio," Trump wrote on Truth Social. "As Vice President, J.D. will continue to fight for our Constitution, stand with our Troops, and will do everything he can to help me MAKE AMERICA GREAT AGAIN."

Vance would eventually get his footing and become a valuable attack dog for Trump in the campaign, but his youth and inexperience were on display in his first speech as the vice-presidential nominee. His remarks hit all the right notes—biographical details, a somber reflection on the assassination attempt, why he believed in Trump and the Trump agenda—but they dragged on for nearly forty minutes, and a handful of delegates could be seen nodding off or checking their phones throughout. He was caught off guard by a spontaneous chant from the crowd—"Drill, baby, drill!"—and clearly was unsure whether to join in. And when he tried to get the speech back on track by praising the "great crowd," a second chant of "Yes we are!" broke out instead.

But one moment from his speech stuck with me. It was when he spoke about his mother, Beverly Aikins, at about the halfway point of his speech, several minutes after he'd first referenced his grandmother, "Mamaw," who had primarily raised him. "Our movement is about single moms like mine, who struggled with money and addiction but never gave up," he said, as the cameras panned to his teary-eyed mother, who was sitting in the VIP box.

Vance's mother was largely an antagonist in his memoir, *Hillbilly Elegy*. He described in detail how she would hit him and how she nearly killed him with her reckless driving. He wrote about his mother demanding he pee in a jar so she could use his urine to pass a drug test and keep her nursing job. She later recalled her son telling her about the memoir over a meal at Waffle House. "He said, 'Mom, I wrote a book, and there's probably some things in it that aren't very favorable,'" she told *The New York Times*. "I just said, 'Will it help you heal?' He said, 'I think it will.'"[21]

Fast-forward nearly a decade, and she was seated in Donald Trump's box at the Fiserv Forum as her son shared her recovery story with the world. As her image flashed on the giant screens by the stage, the crowd started chanting "JD's mom! JD's mom!"

"I'm proud to say that tonight my mom is here, ten years clean and sober. I love you, Mom," Vance said. "And, you know, Mom, I was thinking: It'll be ten years officially in January of 2025, and if President Trump's okay with it, let's have the celebration in the White House!"*

A private person who had spent much of her adult life as an addict, Vance's mother suddenly found herself the center of attention at the biggest political event in the nation. She was surrounded by some of the most powerful people in the world but had no idea who they were. She turned to the man sitting next to her in Trump's box and asked his name.

"Mike Johnson," he said.

"And what do you do here?"

"I'm the Speaker of the House."

"That sounds very impressive," Vance's mother responded, "but I'm not sure exactly what you do."

---

*On April 7, JD Vance followed through on his promise and welcomed his mother and about twenty other members of his family to the White House to celebrate her ten years of sobriety.

By the end of Vance's speech, the logic behind his selection became clear. His job on the ticket wasn't to reassure more traditional Republicans, like Mike Pence had done eight years earlier, and it wasn't to make inroads into Joe Biden's coalition. JD Vance was chosen to reach out to the voters the Trump campaign had determined would win Trump the White House: alienated young men.

"President Trump represents America's last best hope to restore what, if lost, may never be found again: a country where a working-class boy born far from the halls of power can stand on this stage as the next vice president of the United States of America," Vance said.

That Trump campaign goal—getting young men who normally don't vote to show up at the polls—was evident in the selection of speakers and performers leading up to Trump's keynote address on the final night of the convention: Tucker Carlson, Kid Rock, legendary professional wrestler Hulk Hogan, and Dana White, the president of the Ultimate Fighting Championship. Hogan, who noted that he'd known Trump for thirty-five years, took off his suit jacket onstage and ripped off his shirt, revealing a Trump–Vance tank top underneath while shouting it was time to "let Trump-a-mania run wild, brother!" White concluded his remarks by urging the country to elect "a real American badass."

This wasn't a convention designed to woo the suburban woman who voted against Trump in 2020. This wasn't about erasing the gender gap; it was about increasing it—trying to drive up Trump's support among men.

Once Lee Greenwood had finished yet another rendition of his most famous song, the former president—a bandage still covering his right ear—walked up to the microphone and basked in the chants of "USA! USA! USA!" that had broken out. "Friends, delegates, and fellow citizens," Trump began, "I stand before you this evening with a message of confidence, strength, and hope. Four months from now, we will have an incredible victory, and we will begin the four greatest years in the history of our country."

In the days leading up to his speech, Trump's aides had been telling reporters that Trump had entirely rewritten his speech in the wake of the assassination attempt in Butler—just as Trump himself had told me he would do. The aides said he wouldn't mention Joe Biden or Kamala Harris by name, and would instead focus on ending the "discord and division" in the country. And to prove the point, the campaign released excerpts of the speech ahead of time.

"Just a few short days ago, my journey with you nearly ended," Trump was going to say, according to an excerpt of the speech shared with reporters in advance. "And yet here we are tonight, all gathered together, talking about the future, promise, and renewal of America. We live in a world of miracles."[22]

It was to be unlike any address he'd given before.

And for nearly twenty minutes, that was true. Instead of the usual attacks on his political opponents, he actually seemed to reach out to them.

"I am running to be president for all of America, not half of America, because there is no victory in winning for half of America," he began. "Let me begin this evening by expressing my gratitude to the American people for your outpouring of love and support following the assassination attempt at my rally on Saturday."

As Trump began telling the story of what happened to him in Butler, a hush fell over the crowd; there were no yells, or cheers, or boos punctuating Trump's sentences. "The assassin's bullet came within a quarter of an inch of taking my life," he said. "So many people have asked me what happened. 'Tell us what happened, please.' And therefore, I will tell you exactly what happened, and you'll never hear it from me a second time, because it's actually too painful to tell."

Over the next several minutes, Trump re-created the scene from Butler, almost as though he were the narrator in a fairy tale. "It was a warm, beautiful day in the early evening," he said, reading off a teleprompter. "Music was loudly playing, and the campaign was doing really well. I went to the stage and the crowd was cheering wildly. Everybody was happy. I began speaking very strongly, powerfully, and happily."

But then he heard a "loud whizzing sound," and soon his right ear and hand were covered in blood. "There was blood pouring everywhere, and yet in a certain way I felt very safe because I had God on my side," Trump said. "I stand before you in this arena only by the grace of Almighty God. And watching the reports over the last few days, many people say it was a providential moment. Probably was."

He then turned his attention to the other three victims of the shooting: David Dutch, James Copenhaver, and Corey Comperatore. "They were serious Trumpsters—and still are," he said. "But Corey, unfortunately, we have to use the past tense." He then pointed to Comperatore's firefighter gear—which had been wheeled out and displayed onstage to Trump's right—and walked over to it, kissing the helmet. "So now, I ask that we observe a moment of silence in honor of our friend Corey," he said. "There is no greater love than to lay down one's life for others. This is the spirit that forged America in her darkest hours. And this is the love that will lead America back to the summit of human achievement and greatness."

Steve Bannon was watching the festivities from federal prison on an old television through protective glass, listening to Trump's speech over a crackling transistor radio. If he'd had his way, the speech would have ended right there. "The thing at the beginning was amazing," he'd later tell me. "I would have had him go out and hug the fireman, the helmet, kiss it, magnificent. No teleprompter, it's a ten-minute speech, and at ten minutes, the mic is going off."

The mic didn't go off—Trump was just getting started. He spoke for another eighty minutes. The speech didn't end until after midnight on the East Coast. The rest of his remarks were vintage Trump: several riffs on the Democrats' "partisan witch hunts," a meandering story about how he managed to get Dana White, Kid Rock, and "the Hulkster" to show up at the convention, taunts of CBS News's "Deface the Nation," stolen 2020 election claims, and more.

And Trump took a jab at Biden, despite his team making a big deal earlier in the day about how the current president wouldn't be mentioned. "I say it often: If you took the ten worst presidents in the history of the United States—think of it, the ten worst—added them up, they will not have done the damage that Biden has done," Trump said. "Only going to use the term once. Biden. I'm not going to use the name anymore. Just one time. The damage that he's done to this country is unthinkable."

There's no doubt Trump was greatly affected by the attempt on his life—who wouldn't be? But in the end, a seventy-eight-year-old man—particularly a seventy-eight-year-old man like Donald Trump—can only change so much. Especially with so much else in the campaign about to change, Trump's "unity" era was destined to be a short one.

CHAPTER NINE

LOCKED UP

The Republican convention featured a who's who of the extended MAGA universe, with just about every GOP lawmaker, right-wing pundit, and former administration official (in good standing) you could think of in attendance as Donald Trump was nominated for president for the third time. But there was one glaring absence.

As the party descended on Milwaukee in mid-July, Steve Bannon was 925 miles away, locked up at Federal Correctional Institution (FCI) Danbury in Connecticut. The seventy-year-old former chief strategist for Donald Trump—now also known as inmate number 05635-509—was about two weeks into a four-month prison sentence he received after being found guilty on two counts of contempt of Congress. His crime: defying a subpoena and refusing to cooperate with the congressional committee investigating the January 6 attack on the US Capitol.

Bannon's willingness to serve time rather than cave to Nancy Pelosi or Liz Cheney cemented his status as a towering figure in Trump's MAGA movement—and he knew it. "They've made me much bigger than I am," he told *The New York Times* weeks before he reported to prison. "They can't help themselves. I trigger these guys to a level that other people don't."

After losing a last-ditch appeal to the Supreme Court, Bannon, the host of the popular right-wing video podcast *War Room*, prepared for life behind bars. "Do not write a letter to me at all. It will not be read," he told listeners three days before reporting to prison. He urged them to focus their energy on getting Trump reelected: "I don't want you taking time to write a letter. I want you to get to work. This is all about victory."[1]

Bannon showed up at FCI Danbury on July 1, just days after Trump's debate with Joe Biden, and had a final message for the world before he placed himself in federal custody.

"I am proud to go to prison," he told assembled reporters. "If this is what it takes to stand up to tyranny, if this is what it takes to stand up to the [Attorney General Merrick] Garland corrupt criminal DOJ, if this is what it takes to stand up to Nancy Pelosi, if this is what it takes to stand up to Joe Biden, I'm proud to do it."[2]

Danbury is not the kind of prison where you would typically find a nonviolent offender on a relatively minor charge like Bannon. Because he had another pending legal issue—felony charges in New York related to a fraudulent fundraising campaign—he could not be sent to one of the minimum-security prisons, sometimes referred to as "Club Fed," where inmates live relatively comfortably in dormitory-like facilities. No, Bannon would serve his sentence alongside hardened criminals: gangsters, mafiosos, drug smugglers, sex offenders.

It was quite a turn for a man who had made a fortune as an investment banker at Goldman Sachs and created his own Hollywood production company before helping engineer Trump's victory in 2016 and working down the hall from the Oval Office. Members of the January 6 Committee had demanded Bannon's testimony because they believed he was one of the most important, and culpable, figures in the events leading up to the attack on the Capitol.

On January 5, 2021, Bannon seemed well aware of what would unfold the following day.

"All hell is going to break loose tomorrow," Bannon said on his podcast. "It's all converging, and now we're on, as they say, the point of attack." White House phone records uncovered by the committee showed that Bannon's comments that day came shortly after a conversation with President Trump. The two men spoke again at 9:46 p.m. that night and again on the morning of January 6.[3]

Unlike many of Trump's allies, Bannon did not waver in his support for the president after the failed attempt to overturn the 2020 election results. If anything, Bannon became even more devoted to the Trump cause, building *War Room* into the center of the MAGA media ecosystem. The show guided hardcore Trump supporters through all the state election recounts in early 2021, and helped spread the bonkers theory that the former president could be reinstated as president after the votes were counted again. The plan to oust Kevin McCarthy from the speakership in 2023 had been largely hatched on Bannon's show. Trump himself was a regular viewer. Sometimes he tuned in live, other days his assistant Natalie Harp would show him clips—a Bannon highlight reel of sorts. In mid-June

2024, Bannon interrupted an interview to answer his phone. "Hey, Mr. President," he said. "I'm live on TV, can I call you back?"[4]

Bannon lined up an eclectic group of about twenty guest hosts—including his own daughter, Rudy Giuliani's son, and Osama bin Laden's niece—to keep the podcast going while he was behind bars.[5] "I'm not a journalist. I'm not in the media," Bannon said shortly before going to prison. "This is a military headquarters for a populist revolt. This is how we motivate people. This show is an activist show. If you watch this show, you're a foot soldier. We call it the Army of the Awakened."[6]

One of the first things Bannon noticed upon arriving at prison was the lack of places to sit.

"There are no chairs for prisoners in all of Danbury," he recalled.* "The entire thing is to break you psychologically so that you're never comfortable."

He was in a two-story cellblock with eighty-three other men, all of whom shared two showers. His toilet was in his cell. "You're literally on top of each other," Bannon remembered. "It's so hard, just guys on top of you all the time."

Bannon wanted me to know he had it much tougher than others in Trump's orbit who have served time in prison.

"I wasn't in a camp like that pussy [Michael] Cohen," Bannon told me with a laugh, referring to Trump's former fixer who had served time at what *Forbes* had once ranked one of America's "cushiest"

*Bannon would later revise this comment to note that there were a couple of "little plastic shitty chairs," the kind that would accompany an elementary school desk. "There's nothing, like, that you can sit in."

prisons. "I was in a fucking low-medium security with gang-bangers and fucking drugs and stabbings and—Danbury is a rough place."

Bannon also insisted he served time at a rougher place than Peter Navarro, another Trump advisor who was sentenced to prison on contempt of Congress charges.

"Navarro went to a camp, and bitched and moaned the whole time," Bannon told me.

For his part, Navarro claims his prison (the Federal Correctional Institution in Miami) was much more dangerous than Bannon's because he lived in a dormitory-like facility with dozens of other inmates sleeping in bunks. "I had fifty guys who could have shivved me while I slept. Bannon had just one," Navarro told me.

According to Bannon, among the few "amenities" at Danbury is a small room, thirty feet by ten feet, with three TVs behind a glass barrier; inmates could request handheld transistor radios and tune in to listen to the sound from one of the three. In Bannon's description, there was "a Spanish TV, a white TV, and a Black TV."

The "white TV" was almost always tuned to either sports or Fox News.

Inmates were also permitted time outside in the prison yard, a common area shared by the wider prison population from all of Danbury's cellblocks. The movements in and out of the yard were tightly controlled—and they could be tense. Not long after becoming an inmate, Bannon said, he found himself standing around outside with a large group of prisoners, waiting for the steel doors to open so that they could return to their cells. Before long, he said, a commotion broke out among a group of Dominican inmates.

"All of a sudden, they start getting worked up among themselves,"

Bannon told me, laughing as he recalled the scene. "They take a shiv out and fucking rip a guy, right? And there's blood everywhere."

I had to ask: How badly was the guy hurt?

"Fucking hurt!" Bannon claimed. "They took him out in a fucking ambulance, got him out. They fucking ripped him up on the side."

Before long, cops arrived and started asking inmates—including Bannon—what they had seen.

He told them he saw nothing at all. "You just can't," he said. "You can never—[if] you work with a cop, you answer any question a cop asks you, and you're done."

Before reporting to Danbury in July, Bannon had hired Sam Mangel—a federal prison consultant who spent time behind bars after pleading guilty to wire fraud—to give him some tips about navigating life in prison. Mangel had years of experience advising inmates within the federal penitentiary system, working with clients ranging from crypto fraudster Sam Bankman-Fried to Navarro, Bannon's fellow Trump advisor.

"I told him ahead of time, the guards are not your friends," Mangel said. "When you speak to guards, other inmates become suspicious that you're ratting on them. Inmates, especially low-security and up, are naturally very paranoid, suspicious people, because a lot of them are hiding things."

In prison, Bannon spent as much time as he could in the cellblock's computer room, using one of the four PCs—equipped with a two-decade-old Windows operating system—that were shared by the eighty-four prisoners. He would sign up to use the computers for an hour, and then, after a fifteen-minute break, sign up again. Bannon was cognizant of "prison etiquette" about not hogging the computers but said that he would sometimes spend ten hours a day "working on campaign stuff." The devices were not connected to the internet, but he could communicate via email with a few dozen preapproved individuals. The Bureau of Prisons would review the correspondence on its way in and on its way out.

Bannon had a way of keeping up with the news, with the help of his daughter Maureen and his chief financial officer, Grace Chong. "They had a system of sending me, first off, all polling data, everything like that, analytics," he remembered. "They would send it to me, and I'd be able to comment and ask questions." They also sent him images of various news websites so he could see what stories were online even though he didn't have direct access to the internet. "They had the ABC News site [for example]. I'd have fifty stories. I couldn't click on the stories, but I said, 'Send me boom, boom, boom.' And they'd cut and paste and drop it in there."

Early in the evening on July 13, Bannon was standing at one of the computers and writing an email when an inmate he had never spoken to came down to see him from the TV room upstairs.

"A guy that I'd seen a thousand times," Bannon later told me. "He never spoke a word of English. He's one of the Hispanic guys in there."

"Hey, boss," the inmate said to him. "Trump shot."

"What?"

"Trump shot."

Bannon rushed upstairs to the TV room to watch what had happened. He was quickly joined by dozens of other inmates. "It was never as packed as that," Bannon recalled. "All three TVs—the Spanish, the Black, and the white—only time I ever saw that."

Bannon had long feared something like this would happen. I had spoken to him in early June, weeks before his prison sentence began, and he told me the only way Trump wouldn't return to the White House was if the election was stolen or he was assassinated. "I'm very worried," Bannon had told me. The Democrats, the media, "they're giving moral justification that whoever takes [Trump] out is a hero." He even argued Trump's team should individually vet every member of his Secret Service detail.

Five weeks later, he was watching reports out of Butler, Pennsylvania, through the protective glass in the inmate TV room, listening on his prison-issued transistor radio, and convinced his fears were coming true. The Secret Service had failed to protect him. A gunman had taken a shot at Trump.

Had he not been in prison, Bannon would have immediately taken to the airwaves. This was the moment he had been preparing his "Army of the Awakened" for all these years.

"Between now and Election Day, they're going to try to take out so many people," he ominously told the crowd at a Turning Point USA conference earlier that summer. "Are you prepared to fight? Are you prepared to give it all? Are you prepared to leave it all on the battlefield? Ladies and gentlemen, it's very simple: victory or death!"

Lord knows what Bannon would have told his followers to do that evening if he could, and what the ramifications would have been for the country. While Trump himself had called for unity and turned down the temperature, I suspected that his longtime aide's instincts would have led him to do the opposite. *America is lucky that Steve Bannon is behind bars*, I remember thinking at the time.

Shortly after the election, I met with the newly released Bannon at his town house on Capitol Hill to learn more about his time behind bars.

One of my first questions to him was about whether my concerns four months earlier were well founded.

"If [Trump] had not had that reaction, if he had continued the 'Fight! Fight! Fight!' and [declared], 'Fuck them, they tried to kill me,' I think the country would have been on fire," I said, sitting in Bannon's cluttered living room. "And he calmed it down."

"He calmed it down, yes," Bannon said.

"But *you* would have been fanning the flames," I replied.

"Throwing fucking gasoline on it. Fuck yes!" Bannon shot back. "Because it's a base election. . . . I would have revved that thing up to a ten."

"So," I said, leaning in and pointing at him, "there was peace because you were behind bars."

"Yeah, there's no doubt," Bannon said. "And I'm not saying I didn't make that recommendation through code."

Through code.

Yes, Bannon had a way of getting messages to the Trump campaign—and to Trump himself—while he was behind bars. It involved his daughter and his chief financial advisor, as well as Boris Epshteyn, one of Trump's top aides. "I had just a system to get to Boris, kind of in quasi-code, through Mo [Bannon's daughter Maureen] into Grace [Chong]," he said. "Anytime I needed to get to the campaign, we had a system that they could get to them."

I asked him if there was literally a code word that he used. "Well, we had—" he began, before catching himself. "I don't—the Bureau of Prisons could go back through it. *We had a way that they could get to him.*"

Bannon was particularly careful about what he told allies over email. All incoming and outgoing messages were reviewed by the

Bureau of Prisons, of course, but Bannon claims that an investigative officer at Danbury—an official he described as "pure MAGA"—had warned him that his communications were also being reviewed by "Main Justice," otherwise known as the Biden administration.

So with his coded system, he let "the girls"—Maureen and Grace—know which messages were to be passed on to Trump or to those around him. And in the days following the assassination attempt, Bannon let campaign officials know he believed they were making a huge mistake by trying to reduce tensions rather than raise them.

"Trump's going to be Trump. You're not going to have that 'unity,'" he remembered saying. "What you're going to do is blow a huge opportunity to differentiate yourself. And quite frankly, throw down harder that *they tried to assassinate him*. Put it back on them. Get into the thing about the lax security. Double down, *triple* down on this. It's a winner."

Fortunately, the campaign disregarded the advice. As Bannon watched speaker after speaker in Milwaukee who had ripped up their prepared remarks to praise Trump's message of unity, he found himself growing angrier and angrier. "I hated the convention," Bannon told me. "The kumbaya, the cancellation of all the guys who wanted to get up there to fucking throw fucking fists."

"If I had been around, that would have never happened," he said. "Ever."

While much of Bannon's attention for those four months was focused on the world outside Danbury, he also developed a surprisingly close bond with several of his fellow inmates. About halfway through my interview with Bannon at his home in mid-November, he inexplicably stood up and walked out of the room. Returning a few moments later, he slapped a photograph down on the table that showed him standing in the yard with a few other inmates.

"That's prison-yard tough, dude," he said, almost giddy. "Look at that. I'm a fucking beast."

But his attention quickly moved to the other men in the photograph, and I could tell he had genuine affection for them. "That's my cellmate," he said, pointing at one of them. "Twenty-four years in prison. Total fuckin'—Tim Hunsperger, hardest motherfucker I've ever met." He explained that another person in the picture—"the Indian guy"—was a former Goldman Sachs employee who got busted for insider trading. The fourth was a chief financial officer at a construction company busted for fraud.

But Bannon wanted me to know he didn't hang out just with the other nonviolent offenders. "I had murderers, fuckin' mob hitmen, who were my besties," he said. "They were my guys."

Bannon told me one of his closest prison buddies was an Italian guy named Vito who'd been in prison for so long he claimed he once shared a cellblock at the maximum-security federal penitentiary in Marion, Illinois, with John Gotti, the infamous boss of the Gambino crime family. Vito had also served time in the medium-security federal prison in Leavenworth, Kansas, and eventually made his way to the low-security prison in Danbury because of his good behavior. After being locked up for about three decades, Vito got out in April 2025—a year earlier than scheduled—after Bannon helped advocate for his release.

"It was such a powerful thing for me to go through, to see these guys," he recalled.

Bannon was particularly impressed by the way Vito kept his

composure—and his dignity—rather than rotting away in his cell. Prison guards "on the payroll" would regularly smuggle in food for Vito from restaurants in Brooklyn, and they would cook big Italian meals like something straight out of *Goodfellas*. Vito was once sent back to a medium-security prison for several years because he got in a fight with members of an Albanian gang. Why would he risk that? Because they weren't showing enough respect to the Italian Mafia guys. "If you lose your respect," he told Bannon, "it's not worth living."

"[Prison] is meant to break you. It's meant to change you," Bannon told me. "I learned more about human nature and life and myself in prison than I learned in the White House, much more." He made a reference to *The Bridge on the River Kwai*: "Unless you keep yourself together, and your civilization, you'll become a savage. And they want you to become a savage."

In prison, Vito spent a lot of time watching Fox News. "He is the single biggest Trump fan you've ever seen," Bannon told me. "He could literally quote [Trump speeches]. He knew everything about me. Everything. He had read everything."

When Vito was released from Danbury in April 2025, a friend of his girlfriend—whom he'd met while in prison—captured the moment with a cell phone camera. He walked with a swagger away from the razor-wire fence separating the inmates from the outside world, carrying a small black leather bag and wearing a white Sergio Tacchini tracksuit, pristine tennis shoes, and dark sunglasses. His hair was slicked back.

"Come on," Vito said as he gave his girlfriend a hug. "Let's get out of here."

Vito's girlfriend sent the video to Bannon, who watched with gleeful pride at his friend's composure as he experienced freedom for the first time in three decades. "That guy is so impressive," Bannon told me. "Look at that guy's tracksuit, look at the shoes, look at the hair. . . . Walks out, totally precise. These guys amaze me."

Few inmates handled their sentences as well as Vito did. Bannon encountered dozens of men in their early twenties who were facing at least ten years in prison, and often much longer than that.

"Psychologically, they're fucked up, just [because of] the time," he noted. And so they turn to drugs, which Bannon said are "out of control" at Danbury.

In federal prison, every medically able prisoner must perform some kind of work. Like all federal prisons, Danbury has its own inmate education program, and when Bannon arrived to serve his sentence, the prison needed a new civics teacher. The guards who oversaw the inmate education program thought Bannon would be the perfect person to teach American history and government while allowing him to meet his work requirement.

So, the man who stood accused of helping orchestrate an effort to undermine American democracy and to overturn a presidential election now found himself on the federal payroll—prisoners at Danbury get paid about twenty-five cents an hour for their work—teaching civics to fellow convicts.

Bannon's class met up to five days a week, with as many as fifty inmates showing up for the sessions. Whether that impressive attendance had more to do with Bannon's lectures or the sweltering summer heat is anyone's guess—the classes were held in one of the only buildings at the Danbury prison complex with air-conditioning—but

Bannon came away from the experience claiming he learned more from his students than they did from him.

"You can actually get a sense of where the country is in prison. It was amazing," he told me shortly after he was released. "Every Hispanic and Black family in America has someone they know that's incarcerated, that's just the reality. It may not be their son, but it's a cousin, or nephew, or a next-door neighbor. These mass incarcerations are out of control for nonviolent drug charges."

In October, Bannon told me his time in Danbury convinced him that Trump was going to win. In his view, Kamala Harris was never going to be able to connect with those voters because of her record as a prosecutor in California. "No Black or Hispanic men are going to vote for Kamala Harris, because of the mass incarcerations," he told me. "The Black community, the Hispanic community, they literally *hate* her. [Prison] is the most MAGA place I've ever been in my life, *from the minorities.*"*

He also left prison with newfound appreciation for one of the few initiatives from the first Trump administration that he previously didn't like: the criminal justice reforms known as the First Step Act of 2018. The initiative sought to improve conditions in prison and to give inmates more opportunities for education and early release. It was pushed by Trump's son-in-law Jared Kushner, whom Bannon often clashed with, and was one of the few major bills signed by Trump that had overwhelming bipartisan support. The bill passed the Senate by a vote of 87–12. All twelve of the senators voting against

---

*Bannon's grand pronouncement that Harris would not win the votes of any Black or Hispanic men was, of course, far from the truth. According to a Navigator Research postelection survey, Harris won 49 percent of the Hispanic male vote and 71 percent of the Black male vote. Directionally, though, Bannon's broader point stands: Joe Biden did 35 percentage points better than Harris among both groups in 2020.

it were Republicans. Similarly, in the House, every single Democrat voted for it, and the only votes against it were from Republicans.

"Jared was a genius about this. It is our ticket to a massive coalition. Massive coalition," Bannon told me. "Remember, in *Spartacus* the slave revolt starts in a prison, right?"

While Bannon expressed what seemed to be genuine concern for the treatment of the inmates he got to know at the Danbury prison, his compassion for the accused was far from consistent. Not long after he spoke at length with me about his newfound appreciation for the First Step Act, Bannon would praise the Trump administration for flying two planeloads of alleged Venezuelan gang members, without the benefit of a hearing or reasonable notice, to the CECOT prison in El Salvador—a place that actually resembles hell on earth. At CECOT, prisoners have virtually no contact with the outside world. No phone calls. No visits. While Bannon may have had a hard time finding a chair in Danbury, the overcrowded cells in CECOT typically hold more than sixty prisoners who are stacked in metal bunks with no sheets or mattresses. Some prisoners are reportedly allowed outside their cells for only thirty minutes a day.[7] Bannon, however, cavalierly dismissed concerns that some of the people the Trump administration sent there could have been entirely innocent.

"Guess what, if there are some innocent gardeners in there, hey, tough break for a swell guy," Bannon said on *War Room* in March 2025. "That's where we stand. We're getting these criminals out of the United States."

Shortly after 1 a.m. on the final day of his four-month sentence, Bannon was woken up by a prison guard banging on the bars of his cell and letting him know it was time to fill out his discharge paperwork. Given the timing of his middle-of-the-night release, Bannon thought he would be alone as he was discharged. Not so. Several of his fellow inmates came to bid him farewell.

"It was amazing," Bannon recalled. "I didn't even know they knew the time. They get up in the middle of night and come out. Prison has its own system. You can't make it without buddies."

Bannon said his goodbyes, signed the necessary documents, and, at about 3 a.m., walked into the predawn darkness outside the prison. He was a free man.

Prisoner discharges typically don't take place in the middle of the night, but prison authorities wanted to avoid the commotion that would come with Bannon holding a chaotic press conference outside the prison walls, as he had done on the day he was locked up. As he walked out of the prison gate, he was met by his daughter Maureen, who ran over and gave him a hug.

The date was October 29, exactly one week before the 2024 presidential election, and Bannon was ready to get back to work. He had his team announce he would hold a press conference at a luxury hotel in Manhattan later that day. And of course, he'd return to hosting *War Room* immediately.

But first, he had a few calls to make. Aside from a few conversations with his lawyer and one call to his aide Grace Chong, Bannon had not spoken on the phone during his four months behind bars. But within hours of his release—before 6 a.m.—Bannon's phone lit up. Donald Trump was on the line.

"My Steeeeeeve! My Steeeeeve!" Trump said as they both laughed. "You're a convict."

The former president had lots of questions for Bannon about his life behind bars. If Trump lost the election the following week, there was a very real chance that he would end up in prison. How bad was it?

"Let me be blunt," Bannon told him. "It's hard as shit. So we're not going there."

CHAPTER TEN

BIDEN BOWS OUT

At about 8 p.m. on Tuesday, July 16, 2024, Jeffrey Katzenberg received a call from a Biden campaign aide with an urgent request: Would he be able to meet with the president in Las Vegas the following morning? Joe Biden's reelection bid was in free fall, and he wanted to hear ideas from Katzenberg—the former chairman of Walt Disney Studios, a leading Democratic fundraiser, and, for the past year, a co-chair of the Biden–Harris campaign—on how to get it back on track.

Katzenberg knew how deep a hole Biden was in. Not only had the president's devastating debate performance three weeks earlier shocked a nation that already believed he was too old for the job, but the assassination attempt against Donald Trump in Pennsylvania three days earlier had generated a groundswell of goodwill for Biden's Republican opponent. Still, Katzenberg believed there was a path forward—and he wanted to present his plan to the president.

Usually, Katzenberg would just pop over from Los Angeles to Las

Vegas on his private plane—about an hour-long flight. But due to flight restrictions at the Las Vegas airport associated with Biden's visit, that wasn't an option. So Katzenberg, the co-founder of DreamWorks SKG and one of Hollywood's most powerful executives, woke up at 3 a.m. and arranged for a car to take him on the nearly five-hour drive to meet with the president at the Las Vegas hotel where he was staying.

But upon arriving later that morning at Biden's hotel, Katzenberg immediately noticed that the president looked terrible—even worse than he had during the debate. He was coughing. His nose was running. And there were tissues strewn all over the room.

"Thanks for coming down. I really appreciate you," Biden told him, his voice virtually gone. "I know you had to get up in the middle of the night to get here."

Katzenberg proceeded to present his plan, urging Biden to go on the offensive, wage an aggressive campaign against Trump, and put an end to the Democratic hand-wringing over his debate performance once and for all. Biden, he suggested, should do a blizzard of interviews—including late-night comedy programs, political shows, and talk shows. He urged him to appear on *The Jennifer Hudson Show*, a daytime syndicated program more likely to feature celebrities, musical performances, and the stars of online viral videos than a presidential candidate. Katzenberg urged him to make media appearances of all kinds to show people Biden was more than capable of taking the fight to Donald Trump. But as Katzenberg was making the case that Biden could still win despite concerns about his health and age, an enfeebled president was sitting before him, repeatedly coughing and blowing his nose.

"Mr. President, you do not look well, and you do not sound well," Katzenberg finally said. "When did that happen?"

"I woke up with it," Biden replied.

"Have you seen a doctor yet?"

"No."

At this point, the only other person in the room—deputy chief of staff Annie Tomasini, Biden's closest aide—spoke up, telling Katzenberg his time with the president was running out.

"Jeffrey, hurry up," Tomasini said. "The doctor's coming down."

Biden said goodbye to Katzenberg and then briefly saw his doctor. Something was clearly wrong, but the president insisted on plowing ahead with his schedule for the day, which included a radio interview with Univision and a keynote speech at the annual conference of UnidosUS, a Latino advocacy group.

Biden somehow managed to make it through the thirteen-minute radio interview. Although his answers were coherent, his voice sounded incredibly weak, as though he was unable to gather enough breath to complete his sentences. And while the crowd at the conference waited for Biden, his condition continued to worsen. His doctor gave him a COVID-19 test, which quickly came back with a strong positive. Tomasini notified the operations team that they would be flying back to the East Coast as soon as Air Force One was wheeled out from the hangar in which it was being stored to protect it from the sweltering, 120-degree heat.

The Secret Service also prepared in case the president needed to go to the hospital. While the UnidosUS crowd was growing restless and Biden was waiting to be taken to the airport, urgent messages went out over Las Vegas Metropolitan Police Department radios instructing officers to secure not one but two area hospitals for a possible emergency visit by the president of the United States.

"Meet at the Valley Hospital ER parking lot. We're going to meet behind the ER entrances, where the ambulances go," an officer said in one of the transmissions, according to audio later obtained by the *Daily Beast* through a public records request.

"Again, any available units, come down here to Valley Hospital right now," the officer said a short while later. After one of his colleagues let him know four units were on the way, he responded: "I need more."[1]

An hour and twenty minutes after Biden was scheduled to appear, the organizer of the UnidosUS conference walked onstage to make an announcement to the people waiting for him: The president had tested positive for COVID-19 and wouldn't be speaking to the group.

Tomasini was in tears when she called Hunter Biden with the news. The president's health had deteriorated so quickly that she was relieved he "only" had COVID-19. He wasn't taken to the hospital, but he was rushed to Air Force One, which would fly him home to his beach house in Rehoboth Beach, Delaware. The footage of the president shuffling up the stairs to board the plane was painful to watch; he seemed to pause to catch his breath multiple times before disappearing into the aircraft.

Biden looked even worse disembarking the plane, gripping the railing along the stairs tightly and struggling to get into the presidential limousine. As the Trump campaign was celebrating at the Republican convention in Milwaukee that evening, all the public could see of their ailing president was him struggling to walk and appearing to require help from a Secret Service agent to get seated in his limousine.

Upon Biden's arrival in Delaware, the White House released a statement from Biden's doctor. "The President presented this afternoon with upper respiratory symptoms, to include rhinorrhea (runny nose) and non-productive cough, with general malaise," the statement read. "He felt okay for his first event of the day, but given that he was not feeling better, point of care testing for COVID-19 was conducted, and the results were positive for the COVID-19 virus."

Once he got home, he slept for approximately sixteen of the next twenty-four hours, while the political world waited for news. Just about everyone in politics seemed to realize that his candidacy had reached the end of the road, but had Biden himself reached the same conclusion? Ultimately, the decision was still his—and his alone.

The president had had a disastrous week leading up to his COVID-19 diagnosis. On July 9, he was presented with a golden opportunity to right the ship: a three-day NATO conference with leaders from allied countries across the world assembling in Washington, DC. He had touted his work bolstering the military alliance multiple times in his interview with George Stephanopoulos days earlier and even ended that conversation by previewing the upcoming summit. "I guess a good way to judge me," Biden told George, "is you're gonna have now the NATO conference here in the United States next week. Come listen."[2]

But when Biden took the stage at the summit to introduce Ukrainian President Volodymyr Zelensky days later, he failed to meet the moment. "I'd now like to turn it over to the president of Ukraine, who has as much courage as he has determination," Biden declared. "Ladies and gentlemen, President Putin!"

Biden mixed up Zelensky with the murderous dictator who

started the war! It was an especially embarrassing gaffe given that the whole point of the summit was to demonstrate NATO's commitment to Ukraine following Russia's invasion two years earlier. Although he quickly caught the mistake and returned to the microphone to correct it—"President Putin? We're going to *beat* President Putin!"—Biden could not afford that kind of flub. And then, a few hours later, he made another one.

In the days leading up to the NATO summit, White House communications officials had been building expectations for the press conference Biden would hold at the conclusion of the event, at one point even jokingly referring to it as his "'big boy' press conference."[3] The back-and-forth with reporters would mark one of the first times since the debate weeks earlier that the president could put to rest concerns about his mental acuity and ability to think on his feet.

Overall, he performed okay—his advisors told him he did great—fending off question after question about his reelection campaign and pivoting back to his administration's accomplishments and the agreements expected to come out of that week's summit. But in response to the very first question he was asked—about whether he believed Vice President Kamala Harris could defeat Donald Trump if she were the Democratic nominee—Biden stepped on a rake. "Look, I wouldn't have picked Vice President Trump to be vice president did I think she was not qualified to be president," he began. Cameras in the room captured three of his top cabinet officials' reactions to the slipup: Secretary of State Antony Blinken immediately averted his gaze, Defense Secretary Lloyd Austin stared blankly ahead, and National Security Advisor Jake Sullivan leaned forward and worriedly began rubbing his chin.

Biden would have needed to perform just about perfectly to silence the voices calling for him to step aside—and he didn't come anywhere close.

Indeed, several more Democrats released statements in the hours after the press conference urging the president to end his candidacy. The dam was breaking. And a few days later, Representative Adam Schiff of California became the latest in a series of influential Democrats close to former House Speaker Nancy Pelosi to call on Biden to drop out. "A second Trump presidency will undermine the very foundation of our democracy," Schiff said in a written statement, "and I have serious concerns about whether the President can defeat Donald Trump in November."

There were some prominent Democrats who were still standing by Biden and willing to say so publicly, including some of the party's most outspoken progressives. "The matter is closed," Representative Alexandria Ocasio-Cortez of New York told reporters on July 11. "He's in this race, and I support him." Two days later, Senator Bernie Sanders published an op-ed in *The New York Times* saying essentially the same thing. "Enough!" the Vermont socialist wrote. "Mr. Biden may not be the ideal candidate, but he will be the candidate and should be the candidate."[4]

When Biden awoke in Rehoboth Beach on Friday afternoon, he told his inner circle he wanted to convene a meeting the following day at his house there with his most trusted aides: senior advisors Mike Donilon and Steve Ricchetti, Annie Tomasini, his son Hunter (who would join from California via speakerphone), and the first lady.

Donilon and Ricchetti knew they would be asked to provide an update on the state of the campaign, including the latest polling and fundraising numbers. There wasn't much good news to share.

Late Friday evening, Biden chief of staff Jeffrey Zients—who was not invited to take part in the Saturday meeting—received a call from Senator Patty Murray of Washington, the longest-serving Democrat in the Senate. Murray had not been among those publicly criticizing Biden and calling for a change at the top of the ticket, but she bluntly informed Zients that if the president did not end his campaign on his own, she would release a letter the following week publicly calling on him to do so. And her signature wouldn't be the only one on the letter; as many as thirty-five of her Democratic colleagues in the Senate were expected to sign on as well.

The decision to end the campaign may have been Biden's alone. But in practice, as the president battled the coronavirus in Rehoboth Beach, it was already over. Party leaders had abandoned him. The money was drying up. An overwhelming majority of voters believed he was in no condition to serve another four years as president, as did many of his longtime allies in Congress.

As Biden declined—in both his health and his political standing—he became increasingly isolated. His direct contact with key Democrats in Congress had been minimal since his disastrous debate with Trump and had been virtually nonexistent since the previous Saturday, when Democratic Senate Leader Chuck Schumer traveled to Delaware to tell him that even Democratic senators, most of them, believed that Biden would lose if he stayed in the race and he would bring the party down with him. By the time he got sick with COVID in Las Vegas, Biden had only minimal contact with the people running his campaign in Delaware and with the senior aides in the West

Wing running his White House. The core group regularly talking to him had shrunk, essentially, to those who were with him in Rehoboth—Tomasini, Ricchetti, Donilon—along with policy advisor Bruce Reed. The ever-tightening Biden inner circle was made up of people deeply loyal to him who, despite what was obvious to just about everybody else, believed he could still win and serve another four years. Now even they were coming to terms with how bad things really were for Biden.

On Friday evening, as Ricchetti was preparing for the meeting with Biden the following day, he placed a call to Donna Brazile, the former chair of the Democratic National Committee. Brazile had been a stalwart Biden supporter, pushing back for weeks against those in the party who were suggesting he should drop out. But like everyone else, she sensed things were changing.

Ricchetti told Brazile that Biden would be making a final decision about his campaign—a *real* final decision—in the coming days. Given her role as a member of the committee controlling the credentialing of the party's delegates at the upcoming Democratic National Convention, Brazile had a firm grasp on the rules, and had influence with the various activist groups in the party that would play a major role in the event of a contested convention.

He asked Brazile to give him a reality check on Biden's support among the delegates and a refresher on the rules governing the process. *Was there any sign of slipping? How many of the delegates were committed? Could somebody successfully challenge Biden at the convention?* And finally: *If Biden were to drop out, what would the procedure be for nominating his replacement?*

Brazile answered Ricchetti's questions and then got right to work preparing for the possibility of Biden dropping out. Together with

Bakari Sellers, a Democratic official from South Carolina, she began calling state party leaders—and essentially every influential Black leader in the party. Brazile's message to voting delegates was direct: *You need to stand with Biden as long as he's in the race. But if he drops out, we all need to unite behind Kamala Harris.*

In other words, the effort to secure the nomination for Harris had already begun.

But the vice president herself was not involved in that effort. Although she was the obvious heir apparent, Harris had not so much as hinted—publicly or privately—that Biden should drop out of the race as calls for him to do so grew louder. She made that decision out of loyalty to the president, sure, but also out of self-interest. Harris and her top advisors knew that if Biden *did* decide to end his campaign, his endorsement would be the difference between an ugly battle for the nomination at the convention and a simple coronation of his vice president. Even behind-the-scenes whispers could imperil her chances of securing a spot at the top of the ticket.

So for those fateful three weeks in July, Harris kept her head down, remaining loyal to Biden in the expectation that her loyalty would be rewarded down the line. But that devotion had its limits. Harris did not join the chorus of Democratic voices questioning Biden's faculties, but she was not proactively defending him, either. Campaign leadership asked her at one point to call members of Congress to shore up Biden's support among nervous Democrats, but two Harris aides later told me that she declined: Calls to lawmakers, Harris believed, could be misinterpreted as the early stages of an effort to secure the nomination for herself. If she called Democratic members, those members could later disclose that they had spoken to her and misrepresent the purpose of the call.

As for the president himself, Biden still had been speaking to almost no one outside his innermost circle in those fateful final days. Barack Obama had reached out to him, as had Nancy Pelosi—multiple times. He ignored their calls. On July 18, political pundit Mark Halperin reported that Biden was working with historian Jon Meacham to draft a speech announcing his withdrawal from the race, but the scoop was wrong (as was Halperin's reporting that Biden would not endorse Kamala Harris).[5] Meacham had been a friend, an advisor, and an occasional speechwriter for Biden since he launched his 2020 presidential campaign, but the president hadn't been returning his calls for days, either.

As Biden's decision-making process dragged out, a perception began to emerge—including among some senior White House staff—that the president's son Hunter and wife, Jill, were behind his refusal to step aside. "Hunter Biden intensely wants his father to stay in the race," NBC News reported in early July. "And Jill Biden has been adamant that he wouldn't give up."[6]

In one sense, that was accurate: The president's family did not want to let other Democrats drive him out of the race. But at the same time, Hunter insisted that neither he nor Jill Biden were urging President Biden to stay in the race against his own will.

"Mom just kept saying, 'Joe, only you can make this decision,'" Hunter remembered. "I kept saying to him, 'There's one thing everybody's got to remember: You're still the motherfucking president of the United States. You're still the leader of this party. Not President Obama, not Speaker Pelosi, not Hakeem Jeffries, not Chuck Schumer, and *certainly* not the pundit class. You're the one that gets to make this decision.'"

Before Biden's illness forced him from the campaign trail, his family and closest aides still believed that he could weather the storm—in part because he'd done so before. In fact, Joe Biden's entire political career had been riddled with personal and political setbacks, and he'd managed to defy the odds and become the president of the United States. He nearly quit politics in 1972 when his family was hit with tragedy, but forged ahead and became one of the most influential senators of his time. He had ended his first presidential campaign in disgrace following a plagiarism scandal. He ran for president again and lost again twenty years later, but went on to become a two-term vice president. In 2020, he ran yet again and came in fourth place in the Iowa caucuses and fifth in the New Hampshire primary but still managed to bounce back and win the nomination and the presidency.

"The sense was that this is just another of the, I don't know, dozen times in which we were counted out for dead," Hunter later recalled. "How many storms have we weathered? Whether just purely political, the political combined with personal, or the purely personal." Those experiences, he said, led to a sense of calm within the family. They didn't feel an urgency to drop out of the race or even to rush to a decision. "We don't panic," he said. "Not by virtue of that we're some kind of superhuman family. It's just, we've got a lot of fucking practice."

One of Biden's closest advisors also referenced the president's resilience as a reason why, in retrospect, his inner circle was blind to just how deep of a hole he had dug for himself. "We just need the next South Carolina," this person remembered thinking, referring to the state whose Democratic primary voters, after a game-changing endorsement from Representative Jim Clyburn, salvaged Biden's 2020 campaign and propelled him to the White House.

By the time Biden sat down with Mike Donilon and Steve Ricchetti on the porch of his Rehoboth Beach home on Saturday, July 20, that sense of invincibility was gone. Jill Biden, Annie Tomasini, and Anthony Bernal, the first lady's chief of staff, joined for part of the meeting, and Hunter dialed in on speakerphone. The prospect of ending the campaign wasn't explicitly on the agenda, but as Hunter later told me, "I kind of knew."

Donilon kicked off the discussion with an overview of the polling. "I told him exactly what his own pollsters were saying, and they were saying there was no chance that he could win. I told him that," Donilon later told me. He also said to Biden that a "substantial portion" of Democratic senators wanted him out of the race and so did House Democrats, including Pelosi, who, Donilon said, was leading the effort to push Biden out. But even with that grim set of facts, Donilon made the case that Biden should stay in the race.

"I also said to him that it was my view that he was still the best candidate, the best Democrat to win, that he could go forward, but that he needed to understand the kind of race we would have," Donilon said. It would be a race where Biden would be running without many of his big financial backers, without the support of the party leadership, and with a large number of people calling on him to drop out.

"But I felt he could take it to the convention," Donilon told me. "I felt that he could win it at the convention, and that, in my view, while I thought the vice president could win, I still believe that he was the best Democrat to beat Trump."

Ricchetti spoke about the growing opposition Biden was facing within his own party, especially on Capitol Hill. He told Biden about the letter Senator Patty Murray was preparing to release in the coming days calling on him to drop out, noting that an overwhelming majority of Democratic senators were likely to sign it. Ricchetti said there was one bright spot: The party delegates were still standing by Biden, for the most part, and the president's advisors believed he'd be able to fend off any challenge at the convention.

Biden sat in his chair, wearing a mask due to his illness, and took it all in. Had he not contracted COVID-19 days earlier Biden very well could have tried to stick it out. After all, his family was united behind him, and his advisors were still telling him he could win. But getting as sick as he did in Las Vegas had forced his hand.

"God was giving us some signals," one of the advisors with him in Rehoboth later told me. "And then He slapped him in the face with COVID."

After his advisors concluded their presentation, Biden sat quietly for a few moments before asking a question of the group: *If he did decide to drop out, how should he do it?* He instructed Donilon and Ricchetti to draft a statement he could release—if he went through with his decision to call it quits—and the group broke for dinner.

When everyone returned to the porch a couple of hours later, Biden reviewed the draft statement, and the discussion soon turned to how his decision should be announced. He was still too sick to deliver a televised address, so the group resolved to release a written statement and follow up with remarks to the nation a few days later. Biden made clear he would endorse Kamala Harris as his replacement atop the ticket, but that endorsement, the group decided, would come later. Dropping out of the race, his advisors reasoned, was a historic decision—one that needed to stand on its own.

The president seemed to have reached his conclusion. But everyone agreed to sleep on it before officially pulling the plug on his campaign.

The group reconvened the following morning at 11 a.m., and Biden informed them his decision was final: He would announce his withdrawal from the race that afternoon.

But before Biden could execute the plan, he had to make an important call. When National Security Advisor Jake Sullivan patched through a call from the prime minister of Slovenia—to discuss a pending prisoner exchange between Russia, several European countries, and the United States that would include the release of *Wall Street Journal* reporter Evan Gershkovich and former Marine Paul Whelan ten days later—Sullivan had no idea Biden had just decided to end his campaign.

After hanging up with the Slovenian prime minister, Biden called four people to let them know what he had decided. The first call he made was to White House chief of staff Jeff Zients; the second was to his campaign chair, Jen O'Malley Dillon. Only after those calls did he reach out to Vice President Harris.

"Are you sure you want to do this?" she asked. The decision was his alone, she reminded him, and nobody could force him out of the race.

Biden told her his mind was made up. He was dropping out, and the decision had been all his.

At that point, Harris made a request that came across more like a demand: He needed to endorse her. "Of course," Biden responded. He promised his endorsement would come in the next day or two.

No, Harris insisted. It needed to come immediately. Otherwise, she argued, Biden would be opening the door to an ugly fight for the nomination.

Biden agreed to discuss her concerns with his advisors and call her back. The inner circle was adamant that Biden's initial statement stand on its own, but agreed his endorsement of Harris could come shortly thereafter.

Before talking to anybody else at the White House or his campaign, Biden called to give one more person an early heads-up: Representative Jim Clyburn of South Carolina, whose endorsement saved Biden's campaign four years earlier.

At 1:45 p.m., after saying goodbye to Clyburn, Biden convened a call with his senior staff at the White House and the campaign—most of whom had been kept entirely in the dark about his deliberations in Rehoboth over the weekend—to let them know about his decision. But before he could finish speaking, his statement was posted on X for the world to see. The news was out.

"It has been the greatest honor of my life to serve as your President," read the statement, which was published on Elon Musk's X rather than through official White House channels. "And while it has been my intention to seek reelection, I believe it is in the best interest of my party and the country for me to stand down and to focus solely on fulfilling my duties as President for the remainder of my term."[7]

Biden touted what he viewed as his administration's biggest accomplishments—making "historic investments" in infrastructure, passing gun safety legislation for the first time in three decades, overcoming the pandemic and accompanying economic crisis, and strengthening the United States' global alliances—and expressed gratitude to Kamala Harris "for being an extraordinary partner in all this work."

The absence of an endorsement sparked immediate speculation that he would not weigh in on the race to succeed him.

But twenty-seven minutes later, a second post was published from Biden's X account. "My fellow Democrats," it began. "My very first decision as the party nominee in 2020 was to pick Kamala Harris as my Vice President. And it's been the best decision I've made. Today I want to offer my full support and endorsement for Kamala to be the nominee of our party this year. Democrats—it's time to come together and beat Trump. Let's do this."[8]

Over the course of the next several hours, Biden made calls to about fifty of his most important supporters and allies, the people who he believed had made it possible for him to become president of the United States. He called some of closest friends in Congress, labor leaders, a few governors, and others who had been with him through good times and bad. He called them all to say thank you and, in most of the conversations, to put in a good word for Kamala Harris. One person he didn't call, and, in fact, would not talk to for weeks: Barack Obama, the man he had served for eight years as vice president. Obama had been trying to get in touch with Biden for about two weeks, but his calls had not been returned. Obama reached out again after Biden suspended his campaign, but the two men would not end up speaking until shortly before the Democratic National Convention four weeks later.

Not every Democratic leader was thrilled that Harris was all but guaranteed to be the nominee, but most breathed an enormous sigh of relief that the party would not be going into what many believed to be the most important presidential election of their lifetime with an eighty-one-year-old man whose faculties could take a turn for the worse at any time. In a matter of minutes, a race that many Democrats had privately accepted as a fait accompli had become winnable again.

Donald Trump came to the same realization—and he was furious. In a series of statements posted on social media throughout the night on Sunday, he claimed Biden never had COVID, accused the Democratic Party of fraud, and—despite inspiring a mob to attempt to stop the transfer of power four years earlier—said the Democrats were the true threat to democracy.

"The Democrats pick a candidate, Crooked Joe Biden, he loses the Debate badly, then panics, and makes mistake after mistake, is told he can't win, and decide they will pick another candidate, probably Harris," he wrote. "They stole the race from Biden after he won it in the primaries—A First! These people are the real THREAT TO DEMOCRACY!"[9]

CHAPTER ELEVEN

KAMALA RISING

The day after Joe Biden dropped out of the presidential race, Nancy Pelosi was on the phone with Barack Obama. Pelosi had just endorsed Kamala Harris to replace Biden as the Democratic presidential nominee—a move that had caught Obama by surprise.

"Today, it is with immense pride and limitless optimism for our country's future that I endorse Vice President Kamala Harris for President of the United States. My enthusiastic support for Kamala Harris for President is official, personal and political," she said in a statement released around 1 p.m. the day after Biden had dropped out.[1]

The former president wanted to know what had happened. Why had Pelosi issued a statement endorsing Harris so soon? Hadn't he and Pelosi agreed days earlier that party leaders anointing the vice president as Biden's replacement would be a mistake? Weren't they on the same page about the importance of having "a process" for choosing a new Democratic nominee?

"That train has left the station," Pelosi told Obama, according to a person who heard the call.

Pelosi was right: There would be no "process" or competition to choose the Democratic nominee. That much was obvious from the moment Biden issued his statement endorsing his vice president at 2:13 p.m. the day before. Within hours, nearly the entire party apparatus had fallen in line: Establishment figures like Bill and Hillary Clinton had promised to do whatever they could to support Harris, as had progressives like Representative Alexandria Ocasio-Cortez. Virtually every Democrat whose name had been floated as a potential alternative to Harris—Governors Gretchen Whitmer, Gavin Newsom, Andy Beshear, JB Pritzker, Josh Shapiro—quickly made clear that they had no plans to challenge her for the nomination. "The best path forward for the Democratic Party is to quickly unite behind Vice President Harris and refocus on winning the presidency," Shapiro said in a statement early Sunday evening. "The contrast in this race could not be clearer."[2]

This wasn't how Obama and Pelosi had hoped the hours after Biden's withdrawal from the race would play out. The two had been in regular communication as it became clear the president was nearing his decision, and they agreed Harris should not simply be handed the nomination unchallenged. In their view, some kind of mini-primary in which Harris and other potential candidates could compete for the votes of Democratic delegates was essential—not only because it would result in the best nominee but because it would also strengthen that nominee in the process. Therefore, Obama and Pelosi—arguably the two most influential figures in the Democratic

Party—had privately agreed to abstain from making any endorsements.

A source close to Obama insists the former president wasn't angry at Pelosi for abandoning their agreement but rather giving her a good-natured ribbing about her quick change of heart. A source close to Pelosi interpreted the call differently, believing that Obama sounded genuinely irritated that the former Speaker had endorsed Harris. "The Obamas were not happy," a Pelosi confidant told me. This person summed up Obama's message to Pelosi as, essentially, "What the fuck did you just do?"

A senior Biden advisor who also worked in the Obama White House later told me the real reason Obama didn't want to endorse Kamala Harris was because he didn't think she could win. "There's only one Black Jesus," this longtime Democratic operative added contemptuously.

Obama wasn't the only person close to Pelosi who was surprised to learn she had endorsed the vice president. Pelosi had never been a big Harris fan, after all, and had privately made clear in 2020 that she didn't think Biden should choose the Californian as his running mate.

"Kamala?" Paul Pelosi asked incredulously upon answering a phone call from his wife shortly after she made her endorsement.

"Don't start with me," the former Speaker said to her husband. She had no choice. No other candidates had stepped forward—Kamala Harris was it. The only thing Pelosi could do was try to help her win the election.

Obama had actually spoken with Harris the previous day, shortly after Biden announced his withdrawal from the race, to inform her he would not be endorsing her right away. "I want the process to play out a little bit, and it's to your advantage to have the appearance of earning this," a source familiar with the call described Obama as explaining to Harris. "You're obviously the favorite, this is likely going to be you, and I'm going to work hard for whoever the nominee is." Obama's public statement on Biden's decision didn't mention Harris, but simply expressed "confidence that the leaders of our party will be able to create a process from which an outstanding nominee emerges."[3]

In fact, five more days would pass before Barack and Michelle Obama announced their endorsement of Harris, well after the vice president had effectively locked up the nomination and had begun to move forward with her campaign. The former first couple had called Harris on July 24 to let her know an endorsement was forthcoming, but the former president's public silence on the biggest question in Democratic politics prompted widespread speculation—why weren't the party's two most prominent figures endorsing the only real candidate to replace Biden as the party's nominee? Did the Obamas have a problem with Kamala Harris?

The endorsement finally came on July 26, five days after Biden dropped out of the race. "Earlier this week, we got a chance to catch up with a friend who we've known for more than 20 years," the joint statement from the Obamas read. "She's had a pretty busy couple of days, to say the least. But we couldn't be more excited for her—or more thrilled to endorse Kamala Harris as the Democratic nominee for President of the United States."[4]

The endorsement was accompanied by a video; Harris's campaign had filmed her side of the highly choreographed conversation with the Obamas two days earlier. The video looked more than a bit contrived.

"Aw, hi. You're both together," Harris said to start the call. "It's good to hear you both."

The video then showed Harris in a different location holding a speakerphone to her ear.

"I can't have this phone call without saying to my girl, Kamala, I am proud of you," Michelle Obama told Harris. "This is going to be historic."

Then the former president jumped in. "Michelle and I couldn't be prouder to endorse you and do everything we can to get you through this election and into the Oval Office," he said.

"Oh my goodness," Harris replied. "Michelle, Barack, this means so much to me. I am looking forward to doing this with the two of you—Doug and I both—getting out there, being on the road. But most of all, I just want to tell you, the words you have spoken and the friendship that you have given mean more than I can express."

Harris may have exhibited a somewhat stilted giddiness in the video, but the general feeling among her aides was one of frustration—that the Obamas had made her wait so long for the endorsement in the first place. But setting aside the timing or the awkwardness of the phone call, the campaign claimed the video raised $400,000 in just twenty-four hours, a pretty good haul, although a fraction of the $50 million Harris had raised in the first twelve hours after Biden dropped out.

In reality, Obama and Pelosi could have withheld their endorsements of Harris for weeks and it wouldn't have made a whit of difference as far as the nomination went. Harris started furiously working the phones and lining up supporters as soon as Biden dropped out.

Biden had no idea, but when he called Harris to deliver the news that Sunday, her senior advisors were already at the vice presidential residence in Washington having a secret meeting to discuss what would happen if Biden dropped out. The meeting was convened by Tony West, Harris's brother-in-law and confidant, to discuss a subject that they had been intentionally avoiding for weeks. Minyon Moore, the chair of the Democratic National Convention, joined the conversation from Chicago via video conference to explain what the rules would be for selecting a nominee if Biden were to end his campaign.

Harris's senior advisors were meeting out in the pool house and the vice president was making pancakes for her grandnieces in the main house when Biden called. A few minutes later, she broke the news to her brother-in-law and her advisors and they immediately got to work, lining up a list of people for the vice president to call. Her initial outreach was focused on those Democrats who could potentially challenge her for the nomination, including Pritzker, Beshear, Whitmer, and Shapiro. Some asked Harris what the "process" would be for choosing the new nominee.

"This is the process," Harris responded. "I am calling people and asking for their support. I hope to have your support."

Dressed in sweatpants, running shoes, and a Howard University hoodie, Harris reached out to more than one hundred party leaders, including members of Congress, labor organizers, and activists. One such call went to Donna Brazile, the former Democratic National Committee chair, who quickly informed the vice president that she had already been working on Harris's behalf for days and lined up the backing of several state delegations to the Democratic convention.

Harris continued to make calls until about 10 p.m. Sunday night, pausing briefly for lunch (sandwiches and salads) and dinner (pizza) with her family and aides. Just before 5 p.m., CNN correspondent Jamie Gangel reported that Harris and her team had begun to put together a list of potential running mates for two reasons: "To get some challengers, maybe, to go away, who might be considering it. But also to get the party to coalesce around a new team, to create excitement, and to win."[5] Momentum was building. By the time Harris went to bed that night, she had effectively clinched the nomination before anyone else could even think about mounting a challenge.

By Monday morning, Harris had received endorsements from a majority of House and Senate Democrats, and almost half of the Democratic governors around the country. She also raised a record $81 million in the first twenty-four hours of her candidacy—a desperately needed cash infusion after donations to the Biden campaign had all but ground to a halt.[6] Had Biden forged ahead, in fact, his campaign was having so much trouble raising money it would have likely needed to start laying off staff before the Democratic convention. With Harris atop the ticket, money would no longer be an issue.

The Democrats' switcheroo infuriated Donald Trump. Gone was all the "unity" talk from the Republican convention; in its place were false accusations that Democrats were rigging the election and breaking the rules by ousting the candidate he was beating. "It's not over!" Trump posted on Truth Social at 10:19 p.m. on Sunday night. "To morrow Crooked Joe Biden's going to wake up and forget that he dropped out of the race today!"[7]

At 6:24 a.m. the following morning, he still sounded desperate for a return to the status quo. "It's a new day and Joe Biden doesn't remember quitting the race yesterday!" Trump posted. "He is demanding his campaign schedule and arranging talks with Presidents Xi of China, and Putin of Russia, concerning the possible start of World War 3. Biden is 'sharp, decisive, energetic, angry, and ready to go!'"[8]

Trump may have been struggling with the transition, but Harris was moving full steam ahead. She held her first rally as the presumptive Democratic nominee just two days after Biden dropped out of the race and managed to turn out more than three thousand people in West Allis, Wisconsin—a modest crowd compared to a Trump rally, but larger than any Biden had spoken to since announcing his reelection.

"Before I was elected vice president, before I was elected a United States senator, I was elected attorney general of the state of California. And I was a courtroom prosecutor before then," Harris said, weaving some of her own biography into her remarks. "And in those roles, I took on perpetrators of all kinds: predators who abused women, fraudsters who ripped off consumers, cheaters who broke the rules for their own gain. So, hear me when I say: I know Donald Trump's type."

The crowd burst into applause. It had been years since their party had a standard-bearer who could take the fight to Trump with a line like that.

Indeed, the energy among Democrats was palpable. After months of more or less accepting that Biden was shuffling toward certain defeat, the party faithful found in Harris's ascension something they'd been lacking for a long, long time: hope.

On July 26, Fox News released its first battleground-state polls since Biden dropped out, finding Trump and Harris were essentially tied in Wisconsin and Pennsylvania—both places where Biden had been trailing.[9] Speaking at the decidedly pro-Trump Turning Point Action Believers' Summit in West Palm Beach that same day, Trump continued to demonstrate how rattled he was by the new reality, debuting a new analogy for the situation.

"It's like a prizefighter," Trump said. "He's losing badly, ready to be knocked out. And they say, 'Well, wait, let's stop the fight. Let's put somebody else in.' It doesn't work that way, and it's not supposed to work that way. And this really was a coup by the Democrats. This was a coup. Nothing else. He got 14 million votes. I hate to stick up for Biden, but, you know, he didn't want to do what he did."[10]

Once Harris had effectively secured the Democratic nomination, selecting a running mate of her own became one of her top priorities. Vice presidential vetting is typically incredibly involved and painstakingly thorough; the process from which Harris emerged four years earlier began in earnest on April 30 and concluded with her selection by Joe Biden on August 11.[11] With Biden ending his campaign on July 21, he left Harris just twenty-nine days to develop a campaign strategy, vet potential nominees, and make a decision before the Democratic National Convention kicked off in Chicago. Her campaign would need to move quickly.

And it did. Within forty-eight hours, Harris had brought on Eric Holder, the former attorney general in the Obama administration, to spearhead the vetting of potential running mates. Pennsylvania Governor Josh Shapiro, Senator Mark Kelly of Arizona, and Kentucky Governor Andy Beshear were among the first to be contacted by the Harris campaign.

Shapiro, the popular governor of a must-win state who had dominated his Republican opponent by 15 percentage points two years earlier, was an obvious contender. Kelly—a military veteran, an astronaut, and the husband of Gabby Giffords, the gun safety advocate who had been shot and nearly killed while she was serving in Congress—had a remarkable personal story. Beshear, a Democrat who had won two statewide elections in a deep-red state, could help Harris appeal to more moderate voters.

But as the vetting process proceeded, Minnesota Governor Tim Walz emerged as a surprising frontrunner. He had a progressive record, and he didn't come from a key battleground state. But Walz was a former member of the US House who had many allies in Congress—including Nancy Pelosi—advocating on his behalf,[12] and his profile had grown in recent weeks as he became a cable news mainstay. He won plaudits from Democrats by launching a line of attack against MAGA Republicans that seemed to be breaking through, labeling Trump and his acolytes—particularly JD Vance—as "weird."

"These are weird people on the other side," Walz said on MSNBC on July 23. "They want to take books away, they want to be in your exam room, that's what it comes down to. . . . These are weird ideas."

The attack line quickly caught fire in Democratic circles, with other politicians adopting the same line and the Harris campaign using it in press releases.

"Trump is old and quite weird," the Harris campaign said in a flippant press release titled "Statement on a 78-Year-Old Criminal's Fox News Appearance."

Walz also helped his case during his interviews with the campaign's vetting team, winning over Harris and her senior aides by coming across as authentic, down-to-earth, and willing to do anything to help Harris win. Yes, his politics were progressive, but they believed that his biography—he was a former high school football coach who served in the National Guard and came from farm country—would appeal to voters who had doubts about supporting a Black woman from San Francisco.

At around 9 p.m. the night before Harris was set to announce her running mate, I received a tip from a reliable source that she was likely to choose Tim Walz. In fact, the source implied the decision had already been made. Walz had become a serious contender by that point, so the news didn't come as a total shock, but Shapiro was still widely considered the most likely choice. On paper, the Pennsylvania governor couldn't have been a better fit.

Vice presidential candidates rarely make much of a difference in the outcome of the election, but Shapiro seemed like one who could. He was young and media savvy, and he hadn't taken many of the far-left policy positions that dominated Democratic politics during Trump's first term in office. He won a landslide victory two years earlier in the state that would likely tip the race, and he was a compelling speaker whose oratorical style had drawn comparisons to Barack Obama's.[13]

Nevertheless, my source was adamant that Shapiro would not be the pick—so I picked up the phone and called someone close to Shapiro. I let this person know that I had heard Tim Walz was likely to be chosen as Harris's running mate, and I asked if Shapiro had been informed he would not be joining the ticket. He hadn't, according to this source, but he appeared to have a general sense that Harris was likely going to pick someone else.

I later learned that a senior advisor to Shapiro reached out to Harris's team shortly before 11 p.m. that night in an attempt to set up a late-night call between the governor and the vice president. "It was like ten-thirty or eleven o'clock," a top Harris aide told me. "They said, 'The governor really needs to talk to the vice president.' And we were like, 'It's eleven o'clock. No. Is everything okay? Because there's very few people that get to call and say I need to talk to her at eleven o'clock.'" The call never happened.

Harris announced her selection of Walz the following morning, leading Shapiro to issue a lengthy statement of his own implying that he had taken himself out of the running rather than having been rejected. "As I've said repeatedly over the past several weeks," he wrote, "the running mate decision was a deeply personal decision for the Vice President—and it was also a deeply personal decision for me. Pennsylvanians elected me to a four-year term as their governor, and my work here is far from finished—there is a lot more stuff I want to get done for the good people of this Commonwealth."[14]

Later that afternoon, Harris released the same kind of staged, videotaped phone call as she had days earlier when the Obamas endorsed her.

"Hi, this is Tim," said Walz, wearing a black T-shirt and camo hat, when he received the phone call from Harris.

"It's Kamala Harris. Good morning, governor!"

"Good morning, Madam Vice President."

"Listen," Harris said. "I want you to do this with me. Let's do this together. Would you be my running mate, and let's get this thing on the road?"

"I would be honored, Madam Vice President," Walz replied. "The joy that you're bringing back to the country, the enthusiasm that's out there, it'll be a privilege to take this with you across the country."[15]

Trump reacted to the selection in predictable fashion. "TIM WALZ WOULD BE THE WORST VP IN HISTORY!" his campaign said in an email blast to his supporters. "Even worse than Dangerously Liberal and Crooked Kamala Harris—HE'S THAT BAD. He'll unleash HELL ON EARTH."[16]

In reality, though, the Trump campaign was relieved. Top officials had been convinced Harris would select Shapiro—and were worried that he would help her win Pennsylvania.

The day after Harris announced Walz as her running mate, Air Force Two rolled into Detroit, where the presumptive Democratic nominee would hold her biggest rally yet—by far. More than fifteen thousand supporters showed up, according to the campaign, and they were met by a candidate who exuded confidence and seemed to have the wind at her back.[17] She walked onstage to Beyoncé's "Freedom," which had quickly become her unofficial campaign anthem.

> *Hey! I'mma keep running*
> *Cause a winner don't quit on themselves*

"Good evening, Detroit!" Harris began. All she could do was stand and smile; the crowd refused to stop cheering. "We got this," she said, almost to herself. "We're gonna do this. We *are* doing this! We are *doing* this!"

She finally settled the crowd down by reminding them, "We got business to handle," and began working through her prepared remarks. About ten minutes in, however, pro-Palestinian protesters began to disrupt her speech, shouting indiscernibly and distracting Harris. Her crowd of supporters, clearly frustrated, began to chant "Kamala! Kamala! Kamala!" in an effort to drown them out.

The Trump campaign was already hard at work portraying Harris as a far-left radical. How she handled this moment could play right into Republicans' hands—or do the opposite.

"Everyone's voice matters. But I am speaking now," Harris said. "If you want Donald Trump to win, say that. Otherwise, I'm speaking."

At least in that moment, Harris wasn't afraid to stand up to the loudest activists on the fringes of the Democratic Party. Her supporters burst into applause and a new chant broke out: "We're not going back! We're not going back!" At one point, someone in the audience screamed, "I LOVE YOU, KAMALA!"

"I love you back," she answered from the stage, evoking the kind of public engagement that Democratic voters hadn't seen since Obama's 2008 or Bernie Sanders's 2016 campaign.

"We love our country," Harris continued. "And I do believe it is the highest form of patriotism to fight for the ideals of our country."

The visuals were remarkable. An entire airplane hangar overflowing with people, some having to stand outside near where Harris's plane was parked. Hundreds of signs thrust in the air, some featuring "Harris–Walz" and others KAMALA in red, white, and blue lettering. The exuberance was palpable, as if a ten-thousand-pound weight (or eighty-one-year-old nominee) had just been lifted off attendees' chests. This was decidedly not a Joe Biden event.

Trump hated every minute of it. "If Kamala has 1,000 people at a Rally, the Press goes 'crazy,' and talks about how 'big' it was," he wrote on Truth Social the following morning. "And she pays for her 'Crowd.' When I have a Rally, and 100,000 people show up, the Fake News doesn't talk about it, THEY REFUSE TO MENTION CROWD SIZE. The Fake News is the Enemy of the People!"[18]

He was still making outlandishly false allegations about Harris's Detroit rally three days later, absurdly suggesting that her crowd of supporters was actually generated by artificial intelligence. "Has anyone noticed that Kamala CHEATED at the airport?" he wrote. "There was nobody at the plane, and she 'A.I.'d' it, and showed a massive 'crowd' of so-called followers, BUT THEY DIDN'T EXIST!"

He continued: "Same thing is happening with her fake 'crowds' at her speeches. This is the way the Democrats win Elections, by CHEATING—And they're even worse at the Ballot Box. She should be disqualified because the creation of a fake image is ELECTION INTERFERENCE. Anyone who does that will cheat at ANYTHING!"[19]

None of his claims—about AI or faking crowd sizes—had a hint of truth. The photos of the rally in Detroit had no evidence of manipulation, and multiple camera angles confirmed the crowd was legit. But Trump found it profoundly unsettling to see images of his opponent attracting big, enthusiastic crowds.

By the time the Democratic National Convention got underway in Chicago, Trump's lead in the polls had evaporated. The race was a dead heat, and Harris had the momentum. Democrats who had resigned themselves to certain defeat with Biden had begun to believe that Harris was on a path to victory. The switcheroo had worked.

As a result, the convention was a lovefest. The party that had been tearing itself apart over Biden had quickly and seamlessly united behind Harris. Democrats still disagreed on plenty, of course, but after July's turmoil, most lawmakers and voters were desperate to be rowing in the same direction again. For a few short weeks, even the deep divide over Israel and Gaza receded into the background. Harris rejected a demand from some activists to give a pro-Palestinian leader a prominent speaking slot at the convention, and there was barely any blowback.

Progressive figures like Senator Bernie Sanders and Representative Alexandria Ocasio-Cortez *were* chosen to speak in prime time, and they sang Harris's praises even as she very transparently tacked toward the middle. In fact, every night of the convention featured at least one Republican speaker.

Geoff Duncan, the former Republican lieutenant governor of Georgia, spoke on the third night of the convention. As he took the stage, the delegates in the hall were given "USA" signs to hold and small American flags to wave. Convention organizers clearly weren't just trying to win over disaffected Republicans whom Trump had pushed out of the GOP; they were trying to make crystal clear that Americans who were proud of their country were welcome in Kamala Harris's coalition.

"I'm going to focus my attention on the millions of Republicans and independents at home that are sick and tired of making excuses for Donald Trump," Duncan said. "If Republicans are being intellectually honest with ourselves, our party is not civil or conservative. It's chaotic and crazy."

"Let me be clear to my Republican friends at home," he continued. "If you vote for Kamala Harris in 2024, you're not a Democrat. You're a patriot."

Former Representative Adam Kinzinger—a Republican who voted to impeach Trump in early 2021 and later served on the January 6 Committee—made a similar argument when he spoke on the final night of the convention, just minutes before Harris formally accepted the nomination. "I've learned something about the Democratic Party, and I want to let my fellow Republicans in on the secret," Kinzinger said. "The Democrats are as patriotic as us. They love this country just as much as we do. And they are as eager to defend American values at home and abroad as we conservatives have ever been."

When Harris took the stage a few minutes later, she sounded

nothing like the far-left Californian who had run for president in 2019 and was, at one point in her career, ranked as the lawmaker with the most liberal voting record in the Senate.[20] She promised to be tough on crime, crack down on illegal immigration, defend Israel, and stand up to China and Iran. Remove a few sentences criticizing abortion restrictions and touting the "freedom to love who you love," and the speech could have been delivered by George W. Bush at the Republican Convention in 2004.

"Our opponents in this race are out there every day denigrating America, talking about how terrible everything is," she concluded.* "We are the heirs to the greatest democracy in the history of the world. And on behalf of our children and our grandchildren and all those who sacrificed so dearly for our freedom and liberty, we must be worthy of this moment. It is now our turn to do what generations before us have done, guided by optimism and faith, to fight for this country we love, to fight for the ideals we cherish, and to uphold the awesome responsibility that comes with the greatest privilege on earth: the privilege and pride of being an American."

While Harris was highlighting Republican dissidents in Chicago, Trump was working to land a much bigger name on the Democratic side. On the third day of the Democratic convention, my ABC News

*Shortly before Kamala Harris walked onstage to deliver her convention speech, Donald Trump announced that he would be posting about her remarks in real time. "I'm getting ready to be fair but critical of Comrade Kamala Harris," he wrote. "My Play by Play will be on TRUTH Social, starting SOON!" Moments later, he was mocking her for saying "thank you" too much, asking her why she didn't pursue the policies she was talking about while vice president, and accusing her of "causing" Hamas's October 7 attack on Israel. At 11:12 p.m., Trump declared, "SHE HAS LED US INTO FAILING NATION STATUS!"

colleague Aaron Katersky called me with a news tip that he hoped I could help him confirm: Robert F. Kennedy Jr. planned to endorse Donald Trump. According to Aaron's source, Kennedy was planning to appear onstage with Trump in Arizona that Friday.

A Kennedy endorsement of the Republican nominee would be yet another surprising twist in a campaign full of them. Kennedy had initially launched a Democratic primary challenge against Biden but he was now running for president as an independent, fighting to get his name on the ballot in states across the country. He had also had some choice words for Trump in the recent past, calling him "a terrible president" and a "bully."[21] Trump, for his part, had labeled Bobby "a Democrat 'Plant,'" and "a Radical Left Liberal."[22]

"He has no hope as a Democrat because they were able to use their typically Fascist tactics of repression and throw him out of the Party, like a dog, because he was taking primary votes away from the worst President in the history of our Country, Crooked Joe Biden," Trump wrote on Truth Social in April, both insulting the candidate and dialing into his frustrations with the Democratic Party. "So now, Juniors' a so-called Independent, but he's not, he's a Radical Left Lunatic, but trying to have it all ways."[23]

But setting aside recent developments, for most of the previous century a prominent member of the Kennedy family—arguably the most famous family in Democratic Party history—endorsing a Republican for president would have been unthinkable. Even more outlandish would be a Kennedy endorsing a Republican like Donald Trump, who clearly holds in contempt many of the values for which the family stands. The nephew of President John F. Kennedy and the son of Senator Robert F. Kennedy, Bobby had been a liberal Democrat and a dedicated environmental activist for nearly his entire adult life. I've known him for nearly thirty years and first interviewed him in 1997 when some party leaders were trying to recruit him to run for US Senate in New York.

About a decade later, President Barack Obama strongly considered Kennedy to lead the Environmental Protection Agency in his new administration.[24] In recent years, however, Bobby had become an outspoken critic of vaccines, rendering him persona non grata among many Democrats. The primary focus of his work and activism was no longer the environment, but promoting the idea that there is a link between childhood vaccinations and the rise in autism diagnoses, a connection the vast majority of scientific research found deeply lacking. Kennedy's unorthodox views won him a following among some of the same people who supported Trump–and also caught Trump's attention.

In fact, Kennedy had met with Trump at Trump Tower in New York City on January 10, 2017, 10 days before the start of his first term. Kennedy told reporters following the meeting that the president-elect asked him to chair a new "commission on vaccine safety and scientific integrity," but shortly afterward, the Trump transition team put out a statement clarifying that "no decisions have been made." Shortly after he was sworn in, Trump had a second meeting with Kennedy in the Oval Office—which was not on Trump's public schedule and has never been previously reported—and appeared to be persuaded to move forward with the idea of a new task force on autism and vaccines that Kennedy would lead.

Not long after meeting with Kennedy, however, Trump sat down with Microsoft co-founder Bill Gates, who had spent billions of dollars through his Gates Foundation to combat diseases worldwide and expand access to life-saving vaccines. Trump asked Gates what he thought about Bobby's task force idea.

"That would be a terrible mistake," Gates told the president, arguing Kennedy had no credibility on the issue.

"Fauci and Collins told me the same thing," Trump responded, referring to Dr. Anthony Fauci and Dr. Francis Collins, two top officials at the National Institutes of Health.

Trump told Gates he would hold off on the idea of creating a task force on autism if Fauci and Collins would give Kennedy a chance to discuss his views on vaccines with them. And sure enough, Fauci soon received a call from the office of Jared Kushner, Trump's son-in-law and senior advisor. Fauci later told me Kushner asked him to "set up a meeting and just listen to what Bobby has to say." Arrangements were made for Kennedy to come to Building 31 of the National Institutes of Health on May 31, 2017. He was escorted into a conference room, where he delivered a PowerPoint presentation to Fauci, Collins, and a select group of NIH experts.

"Before we start," Kennedy said, "I want some ground rules. Every time I speak to people like you, all you do is interrupt me, and I never get a chance to fully explain my point—so no interruptions."

With that, Kennedy began his presentation. The first PowerPoint slide he projected onto the screen listed a number of adverse health conditions Kennedy said had been proven to be caused by vaccines, leading Fauci to raise his hand to speak.

"Is there any data associated with that slide?" he asked. "Because I'm not aware of any—"

"There you go!" Kennedy said, cutting Fauci off mid-sentence. "You are doing exactly what everybody else does. You've got to let me talk or I will never get through my presentation."

Kennedy finished the remainder of his presentation without interruption. Collins later told me Kennedy spoke nonstop and barely took time to breathe, citing discredited studies and ignoring well-established evidence on the effectiveness of vaccines. After Kennedy finished his lengthy presentation, he had a spirited discussion with Fauci, who took issue with just about everything Kennedy had to say. The meeting lasted nearly two hours, with nothing having been resolved. Trump did keep his word to Gates, however, and Kennedy was not appointed to any new task force on vaccines.

Now, nearly seven years later, my colleague Aaron Katersky was hearing that Kennedy was going to endorse Donald Trump for president. Could it be? I called Bobby to ask him.

"I've been told with great specificity that you're going to be in Arizona on Friday with Trump, and you're going to endorse him," I said.

"I will not confirm or deny that," Kennedy told me. "We are not talking about any of that."

I followed up. "Are you going to be in Arizona on Friday?"

"Jon, do you think I'm stupid?" he responded. "I'm not answering the question."

I tried a different approach, asking him about Kamala Harris and the Democratic convention.

"I think it was a coronation. It's not democracy," he told me. "Nobody voted. Who chose Kamala? It wasn't voters."

He complained about the way the news media—myself included—had neglected to cover his presidential campaign, and he complained about being excluded from debates. "That's a central problem with democracy, and you are at the center, core of it, Jon," he said. "Is that what you wanted to do with your career?"

He then turned his attention to Harris. "She went in four weeks from being the worst liability for the Democratic Party, according to you, to the second coming of Christ," he said. "Without giving one interview, without showing up for a debate, without a single policy that anybody thinks isn't ridiculous. It's not democracy."

I had never actually said Kamala Harris was "the worst liability for the Democratic Party" or "the second coming of Christ." In fact, I had never said anything remotely like either of those statements, but Kennedy wasn't only personally attacking me—he was complaining about what he perceived as the mainstream news media's uncritical coverage of Harris.

I asked him about the Republican nominee. During Trump's first term, Bobby had argued his administration was "essentially destroying 30 years of my work on environmental issues."[25] What did Kennedy think about Trump labeling climate change "a hoax"?

"I am not going to talk about Donald Trump with you," he shot back.

He didn't need to. As that conversation made clear, Kennedy's MAGA transformation was already well underway. I was quickly able to confirm that his endorsement of Trump was indeed forthcoming. Just as Aaron Katersky had heard, Bobby appeared onstage with the Republican nominee in Arizona that Friday. "I was a ferocious critic of many of the policies during his first administration, and there are still issues and approaches upon which we continue to have very serious differences," Kennedy said. "But we are aligned with each other on other key issues, like ending of forever wars, ending the childhood disease epidemics, securing the border, protecting freedom of speech, unraveling the corporate capture of our regulatory agencies, and getting the US intelligence agencies out of the business of propagandizing and censoring and surveilling Americans and interfering with our elections."

Kennedy's endorsement may have been driven by those issues, but his decision to align himself with Trump was also clearly driven by grievance and resentment—and he may have had some legitimate reasons to be angry. His campaign *had* been effectively ignored by most mainstream news outlets, and the Democratic Party *had* never given him—or anyone else—a chance to wage a real primary campaign against Biden.

There was also a deeply human element to Kennedy's endorsement. Trump made him feel valued and listened to; Harris couldn't be bothered to give him the time of day. "Following my first discussion with President Trump, I tried unsuccessfully to open similar discussions with Vice President Harris," Bobby said during his endorsement speech. "Vice President Harris declined to meet or even to speak with me."

What Kennedy said about Harris's "coronation" wasn't entirely off base, either. Four years after being elected vice president, she had captured the Democratic nomination without giving a single interview or participating in a single debate, after flaming out before any votes were cast during the 2020 Democratic presidential primary. Now, she was drawing huge crowds and gliding through the convention as she rose in the polls. "Vice President Harris has not appeared in a single interview or an unscripted encounter with voters for 35 days," Kennedy said while endorsing Trump. "This is profoundly undemocratic. How are people to judge when they don't know whom they are choosing?"

Since becoming the nominee, Harris truly hadn't faced any substantive questions. She hadn't been pressed on whether the Joe Biden

America saw on debate night was the same Joe Biden she had been having lunch with every week for years. She hadn't explained why voters should view her as anything other than a direct extension of the Biden administration. She hadn't explained how and why she evolved from a far-left progressive in 2019 to a moderate pragmatist in 2024.

She had not been tested, but she would be—and soon. Trump had clearly struggled out of the gate to adapt to his new opponent and had not figured out how to run against her. Not yet.

CHAPTER TWELVE

"THE WEAVE"

On a Thursday afternoon at the end of August, I was sitting in a meeting at the ABC News Washington bureau when my phone began to ring. I was about to send the call to voicemail, but then I saw the name on the screen: Donald Trump.

I had last spoken to Trump on July 15, two days after a would-be assassin had attempted to kill him in Butler, Pennsylvania—and six days before Joe Biden had turned the race for the White House upside down by ending his campaign. Then, Trump was the clear favorite and his advisors were predicting a landslide victory. Now, Kamala Harris had energized the Democratic Party and quickly eaten into Trump's formidable lead. The two were set to face off in a debate hosted by ABC News two weeks later.

I was surprised to see that Trump was calling. Just a few days earlier, he had some choice words for me—on both social media and the campaign trail. The first swipe had come the previous Sunday, hours after I'd interviewed Republican Senator Tom Cotton on ABC

News's *This Week* and asked him some pointed questions about Trump's declining poll numbers and the surprising promise Trump had recently made that he would be "great for women and their reproductive rights."[1] The interview with Cotton was somewhat contentious, but not excessively so. I didn't expect it to attract Trump's attention, but it did.

"I watched ABC FAKE NEWS this morning, both lightweight reporter Jonathan Carl's(K?) ridiculous and biased interview of Tom Cotton (who was fantastic!), and their so-called Panel of Trump Haters," he wrote on Truth Social. "Why would I do the Debate against Kamala Harris on that network?"[2]

Trump had apparently been privately complaining about my interview all day, calling both Cotton and Reince Priebus, who was his former chief of staff and had been a panelist on the show, to vent about it.

"What's wrong with him?" Trump asked Priebus, referring to me. "I've known him for a long time, right?"

"He used to work at the *New York Post*," Priebus replied. "You have known him for years and years and years."

"Yeah, yeah. I know him. He was a good guy," Trump continued. "He used to be a good guy. I don't know what happened to him, but these guys are the worst."

Trump's running mate, JD Vance, also jumped in to criticize my interview with Senator Cotton. Vance took issue with the fact that during the interview, I said that Kamala Harris's views on private health insurance had changed. During her first presidential bid in 2019, she had supported a Medicare-for-All system. Five years later, her campaign said she no longer did.

In criticizing me, Vance made a good point, texting me: "Jon, I

President-elect Donald Trump and President Biden walking along the White House Colonnade on November 13, 2024.

Official White House Photo by Adam Schultz

Donald Trump alongside his attorney Todd Blanche on May 13, 2024, at the Manhattan Criminal Courthouse. Trump used the stakeout camera in the hallway outside the courtroom as his campaign stage while his criminal trial was underway.

Photo courtesy of ABC News

Todd Blanche went from the hallway outside the courtroom in New York to the Oval Office. He was sworn in as the deputy attorney general on March 6, 2025.

Official White House Photo

President Biden with his son Hunter, along with Hunter's son, Beau, and Hunter's wife, Melissa, at the airport in Wilmington, Delaware, on June 11, 2024. A jury had just found Hunter guilty on charges related to his purchase of a firearm.

Photo courtesy of ABC News

President Joe Biden and his national security team, including Vice President Kamala Harris, in the White House situation room on July 14, 2024, discussing the attempted assassination attempt on Donald Trump in Butler, Pennsylvania.

Official White House Photo by Adam Schultz

The debate that ended Joe Biden's reelection campaign. Biden and Trump on June 27, 2024.

Photo courtesy of ABC News

President Biden meets with Ukrainian President Volodymyr Zelensky at a NATO summit in Washington, DC, on July 11, 2024. Biden didn't help his case when he mistakenly introduced Zelensky as Vladimir Putin.

Official White House Photo by Oliver Contreras

I had a one-on-one meeting with Kamala Harris in her West Wing office on May 2, 2024.

Official White House Photo by Lawrence Jackson

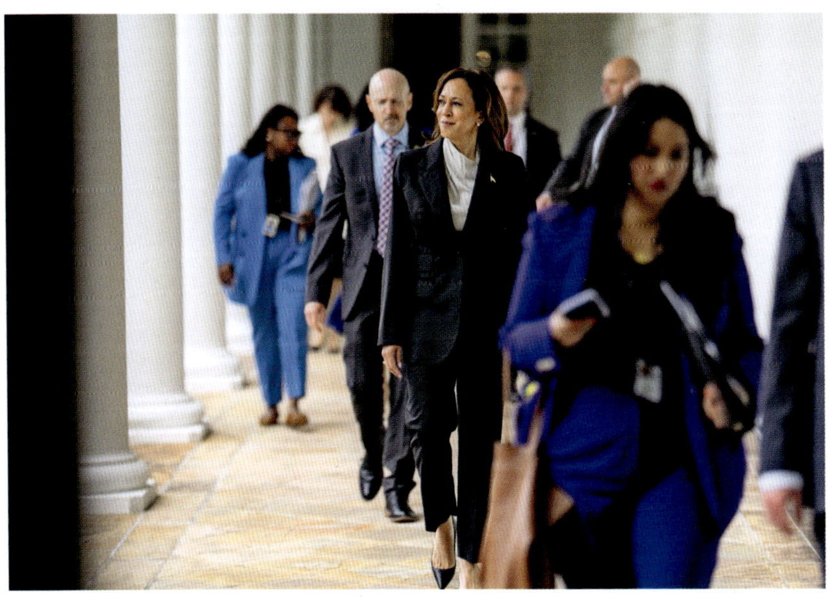

Kamala Harris walking through the White House Colonnade on July 22, 2024— the day after Biden ended his presidential campaign and Harris started hers.

Official White House Photo by Lawrence Jackson

I interviewed Steve Bannon on June 29, 2024. Two days later, he went to prison to begin serving a four-month sentence for contempt of Congress.

Photo by Ian Sbalcio for ABC News

Steve Bannon in the prison yard at the federal prison in Danbury, Connecticut, with his cellmate, Tim Hunsperger.

Photo courtesy of Steve Bannon

Donald Trump at a McDonald's in Pennsylvania on October 21, 2024.
Photo courtesy of ABC News

Donald Trump puts on a safety vest and jumps in a garbage truck in Green Bay, Wisconsin, on October 30, 2024.
Photo courtesy of ABC News

Donald Trump's rally at Madison Square Garden on October 27, 2024.
Photo by Jonathan Karl

The president's men: Stephen Miller, Kash Patel, Pete Hegseth, and Dan Scavino on February 21, 2025.

Official White House Photo by Joyce N. Boghosian

President Donald Trump in the Oval Office with Scott Bessent, Howard Lutnick, Doug Burgum, and Sean Duffy.

Official White House Photo by Joyce N. Boghosian

President Biden invited President-elect Trump to the White House after the election. The two men met for nearly two hours in the Oval Office on November 13, 2024, along with outgoing chief of staff, Jeff Zients (right), and incoming chief of staff, Susie Wiles (left).

Official White House Photo by Adam Schultz

Trump poses for a photo with Biden and First Lady Jill Biden on November 13, 2024. The First Lady also invited Melania Trump, but Mrs. Trump declined.

Official White House Photo by Adam Schultz

More than 1,500 people were convicted in connection with the January 6 attack on the US Capitol. On the first day of his second presidency, Trump pardoned or commuted the sentences of all of them.

Photos courtesy of ABC News

All hail the chief: President Trump's first cabinet meeting, February 26, 2025.

Official White House Photo

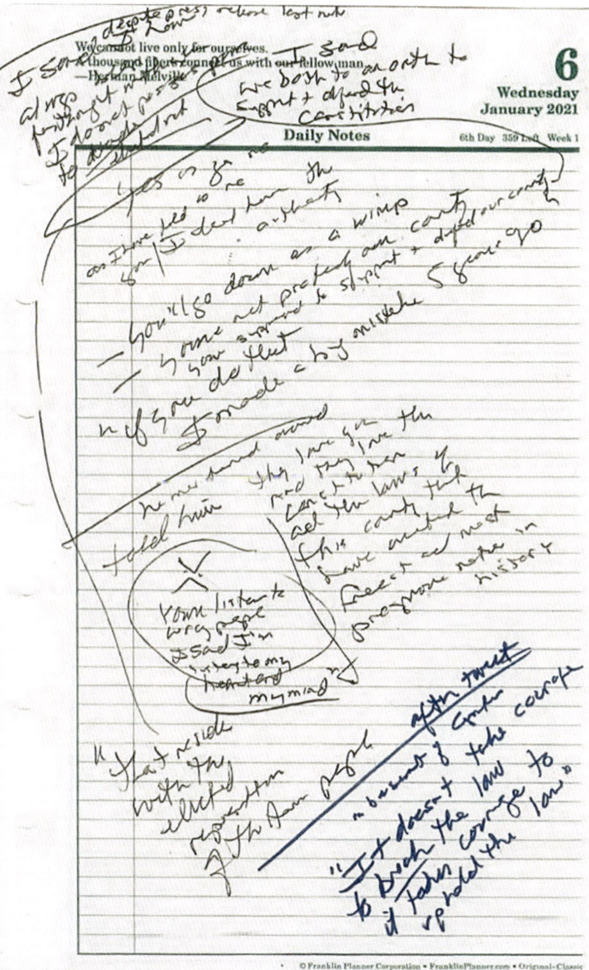
We cannot live only for ourselves. A thousand fibers connect us with our fellow man.
—Herman Melville

6
Wednesday
January 2021

Daily Notes

6th Day 359 Left Week 1

You'll go down as a wimp

"It doesn't take courage to break the law it takes courage to uphold the law."

© Franklin Planner Corporation • FranklinPlanner.com • Original-Classic

Mike Pence's notes on his phone call with Donald Trump on the morning of January 6, 2021. "You'll go down as a wimp," Trump tells him. "I made a big mistake five years ago" [when he picked Pence as his running mate]. Pence's response: "It doesn't take courage to break the law. It takes courage to uphold the law."

Vice President Mike Pence presiding over the counting of the electoral votes on January 6, 2021.
Official White House Photo by Myles Cullen

President Donald Trump with Susie Wiles on March 20, 2025.

Official White House Photo by Daniel Torok

Representative Marjorie Taylor Green (on left) cheers after Robert F. Kennedy Jr., was sworn in as Secretary of Health and Human Services on February 13, 2025.

Official White House Photo

Attorney General Pam Bondi escorts President Trump during his visit to the Department of Justice on March 14, 2025.

Official White House Photo

Boris Epshteyn walking the halls of the Justice Department with President Trump on March 14, 2025.

Official White House Photo

Elon Musk holds court at the Pentagon on March 21, 2025.

DOD photo by US Senior Airman Spencer Perkins

"You don't have the cards." Donald Trump and Volodymyr Zelensky in the Oval Office on February 28, 2025.

Official White House Photo by Daniel Torok

President Trump at Fort Bragg in North Carolina on June 10, 2025.

Official White House Photo

After Trump's visit, the Army launched a "review" of how Trump campaign merchandise came to be sold on base during Trump's speech.

Photo by Mary Bruce, ABC News

Trump watching Trump, April 9, 2025.

Official White House Photo by Joyce N. Boghosian

respect you, but I think it's very important for you guys not to say Kamala Harris's opinion has changed when she refuses to sit for an interview to explain what changed, and why," Vance wrote. "You can't reward her for hiding from the media!"

"That's fair," I texted back. "I said what I said because her campaign says that is no longer her position and she hasn't repeated it for five years. And it wasn't the position of the Biden-Harris administration for the past 3½ years. But she does have to answer questions about exactly where she stands now that she is the presidential nominee, and I look forward to asking them. As you can imagine, I won't shy away from doing so."*

I was still on Trump's mind the following day, when he held a campaign event at a Vietnamese restaurant in Falls Church, Virginia, about twenty minutes away from my home. In light of his Truth Social post, a reporter asked him if he was still planning to participate in the ABC News presidential debate scheduled for September 10. Before addressing the question, Trump went after me again.

"I watched this weekend, and it's the worst of all networks," Trump said. "They had this Jonathan Karl, who's a lightweight, and he was asking questions of Tom Cotton, who was fantastic, by the way. Only a total pro could have gotten through that interview."

Trump continued to lash out at ABC News for several minutes. "When you see the level of hatred in that room," he said of the roundtable. "When you see Jonathan Karl, who's terrible—I mean, he's just terrible. He's just an average person, but they tell him what to do."

*I never got a chance to ask those questions of Kamala Harris or her running mate, Tim Walz. I pushed repeatedly to interview both of them over the next three months, but neither agreed to sit down with me. In contrast, I did interview Vance multiple times over the course of the campaign and regularly talked to Trump over the phone.

Trump added that he was "thinking about" skipping the debate with Harris, and that he would much rather do it on another network.

I later learned that Trump had originally planned to formally withdraw from the ABC News debate in the Truth Social post attacking me, but that his advisors had convinced him to hold off—at least for the moment. Instead, he rewrote his statement to focus on me, pretending he didn't know how to spell my name and hinting that he *may eventually* decide not to participate in the debate.

After the barrage of insults, I decided to send Trump a text message. "I hope you had a chance to see my interview with Bernie Sanders on Sunday (which was right before Tom Cotton)," I texted him, referring to some questions I had asked Sanders about Kamala Harris. "Many people say that was a much tougher interview." I did not expect to hear back from him and didn't—at least not right away.

When my cell phone rang on Thursday, however, I quickly realized Trump wasn't calling to complain—he seemed to just want to chat. Any talk of skipping the ABC News debate was in the rearview mirror.

"What's happening?" he asked me after I answered the phone. He told me he was returning my call, but I had not called him. Perhaps he was referring to my text two days earlier?

We discussed an interview that Harris and her running mate, Tim Walz, would be doing that night with Dana Bash of CNN—Harris's first interview since Biden dropped out as the Democratic presidential nominee more than five weeks earlier. CNN and many of its competitors were treating the interview as a major, prime-time news event. After all, Harris had barely answered any questions from reporters since becoming the Democratic presidential nominee. Trump told me he couldn't believe how much hype there was for the conversation and suggested Walz was joining only "so he could save her."

"I never knew she had that problem where she can't do an interview," Trump told me. "Does she have that problem debating, too?"

I noted that Harris had participated in debates during the Democratic presidential primary in 2019, and that she had performed pretty well. "You remember how she went after Biden?" I asked, referring to the Democratic primary debate where Harris attacked Biden for opposing federally mandated school busing to combat racial segregation. "She's pretty aggressive in a debate. How do you feel about debating her?"

"I never found her good or bad in the debate," Trump responded. "She wasn't like, she wasn't horrible, right? She did the thing with the bus, and she hit Biden harder than anybody, and he was so unable to respond that he picked her. That whole thing is crazy."*

Trump's tone was chatty, not at all combative. He bounced from topic to topic, sometimes mid-sentence. He did eventually turn to my interview with Cotton days earlier, but with none of the anger he had expressed just a couple of days earlier. "You hit our friend Tom Cotton very hard the other day," he said. "I mean, he was very capable of handling himself, but you hit him quite hard. I was surprised a little bit, but that's all right."

As Trump started to say goodbye, he finally got around to what was likely the real reason for the call. "Jon, you take care of yourself. Be fair," he said. "Oh! So, we're going to do the debate. Are you going to be involved in the debate?"

---

*During a primary debate on June 27, 2019, Harris had criticized Biden—in deeply personal terms—for his decades-old relationships with pro-segregation senators and his opposition to federal busing programs to enforce racial integration in public schools in the 1970s. "I do not believe you are a racist," she began, "[but] it was hurtful to hear you talk about the reputations of two United States senators who built their reputations and career on the segregation of race in this country." Harris went on to tell the story of a little girl in California who was able to attend an integrated school because of a busing program: "And that little girl was me."

I told him I would be co-anchoring the pre- and post-debate shows on ABC, but that the debate itself would be moderated by my colleagues David Muir and Linsey Davis. And I told him I'd like to talk to him again after it was over.

"Call me in a week or so. Call me right after," Trump said. "We'll do something at Mar-a-Lago. We'll do some camera work."

The vitriol from a few days earlier had vanished. Trump was inviting me to his home. "You were fantastic, and you got to be okay," he said before reminding me one last time not to believe the polls. "You know, I way under-poll. Nobody has ever under-polled like me. I don't know if that's a nice thing or not a nice thing, but it's a fact."

Trump had been bragging about his lead over Biden in the polls for nearly a year, but his advantage had evaporated within weeks of Harris taking over atop the ticket—and it was driving him nuts. "We spent all of our time, and a great deal of money, fighting Crooked Joe, then they unceremoniously dumped him and threw in an even worse person, Kamala, a Radical Left Marxist," he complained on Truth Social on August 25—more than a month after Biden had left the race.[3]

Top officials on Trump's campaign had been insisting they had a plan to take on the new Democratic nominee. "Rest assured, we are 100 percent ready," Tony Fabrizio, Trump's pollster, said when asked about Harris during an event on July 17—days *before* Biden dropped out. The former president's team was not only prepared with videos and other digital ads targeting Harris; it had a simple message to deploy against her: Biden's failures were Harris's failures. Voters frustrated with the administration's approach to inflation, immigration, and crime—to say nothing of the disastrous withdrawal from

Afghanistan—should hold those issues against Biden's loyal vice president as much as they did against him.

But just because Trump's *campaign* had a plan for Harris didn't mean Trump himself was on board with it. In fact, he and his allies spent much of August obsessing over the Democrats' switch at the top of the ticket, insisting that the maneuver had broken some rule. "It was a coup by people that wanted him out," he said during a mid-August event that was theoretically about inflation. "They didn't do it the way, not the way they're supposed to do it."[4]

Days earlier, at a campaign event in Bozeman, Montana, Trump told his supporters about the "terrible thing" the Democrats did: "The first coup in the history of our country."

"I hear [Biden] is going to make a comeback at the Democrat convention," Trump mused. "He's going to walk into the room and he's going to say, 'I want my presidency back. I want another chance to debate Trump. I want another chance.'"

There would be no miraculous Biden comeback, of course, but it was telling that Trump kept fantasizing about one. He knew how to campaign against an elderly eighty-one year-old career politician with serious political baggage. A fifty-nine-year-old woman of Indian and Jamaican descent was proving to be more of a challenge. Nowhere was that more obvious than during Trump's appearance at a National Association of Black Journalists (NABJ) event in Chicago in late July.

Trump's decision to show up to the conference was gutsy, and it presented him with an opportunity to go after Harris, who had not accepted the invitation to appear at the NABJ's annual convention.* But even before his plane landed in Chicago, Trump was having

*Harris eventually did an interview, via video link, with NABJ later in the summer, but she was a no-show at the group's annual convention.

second thoughts. He may have believed the appearance was a good idea at one point—no president had done more for Black people than Trump, he often claimed—but now he was demanding to know why it was on his schedule. Some members of the NABJ were already expressing outrage that he had been invited to speak, and Trump had begun to suspect that he was walking into a trap.

Once Trump arrived at the venue, his team started making demands. The NABJ had announced they would have a team doing a live fact-check of Trump's comments. Justin Caporale, Trump's deputy campaign manager, insisted there could be no fact-checking. The NABJ addressed those concerns by explaining that the fact-checking would appear only on the organization's website and not on-screen during the live television broadcast of Trump's interview. But Caporale somehow found out that my ABC News colleague Rachel Scott, who would be introducing and interviewing Trump along with two other journalists, planned to mention the fact-checking in her opening remarks. Caporale now demanded that Rachel edit her remarks to take out any reference to fact-checking. She refused, and so did the NABJ leadership.

The event was scheduled to start at noon, but Trump's arrival onstage had already been delayed a few minutes due to an issue with the sound system. Now, the standoff over fact-checking was delaying it further. Trump was waiting in a nearby holding room; Rachel was standing a few feet behind the stage waiting with the two other journalists who would join her in interviewing Trump: Harris Faulkner of Fox News and Kadia Goba of *Semafor*. On the other side of the curtain, the crowd of two thousand NABJ members in the audience was growing restless; they had no idea what was holding things up.

Caporale told NABJ President Ken Lemon that unless Rachel

dropped the reference to fact-checking, Trump would leave the event and there would be no interview. To make clear he was serious, Caporale got Susie Wiles, Trump's campaign co-chair, on the phone, and she told Lemon the same thing. At 12:33 p.m., Rachel received a text from Trump campaign advisor Jason Miller: "Gimme a shout about this fact-checking thing." She told him to discuss it with the NABJ, and then she told the group's leadership that *she* would not participate in the interview if the reference to fact-checking was removed from her introductory remarks.

The two sides, it seemed, had reached an impasse. Caporale returned to Trump's holding room, leading Rachel to assume the former president was going to leave. As Lemon began typing up a new set of remarks explaining why the event had been canceled, Trump's deputy campaign manager came running back.

"Fuck it," Caporale told Rachel. "Let's go."

And so a few minutes later, Rachel found herself onstage with Faulkner and Goba, teeing up the conversation with the former president. "As journalists, we use opportunities like these both to inform our reporting but also to help voters understand the choices that they face in a consequential and historic election year," she said. "NABJ has partnered with PolitiFact to fact-check this conversation in real time. You can access that feed on social media using the hashtag #NABJFactCheck. *Again, the hashtag is #NABJFactCheck.*"

"Mr. President, we so appreciate you giving us an hour of your time," Rachel began before asking her first question.

"I want to start by addressing the elephant in the room, sir. A lot of people did not think it was appropriate for you to be here today. You have pushed false claims about some of your rivals, from Nikki Haley to former President Barack Obama, saying that they were not born in the United States, which is not true. You have told four congresswomen of color who were American citizens to go back to where they came from. You have used words like 'animal' and 'rabid' to describe Black district attorneys. You've attacked Black journalists, calling them 'a loser,' saying the questions that they ask are 'stupid and racist.' You've had dinner with a white supremacist at your Mar-a-Lago resort. So my question, sir, now that you are asking Black supporters to vote for you, why should Black voters trust you after you have used language like that?"

"Well, first of all, I don't think I've ever been asked a question in such a horrible manner. First question, you don't even say 'Hello. How are you?'" Trump began as the crowd responded with a mix of laughter and jeers. "Are you with ABC? Because I think they're a fake news network, a terrible network, and I think it's disgraceful that I came here in good spirit. I love the Black population of this country."

The conversation only went more off the rails from there. "For you to start off a question-and-answer period—especially when you're thirty-five minutes late because you couldn't get your equipment to work—in such a hostile manner, I think it's a disgrace," Trump continued, lying about the primary reason for the delay. "I really do think it's a disgrace."

But Trump's most explosive comment of the day came in response to a question a few moments later, prompted by Republicans who in recent days had claimed Biden selected Harris as his running mate in 2020 only because of her race. "Sir, do you believe that Vice President Kamala Harris is only on the ticket because she is a Black woman?" Rachel asked.

"Well, I can say no, I think it's maybe a little bit different," Trump began. "She was always of Indian heritage, and she was only promoting Indian heritage. I didn't know she was Black until a number of years ago when she happened to turn Black and now she wants to be known as Black. So I don't know. Is she Indian or is she Black?"

"She has always identified as a Black woman," Rachel responded.

"But you know what—"

"She went to a historically Black college."

"I respect either one," Trump said, "but she obviously doesn't, because she was Indian all the way and then all of a sudden she made a turn and she became a Black person."

Suffice it to say, questioning Kamala Harris's race—*all of a sudden she made a turn and she became a Black person*—was not part of the campaign playbook. Rachel had asked tough and fair questions, but Trump had gone seriously off script—and there would be plenty more self-inflicted wounds to come. The relatively subdued, disciplined Trump who had emerged over the course of the summer—particularly in the days following the attempt on his life—was gone.

"When I got hit, everybody thought I was going to be a nice guy, and they thought I'd change," he told a rally crowd in Harrisburg, Pennsylvania, on July 31. "They all said, 'Trump is going to be a nice man now. He came close to death.' And I really agreed with that—for about eight hours or so."

As Trump was veering off message and watching his lead in the polls slip away, he was getting no help from his new running mate. Just a few days after the Republican National Convention drew to a close, a video clip from 2021 resurfaced in which JD Vance, then running for US Senate, insulted women who don't have children.

"We are effectively run in this country—via the Democrats, via our corporate oligarchs—by a bunch of childless cat ladies," he told then–Fox News anchor Tucker Carlson, "who are miserable at their own lives and the choices that they've made, and so they want to make the rest of the country miserable, too." He named names, too, including Representative Alexandria Ocasio-Cortez and . . . Vice President Kamala Harris.

The Trump campaign, already wary of its standing with women, needed to be driving home the message that Harris would represent a continuation of Biden's failed policies. Instead, Vance had handed the Democratic base a rallying cry.

And the comment wasn't just offensive to "childless cat ladies" on the left. At least some of Trump's allies on the right took umbrage with it as well.

On Fox News, for example, former Representative Trey Gowdy, a Republican, reacted to Vance's comments by telling the story of two Catholic nuns he had recently met. They didn't have children, Gowdy noted, but they loved America and were living lives of service to others. "And it's not just Catholic nuns," Gowdy continued. "Some of the finest people I know don't have children: teachers and guidance counselors and lawyers and doctors. And they love other people's children enough to teach and guide and protect and minister to them. Some people choose not to have children. Others desperately want them, but they can't."[5]

Vance later tried to downplay the comment, but it was far from a one-off aside. Also in 2021, for example, he had delivered a speech at the Intercollegiate Studies Institute's "Future of American Political Economy" conference on the "civilizational crisis" facing the United States. One of his proposed solutions was to award children the right to vote, with their parents controlling the ballots. "When you go to the polls in this country as a parent, you should have more power," he said. "You should have more of an ability to speak your voice in our democratic republic than people who don't have kids. Let's face the consequences and the reality. If you don't have as much of an investment in the future of this country, maybe you shouldn't get nearly the same voice."[6]

I interviewed Vance for ABC's *This Week* in early August, as the controversy surrounding his proposal for extra votes for parents and his comments about "childless cat ladies" were drawing criticism from both the left and the right. I read him his own words from that 2021 speech and asked him to explain why he was suggesting that parents should "have more power" at the polls than Americans without children. He said it was just a "thought experiment" and he never intended it as a serious policy proposal.

I read him another quote from the speech, in which he predicted *The Atlantic* magazine and *The Washington Post* would "come out and say, 'Well, doesn't this mean non-parents don't have as much of a voice as parents? Doesn't it mean that parents get a bigger say in how our democracy functions?' Yes, absolutely."

That sounded like more than a thought experiment. "Do you regret saying that?" I asked him. "Do you take that back?"

"Look, Jon," Vance replied. "I'm talking about a thought experiment here. And do I regret saying it? I regret that the media and the Kamala Harris campaign has, frankly, distorted what I said."

"I just read your words," I replied. "How's that distorting what you said?"

"Because they have turned this into a policy proposal that I never made," he said. During his year and a half as a US senator, he noted, he had not introduced a bill to give parents more voting power.

That was not the only time during the campaign that Vance had needed to walk back a "thought experiment." A few weeks earlier, in late July, as Trump and his campaign were desperately trying to distance themselves from the Heritage Foundation's "Project 2025"—a road map full of unpopular, ultraconservative policy proposals—Heritage Foundation president Kevin Roberts revealed that Vance had written the foreword of his upcoming book. "Roberts is articulating a fundamentally Christian view of culture and economics," Vance wrote glowingly. "Recognizing that virtue and material progress go hand in hand."

A spokesman for Vance quickly backtracked when asked about the senator's relationship with Roberts and the Heritage Foundation. "The foreword has nothing to do with Project 2025," he said. "Senator Vance has previously said that he has no involvement with it and has plenty of disagreements with what they're calling for. Only President Trump sets the Trump policy agenda."[7]

Even some of the very voters Vance was seemingly chosen to shore up for Trump—younger, disaffected men—seemed to be turned off by what they were hearing. "You want me to pay more taxes to take care of other people's kids?" Dave Portnoy, the founder of Barstool Sports, said in response to a video of Vance talking about his support for the child tax credit. "We sure this dude is a Republican? Sounds like a moron."[8]

Ben Domenech, a prominent right-wing commentator, even suggested in a column for *The Spectator* that Vance might not be long for the Republican ticket. "His particular brand of conservatism is exactly what Harris–Walz want to run against, not the Trump record on economy, the border, and security," Domenech wrote. "The world where Vance made sense as a choice disappeared the minute Joe

Biden was knifed by his fellow Democrats in favor of Harris. . . . There is a non-zero possibility that Donald Trump could decide to move on from J.D. Vance in the aftermath of the upcoming Democratic National Convention. As of this morning, Trump is losing this race—and he knows it."[9]

As the criticism mounted, Trump himself seemed to be having second thoughts about his running mate. On at least one occasion, Trump told people that Phil Ruffin—an eighty-eight-year-old Las Vegas casino magnate and one of his oldest friends—had suggested Vance should be replaced on the ticket, and while Trump didn't say he was considering such a move, he said his friend Phil was almost never wrong.

Publicly, Trump had begun dismissing the importance of the vice president at all. Asked about Vance in the NABJ interview, for example, he replied that a president's running mate "does not have any impact."

"Historically, the choice of a vice president makes no difference," he said. "You're voting for the president. You're voting for me. If you like me, I'm going to win. If you don't like me, I'm not going to win."

For some of Trump's allies—and perhaps Trump himself—Vance had become a convenient scapegoat on whom to blame the campaign's slide in recent weeks. But as the conservative *Wall Street Journal* editorial board noted on August 7, Trump's running mate was merely a symptom of the underlying problem with the GOP ticket. "Republicans are wondering if Donald Trump made a mistake in choosing J.D. Vance as his running mate," the editorial read. "But the more urgent and consequential question for Republicans with 90 days left in the campaign is whether Mr. Trump is going to blow another presidential race he should win."[10]

Indeed, at times Trump seemed as though he were *trying* to throw the election.

Three days after the NABJ convention, for example, Trump held an event in Georgia, a key swing state that he'd lost in 2020 by fewer than twelve thousand votes. But instead of training his fire exclusively on Harris and the Democrats, Trump decided to go on an extended rant targeting Brian Kemp, the state's popular Republican governor, and his wife. Why? Because Kemp didn't go along with Trump's effort to overturn the 2020 election, and because Kemp's wife had suggested months earlier that she was going to write in her husband's name rather than vote for Trump.

"He's a bad guy. He's a disloyal guy. And he's a very average governor," Trump said about Kemp. "Little Brian, little Brian Kemp. Bad guy."

Kemp responded in a post on X. "My focus is on winning this November and saving our country from Kamala Harris and the Democrats—not engaging in petty personal insults, attacking fellow Republicans, or dwelling on the past," he wrote. "You should do the same, Mr. President, and leave my family out of it."[11]

Trump, losing ground to the new Democratic nominee, was spending time and energy three months before the election sparring with a governor from his own party who had a 64 percent approval rating in a state he needed to win.[12] There isn't a campaign operative in the world who could tell you with a straight face that this was smart politics.

Speaking of campaign operatives, the two leading Trump's team, Susie Wiles and Chris LaCivita, were beginning to face some serious questions as their boss began to slip in the polls. Corey Lewandowski, Trump's first campaign manager in 2016, tried to convince the former president that LaCivita was personally enriching himself off the campaign, and Kellyanne Conway, another onetime Trump campaign manager from 2016, was trying to work her way back into Trump's inner circle.

Steve Bannon was still imprisoned in Danbury, Connecticut, during this period, but he was spending as many as ten hours a day on the computer, keeping up with current events by reading emails from his allies. According to Bannon, as Trump began to spiral, Lara Trump—the former president's daughter-in-law and Republican National Committee co chair—was so concerned about the state of the race that she reached out to someone on Bannon's team in the hopes of setting up a call with him to discuss firing LaCivita and replacing him with Conway.

Lara Trump, however, doesn't remember things going down that way. "I never reached out to Steve Bannon," she later told me. "Kellyanne and I definitely met with the president, that's fact, for sure, but I never at all considered calling Steve Bannon to get his support on any front on anything."

"There's a possibility that other people, maybe, reached out to him and said it was on my behalf," she continued, "but I can promise you I never once attempted to contact him. To be honest, I didn't even know where he was incarcerated."

Whether the request for a call was legitimate or not, Bannon wasn't interested in helping oust LaCivita in favor of Conway, with whom he had worked on Trump's 2016 campaign. "Kellyanne is a disaster," he told me. "She's divisive. She's also a fucking moron."

I reached out to Kellyanne Conway to get her version of events. She declined to comment.

But *The New York Times* reported that Conway and Lara Trump did meet with the president at his club in Bedminster, New Jersey, on

August 2. Lara confirmed the meeting took place but said the group didn't discuss replacing any senior campaign aides. Conway did, however, post a picture of herself standing next to Donald Trump on X with the caption, "Quite the visit today with @realDonaldTrump in #NJ."[13]

After *New York Times* reporter Maggie Haberman published her reporting about the meeting in Bedminster, she received what she described as an angry phone call from the former president. "Trump denied that he was making any changes to his team, saying he was 'thrilled' with his top advisers, Susie Wiles and Chris LaCivita, and asking why he would even want to make such a change," she wrote.[14]

In fact, there would be no changes to Trump's campaign team—or to his self-destructive behavior. As Harris's lead in national polling continued to grow over the next few weeks—and she pulled ahead in several key battleground states—Trump could be found musing about jailing Facebook founder Mark Zuckerberg, joking about the civilian Medal of Freedom being "much better" than the Congressional Medal of Honor because recipients of the latter are generally either dead or "in very bad shape," baselessly claiming the massive crowds showing up at Harris's rallies were generated by artificial intelligence, praising the fictional serial killer Hannibal Lecter as a "wonderful man," and obsessing over an illustration of Harris on a recent cover of *Time* magazine. "I saw a picture of [Harris] on *Time* magazine today. She looks like the most beautiful actress ever to live," he told Elon Musk during a meandering, glitchy two-hour-long conversation on X Spaces. "Actually, she looked very much like our great first lady, Melania."*

*In another, separate rant on the *Time* magazine cover, Trump later declared, "I am much better looking than her. I think I'm much better. I'm a better-looking person than Kamala."

These seemingly random asides were catnip for journalists and cable news producers, and they were immensely frustrating to many of Trump's own supporters and aides, who wished he would just stay on message. But Trump himself believed they served a purpose. "You know, I do the weave," he said at a rally in Johnstown, Pennsylvania, on September 1. "You know what the weave is? I'll talk about like nine different things, and they all come back brilliantly together. And it's like, friends of mine that are, like, English professors, they say, 'It's the most brilliant thing I've ever seen.'"

Trump added: "The fake news, you know what they say, 'He rambled.' It's not rambling. What you do is you get off a subject to mention another little tidbit, then you get back on to the subject, and you go through this and you do it for two hours, and you don't even mispronounce one word."[15]

Weeks earlier, Trump's campaign had put together an event focused on the economy, complete with three tables covered with groceries and charts showing how much prices had risen. He managed to stay on message for a few minutes, but before long was discussing the Democrats' Biden "coup," railing against the "crooked" prosecutors going after him, and calling Kamala Harris "not intelligent."

Toward the end of Trump's press conference, a reporter asked him about some unsolicited advice former South Carolina Governor Nikki Haley had offered Trump, saying he should mellow out a bit and focus on running a more disciplined campaign. "I think I'm doing a very calm campaign. I mean, we're here. There's no shouting," he responded. "Some of you will say, 'He ranted and raved.' I didn't rant and rave."

The bottom line: Trump had no desire to take advice from somebody whom he had beaten badly in the Republican primary. "I have to do it my way," he said. "You know, I ran against her and I did it my way. People said I should maybe do it a different way, but I won in South Carolina by numbers that nobody's ever seen before."

As the fall campaign got underway, Trump would continue to do it his way, chaotically weaving through controversies and self-created campaign crises in a manner that some of his allies feared would doom his campaign.

CHAPTER THIRTEEN

CATS AND DOGS

Four days before the ABC News debate between Donald Trump and Kamala Harris, former Vice President Dick Cheney did something he had never done before: endorse a Democrat. For more than half a century, Cheney had been a die-hard Republican serving in some of the most prominent positions in American politics: White House chief of staff, the third-ranking Republican in the House of Representatives, secretary of defense, and, from 2001 to 2009, perhaps the most powerful vice president in US history. His reputation as a hard-edged partisan had turned him into a Democratic bogeyman, the Darth Vader of the GOP.

But by 2024, Dick Cheney wasn't just backing the Democratic nominee for president—he was doing so with a scathing rebuke of his own party's candidate.

"In our nation's 248-year history, there has never been an individual who is a greater threat to our republic than Donald Trump," Cheney said. "He tried to steal the last election using lies and violence to keep himself in power after the voters had rejected him. He can never be trusted with power again."[1]

Despite his lifelong history as a party-line Republican, Cheney's endorsement of Kamala Harris wasn't all that surprising by the time September rolled around. His daughter Liz had worked tirelessly following the January 6 attack on the US Capitol building to banish Trump from the Republican Party, an act of defiance that destroyed her career as a Republican leader in Congress. In August 2022, the younger Cheney was ousted from her House seat in Wyoming by a relatively unknown primary challenger who had the backing of Trump and his allies.

Liz Cheney had endorsed Harris on September 4, and her father's decision to do the same two days later served as a stark reminder that the pre-Trump Republican Party was dead. Among those who had declared Trump unfit for office were Mitt Romney, the GOP's 2012 presidential nominee; the family of John McCain, the GOP's 2008 nominee; and Paul Ryan, the former Speaker of the House and 2012 Republican vice presidential nominee. Even Mike Pence, Trump's former vice president, had declared he would not be backing his former running mate, saying, "I believe anyone that puts themselves over the Constitution should never be president of the United States." And former President George W. Bush and former First Lady Laura Bush had also put out word that they wouldn't be endorsing Trump, either.[2]

As the old Republican leaders went into political exile, Trump enjoyed a level of devotion from rank-and-file GOP voters that few, if any, of them ever had. Kamala Harris may have had a slight lead in most polls, but those same polls showed that over 90 percent of Republican voters were committed to Trump. That wasn't going to change because of anything Dick Cheney, Mitt Romney, or anybody else from the old Republican Party had to say.

Harris prepared for her debate with Trump as though it would be the decisive moment in the campaign. In the weeks leading up to the event, top officials from her campaign reached out to ABC about the precise measurements of the stage that would be built for the candidates at the Constitution Center in Philadelphia. ABC provided the measurements to both the Harris and the Trump campaigns. The Trump team didn't have much use for the information; Harris's campaign, however, used it to construct an exact replica of the set.

The vice president's debate prep was extensive, with her and a handful of key advisors hunkering down at the Omni William Penn Hotel in Pittsburgh for five days. The sessions were led by Karen Dunn, a lawyer who helped prepare Hillary Clinton to debate Trump in 2016, and Philippe Reines, who reprised his role as Trump's stand-in from eight years earlier as well. Reines took on the role as if he were a Method actor, mimicking Trump's character and mannerisms—down to the "boxy suit" and "long tie."[3] During the mock debates, Reines, who has compared debating Trump to being onstage with a malfunctioning appliance, repeatedly interrupted Harris, abused the debate rules, and tried to dominate the practice sessions.

When the day of the debate rolled around, Harris and her team arrived at the Constitution Center early to examine every detail of the set, from the positioning of the lecterns and the placement of the cameras to the feel of the carpet. Unlike Biden, who had skipped the opportunity to check out the stage before his debate with Trump,

Harris wanted to know exactly what she was getting into. Her team also closely inspected the hold room where she would be before the debate started, demanding changes to how the furniture was arranged.

About ninety minutes before the debate, Trump and his aides showed up to inspect the set. Tulsi Gabbard, the former Democratic congresswoman who would eventually become Trump's director of national intelligence, stood behind Kamala Harris's lectern, while Trump stood in position behind his lectern and watched a live video feed on an iPad, giving him a chance to see how he and Harris would look on TV.

"Is there going to be a handshake?" Trump asked his team. "Do I shake her hand?"

"No, Mr. President, I don't think you should shake her hand," Jason Miller responded. "You didn't shake Biden's hand. And I'm sort of suspicious about these things."

Trump's entourage in the hours leading up to the debate included Laura Loomer, a far-right activist and conspiracy theorist known for provocative stunts and spreading hate and disinformation. On September 8, she had responded to a post from Kamala Harris about her Indian heritage with a string of crude and racially charged stereotypes about India. "If @KamalaHarris wins," Loomer wrote on X, "the White House will smell like curry & White House speeches will be facilitated via a call center and the American people will only be able to convey their feedback through a customer satisfaction survey at the end of the call that nobody will understand."[4] Two days later, cameras captured her exiting Trump's plane shortly after it landed in Philadelphia ahead of the debate.

Among the outrageous things Loomer had been promoting on

social media before the debate was a slanderous narrative about Haitian immigrants in Springfield, Ohio, who, she claimed, were "kidnapping and killing people's cats and dogs." For good measure, she added that "those Haitians are eating humans too. Haitian Cannibals."[5] None of it was true, but Loomer was not the only influencer on the right pushing the narrative. In fact, Trump's running mate was leading the charge.

"Months ago, I raised the issue of Haitian illegal immigrants draining social services and generally causing chaos all over Springfield, Ohio," JD Vance tweeted on the morning of September 9, the day before the debate. "Reports now show that people have had their pets abducted and eaten by people who shouldn't be in this country. Where is our border czar?"[6]

To Vance, it didn't matter that those "reports" were coming from anonymous online accounts with names like "End Wokeness" and "The Black Insurrectionist." In fact, the Republican vice presidential nominee talked up the absurd "reports" the following day—the morning of the debate—with an astonishing argument: Whether or not the specific tales about dogs and cats were true was largely irrelevant; what mattered was that the stories were bringing attention to the difficulties associated with the large influx of migrants settling in a Midwestern town.[7] "It's possible, of course, that all of these rumors will turn out to be false," Vance wrote. "[But] don't let the crybabies in the media dissuade you, fellow patriots. Keep the cat memes flowing."*

*Vance would go on to make an even starker version of this argument days later, in an interview with CNN's Dana Bash. "The American media totally ignored this stuff until Donald Trump and I started talking about cat memes," he said. "If I have to create stories so that the American media actually pays attention to the suffering of the American people, then that's what I'm going to do."

Back at the Constitution Center, my ABC News colleagues David Muir and Linsey Davis kicked off the debate with an explanation of the rules for the night. The ninety-minute showdown would feature two commercial breaks, and candidates would be given two minutes to answer each question. There would be no live studio audience, and each candidate's microphone would be turned on only when it was his or her turn to speak. The Harris team had objected strongly to the muting of the microphones, hoping an open mic would make Trump sound like a bully, but the rules had been agreed to back when Biden was still the Democratic nominee.

Muir then introduced the candidates, noting that this would be the first time they had ever met in person. Trump ambled toward his lectern on stage right and began to settle in, but Harris walked purposefully over to Trump's side of the stage to meet him. "Kamala Harris," she said by way of introduction. "Let's have a good debate."

"Nice to see you," Trump replied, shaking her outstretched hand. "Have fun."

The first question went to Harris.

"When it comes to the economy, do you believe Americans are better off than they were four years ago?" Muir asked.

She seemed a little nervous, but handled her response fine, promising to "lift up" the middle class and hitting on an issue that would loom large after the election: Trump's pledge to implement tariffs on the United States' trading partners around the world. "My opponent has a plan that I call the Trump sales tax, which would be a 20 percent tax on everyday goods that you rely on to get through the month," she said, adding that some economists believed the policy would cost middle-class families up to $4,000 a year. But she didn't address the heart of the question: whether Americans were better off under Biden.

Trump disputed her "sales tax" label in his response, but he didn't back away from his promised levies. "We're doing tariffs on other countries," he said. "Other countries are going to finally, after 75 years, pay us back for all that we've done for the world. And the tariff will be substantial in some cases."

And so the debate went. For the first thirty minutes, the candidates' back-and forth was fairly conventional. Harris deflected questions about the Biden–Harris administration by attacking Trump's proposals and his own White House record. Trump argued that Biden, and by extension Harris, had destroyed the great economy he had built as president. "We handed them over a country where the economy and where the stock market was higher than it was before the pandemic came in," Trump said. "Nobody's ever seen anything like it."

Trump landed a particularly potent blow a few minutes into the debate, drilling down on one of Harris's key vulnerabilities: the fuzziness of her own political beliefs. Five years earlier, she had campaigned for president as an unabashed progressive, supporting a slightly modified Medicare for All health-care plan[8] and the decriminalization of illegal border crossings.[9] Now she was attempting to run as a moderate.

"She has no policy," Trump said. "Everything that she believed three years ago and four years ago is out the window. She's going to my philosophy now. In fact, I was going to send her a MAGA hat. She's gone to my philosophy. But if she ever got elected, she'd change it, and it will be the end of our country. She's a Marxist; everybody knows she's a Marxist."

Indeed, Harris often found herself on the back foot early in the debate, confronted—by both Trump and the moderators—on her shifting positions and the Biden administration's various failures. "We know that illegal border crossings reached a record high in the Biden administration," David said at one point. "This past June, President Biden imposed tough new asylum restrictions. We know the numbers since then have dropped significantly. But my question to you tonight is, why did the administration wait until six months before the election to act—and would you have done anything differently from President Biden on this?"

These were good questions, and Harris didn't have good answers—so she tried to change the subject instead. After briefly mentioning a bipartisan border security bill that had died in Congress earlier in the year—in part because Trump had urged Republicans to vote it down—Harris baited Trump, saying something she knew would infuriate him.

"I'm going to actually do something really unusual, and I'm going to invite you to attend one of Donald Trump's rallies," she began. "Because it's a really interesting thing to watch. You will see during the course of his rallies, he talks about fictional characters like Hannibal Lecter. He will talk about windmills cause cancer. And what you will also notice is that people start leaving his rallies early out of exhaustion and boredom."

David turned to Trump for a response, attempting to bring the conversation back to the subject of border security. But there was no going back: Trump could have pointed out that his opponent had completely evaded the question, but instead he took Harris's bait.

"First, let me respond as to the rallies," Trump began, clearly flustered. "She said people start leaving. People don't go to her rallies. There's no reason to go. And the people that do go, she's busing them in and paying them to be there. And then showing them in a different light. So, she can't talk about that. People don't leave my rallies. We have the biggest rallies, the most incredible rallies in the history of politics."

Only once that was out of his system did Trump return to the topic at hand—kind of. Rather than focusing on the record number of illegal immigrants crossing the border and the Biden–Harris administration's undeniable negligence on the issue, he followed Laura Loomer and JD Vance down the Springfield, Ohio, rabbit hole. "Look at what's happening to the towns all over the United States," he said. "A lot of towns don't want to talk about it because they're so embarrassed by it. In Springfield, *they're eating the dogs*. The people that came in. They're eating the cats. They're eating—they're eating the pets of the people that live there. And this is what's happening in our country. And it's a shame."

A grin began to form on Harris's face. Her plan to throw Trump off his game had worked even better than she could have anticipated.

Had the former president really just blurted out a completely unsubstantiated and easily debunked internet rumor on live television? My mind immediately jumped to those tens of millions of Americans tuning in who *hadn't* been following the bizarre rumors about Springfield. What would Trump's rant about vicious immigrants eating cats and dogs sound like to them? How many people would believe that this was really happening?

Thanks to Hannah Demissie, an ABC News embed reporter on the Trump campaign, David Muir was prepared. The day before the debate, Hannah had reached out to local officials in Springfield to determine whether there was any validity to the story—and there wasn't. As Springfield city manager Bryan Heck told Hannah, "There have been no credible reports or specific claims of pets being harmed, injured, or abused by individuals within the immigrant community."

"I just want to clarify here," David interjected. "You bring up Springfield, Ohio. And ABC News did reach out to the city manager there. He told us there have been no credible reports of specific claims of pets being harmed, injured, or abused by individuals within the immigrant community."

Trump didn't want to be corrected.*

"Well, I've seen people on television," he began. "The people on television say, 'My dog was taken and used for food.' So maybe he said that, and maybe that's a good thing to say for a city manager."

They went back and forth a few more times before David moved on. "Again, the Springfield city manager says there's no evidence of that," he concluded.

But Trump couldn't let him have the last word: "We'll find out."

Harris couldn't believe her luck. "Talk about extreme," she said with a laugh. "This is, I think, one of the reasons why in this election I actually have the endorsement of 200 Republicans who have formerly worked with President Bush, Mitt Romney, and John McCain, including the endorsement of former Vice President Dick Cheney and Congressmember Liz Cheney."

From that point forward, Harris was firmly in control of the debate. She had effectively deflected the toughest question she would be

---

*The Trump campaign later claimed that ABC had agreed moderators would not fact-check either candidate during the debate, but that was not true. "We're not making a commitment to fact-check everything, or fact-check nothing, in either direction," ABC News's political director Rick Klein told *The New York Times* two days before the debate. "We're there to keep a conversation going, and to facilitate a good solid debate, and that entails a lot of things in terms of asking questions, moving the conversation along, making sure that it's civilized."

asked that night, using it to goad Trump into shouting absurdly false claims about Haitian immigrants and knock Trump off balance.

Another thing that seemed to be bothering Trump was the lack of a studio audience. Trump thrives on the reactions of those around him, but the only people in the studio with him during the debate were Harris, the moderators, and the camera crew. There was no crowd to laugh at his punch lines or to boo him and serve as a foil.

He was able to walk back to his holding room during the two commercial breaks, but there would be nobody there until the debate was over. He couldn't even check his phone or turn on the television to see what political commentators were saying about him on cable television. Under the rules that had been agreed to by both campaigns, the candidates were not allowed to talk to their aides, access their electronic devices, or watch any television until after the debate. They couldn't even read through briefing materials during the break. Trump did have his briefcase, the one you see carried by his personal aide Walt Nauta wherever Trump goes, but, as I had learned, the only thing Trump puts in that briefcase is the makeup—lots of makeup—that he often puts on himself before his TV appearances.

When the debate was over, Linsey and David said good night to the 67 million viewers who had tuned in, and the candidates made their way off the stage without saying anything to each other. When Trump reached his holding room, he was greeted by his entourage of supporters and advisors—including Susie Wiles, Chris LaCivita, Boris Epshteyn, and Representative Matt Gaetz—who leapt to their feet in applause when he walked in. When one aide told Trump that he had totally dominated the debate, the former president quickly turned to him. "I need you in the spin room saying that right now," he said, referring to the large convention space a block away from the debate site where television networks and reporters from news organizations all over the world were waiting to interview campaign surrogates after the debate.

Trump then decided to make the trip to the spin room himself. He'd done the same after the presidential primary debates in 2016, but never after a general election debate. Trump clearly thought that the debate had not gone his way and that he needed to salvage the narrative himself. Before Trump walked out to talk to reporters, he was greeted by JD Vance, who took the opportunity to give his running mate a pep talk.

"The story they are going to try to spin, because you have all the momentum, is she stopped the momentum," Vance told Trump. "It's bullshit."

"I think I killed her," Trump said.

"I think you killed her," Vance replied.

"I'm getting calls from congressmen saying, 'It's the best I've ever seen.'"

As Trump walked out into the convention space to the awaiting reporters and television anchors, there was one more person waiting to give him morale boost: Senator Marco Rubio.

"What did you think?" Trump asked Rubio.

"Good," Rubio replied. Pointing to the reporters gathered in the convention hall, he added, "I think the way people here analyze it and the way real voters analyze it is very, very different."

"I thought it was the best," Trump responded, clearly appreciating the affirmation. "We love you, man. Thanks, Marco."[10]

Rubio and Vance were trying to cheer Trump up because he needed to be cheered up. For all the bluster, Trump's advisors, and Trump himself, knew the debate hadn't gone well. But admitting defeat is not the Trump way.

"So, we thought it was our best debate ever, that it was my best debate ever," Trump boasted to reporters minutes after the pep talks from Vance and Rubio.

"If you're so confident you won tonight, why are you here?" one reporter asked. "Why not let the performance speak for itself?"

"Well, I think it did," Trump shot back. "But people said, 'Would I come here?' And I made an obligation to a couple of people that I'm going to do their show. But it was—I thought it was a great night."

Kamala Harris, meanwhile, was having a very different post-debate experience. Just minutes after the debate concluded, her campaign received a surprising jolt of what seemed to be great news. Taylor Swift, the biggest pop star on the planet, had endorsed her.

"Like many of you, I watched the debate tonight," Swift wrote in her Instagram post. "I will be casting my vote for Kamala Harris and Tim Walz in the 2024 Presidential Election. I'm voting for @kamalaharris because she fights for the rights and causes I believe need a warrior to champion them. I think she is a steady-handed, gifted leader and I believe we can accomplish so much more in this country if we are led by calm and not chaos." The endorsement was accompanied by a photo of Swift holding her Ragdoll cat, Benjamin Button, and in a final jab at JD Vance, she signed the post, "Taylor Swift, Childless Cat Lady."[11]

Neither Harris nor anyone on her campaign had any idea Swift's endorsement—arguably the biggest one she could get—was coming. If they had, they would have asked her to hold off for a day or two. Coming when it did, the news could only do one of two things: get buried by Harris's dominant debate performance or distract from it.

The vice president heard about Swift's endorsement while she was en route from the Constitution Center to Cherry Street Pier in Philadelphia, where she would be stopping by a watch party for supporters. Harris and her senior advisors huddled to discuss how much she should lean into the Swift news, and ultimately opted for a lighter touch. She wouldn't mention the news onstage, but her campaign would play a Taylor Swift song as she concluded her remarks. The group settled on "The Man."

I'm so sick of running as fast as I can
Wondering if I'd get there quicker if I was a man

Donald Trump and Kamala Harris had never met until the debate, but just hours after first shaking hands onstage, they found themselves doing the same once again, this time at Ground Zero in New York City to commemorate the twenty-third anniversary of the September 11 attacks. The ceremony featured a remarkable lineup: Senator Kirsten Gillibrand, Senator Chuck Schumer, Vice President Kamala Harris, President Joe Biden, former Mayor Michael Bloomberg, former President Donald Trump, and Senator JD Vance, all of them standing together.

Like the day before, Laura Loomer was traveling with the Republican nominee and his team, and like the day before, the far-right activist was causing problems. Although she'd later deny it, Loomer had shared a video in June 2023 that declared "9/11 was an Inside Job!" and heavily implied that then–Defense Secretary Donald Rumsfeld had been involved in the attacks.[12] When asked why the former president decided to bring her to the Ground Zero event, neither the Trump campaign nor Loomer herself responded. "To the many reporters who are calling me and obsessively asking me to talk to them today, the answer is no," Loomer would later say. "I am very busy working on my stories and investigations and don't have time to entertain your conspiracy theories."[13]

Her "stories," though, were actually just more conspiracy theories. At 12:25 a.m. on September 11, mere hours after the debate concluded, Loomer trotted out one of the oldest Trump tricks in the book, accusing Kamala Harris of having her answers fed to her by someone offstage. "Interesting choice of earrings tonight, @KamalaHarris," she wrote, comparing the vice president's jewelry to a secret communications device known as the Nova H1 "audio earring." Trump top aide Jason Miller got in on the crazy talk later that day, posting a story from the right-wing outlet *Just the News*: "Company responds to theory Harris wore audio earrings at debate: 'The resemblance is striking.'"[14]

Although Trump and his allies continued to insist he had swept the floor with Harris the night before, their actions—sending Trump to the spin room, complaining about the moderators, spreading conspiracy theories—made it obvious what they really thought about his performance. They needed someone—or something—to blame.

Enter the "Black Insurrectionist," the X account that, days earlier, had been instrumental in spreading the rumors about Haitians eating pets in Springfield, Ohio. This time, the X user claimed that a whistleblower had reported in an affidavit that ABC News had colluded with the Harris campaign, giving it the moderators' questions in advance and promising to fact-check Donald Trump while ignoring Harris's false statements.*

---

*The Associated Press would later report that the "Black Insurrectionist," who was responsible for spreading the false claims, was actually a white man from upstate New York. "The

For three days, that's all the user had: a claim that some anonymous whistleblower had filed an affidavit with an allegation. On September 15, the account posted a "document," but it was riddled with typographical and factual errors and lacked any evidence to support its claims. That didn't stop some of the largest right-wing accounts on X from sharing the allegations.[15]

Elon Musk responded to the assertion with two exclamation points—"!!"—ensuring it could be seen by his two hundred million followers.[16] Republican Senator Ted Cruz jumped on the story, too, acknowledging that he had no idea whether it was true but reposting it to his six million followers on X anyway. "If this is accurate—and I do not know that it is—it would constitute one of the gravest violations of journalist ethics in presidential debate history," he wrote. "If true, multiple senior people at @abc should be fired."[17]

GOP Representative Marjorie Taylor Greene added another dimension to the conspiracy. "The ABC whistleblower who claimed Kamala Harris was given debate questions ahead of the debate has died in a car crash according to news reports," she tweeted. She did not cite any news reports, and her claim was completely bogus. Within hours, even Greene would acknowledge as much: "This story appears to be false and I'm glad to hear it."[18] Her original post, which she did not delete, garnered more than 4.5 million views. The follow-up clarification received just 520,000.

As they had with the Haitian migrants story days earlier, people

---

Black Insurrectionist account is linked directly to Jason G. Palmer, who has his own questionable backstory, starting with the fact that he isn't Black," reported Brian Slodysko, who interviewed a half-dozen people who knew the man. "The records and personal accounts offer a portrait of an individual who has repeatedly been accused of defrauding business partners and lenders, has struggled with drug addiction and whose home was raided by the FBI over a decade ago. He also owes more than $6.7 million in back taxes to the state of New York." The account was deactivated weeks before the 2024 election.

in positions of authority who knew better—or should know better—were spreading easily debunked disinformation to score cheap partisan points or spin Donald Trump's bad debate performance. And in both instances, there were real-world ramifications.

Schools in Springfield, Ohio, were forced to close multiple times in September 2024 due to bomb threats, and the city would later sue a neo-Nazi group for alleged intimidation of government officials.[19] My ABC News colleagues and I were also bombarded by hateful and threatening messages following the fake "affidavit." Several days after the debate, I spoke to a group of West Point cadets who were visiting Washington, and the misinformation had spread so widely that even these brilliant and honorable students had heard about it. At least a few of them believed it, too.

One of the otherwise responsible people who had lent their credibility to this nonsense was Bill Ackman, the highly successful founder of Pershing Square Capital Management and a prominent Trump supporter. Ackman posted the fake "whistleblower" affidavit on his X account, alongside a lengthy open letter saying he found the claims "credible" and demanding an investigation.[20] I had met Ackman before and spent some time with him, finding him to be a serious and, I believed, intelligent person. When I saw he was at the forefront of spreading disinformation that slandered my colleagues, I sent him a text message.

> Greetings Bill–Jon Karl here. I am reaching out solely on a personal level as someone who has a great deal of respect for you. I was surprised to see you circulate and publicize an "affidavit" that made clearly bogus claims about the debate.

> Did you make any effort to verify its authenticity before lending your credibility to something that is entirely without credibility?
>
> The result has been more disinformation, more conspiracy nonsense and more death threats for my colleagues.
>
> As [Ohio Republican Governor] Mike DeWine said recently about another claim without any merit, there's a lot of garbage on the internet. That's not new and wouldn't matter much if otherwise serious people didn't tell millions of people that the garbage should be taken seriously.

Ackman never responded to my texts. But a month later—a full month later—he finally acknowledged the obvious: "It seems pretty clear that the alleged @abc whistleblower debate story claiming that @KamalaHarris was given questions in advance and other advantages was a fake."[21]

That was it. No apology for helping to spread the lies, or for waiting so long to correct the record.

Five days after the debate, Trump was still stewing about Taylor Swift's endorsement of Kamala Harris. In a one-sentence post on his social media platform, Trump said simply, "I hate Taylor Swift."*

The feeling was probably mutual, but Swift didn't show much love

*Trump was still thinking about the endorsement months after winning the election, boasting about his response to it while traveling home from the first major foreign trip

for Kamala Harris after her post-debate endorsement. The Harris campaign team tried to reach out to the pop star. Maybe she could appear in a campaign ad? Maybe she could perform at a campaign event? There were many possibilities—after all, Swift was massively popular with an important group of voters who could help Harris win the election: young women. But the Harris campaign got no answer. They couldn't even get a response from Taylor Swift's spokesperson, Trina "Tree" Paine, sending her several messages but never receiving an answer.

On September 15, the world—almost—changed again. While Trump was playing golf at the Trump International Golf Club in West Palm Beach with his golf buddy and future Middle East envoy Steve Witkoff, the Secret Service thwarted another assassination attempt. Two months after he was shot in Butler, Pennsylvania, Trump came frighteningly close to losing his life to another gunman, as Ryan Routh allegedly hid in the bushes just three hundred yards from Trump with a fully loaded assault rifle.

Trump was preparing to putt on the fifth hole when a Secret Service agent shouted "gun" after seeing Routh's rifle sticking out of the bushes. Routh fled the scene by car after agents fired at him, and he was arrested one hour later when he was pulled over in nearby Martin County.

Routh's motive for the planned attack remains unclear, though he lashed out against Trump in a rambling self-published book titled *Ukraine's Unwinnable War: The Fatal Flaw of Democracy, World*

---

of his second term in a post on Truth Social: "Has anyone noticed that, since I said 'I HATE TAYLOR SWIFT,' she's no longer 'HOT?'"

Abandonment and the Global Citizen—Taiwan, Afghanistan, North Korea and the End of Humanity. He said he voted for Trump in 2016 but was disappointed by his presidency, and Routh's recent years were occupied by his delusional attempt to help Ukraine in its war with Russia.

After the thwarted assassination attempt, Elon Musk wrote a statement on X, saying, "And nobody is even trying to assassinate Biden/Kamala?"

It was a grossly irresponsible thing to say that could have been seen as inviting an assassination attempt of Trump's Democratic rivals. Several hours later, Musk deleted it, insisting he had been joking: "Well, one lesson I've learned is that just because I say something to a group and they laugh doesn't mean it's going to be all that hilarious as a post on X," he wrote.

But a few weeks later, he talked about it again in an interview with Tucker Carlson.

"I made a joke, which I realized—I deleted—which is like: Nobody's even bothering to try to kill Kamala because it's pointless. What do you achieve?"

After Musk said those words, both he and Carlson doubled over in laughter.

"It's deep and true though," Carlson said as he continued to laugh uncontrollably.[22]

As evidenced by the great lengths Trump's allies went to explain away her performance, the debate was a high point for Kamala Harris and her campaign. But while she got a slight boost in some of the national polls, the momentum didn't last. A little-noticed interview Harris did with a local ABC News affiliate in Philadelphia three days after the debate helps explain why.

The conversation with reporter Brian Taff—just Harris's second sit-down interview in the nearly two months since she became the presumptive Democratic nominee—lasted only eleven minutes. Far from the confident and forceful candidate viewers saw accepting the nomination in Chicago or debating Donald Trump in Philadelphia, Harris seemed tentative and nervous, offering meandering and unconvincing answers to Taff's straightforward questions.

"At the debate the other night, you talked about creating an opportunity economy," Taff began. "I wonder if we can drill down on that a little bit. When we talk about bringing down prices and making life more affordable for people, what are one or two specific things you have in mind for that?"

The question couldn't have been any easier: Talk about your plan for the economy, the issue voters repeatedly say is their top priority heading into the election. But rather than dive right in, Harris filibustered for several minutes about her own middle-class upbringing, throwing in some niceties about Americans' "beautiful character" and their "ambitions and aspirations and dreams." She eventually got around to mentioning two policy proposals: a $50,000 tax deduction for entrepreneurs who start a small business, and $25,000 in down-payment assistance for first-time homebuyers.

Setting aside the economic merits of either proposal—and there were reasons to doubt the economic sense of both ideas—neither would have any direct impact on the vast majority of Americans. There was nothing in Harris's answer to offer hope for working families living paycheck to paycheck and struggling to pay rising grocery bills, or for construction workers who hadn't seen their real wages increase in years.

Just about every answer Harris gave in that interview followed the same pattern—bland, inoffensive, and forgettable. How is she different from Joe Biden? She offers a "new generation of leadership." How can she make inroads with people who've voted for Trump in the past? Her "lived experience" tells her that the "vast majority of us as Americans have so much more in common than what separates us." What is one fun fact about her she'd like the American people to know? She loves her family and loves to cook.

In football terms, Harris was approaching the interview—and the campaign—as though she were running out the clock. Already in the lead, she didn't need to take any risks to advance the ball down the field. As long as she avoided any major mistakes, she would end up victorious. She could steer clear of most interviews, and deliver milquetoast answers during those she did. She could delay releasing a policy platform and campaign on amorphous feelings like "joy" and "unity" instead. She could avoid making the difficult decision to distance herself from the unpopular administration in which she served in the hopes that her standard answer to such questions—"I'm obviously not Joe Biden"—would suffice.

But all those decisions were based on the assumption that Harris *was*, in fact, winning. And by the time she realized that she wasn't and tried to change course, it was too late. She thought that she was running out the clock, but in reality, the clock was running out on her.

CHAPTER FOURTEEN

CLOSING ARGUMENT

The final weeks of Donald Trump's 2024 presidential campaign were filled with a mix of highly effective political showmanship, unforced errors, and flat-out embarrassments that would have likely doomed any other candidate's chances. His Madison Square Garden rally in New York City nine days before the election showcased all three.

Even putting the rally on his schedule was a bold and unexpected move. It almost seemed as if Trump had as many criminal convictions in Manhattan as he had voters in the 2020 election. He lost the borough to Joe Biden by more than 70 percentage points. But as a born-and-bred New Yorker, Trump wanted to prove to the world that he could turn the most iconic arena in America's largest city into Trump country—at least for a night.

He pulled it off and almost lost the election in the process.

I spoke with Trump the night before the rally, hoping to figure out why he had decided to host a major campaign event in New York—a state that not even his own aides thought he had a chance of winning. After all, the most important asset a presidential candidate had at this point in the race was his or her time—and Trump appeared to be wasting it. But before I could say much, Trump began asking me questions instead.

"How do you see it?" Trump asked. He was referring to the election, not the upcoming rally.

I told him basically the same thing I had been telling ABC News viewers for the past week: I thought the race was very, very close. The momentum had certainly shifted back toward Trump in recent days after Harris's initial surge, and he now had a very narrow lead in most national polls. That said, just about every battleground state poll found Trump and Harris in a statistical tie. He could win them all, or he could lose them all.

"That's interesting, because some think it's a blow-away," Trump told me. "We're up a little bit in the popular vote, but that equates to killing it in the swing states."

He continued, taking a dig at Harris: "And from what I'm understanding, there's not a lot of enthusiasm for her, which there shouldn't be. She's a fucking dud."

Trump then turned away from his phone and said something to the people with him on his plane. "Jonathan Karl thinks it's going to be a close election," I could hear him say. Then he began talking to me again: "I'm here with Susie [Wiles] and Chris [LaCivita]."[1]

I had no idea when I called him that Trump was sitting with his top two campaign aides, but before long, I found myself speaking with LaCivita. The longtime GOP operative said something about the race being a blowout, but I couldn't really hear him over his own laughter as he handed the phone back to Trump. They were feeling good—and cocky, too.

Just a few days earlier, John Kelly, Trump's former White House chief of staff, had issued a dire assessment of the man whom he had served, calling him a fascist who didn't understand American values. "It's a very dangerous thing to have the wrong person elected to high office," Kelly warned in an interview with *The New York Times*.[2]

Kelly said Trump had told him, more than once, "You know, Hitler did some good things, too."

Kelly, of course, was not just another Trump critic: He had been Trump's longest-serving chief of staff and was a retired four-star Marine general who had devoted his life to serving his country. He had seen lots of combat, at one point serving nearly two consecutive years in Iraq's Anbar province, one of the deadliest places in the country at the time. Kelly was also the highest-ranking military officer to lose a child in Iraq or Afghanistan; his twenty-nine-year-old son Robert had been killed while leading his platoon on a combat patrol in Afghanistan's Helmand province in 2010. In the face of such a brutal personal loss, he carried on with characteristic selflessness.

"We are only one of 5,500 American families who have suffered the loss of a child in this war," Kelly wrote in 2011 when asked about the pain of losing a son. "The death of my boy simply cannot be made to seem any more tragic than the others."[3]

Kelly agreed with the vast majority of Trump's policies, and he had worked to enact them for two years before he left the White House in January 2019. But he also had an unvarnished look at how Trump approached the presidency and was gravely concerned about the prospect of Trump returning to the Oval Office. I asked Trump about Kelly's comments during that late-October phone call.

"He's a fucking loser, always has been," Trump said. "He's a bully who turned out to be a weak guy. He couldn't take the pressure at all. He was terrible." He then quickly pivoted to another topic, sounding more bored with the question than angry about being labeled a fascist.[4]

But Kelly's comments were part of a pattern. As Trump stood at the precipice of the unlikeliest return to power in American history, the most dire warnings about what that would mean were often coming from military leaders whom he had put in high-ranking positions in his first administration.

In the early days of the first Trump White House, the president surrounded himself with a number of decorated military officers who had waged war and earned the stars on their shoulders. At a luncheon shortly after his first inauguration, Trump had pointed with pride to Kelly and Defense Secretary James Mattis, describing them as "my generals." He said they were straight out of central casting. "If I'm doing a movie, I'd pick you generals."

Trump would soon learn, however, that the retired military officers he entrusted to implement his agenda were not really *his* generals, after all; they had each sworn an oath to the Constitution, not the president.

Kelly wasn't even the first Trump general who would go on to call him a fascist. Mark Milley, whom Trump appointed as chairman of the Joint Chiefs of Staff in 2019, told Bob Woodward in 2023 that Trump is "fascist to the core" and "the most dangerous person to this country."[5] Three years earlier, as Trump was running for reelection, Mattis had accused the president of making "a mockery of our Constitution" and described him as "the first president in my lifetime who does not try to unite the American people."[6]

By October 2024, those generals were nowhere near Trump's inner circle. Their warnings garnered plenty of media attention, but they had no discernible impact on the race—and were either dismissed or mocked by most of Trump's supporters.

I arrived at Madison Square Garden in the afternoon on Sunday, October 27, and almost immediately spotted an old friend named Deroy Murdock. I hadn't seen him in years, but I had actually gone to Madison Square Garden with him three decades earlier—to see a Grateful Dead concert. Back then, Deroy was a die-hard Deadhead, but he had little use for politicians of any kind. He was nominally a Republican, but he was also a Black, gay libertarian who didn't trust either major political party. Still, here he was, at Trump's rally, looking every bit as excited as he had been to see the Grateful Dead's Jerry Garcia thirty years earlier.

Trump's campaign had assembled more than thirty speakers and performers for the event, including five members of the Trump family and an eclectic mix of MAGA celebrities ranging from the late wrestler Hulk Hogan and former Fox News host Tucker Carlson to Rudy Giuliani, the nearly bankrupt former mayor of New York, and Elon Musk, the world's richest man. I had arrived at the Garden hours before the programming was set to begin, but the arena was already packed.

That Trump could draw a crowd like this in the middle of Manhattan was remarkable, but even more impressive was that crowd's devotion to the Republican nominee. These people were willing to endure New York traffic, crowded subways, painfully long lines, and a phalanx of security—all to sit and watch more than six hours of political speeches. With all that energy inside the arena, it felt like Trump was running a winning campaign.

But then the featured guests began to speak.

The tone of the evening was dark and resentful, at times outright hateful. One speaker referred to Kamala Harris as a prostitute, saying "her and her pimp handlers will destroy our country." Another, holding up a crucifix for the crowd to see, called Harris "the antichrist" and "the devil." Tucker Carlson mocked the Democratic nominee's mixed-race heritage, labeling her a "Samoan Malaysian, low-IQ, former California prosecutor."*

Virtually nothing said by the parade of speakers that night was designed to appeal to anyone who wasn't already enthralled with—and voting for—Donald Trump. *The New York Times* called it "a carnival of grievances, misogyny and racism."[7] A comedian named Tony Hinchcliffe—somewhat well-known online for his podcast *Kill Tony* but far from the mainstream—delivered particularly vulgar and racist remarks. At one point, he gestured toward a Black person in the audience and made a crack about carving watermelons with him. A few minutes later, he mocked Latinos who "love making babies"—because "they come inside, just like they did to our country." But he was only getting started.

"I don't know if you guys know this, but there's literally a floating island of garbage in the middle of the ocean right now. Yeah. I think it's called Puerto Rico," Hinchliffe said. As the joke bombed, he reacted to the boos. "Okay, we're getting there. Now, again, normally I don't follow the national anthem, everybody. This isn't exactly a perfect comedy setup."

Hinchcliffe was right about that, of course: His brand of humor was a better fit for the 1 a.m. hour on Comedy Central than it was for

*Harris's father was from Jamaica and her mother was from India, as Carlson surely knew.

the opening act of a presidential campaign event. Podcaster and Ultimate Fighting Championship commentator Joe Rogan had suggested months earlier on an episode of *The Joe Rogan Experience* that Trump hire Hinchcliffe to write "bangers" for him during the campaign, but quickly made clear he was joking: "Do you know how fucking insane that would be?"[8]

Insane or not, the Trump campaign *did* invite Hinchcliffe to speak, and aides quickly found themselves distancing their boss from the comedian's remarks.* "This joke does not reflect the views of President Trump or the campaign," a Trump spokesperson said in a statement on his joke about Puerto Rico. Even Trump himself would later admit that Hinchcliffe "said some bad things" and that he probably "shouldn't have been there."[9]

The Madison Square Garden spectacle was put on and paid for by the Trump campaign, of course, but it arguably could have been an in-kind contribution to Kamala Harris, providing her campaign with vivid and fresh examples of extreme and offensive rhetoric that seemed sure to alienate the race's last remaining undecided voters. The Harris campaign immediately got to work making sure the more than three hundred thousand Puerto Rican voters in Pennsylvania knew what the Trump rally speaker had said. Nicky Jam, a Puerto Rican singer who had backed Trump weeks earlier, rescinded his endorsement following the remarks.[10]

But the Hinchliffe comments ultimately did little, if anything, to change the trajectory of the race. Trump would go on to secure more

---

*After much speculation about the process, Marc Caputo would later report for *The Bulwark* that the Trump campaign *had* vetted Hinchcliffe's remarks, even getting him to remove a joke calling Kamala Harris a "cunt." But that just raised other questions: Did the vetting team let the other "jokes" through?

of the Hispanic vote in 2024 than he did in 2020 and, according to exit polls, the most ever for a Republican presidential candidate.[11]

What the offensive remarks did do, however, is overshadow and distract from comments made at the Madison Square Garden rally that telegraphed what Trump would do if he got back to the White House. For example, Stephen Miller—who would become the architect of Trump's domestic policy agenda—proudly declared that "America is for Americans and Americans only." Trump himself praised Robert F. Kennedy Jr., promising he would let him "go wild" on health, food, and medicine, foreshadowing his plan to make Kennedy the secretary of Health and Human Services. And Elon Musk took the stage with the future commerce secretary Howard Lutnick and promised to cut "at least $2 trillion" in federal spending in a single year, previewing just how far-reaching his ambitions to dismantle the government would be (even as they would fall far short of Musk's goal).

Trump's Madison Square Garden rally came along as the Harris campaign was increasingly desperate for something to change the dynamics of the race. While Trump and his top aides were growing increasingly confident—predicting a blowout in casual conversations with journalists—Harris's advisors had begun to worry that Trump had built up an insurmountable lead heading into the final stretch of the campaign. The energy and momentum that Harris had enjoyed in the weeks after she replaced Biden as the Democratic nominee were gone.

In a last-ditch effort to recapture some momentum, the Harris campaign was practically begging for another debate with Trump.

The Democratic nominee's top aides approached NBC News first, but the network would not announce a contest unless both candidates agreed to participate—and Trump refused. The Harris campaign went to CNN next, and the network quickly announced that both candidates were invited to a debate in Atlanta on October 23. Harris publicly accepted the offer, but once again, Trump refused.

Harris was so desperate to shake up the race, in fact, that she had two of her top campaign advisors quietly reach out to Fox News to inquire about the possibility of a debate, even though she and her team firmly believed the network was heavily biased against her.

Fox had already proposed a debate weeks earlier. The morning after the September 10 contest between Trump and Harris hosted by ABC News, Fox News host Steve Doocy put the offer to Trump directly in a live interview on *Fox & Friends*, asking if he would agree to a debate hosted by Fox News anchors Bret Baier and Martha MacCallum. Before Doocy could list the three proposed dates, however, Trump cut him off. "Well, I wouldn't want to have Martha and Bret," he said. "I'd love to have somebody else other than Martha and Bret." He said he'd rather do a debate hosted by one of Fox's more Trump-friendly prime-time anchors, mentioning Sean Hannity, Laura Ingraham, or Jesse Watters.

Any of those three would obviously be a nonstarter for Harris, but the suggestion didn't really matter because at that point the Democratic nominee had no interest whatsoever in a Fox News debate, regardless of who was moderating. A few weeks later, though—with her campaign on the ropes and talks with NBC News and CNN stalling out—the situation had changed. Harris advisors Stephanie Cutter and Brian Fallon reached out to Bret Baier and Fox News president

Jay Wallace directly, letting them know Harris was now open to a debate hosted by Fox. Trump, however, still wasn't interested. After toying with the idea for a few days, he officially rejected it.

Once another debate had been ruled out, Harris moved ahead with her backup plan: a one-on-one interview with Bret Baier. This represented a marked shift for Harris, as she had never done an interview with Fox News in her entire career. But Harris needed significant, attention-grabbing moments if she wanted to have any chance of winning the election, and one more bland, sit-down interview with a friendly journalist was not going to provide any sparks. She needed a confrontation.

Harris's interview with Baier was scheduled to take place October 16 in Washington Crossing, Pennsylvania, where George Washington launched his clandestine journey across the Delaware River and into New Jersey during the Revolutionary War. Harris herself approached the conversation as though she were heading into enemy territory.

The parameters for the interview were strict. It would be pretaped, last twenty minutes, and air on Baier's show that Wednesday evening at 6 p.m. The conversation itself was scheduled to take place at 5 p.m.—shortly after Harris held a rally at a nearby park—meaning Baier would not have much time between taping the interview and anchoring his show. Fox News producers, therefore, had asked the vice president to arrive a few minutes early to ensure the interview could start promptly at 5 p.m.

Harris's rally ended around 4:30 p.m., and she went to a room down the hall from where Baier would interview her. By 5 p.m., however, the vice president was in her holding room and had still not shown up for the interview. As Baier sat anxiously in his chair, looking at his watch and exchanging worried looks with his producers, he reminded Harris's aides that 5:18 p.m. was the cutoff: If Harris wasn't seated for the interview by then, it would not air that night.

Harris finally walked down the hall and into the room at about thirty seconds past 5:17 p.m. There would typically be a little small talk between the anchor and the candidate before an interview like this—particularly because Baier had never met Harris before—but the vice president had left them no time for that.

"Madame Vice President, thanks for being here," Baier said as Harris sat down and the Fox News crew set up her microphone. "Lovely event outside."

As soon as her microphone was in place, Harris, who had still not greeted Baier, said her first words to him.

"You ready?"

A Harris advisor later told me the last-second arrival was intentional—an effort to "ice the kicker," so to speak, like when a football coach attempts to get inside an opposing kicker's head by calling a time-out immediately before he attempts a field goal. And if Baier had planned to ease into the interview with a noncontrontational question, Harris's attempted "icing" changed his approach.

"Voters tell pollsters all over the country and here in Pennsylvania that immigration is one of the key issues that they're looking at this election, and specifically the influx of illegal immigrants from more than 150 countries," he began. "How many illegal immigrants would you estimate your administration has released into the country over the last three and a half years?"

The interview was contentious—arguably the only tough questioning Harris faced during her entire presidential campaign—but it was also one of her better interviews, because Baier's aggressive questioning forced her to match his intensity. The friendlier interviews were what got Harris into trouble.

A week before she sat down with Fox News, Harris had a decidedly warmer reception on ABC's *The View*. Co-host Sunny Hostin, whose support of Harris was no secret, asked the Democratic nominee what seemed to be an easy—and obvious—question: "If anything, would you have done something differently than President Biden during the past four years?"

The question presented Harris with a golden opportunity to reassure the more than 56 percent of voters who didn't approve of Biden at the time that, although she served in his administration, her presidency would not be a continuation of his. She opted not to do so.

"There is not a thing that comes to mind," Harris replied. "And I have been a part of most of the decisions that have had impact."

Harris went on to tick through a laundry list of the Biden administration's initiatives, seemingly oblivious to the fact that she also had just saddled herself with every Biden administration failure, from the deadly and chaotic withdrawal from Afghanistan to the mess at the southern border. The Trump campaign predictably used the video clip of Harris's answer over and over again in television ads, playing it at rallies, and posting it all over social media as evidence that Harris would be no different from the deeply unpopular president she served.

Following her stumbles on *The View*, Harris's campaign sought out some less conventional interviews for the vice president. She sat down for forty minutes with Alex Cooper, the host of *Call Her Daddy*, a podcast popular with young women, and she offered to do the same on *New Heights*, a podcast hosted by brothers and NFL stars Jason and Travis Kelce. The Kelce brothers, however, rejected the offer, even though Travis's girlfriend, Taylor Swift, had endorsed Harris weeks earlier. Their producer explained they do sports, not politics.

The vice president's aides were also unable to book her on *The Joe Rogan Experience*, which had a much larger—and more male—fan base than Cooper's *Call Her Daddy*. Harris's team knew she was bleeding support with young men, so they made it a priority to get her on Rogan's show, even offering to make a special trip to Texas—under the guise of highlighting the state's restrictive abortion policies—so she could record at Rogan's studio in Austin. But the podcaster's team played coy with his schedule, and Rogan ultimately decided to sit down instead with Trump for three hours on the day Harris was in Texas. Rogan's conversation with Trump quickly racked up tens of millions of views and downloads.

As Harris struggled to shake up the trajectory of an election her aides feared was slipping away, the Trump campaign took aim at a relatively minor detail in Harris's biography: her claim to have worked at McDonald's during one summer while she was a college student.

"I did the French fries, and I did the ice cream," Harris said at a 2019 event in Las Vegas in support of a fifteen-dollar minimum wage.[12] The comments had little, if any, impact on her failed 2020 presidential campaign and were quickly forgotten—but not by Donald Trump.

Four years later, Trump saw a golden opportunity in Harris's claim, accusing her of lying about her time at McDonald's. He had no evidence she wasn't telling the truth, but Harris, despite her best efforts, had no evidence that she was. The Harris campaign reached out to the fast-food chain's corporate headquarters in Chicago, hoping their records would provide proof of employment, but Harris's stint at a California franchise had come four decades earlier and she had only worked there a matter of weeks. There were no records. Harris even sent someone to search through boxes she had in storage back home because she thought one of them might contain an old McDonald's uniform. No luck.

As Harris looked for evidence to prove where she had worked so many years ago, Trump refused to let the matter go, ensuring the Democratic nominee continued to face questions about it.

"I just want to ask you, yes or no: At any point in your life, have you served two all-beef patties, special sauce, lettuce, cheese, pickles, onions—" MSNBC's Stephanie Ruhle asked Harris in late September.

"On a sesame seed bun?" Harris interjected jokingly, before standing by her claims about her employment history. "Part of the reason I even talk about having worked at McDonald's is because there are people who work at McDonald's in our country who are trying to raise a family."

A few weeks later, Trump stopped by a McDonald's franchise in Bucks County, Pennsylvania, and, with television cameras following him, asked if he could do some work. The whole event was staged—the store was closed to accommodate Trump's visit, and the "customers" were vetted—but the staging was perfect. Trump donned a McDonald's apron over his white shirt and red tie, operated the fryers, and worked the drive-through.

"I've now worked for fifteen minutes more than Kamala," he said to reporters as he stuck his head out of the drive-through window. "She never worked here."

The stunt went viral on social media, with some users assuming the photographs were generated by artificial intelligence before learning that no, Trump really *had* stopped by to do some work at a Mc-

Donald's in Pennsylvania. The Republican nominee was still buzzing about it when I talked to him the following day.

"We had a great day yesterday," he told me over the phone. "We had a thing called McDonald's, which some people are now attributing to be one of the greatest events in history, actually."[13]

Well, not quite. But it was one of the best political stunts I could remember—until he surpassed it ten days later.

Trump's next playful antic came on October 30, this time mocking Joe Biden. Appearing via video chat with a group of Latino voters the night before, Biden had attempted to lash out at Tony Hinchcliffe, the comedian who had called Puerto Rico a "floating island of garbage" at Trump's Madison Square Garden rally days earlier. But the words didn't come out quite right.

"The only garbage I see floating out there is his supporters," Biden began. "His—his demonization of Latinos is unconscionable, and it's un-American."

The White House immediately tried to clarify the president's remarks—adding a possessive apostrophe to "supporter's" in the official transcript—but the damage was already done. Not only had Biden completely stepped on the news cycle that Kamala Harris was hoping to generate with a big speech that night outside the White House at the Ellipse—the same site where Trump had urged his supporters to march to the Capitol on January 6, 2021—but he had presented the Republican nominee with another opportunity to rile up his supporters. *The president of the United States thinks that you're garbage.**

*Biden himself tried to walk back the comments the next day, writing on social media, "Earlier today I referred to the hateful rhetoric about Puerto Rico spewed by Trump's supporter at his Madison Square Garden rally as garbage—which is the only word I can think of to describe it. His demonization of Latinos is unconscionable. That's all I meant to say. The comments at that rally don't reflect who we are as a nation."

Trump leaned into the opportunity the following day.

Donning an orange safety vest over his trademark white shirt and red tie, the Republican nominee stepped off his plane in Green Bay, Wisconsin, and declared, "Two hundred and fifty million people are not garbage." He then climbed into a large garbage truck with the Trump campaign logo emblazoned on the side. Sitting in the passenger seat, Trump addressed the television cameras. "How do you like my garbage truck?" he asked the assembled reporters. "This truck is in honor of Kamala and Joe Biden."

Once again, Trump had managed to hammer home a message far more effectively with a single image than either his campaign or Harris's could have done with hundreds of press releases or campaign speeches.

But setting aside the creative stunts, Trump wasn't acting like a candidate who was heading toward victory. The former president's advisors encouraged him to focus on what they believed was a winning message—that life in America was better when he was president, with lower inflation, fewer wars, and a more secure border—but Trump himself was constantly stepping on that message with odd tangents and controversial diatribes.

During a campaign rally in suburban Pennsylvania, for example, Trump abandoned a planned question-and-answer session with future Secretary of Homeland Security Kristi Noem and decided to dance onstage instead. Two medical emergencies in the crowd had interrupted the event, triggering Trump's walk-off song—the Village People's "Y.M.C.A."—but the former president opted to keep the rally going. "Let's not do any more questions," Trump said. "Let's just listen to music. . . . Who the hell wants to hear questions, right?" And for the next forty minutes, Trump swayed back and forth onstage to an eclectic collection of songs: "God Bless America," "Ave Maria," Andrea Bocelli's "Con te partirò," Rufus Wainwright's cover of "Hallelujah," and "Memory" from the musical *Cats*.

"Hope he's okay," Harris wrote on X, sharing a video clip of the bizarre rally.[14]

As odd as that event was, Trump outdid himself days later at a rally in Latrobe, Pennsylvania, where campaign strategist Jason Miller told reporters that the Republican nominee would begin previewing his closing argument. When Trump took the stage, he veered dramatically off script, telling a crude story about golfing legend Arnold Palmer, who was born in Latrobe, and what he looked like when he was naked in the shower.

"Arnold Palmer was all man, and I say that in all due respect to women—and I love women," Trump said. "But this guy, this guy, this is a guy that was all man. This man was strong and tough. And I refuse to say it, but when he took showers with the other pros, they came out of there, they said, 'Oh my God, that's unbelievable.'"

"I had to say [it]," he continued. "We have women that are highly sophisticated here, but they used to look at Arnold as a man."

And for the next ten minutes or so, Trump went on about Arnold Palmer—and his manhood. Not exactly the closing argument that anybody, especially his own advisors, expected him to preview.

Trump's closing argument was also repeatedly overshadowed by his increasingly harsh—even violent—rhetoric. In an interview with Fox News's Maria Bartiromo that aired on October 13, Trump argued that he was more concerned about domestic election interference than any foreign threats. "I think the bigger problem are the people from within," he said. "We have some very bad people. We have some sick people, radical left lunatics. . . . And it should be very easily handled by—if necessary, by National Guard, or if really necessary, by the military, because they can't let that happen."[15]

Trump would later walk back his comments about deploying the military against his political opponents, but he continued to refer to them as "the enemy within." "We have two enemies," he told Bartiromo when asked about the possibility of bureaucrats undermining him during a second term. "We have the outside enemy, and then we have the enemy from within. And the enemy from within, in my opinion, is more dangerous than China, Russia, and all these countries. Because if you have a smart president, he can handle them pretty easily. . . . But the thing that's tougher to handle are these lunatics that we have inside, like Adam Schiff."

"They are so bad and frankly, they're evil," Trump said of his opponents at a town hall in Pennsylvania the following day. And in an interview with the Catholic television network EWTN on October 17, he did it again. "When you see the radical left programs that they're espousing," he began, "we have a true enemy from within. They hate when I say that, but whether we like it, and I think in many ways, it's more dangerous from the outside enemies that we have."[16]

Once again, this was not the closing argument that Trump's campaign advisors had envisioned for their candidate.

On October 31, I called Robert F. Kennedy Jr. to ask him about some controversial health-policy recommendations I had heard he was making to Trump's transition team, including his suggestion that Trump name Florida's surgeon general, known for his opposition to vaccines, as the surgeon general of the United States. He essentially confirmed the story, but before I could hang up the phone, he changed the subject and spent about ten minutes lecturing me about the media's treatment of Donald Trump.

"Calling Trump Hitler at a time when there's so many assassins out there and potential assassins is just—you guys are really irresponsible," he told me. "It's not journalism. It's just slander."

"Just for the record, I've never called him Hitler, or anything like that," I responded. "I never did. ABC never did."

Kennedy ignored my pushback and kept going.

"[Trump] will definitely win if all the votes are counted," he declared. "I don't think he can lose."

I needed to get back to work and had no desire to get into a long discussion with Kennedy about voter fraud, so I tried to wind down the conversation. "Anyway. All right, well, we will see," I said. "No matter what happens, half the country is going to be totally distraught, so Lord knows. But we'll see. All right, thanks. I appreciate it. Bye."

But within two minutes, Kennedy called me back.

"You just said that half the people in the country are going to be really upset [after the election], and I understand that, because the demonization that the media has done on Trump," he began. "But Trump is surrounded by really, like, incredible people who have the values that I had in the Democratic Party growing up. They want to end the wars. They want to make sure that the Constitution is protected, that we have free speech, that we end the weaponization of federal agencies, that we protect kids' health."

As he was telling me about these "incredible people," Kennedy was about to take the stage at a Trump event in Arizona with Tucker

Carlson, the right-wing provocateur who had grown a following by mocking and denouncing the values of the Democrats whom Bobby Kennedy Jr. had grown up with. He kept talking. "Everybody I knew that I grew up with is really terrified of Donald Trump because they think he's going to be a dictator," he told me. "You know, it's just not going to happen. He's going to be a good president."

As Kennedy started to lecture me again about how "the media" was dividing the country and demonizing Trump, I decided to interject. Didn't he hear Trump calling his opponents "evil" and "the enemy within"? "You say the country is divided because of the way the media demonizes Trump, but you hear what Trump says," I said. "He says that we're not going to have a country anymore if the other side wins."

"Trump is an entertainer. He says things that are outrageous, deliberately," Kennedy said, adding that the Trump he had endorsed was much different from the one who had been president from 2017 to 2021. "The last time around, you know, he was surrounded by lobbyists and all these kind of people who did bad shit. He doesn't want to do that again."

A few minutes after our call ended, Kennedy took the stage in Glendale, Arizona, and recounted parts of our conversation, describing what he had told "one of the anchors of ABC" about how the news media is dividing the country. He didn't mention anything about Trump's own divisive rhetoric, of course, but when Trump took the stage, he illustrated my point more vividly than I ever could.

Tucker Carlson had just asked Trump whether he thought it was "weird" for Liz Cheney, the longtime Republican lawmaker and daughter of former Vice President Dick Cheney, to support his Democratic opponent. Trump made some comments about Harris's decision to campaign with Cheney, but eventually turned toward his policy disagreements with the Wyoming Republican. Cheney has always had a hawkish foreign policy, and was generally more willing than Trump—or at least this version of Trump—to support American military action abroad. Those are legitimate differences of opinion, worth debating vigorously.

But that's not what Trump was interested in doing.

"She is a radical war hawk," he said of the former congresswoman who'd had to hire private security years earlier after receiving death threats. "Let's put her with a rifle standing there with nine barrels shooting at her, OK? Let's see how she feels about it, you know, when the guns are trained on her face."

The Sunday before the election, I appeared on *Good Morning America* and summed up the view from many of Trump's advisors both inside and outside the campaign.

"The Trump campaign's closing argument is a pretty basic one," I said. "It's that things were better when he was president than they are now. He says it at every rally now. 'Are you better off today than you were four years ago?' The crowd screams 'NO.' Now, to be clear, exactly four years ago, we were in the middle of a pandemic that had shut down our economy, and thousands of people were dying. That's not literally what he means. But he means pre-pandemic; we had low inflation, economic growth. The world was not, in Trump's words, 'on fire.'"

That was a pretty compelling closing argument, especially given how closely Harris had tied herself to Biden's record.

"That said," I continued, "Trump's own message once he gets past that opening line is all over the place. It's seeing Liz Cheney with guns in her face. It's the rally we saw at Madison Square Garden, and the talk of the 'enemy within.' It's nowhere near as disciplined as his campaign would like to see it."

Several minutes after the segment ended, I ducked into a small office at Times Square Studios, where *Good Morning America* was broadcast. The time was 7:28 a.m., and I decided to call Trump. He had been campaigning in Pennsylvania until about midnight the night before, but I figured he would already be awake. Trump never seems to sleep.

"Hello, Jonathan," he answered, sounding groggy. Maybe I *had* woken him up.

"Hey, President Trump," I responded. "How are you holding up?"

"I think very good," he said, his voice as scratchy and tired as I had ever heard it. "The voice is in great shape."

It turned out Trump had already been awake for a while. He had just watched me on *GMA* and was not happy about what he saw.

"I just watched," he told me. "You said I didn't have a message. I have a tremendous message, but you don't—you just can't do it, Jon, just can't do it. It's too bad. I just watched specifically to see, and you said, you know, my message was all over the place. It's not."

"Well, it's a little bit of the weave," I said, referring to the label Trump himself had given to his tendency to jump from topic to topic.

"Look, the weave got me elected president," he shot back. "Yeah, that's one of those things. But the weave is a good thing. Nobody else can do it. Very few people can."[17]

Shortly after we said our goodbyes, Trump departed for his first campaign event that day, a 10 a.m. rally in Lititz, Pennsylvania—and he was in a noticeably sour mood. His lack of sleep may have had something to do with it, or he could have been upset by a *Des Moines*

Register poll released the night before that found him losing to Harris in solid-red Iowa (the poll turned out to be wildly inaccurate). One of Trump's advisors later told *Washington Post* reporter Josh Dawsey that he was agitated that morning because of his phone call with me.

Whatever the reason, Trump was clearly angry about something when he took the stage for his first rally of the day. His aides had loaded a speech into the teleprompters, but he went off script almost immediately—and let the crowd know it. "I tell you what, I love being off the stupid teleprompters because the truth comes out," he said. "The truth comes out, and at least you find out that it's nice to have a president that doesn't have to use teleprompters."

Trump then began complaining about the bulletproof glass that now surrounded him at all his outdoor events, which was something the Secret Service had insisted upon following the two attempts on his life in recent months. He noted that there was a little space between the glass on one part of the stage, but that any would-be assassin would need to be positioned behind the press area to take advantage of it.

"I have this piece of glass here, but all we have really over here is the fake news," he said. "And to get me, somebody would have to shoot through the fake news. And I don't mind that so much. I don't mind, I don't mind that."

The comments were remarkably irresponsible, especially considering that many of the reporters standing there that day had been with Trump in Butler, Pennsylvania, months earlier.

After bouncing around to a few other topics, Trump returned once again to the bulletproof glass, this time stepping into a gap on the stage as though he were acting out a death wish. He pointed to a horn set atop a pole by a nearby airstrip. "It's right in the field where you might have a sniper," Trump said. "See this? And I have no glass here."

Trump began to turn back and forth to demonstrate the gap in the protective glass. "Glass here," he said. "There's nothing over there."

Then he pointed to the press area in front of him. "They're my glass," he said. "See? Those people are my glass."

Although Trump himself remained as unpredictable as ever in the final weeks of the election, his campaign team was far more disciplined, blanketing the airwaves with arguably the most effective ad of the 2024 race.

Anyone who lived in a swing state and watched even a few minutes of baseball, football, or NASCAR likely saw it. The ad highlighted comments Harris made expressing support for taxpayer-funded transgender surgeries for undocumented immigrants in prison, and it featured a potent tagline: "Kamala is for they/them, President Trump is for you."

The Trump campaign spent tens of millions of dollars to run the ad, airing it more than fifty thousand times.[18] The comments from Harris came in 2019, when she was running as a progressive in the Democratic presidential primary, but they played differently in a general election five years later. "Every transgender inmate in the prison system" should have access to gender-transition treatments, Harris said in the clip. Then a narrator hammered the point home: "Even the liberal media was shocked Kamala supports taxpayer-funded sex changes for prisoners and illegal aliens."

The interview was first uncovered by Alex Pfeiffer, a former producer for Tucker Carlson's show on Fox News, who brought it to the attention of Trump campaign pollster Tony Fabrizio.* The campaign knew it had struck gold, and according to Fabrizio, the ad was created within twenty-four hours of Pfeiffer finding the clip. An analysis conducted by a super PAC aligned with Harris's campaign found that the ad shifted the race 2.7 percentage points toward Trump in markets where it was aired.[19]

In mid-October, former President Bill Clinton spent two days campaigning for Harris in North Carolina and kept getting questions about why Harris thought taxpayers should be paying for prisoners to get transgender surgeries. He had no idea what the voters were talking about, but figured they were getting their information from a Trump ad. He called Jen O'Malley Dillon, who was now Harris's campaign manager, to tell her what he was hearing and suggest that Harris respond to the ad, because it was doing real damage.

The Harris team knew how much money the Trump campaign and its affiliated super PAC were spending to run the ad. I later learned that the Harris campaign *had* created an ad responding to it, pointing out that the policy that enabled prisoners to receive transgender surgeries had been on the books while Trump was president. But the ad didn't perform well when tested by a focus group, and it was never aired.

When Bret Baier had asked Harris about her position on the issue during their Fox News interview, however, the Democratic nominee fell back on the same response that had proved ineffective in focus groups. "I will follow the law, and it's a law that Donald Trump actually followed," she said. "I think, frankly, that ad from the Trump campaign is a little bit of like throwing stones when you're living in a glass house."

"The Trump aides say that he never advocated for that prison

*Pfeiffer would go on to be named the Trump administration's principal deputy communications director.

policy, and no gender-transition surgeries happened during his presidency," Baier responded.

"Well, you know what, you've got to take responsibility for what happened in your administration," Harris said.

"Yeah," Baier responded. "No surgeries happened in his presidency."

Harris had no good answer for Baier, because she had no good answer on the topic more broadly. Why *did* she tell a transgender activist in 2019 that she thought taxpayers should pay for illegal immigrants' gender-transition surgeries? Did she still believe that? If not, when did she change her mind, and why?

Harris could never come right out and admit what was likely the truth—she had concluded that the issue was politically helpful in 2019 and politically harmful in 2024—but a senior advisor to her campaign later told me that Harris decided she would try to mitigate the damage on the issue by saying she was opposed to biological men playing in women's sports if she was asked about the topic. But in the final weeks of the campaign, no interviewer or reporter asked her that question, perhaps because even then Harris rarely held open press conferences and had only limited interactions with the journalists covering her campaign.

And so in the end, neither Harris nor her campaign did anything to address the most ubiquitous and devastating attack ad against her.

During the final days of the race, Harris's advisors touted the campaign's massive get-out-the-vote efforts as the key to victory, giving reporters daily updates on the millions of doors volunteers had knocked on and text messages they had sent encouraging swing state voters to go to the polls on Election Day.

The Harris team eventually boasted of knocking on fifty million doors, and financial disclosure reports later showed that they spent more than $275 million in the final weeks of the campaign.[20] The Trump campaign, meanwhile, had essentially outsourced its get-out-the-vote efforts to Elon Musk and Charlie Kirk, the founder of the Turning Point USA campus organization. Neither man had run a political operation on the scale of a presidential campaign, but thanks to Musk, what they lacked in experience they made up for in money.

Days after Musk endorsed Trump, *The Wall Street Journal* reported that the tech mogul planned to spend $45 million a month to support the president's campaign via a super PAC.[21] The sudden surge of cash from a single donor would be unprecedented, and within days, Musk shot down the reports as ridiculous. "I am not donating $45 million a month to Trump" he said in an interview with conservative commentator Jordan Peterson.[22]

"I am making some donations to America PAC, but at a much lower level," he posted on X. "The key values of the PAC are supporting a meritocracy & individual freedom."[23]

By the end of the year, though, it was clear Musk was spending much *more* than $45 million a month to help elect Trump. According to Federal Election Commission filings, Musk had spent a whopping $288 million supporting Trump and, to a lesser extent, other Republican candidates—an average of more than $70 million per month.[24]

In the final weeks of the election, Musk's PAC was burning through so much cash that it resorted to simply giving it away. Beginning in mid-October, America PAC claimed it would start giving out $1 million every day to a randomly selected swing-state voter who signed a petition online "in support of the Constitution, especially freedom of speech and the right to bear arms."

"So, I have a surprise for you, which is that we are going to be awarding a million dollars randomly to people who have signed the petition every day from now until the election," Musk told a crowd in Pennsylvania on October 19.

Democrats immediately criticized the plan, arguing it was tantamount to buying votes in the final days of the election. The gambit also prompted local and federal investigations. Days before the election, Philadelphia District Attorney Larry Krasner sued Musk for conducting an illegal lottery, forcing Musk's representatives to reveal the process for the million-dollar giveaways in court.

But one day before the election, a Philadelphia judge allowed the effort to proceed, in part because Musk's representatives admitted in court that the giveaways were built on a lie. Musk's giveaway wasn't technically a lottery, because "winners" were not random; they were vetted by America PAC officials and chosen based on their potential effectiveness as spokespeople for Musk's organization.

"The $1 million recipients are not chosen by chance," Musk's lawyer Chris Gober explained in court. "We know exactly who will be announced as the $1 million recipient today and tomorrow."[25]

"The opportunity to earn," added Chris Young, the treasurer of Musk's super PAC, "is different from the chance to win."[26]

Musk's burgeoning political operation dealt with some other growing pains in the weeks before the election, as paid contractors spread across battleground states to campaign door-to-door for Trump. According to reporting from *Wired*, some door knockers who were part of the operation were flown to Michigan, driven around the state in the back of a U-Haul van, forced to meet quotas to have their housing paid for, and didn't even know they were helping elect Trump.[27] Some Harris campaign officials read the reports with glee, viewing Musk's inept get-out-the-vote effort as a sign Harris could still come out ahead on Election Day.

But as it turned out, there was some method to Musk's madness. His efforts focused largely on people who don't usually vote—or who had never voted before—assuming, correctly, that most of them would vote for Trump if they made it to the polls. The strategy was unusual in campaign circles—the final days of the race had historically been about activating voters campaigns knew they could count on—but America PAC's efforts with Amish communities, for example, may have paid dividends in Pennsylvania. The operation gave financial support for local organizers, providing them with computers, Starlink satellite internet access, and drivers to take voters to the polls.[28]

Perhaps more consequential were the secretive ad campaigns supported by Musk. In the month before the election, for example, Musk donated more than $20 million to a shadowy entity named RBG PAC, which pumped out ads intended to reassure voters that Trump's abortion position was in line with that of Ruth Bader Ginsburg, the late Supreme Court justice.[29] Ginsburg's granddaughter told *The New York Times* that the effort was "appalling" and "an affront" to her grandmother's legacy.[30]

In Jewish and Muslim communities, Musk bankrolled competing ads that offered diametrically opposing views of Vice President Kamala Harris's Middle East policies. In areas of Michigan with large Arab and Muslim populations, a PAC funded by Musk ran ads touting Harris's reliable support for Israel. The PAC sent out mail ads purportedly in support of Harris, arguing that she "leans on Jewish husband Doug Emhoff to advise on high-level pro-Israel policies" and describing the vice president and second gentleman as "the ultimate pro-Israel power couple."[31]

Voters in Pennsylvania were targeted by the same PAC with an entirely different message. "In Jewish communities throughout America, questions are being asked: Why did Kamala Harris support denying Israel the weapons needed to defeat the Hamas terrorists who massacred thousands?" the narrator in one video ominously said. "And why did Harris show sympathy for college protesters who are rabidly antisemitic?"[32]

Even with Musk dumping millions into the campaign, Harris had a larger and more experienced army of political operatives and volunteers reaching out to voters in the battleground states, relentlessly knocking on doors, making phone calls, and sending potential voters multiple text messages every day. Harris's aides entered the final days of the election nervous but confident about the Democrat's chances because they thought their campaign's ground game—the person-to-person effort to get people out to vote—was superior.

Indeed, if you were counting the number of door knocks, phone calls, and text messages, Harris was winning. But as I listened to the Harris campaign summarizing their get-out-the vote effort on Election Day, I couldn't help but wonder: Does anybody really like it when strangers knock on their door or when their phone gets bombarded with unsolicited text messages? Was the Harris campaign's highly touted grand game motivating voters, or just annoying them?*

*But in the end, voter turnout was neither the problem nor the solution for Kamala Harris. After the election, a study by the nonpartisan Pew Research Center showed that people who didn't vote preferred Trump by an even larger margin than those who voted. The bottom line: If every single eligible voter in America cast a ballot, it's likely Trump's victory would have been bigger than it was.

CHAPTER FIFTEEN

MEET THE NEW BOSS

As the votes were counted on election night, an inmate at the Tallahatchie County Correctional Facility in Tutwiler, Mississippi, lay on the floor of his prison cell. He pressed his ear against the crack under the heavy metal door, straining to hear the sound emanating from a television in the nearby guard station. There were few people in the world who had more personally riding on the results of the election than this inmate. His name: Enrique Tarrio. A leader of the Proud Boys militia group, Tarrio was less than two years into the twenty-two-year prison sentence he received after being convicted of seditious conspiracy against the United States for his role in the January 6 attack on the US Capitol.

There were hundreds of January 6 defendants, but prosecutors considered Tarrio to be the worst of the worst—and he was sentenced accordingly. Although he wasn't on the Capitol grounds that day—he had been arrested forty-eight hours earlier on unrelated charges and ordered to leave Washington—the Justice Department said he organized and inspired the most violent of the men who charged into the building wearing body armor and tactical gear, smashing windows, and beating police officers along the way. As Tarrio lay on the floor straining to hear the election night coverage, he believed the results would determine whether he would spend the next two decades of his life in prison or be set free.

"If Trump won, I was one hundred percent certain he would give me a pardon," Tarrio later told me.[1]

Tarrio had been listening to the election returns on a small transistor radio he had bought from the prison commissary, but its single AAA battery died sometime around 11 p.m., before it became clear who would win. Tarrio called out to the nearby prison guards and pleaded with them to turn up the sound on the television they were watching, and one of them—"one hundred percent MAGA," Tarrio told me—obliged. Before long, the voices of CNN anchors could be heard echoing down the concrete hall of his cellblock. At 2:05 a.m., CNN projected Trump as the winner of Pennsylvania, and Tarrio knew the election was effectively over.* He leapt to his feet and began banging on the door of his cell in celebration, quickly joined by his fellow inmates, who had come to know him as one of the ringleaders of the January 6 attack. Within minutes, the prison was erupting with the noise of inmates hollering and pounding on their enclosures to mark Donald Trump's victory over Kamala Harris.

While Enrique Tarrio was spending the night in prison, the world's richest man, Elon Musk, was settling in a few hundred miles away at

*Fox News had projected Trump the winner at 1:46 a.m., but Tarrio had no way of knowing that from his prison cell.

Mar-a-Lago, where he would be a live-in guest for most of the next two and a half months.

"Let me tell you, we have a new star," Trump proclaimed in his election night victory speech at the Palm Beach Convention Center in West Palm Beach, Florida. "A star is born, Elon. No, he is. Now he's an amazing guy."

Musk had already had dinner with Trump earlier that night on the patio at Mar-a-Lago, and he'd finagled his way into the Trump family's election night photo alongside the president-elect, all of his children, and half a dozen grandchildren. Musk—a newcomer to Republican politics who had originally supported Ron DeSantis in the Republican presidential primary—seemed to have firmly entrenched himself in Trump's inner circle. As Donald Trump Jr.'s seventeen-year-old daughter Kai would put it in a social media post a few days later, Musk was "achieving uncle status 😂."[2]

He would eventually have a seismic falling-out with Trump, but after the election, Musk carried himself around Mar-a-Lago like a man who had made Trump's victory possible. After all, he had spent nearly $300 million helping elect Trump and Republican congressional candidates. As Musk would later say, "Without me, Trump would have lost the election."[3]

In a measure of his newfound prominence, Musk joined Trump for at least two calls with foreign leaders on November 6, 2024, the day after the election: one with Turkish President Recep Tayyip Erdoğan, and one with Ukrainian President Volodymyr Zelensky. At one point during the latter call, Trump handed the phone over to Musk so Zelensky could personally thank the SpaceX CEO for his company's Starlink internet service, which had made the call from his war-battered country possible.

Trump got off to a quick start staffing his second administration, announcing on November 7 that Susie Wiles, the co-chair of his campaign, would become the first woman to serve as White House chief of staff. But much of the plan for what he would do upon taking office was already in place. The morning after the election, Trump's policy advisors, including future deputy chief of staff Stephen Miller, distributed a document to the transition team titled "50+ Potential 'Day One' Actions." While not all "day one" priorities, the list included many executive orders that Trump would, in fact, go on to sign early in his second term, including:

- "Free January 6 political prisoners"
- "Begin the largest deportation operation in American History"
- "Implement tariffs"
- "Create Government Efficiency Commission"
- "Defund colleges that do not take appropriate actions" to fight antisemitism

Miller had been planning for Trump's second term for months, if not years. In the transition team's policy meetings, he explained that the president would rely on an obscure piece of legislation—the Alien Enemies Act of 1789, which hadn't been invoked since World War II—to deport a massive number of undocumented immigrants without getting bogged down by inconveniences like deportation hearings and other procedural protections. The "Day One" list also called for the firing of several high-ranking government officials who would traditionally continue serving in a new administration, including FBI Director Christopher Wray, special counsel Jack Smith, and Securities and Exchange Commission chairman Gary Gensler. All three men saw the writing on the wall and resigned from their posts before Trump took office.

The Trump transition team's official office was situated a few miles away from Mar-a-Lago—in what had been the campaign's headquarters—but the key decisions that would shape the incoming administration were being made within the ornate and gold-accented walls of Trump's private club. As Musk and virtually everyone else looking to influence the president-elect or get a top job knew, proximity to Trump mattered more than anything else. As always, the key was to be the last person to speak with him before he made a decision.

Take, for example, Trump's selection of Susie Wiles as his chief of staff. While the president-elect was meeting with his campaign co-chair on November 7 to offer her the job, two other contenders, Linda McMahon and Brooke Rollins, rushed over to Mar-a-Lago in a last-ditch effort to derail the pick. Various Trump aides, most of whom had worked for Wiles during the campaign, managed to impede the two women on their way to see Trump. They were delayed by various transition officials coming over to talk to them and even a phone call with Vice President-elect JD Vance. By the time McMahon and Rollins could get in to see Trump, it was too late. He had already asked Wiles to be chief of staff. They would have to settle instead for secretary of education and secretary of agriculture, respectively.

Another Trump ally who quickly realized he'd need to prioritize time at Mar-a-Lago during the transition was Robert F. Kennedy Jr. The day after the election, Kennedy and his entourage—far-right pundit Tucker Carlson, former Democratic Representative Tulsi Gabbard, and Amaryllis Fox Kennedy, his daughter-in-law and former campaign manager—spent at least eight hours at Trump's club. Joe Biden was still the president, but for all intents and purposes,

1100 South Ocean Boulevard in Palm Beach was the center of the political universe.

So much so that Howard Lutnick—Trump's billionaire friend from New York, who was leading the transition—ended up working primarily from Mar-a-Lago. Besides Trump's office on the second floor, the club has very few workspaces, so Lutnick set up his operation in the closest thing to a private meeting area: the "Tea Room," located next to the living room that operated as the main lobby. The Tea Room, added to the club after Trump purchased the property in 1985, is relatively modern and bland compared with the rest of the club, but it did the job.

Lutnick was the chairman of Cantor Fitzgerald, the New York–based financial firm that was housed in the North Tower of the World Trade Center when it was attacked on September 11. Nearly 660 of its employees were killed that day, including Lutnick's younger brother, Gary. Lutnick had long been a Democrat—he hosted a fundraiser for Hillary Clinton in 2015—but by 2024, he was all in for Trump.[4] One month after the Republican National Convention, Trump named him co-chair of his presidential transition team, a role he would share with Linda McMahon, a fellow billionaire and co-founder of World Wrestling Entertainment.

Trump had little interest in the transition, but Lutnick took the job seriously, methodically compiling lists of names to fill various cabinet positions and other key posts. The suggestions were strictly notional—Kevin McCarthy was listed as a potential secretary of state and Aileen Cannon, the Florida judge who had thrown out the classified documents case against Trump, was named as a potential attorney general—because Trump, a bit superstitious about making plans before winning the election, didn't want anything to do with the transition until he was president-elect. "I don't like to talk about transition until I win," Trump told me in late October when I asked him about the planning that was underway. "When we win, you and I will talk about it. But until you win, I don't like talking about transition."[5]

Since Congress passed the Presidential Transition Act of 1963, major-party presidential nominees have generally set up formal transition operations months before their respective elections, complete with office space provided by the federal government and access to FBI resources for the purpose of conducting background checks on potential cabinet nominees. The idea is to allow the president-elect to hit the ground running after his or her victory in November and get a head start on the massive task of setting up an administration.

In 2016, the Trump transition team was set up in federal government offices just two blocks from the White House—but Trump himself ultimately ignored the vast majority of the work those staffers did. Eight years later, Trump initially declined federal transition assistance, including not only the office space but the ability to ask the FBI to conduct background checks on potential appointees.* Why? In part because he didn't trust the FBI, and in part because accepting federal transition assistance also required accepting limits on the amount of outside money he could raise for the effort. As a result, Lutnick and his team were operating entirely on their own. In the weeks leading up to the election, they were working primarily out of the Cantor Fitzgerald offices in midtown Manhattan.

Within hours of Trump's victory, however, Lutnick had made his

*Trump did eventually sign an agreement that enabled his transition team to request FBI background checks, but not until December 3—well after he had announced most of his cabinet picks.

way to Mar-a-Lago, working in the Tea Room, which was just steps away from the bar and outdoor patio by the swimming pool. He had a conference table installed in the Tea Room, as well as several large television screens that he used for presentations to Trump about potential nominees. One monitor would display bullet points—no more than five—describing a candidate's qualifications, while a second screen would be loaded up with video clips of his or her recent TV appearances. A third monitor would feature a large photograph of the candidate—a headshot—so that Trump could visualize whether he or she looked the part; whether they were, in Trump's mind, out of "central casting."

Although he hadn't wanted to think or talk much about the transition before the election, Trump clearly had more opinions about who would serve in his second administration than he'd had about who would serve in his first. In 2016, when he was still new to Republican politics, Trump was forced to rely on advice from others as he scrambled to staff the federal government. That's how a number of people who were not ideologically aligned with Trump or unflinchingly loyal to him—James Mattis, Gary Cohn, Mike Pompeo, Rex Tillerson, Nikki Haley, John Kelly—ended up with top roles in his first administration.

Trump wasn't going to let that happen again. "The difference between now and before is I know everybody now, and when I first came I knew nobody," Trump told me during a phone conversation on October 21, 2024. "We had a lot of great people. But I didn't know people. Had to rely on recommendations. Now I know people, so it's good." Days after that call, he would make a seemingly unprompted announcement on Truth Social: "I will not be inviting former Ambassador Nikki Haley, or former Secretary of State Mike Pompeo, to join the Trump Administration, which is currently in formation."[6]

Although Trump was generally only selecting people he knew personally for high-level roles, they still needed to be vetted. And without access to FBI background checks, Lutnick scrambled to cobble together a team of lawyers tasked with digging into the personal histories of potential candidates for high-level positions in the incoming administration. The finalists would be summoned to Mar-a-Lago and meet with Trump for an in-person interview in his office upstairs. In the weeks after the election, the Mar-a-Lago living room became the crossroads of the MAGA world.

On any given day, you could spot billionaire donors, Republican politicians, right-wing pundits, pro-Trump influencers, and other would-be cabinet secretaries hustling in and out or just hanging around. One of those seen regularly at Mar-a-Lago in the weeks after the election was Kash Patel, a deeply committed Trump loyalist who served in the first administration and wrote three children's books about Donald Trump's battles with his political enemies (a trilogy titled *The Plot Against the King*). Patel would often be seen hanging around the club's living room, ready whenever Trump walked by to make his pitch to be the director of the FBI. Paul Manafort, the former chairman of Trump's 2016 campaign who did time in prison for tax and bank fraud, was spotted at the club, too, bringing his own candidate to be FBI director.

Some aspiring candidates for top jobs in Trump's White House struggled with the president-elect's process. One prospective cabinet secretary, for example, flew to Palm Beach from Texas a few days after the election because he had been told to be ready to meet with

Trump at any time. This person, a business leader and major Republican donor who had served in the first Trump administration and who spoke to me on the condition that I not reveal his name, told me he stayed at a nearby hotel for two days before finally being invited to see Trump the following morning at 9:30 a.m. Upon showing up at Mar-a-Lago, he sat down on a couch in the living room next to a candidate for attorney general—and he waited. Several other potential nominees came and went over the next several hours, all waiting for an audience with the president-elect.

It wasn't until 12:30 p.m. that this potential cabinet member was called in to see Trump. The meeting went well, he later told me, but he was taken aback when the president-elect started asking him questions about a different role than the one he had been talking to Lutnick and the transition team about.

One of the people this cabinet finalist had been sitting near in the Mar-a-Lago living room downstairs was a Fox News weekend anchor, whom he assumed was in town to conduct a television interview with Trump. Like the rest of the world, he was stunned to hear later that night that the president-elect would be nominating that Fox News weekend anchor—Pete Hegseth—to serve as secretary of defense.

In fact, the only person involved with the Trump transition team who had been seriously considering Hegseth as a candidate to run the Pentagon seemed to be Trump himself. Hegseth had served honorably in the Army—including combat tours in Iraq and Afghanistan—and he had degrees from both Princeton and Harvard, but for most of the past decade, he had been a pro-Trump talking head on Fox News, most recently as the co-anchor of one Trump's favorite programs, *Fox & Friends Weekend*. He hadn't been considered by the transition team for any senior government position, let alone for defense secretary. For that role, Lutnick's operation had compiled a list of candidates that included Florida Governor Ron DeSantis and US Senator Joni Ernst from Iowa, a former commander in the US Army Reserve with more than twenty years of service under her belt and a widely respected member of the Senate Armed Services Committee.

Instead, Trump did what he so often does and went with his gut, selecting the guy he liked to watch on TV who would stand up to the military leaders Trump believed had undermined him in the final months of his first administration. The lack of any background check, however, created some serious complications for Trump and his team. Hegseth would eventually be confirmed by the Senate—barely, with Vice President JD Vance breaking a 50–50 tie—but not before a devastating string of allegations about his past came to light, almost all of them unknown by the Trump transition team.

Two days after Trump announced his intent to nominate Hegseth, *Vanity Fair* reported that the Trump transition team was scrambling to investigate a sexual assault allegation from several years earlier.[7] Hegseth, who'd been married three times before turning forty years old, maintained the encounter was consensual, but local police investigated the incident at the time, and Hegseth's own lawyer confirmed that Hegseth had paid the accuser a settlement as part of a nondisclosure agreement.[8] Weeks later, *The New Yorker* published a story detailing Hegseth's alleged financial mismanagement and struggles with alcohol while president of Concerned Veterans for America and as a host on Fox News.[9] In late November, *The New York Times* obtained an email that Hegseth's own mother had sent him in 2018. "You are an abuser of women—that is the ugly truth and I have no respect for any man that belittles, lies, cheats, sleeps around and uses women for his own power and ego," it read. "On behalf of all the women (and I know it's many) you have abused in some way, I say... get some help and take an honest look at yourself."[10]

Mrs. Hegseth told the *Times* that she had immediately followed up to apologize to her son, because she had fired off the original email "in anger, with emotion."[11]

The controversy surrounding Hegseth overshadowed another cabinet pick Trump had made earlier on the same day: South Dakota Governor Kristi Noem to be secretary of Homeland Security. Like Hegseth, Noem had not been on the transition team's list of possible candidates and had not gone through vetting for the job. When a surprised Trump advisor asked the president-elect why he had decided to nominate Noem to be secretary of Homeland Security, he had a simple answer. "I did it for Corey," he said. "It's the only thing Corey asked me for."

Trump was referring to Corey Lewandowski, the Republican operative who had served as his first of three campaign managers during his 2016 run for the White House. Lewandowski was not well liked among Trump's advisors, but his loyalty to Trump had never wavered—and he had developed a close personal relationship with Governor Noem.

That Trump would offer Noem a high-profile job was no surprise. She had long been a defender of his, and in 2020 she had gifted him a model of Mount Rushmore with five faces etched into the side: George Washington's, Thomas Jefferson's, Teddy Roosevelt's, Abraham Lincoln's, and... Donald Trump's.[12] The former president kept it on display in his Mar-a-Lago office for years.

But secretary of the Department of Homeland Security is one of the most consequential positions in any presidential administration, and it would only take on even more importance in Trump's, given the agenda he was planning to pursue. And the reviews of Noem's tenure as governor of South Dakota were mixed at best, marked by ethics concerns and allegations she used taxpayer resources to boost her national political profile. She had so alienated South Dakota's Native American leaders that all nine of the nationally recognized tribes banned her from their lands, effectively forbidding the governor from entering approximately 17 percent of the state.[13] And then there was the controversy surrounding a book she published in 2024, in which she wrote about shooting her family's fourteen-month-old dog Cricket because she was misbehaving and stated that she had met with North Korean leader Kim Jong Un (she later acknowledged no such meeting happened).

Was Noem really qualified to run the sprawling agency that includes Immigration and Customs Enforcement (ICE), the Federal Emergency Management Agency (FEMA), the Transportation Security Administration (TSA), the Cybersecurity and Infrastructure Security Agency (CISA), and the Secret Service? Even some of Trump's closest allies were uncomfortable with putting her in charge of all that.

"We still got the global war on terror," an exasperated Steve Bannon told me two days after Trump made the announcement. "She runs the whole thing? She runs the fucking Secret Service? It's all of it. It's the global war on terror. It's all that. What are you talking about? She's never been in law enforcement!"

But Bannon didn't put the blame on Trump for making what he considered a terrible choice. He blamed Lewandowski for convincing the president-elect to do it.

“This motherfucker asked for somebody who’s obviously unqualified—and it’s dangerous,” Bannon said. “This is dangerous. What are you doing?”

Pete Hegseth was far from the only Fox News personality to be angling for a job in the second Trump administration—and far from the only one to eventually make it into government.* Sean Duffy, a former Republican member of Congress and Fox Business anchor, was interested in a role, and Trump enjoyed watching him on television. More importantly, Trump was a big fan of Duffy’s wife, Rachel Campos-Duffy, who had been working alongside Hegseth as the co-host of *Fox & Friends Weekend*.

Duffy’s top choice for a cabinet role was US Ambassador to the United Nations. He had no foreign policy or diplomatic experience, but he found the job appealing for a completely unrelated, logistical reason: It was based in New York, due to the location of the UN headquarters. Not only would he not have to uproot his nine children and move to Washington, DC, but Rachel could continue anchoring *Fox & Friends Weekend* from the show’s studios in Manhattan.

*As of late May 2025, the Fox-to-White House pipeline included Defense Secretary Pete Hegseth, Transportation Secretary Sean Duffy, Director of National Intelligence Tulsi Gabbard, former National Security Advisor Mike Waltz, special envoy for Ukraine and Russia Keith Kellogg, ambassador to Israel Mike Huckabee, State Department spokeswoman Tammy Bruce, ambassador to Greece Kimberly Guilfoyle, deputy special envoy to the Middle East Morgan Ortagus, US attorney for the District of Columbia Jeanine Pirro, and senior counsel to the Assistant Attorney General for the Civil Rights Division of the Justice Department Leo Terrell. Trump also appointed Maria Bartiromo and Laura Ingraham to the board of the Kennedy Center for the Performing Arts, and Mark Levin to the Homeland Security Advisory Council.

Alas, Trump had already decided to offer the United Nations job to Representative Elise Stefanik.*

Reince Priebus, Trump's former White House chief of staff, suggested that Trump make Duffy secretary of transportation instead. This was an odd recommendation. Duffy had a colorful biography—in addition to his Fox Business experience, he had been a reality TV star on MTV's *Real World*, served four terms in the House of Representatives, won three lumberjack world championships, and worked as a local prosecutor in Wisconsin and a lobbyist in Washington—but he had no relevant experience for the job. When Trump asked a friend of Duffy's if he knew anything about transportation, the friend answered, "Of course he does, he has nine kids!" Moving a family that large around, the friend joked, requires at least some transportation expertise.

Unsurprisingly, Duffy's name had not been on the transition's list of possible transportation secretaries. Lutnick had recommended a former senior executive at Uber named Emil Michael for the role, and Elon Musk had seconded that suggestion, believing Michael's experience at a big tech company that had revolutionized urban transportation would make him an ideal candidate to shake up the federal agency. Trump, however, had never heard of the guy—and that made him a nonstarter.

When Lutnick found out Trump was leaning toward Duffy for the role, he tried to shut the idea down. Making a case against him on the

---

*Trump tapped Stefanik to serve as the US ambassador to the United Nations, but in March 2025 he withdrew her nomination due to concerns about Republicans' narrow majority in the House of Representatives. If she were confirmed, her seat in upstate New York would remain vacant until it could be filled in a special election—which was not guaranteed to go the GOP's way. Instead, Trump decided to remove Mike Waltz as his national security advisor and renominate him for the UN role.

merits wasn't working—*sir, the man has no relevant experience*—so Lutnick tried to appeal to the president-elect's ego instead, tasking his team with searching through Duffy's hundreds of television appearances to find any criticism of Trump. It took a while, as Duffy and his wife, Rachel, were unabashed Trump enthusiasts and had been for years. Lutnick's team had to go back nearly a decade—to the early days of the 2016 Republican presidential primary—to find anything Duffy had said that was remotely negative about Donald Trump. He finally found a September 2015 interview in which the then-congressman had said he didn't believe Trump was a real conservative and didn't think he would win the party's nomination.[14] But even back then, Duffy had praised Trump for "boldly speaking and saying things that the conservative wing wished that their leaders would say."

As weak as Lutnick's effort to dig up dirt turned out to be, that one stray comment from almost ten years earlier nearly cost Duffy the job. Trump, reconsidering the pick, called Duffy and his wife, Rachel, and they were able to convince the president-elect that Sean had long since changed his views on Trump's conservative bona fides. On November 18, Trump made his decision final: "The husband of a wonderful woman, Rachel Campos-Duffy, a STAR on Fox News, and the father of nine incredible children, Sean knows how important it is for families to be able to travel safely, and with peace of mind."

In those initial weeks after the election, no decision would hold more weight for Donald Trump than who would serve as his attorney general. He believed that both Jeff Sessions and William Barr had betrayed him while serving in the role during his first administration—

Sessions for recusing himself from the Justice Department's Russia investigation; Barr for contradicting Trump's false claims of widespread election fraud in late 2020—and he wanted to ensure his next pick would prioritize loyalty above all else.

The transition team's initial list of AG candidates included several lawyers with impressive credentials: Jay Clayton, a longtime partner at Sullivan & Cromwell who had served as chairman of the Securities and Exchange Commission during Trump's first term; Robert Giuffra, another Sullivan & Cromwell partner who would go on to lead Trump's appeal of his criminal conviction in New York; and Andrew Bailey, the attorney general of Missouri who staunchly defended the former president during his legal travails in 2023 and 2024.

One by one, these finalists met with Trump in his second-floor Mar-a-Lago office, sitting across his enormous desk alongside Vice President–elect Vance, Elon Musk, and Boris Epshteyn, the Moscow-born graduate of Georgetown University Law Center who had gone to college with Trump's son Eric and whose counsel Trump had come to rely on after leaving the White House in early 2021. As Trump spoke to the candidates, he didn't seem to find quite what he wanted in an attorney general. Clayton and Giuffra had sterling credentials and either one would easily be confirmed by the Senate—but Trump wasn't looking for sterling credentials or an easy confirmation. He was looking for fealty.

He found it in Matt Gaetz.

The four-term representative from Florida was undoubtedly one of Trump's most unwavering defenders in Congress—he had even proposed making Trump Speaker of the House in early 2023—but he wasn't anywhere *near* Lutnick's lists for a job in the Trump administration. Gaetz had been the subject of a federal investigation into child sex trafficking years earlier, and although that probe was closed in early 2023 without any charges being filed, the House Ethics Committee was investigating similar allegations—and its report was about to be released.

Gaetz was a near-constant presence at Mar-a-Lago in early November, and deeply involved in the transition team's search for an attorney general. He had a law degree from William & Mary, but he wasn't exactly known in Washington for his legal prowess or law enforcement credentials. As Republican Senator Markwayne Mullin of Oklahoma, who served with Gaetz in the House, put it, "I didn't even know he was an attorney until after he was appointed attorney general."[15]

Trump made his decision official on the afternoon of November 13, 2024. "Matt will end Weaponized Government, protect our Borders, dismantle Criminal Organizations and restore Americans' badly-shattered Faith and Confidence in the Justice Department," the president-elect wrote on Truth Social.[16]

The decision to nominate Gaetz for attorney general came as a shock to just about everyone in Washington, including most of Trump's allies. But Boris Epshteyn wasn't surprised, and neither was Steve Bannon, because they knew what Trump was looking for in an AG: someone loyal who was willing to unleash the power of the Justice Department on his enemies. "The hunted are about to become the hunters," Bannon declared ominously a few days before Gaetz was selected.

That sentiment was widespread among MAGA influencers in the days following the election. "Here's my current mood," Mike Davis, a legal advisor to Trump, posted on X on November 6. "I want to drag their dead political bodies through the streets, burn them, and throw them off the wall. (Legally, politically, and financially, of course.)"[17]

Gaetz, the self-described firebrand who had helped spearhead Trump's efforts to overturn the 2020 election and Republican efforts to tarnish the Biden family's reputation, was just the guy for the job. But the effort to convince Trump of that was shrouded in secrecy. Gaetz subtly positioned himself for the job as he helped the transition team compile a list of potential candidates. Bannon spoke with Epshteyn about the push, but when they talked about Gaetz, they didn't mention his name, instead using a code word, even in private messages. Not even Trump's incoming chief of staff, Susie Wiles, knew Gaetz was under consideration.[18] If other factions within Trump's orbit caught wind of what Gaetz and his allies were planning, they would do everything they could to talk the president-elect out of it before he made anything official.

The blowback to Gaetz was intense, as everyone involved knew it would be, but Trump was prepared to dig in for an ugly fight to get his man installed at the DOJ. Republican senators were quick to voice their concerns about the nomination, as even Trump-friendly lawmakers questioned the president-elect's judgment. But as one top Trump lieutenant told me at the time, the president's inner circle had plans to ensure GOP senators fell in line by the time confirmation votes rolled around.

"The president gets to decide his cabinet. No one else. That's just the way it is," this advisor told me. "There's votes coming. And if you are on the wrong side of the vote, you're buying yourself a primary. That is all. And there's a guy named Elon Musk who is going to finance it."

Indeed, as opposition to Gaetz solidified on Capitol Hill, Musk himself tried to put pressure on wobbling Republicans. "Matt Gaetz has 3 critical assets that are needed for the AG role: a big brain, a spine of steel and an axe to grind," he wrote. "He is the Judge Dredd America needs to clean up a corrupt system and put powerful bad actors in prison. Gaetz will be our Hammer of Justice."[19]

Ultimately, however, Gaetz's personal scandals—and his history of antagonizing fellow Republicans—proved too big a hurdle for him to overcome. Once it became clear to Trump that his pick didn't have the votes—and would never have the votes—he asked him to withdraw his name from consideration. Gaetz complied, and Trump quickly announced his intent to nominate Pam Bondi, the former attorney general of Florida, instead.

"I greatly appreciate the recent efforts of Matt Gaetz in seeking approval to be Attorney General," Trump wrote on Truth Social. "He was doing very well but, at the same time, did not want to be a distraction for the Administration, for which he has much respect. Matt has a wonderful future, and I look forward to watching all of the great things he will do!"[20]

Gaetz would go on to host a show on the far-right One America News Network. But for those eight short days between his announcement as AG nominee and his withdrawal from consideration, the faction of the Republican Party represented by Bannon and Boris Epshteyn was ascendant, and Boris himself was on top of the world. He had helped select not only the attorney general but also many of the lawyers who would serve in the top ranks of the Justice Department. He'd come a long way from his days after law school as a newly minted lawyer at Milbank Tweed, one of America's oldest and most respected law firms.

Boris had worked on Trump's 2016 campaign and, for a brief time, inside the first administration. But Boris truly emerged as a key player in Trump's inner circle in the aftermath of the 2020 election, when he volunteered to help the president in his effort to overturn the results. Most major players from the White House abandoned Trump when the disgraced former president was exiled to Mar-a-Lago in early 2021, but Boris remained right by his side.

He was there on the night of the 2022 midterms, sitting next to Trump as the former president's handpicked candidates lost winnable races one by one. He was there a week later, when Trump, against the advice of many of his allies, launched his third bid for the White House from the ballroom at Mar-a-Lago. He was there in courtroom after courtroom as Trump became the first former president to be indicted—four times over.

And because he was there when times were bad, Boris had built up a tremendous amount of goodwill with the president-elect. Whenever Trump was under fire, Boris would offer him the counsel he most wanted to hear: He needed to hit back, and hit back hard. He wasn't the lead defense attorney for Trump in any of his criminal cases, but, in a way, he had a more important role: recruiting and organizing the former president's army of lawyers.

Boris is deceptively shrewd. His legal efforts helped Trump fend off an avalanche of legal trouble and, by extension, make it back to the White House. There was no question he would be by the president-elect's side as he was making decisions about his second administration.

I've known Boris for a long time, and he's never once said anything to me—on the record or off—even remotely critical of Trump. He has a booming voice, and is rarely seen in anything other than a three-piece suit with a bright pocket square. If you spend much time with him, you'll likely see him take a call and start talking in Russian. When he hangs up, he'll tell you he was talking to his mother.

He attacks the news media relentlessly, but he's gregarious and friendly when he wants to be. When in Washington, he takes most of his meetings over lunch at The Palm, an old-school steak house that has served as a gathering place for politicians and influence peddlers of all kinds for decades. On the walls of the restaurant are caricatures of famous and influential people who have dined there over the years: former presidents, Supreme Court justices, secretaries of state, congressional leaders. But as Boris will make sure to show you, there's a drawing of him, too—on the left as you walk in, right above the coatrack.

As Boris was riding high after the Gaetz nomination, his enemies within Trumpworld—and there are many of them—launched an effort to take Boris down. I began hearing unconfirmed reports of Boris using his proximity to the president-elect to enrich himself; of him shaking down potential candidates for jobs in the incoming White House for cash. A couple of people close to Trump told me they had heard that one of Trump's recent cabinet picks had paid Boris $50,000 before being selected; others said that was just one of many Boris shakedowns. I looked into the allegations and could find no proof that any such payments occurred, but the rumors were persistent—and they were coming from people close to Trump.

I was planning a trip to Palm Beach a few weeks after the election and figured I should talk to Boris about these rumors—and about the transition more broadly—directly and in person. Shortly after 8 a.m. on Saturday, November 16, I sent him a text message asking him to call me.

KARL: Good morning, Boris. Please give me a call when you have a moment.

EPSHTEYN: Text please

KARL: I'm going to be in Palm Beach weds/thurs–can we get together? And would love to stop by MAL [Mar-a-Lago]

EPSHTEYN: No

My phone rang five minutes later.

"Why do you want to meet?" Boris demanded.

"I think that's obvious," I said. "I'm going to be down there and want to get the lay of the land from you."

"I don't have the time," he said. "And I'm certainly not having journalists going to Mar-a-Lago. Also, you haven't been good to us."

Boris spent a few more minutes complaining about my reporting, but eventually agreed to meet in Palm Beach later in the week. The conversation ended with Boris telling me he had to go because I had interrupted a phone call he was having with his mother.

I flew down to West Palm Beach the following Wednesday. By Thursday morning, when I was supposed to see Boris, Matt Gaetz's brief time as Donald Trump's choice to be attorney general had come to an end, and Boris needed to push our meeting back a day.

So instead, I made a stop on a yacht docked near Mar-a-Lago. Let me explain . . .

Days earlier, Steve Bannon had told me that if I wanted to know what was truly happening with the Trump transition, I needed to go see a longtime Republican fundraiser named Caroline Wren at what he called the Alternative Transition Headquarters, a yacht docked on the Intracoastal Waterway that was serving as the *real* MAGA operation in Palm Beach, where true believers were making plans for Trump's imminent takeover of Washington. I had actually known Wren for a while; she had worked for Mitt Romney's 2012 presidential campaign before becoming a warrior in the MAGA movement.

I made my way to the private dock in a quiet neighborhood of multimillion-dollar Palm Beach mansions that was about an eight-minute drive from Mar-a-Lago. I was met by a man who introduced himself as Captain Scott, and he escorted me to the boat he operated for an affable, retired Pennsylvania coal magnate named John Rich. Rich wasn't particularly political, but he had become a member at Mar-a-Lago shortly after Trump won the presidency in 2016. He made his yacht available to the president's allies, both as a meeting place and, when needed, as a place to stay. Kari Lake, a failed Republican candidate for governor and US Senate from Arizona, would sometimes stay overnight on the boat when she came to see Trump.

The merry band of Trump supporters who had convened on John Rich's yacht in November 2024 were pushing to ensure top jobs in the incoming administration went to die-hard MAGA candidates. This was the group lobbying—and ultimately succeeding—to get Trump to tap Kash Patel as FBI director and Scott Bessent, a hedge fund manager and regular guest on Steve Bannon's *War Room* podcast, as treasury secretary. They had also been quiet boosters of the stealth, and ultimately doomed, campaign to make Matt Gaetz the next attorney general.

During the day, Rich's yacht served as a workspace for well-connected Trump operatives and a meeting place for potential candidates to serve in the administration. And after dinner at Mar-a-Lago wrapped up, a group would make its way back to the boat for the after-party.

Before long, I learned that John Rich and Captain Scott were not fans of Boris Epshteyn—not for political reasons, but for personal ones. A few nights before I arrived in Palm Beach, Rich was having dinner at Mar-a-Lago, as usual, when he saw Trump at his table on the club's patio with Elon Musk. As dinner was winding down, Rich decided to head over to offer Musk a gift. Rich owns an impeccably restored electric car from 1912 that originally belonged to Thomas Edison, and he figured that the man who owned Tesla and brought electric cars into the twenty-first century would appreciate it. But as the coal magnate walked over to make the offer, he was intercepted by Boris, who informed him that neither Musk nor Trump wanted to be bothered. Rich was taken aback—*who was this guy to tell him what to do?*—and stormed out of the club. He kept his Thomas Edison electric car.

On Friday morning, I headed to the Four Seasons hotel in Palm Beach for my meeting with Boris. We were scheduled to meet at 10 a.m., but at 10:15, Boris let me know he was running late and asked me to wait for him at a small table down a hallway away from the lobby. He still hadn't arrived by 11 a.m., so I gave him a call. He told me he needed to cancel.

I offered to stick around for a while and suggested Boris stop by whenever he had a few minutes. He agreed, saying he'd try to be there by 2:15 p.m. But he insisted I leave the Four Seasons and return a few hours later.

What I didn't realize at the time was that Boris was facing withering attacks from within Trump's inner circle. Some of those unconfirmed allegations of grifting were about to be reported by a right-wing writer named John Solomon in his news outlet, *Just the News*. Solomon had informed the Trump transition team the previous day that he had evidence—including text messages—of Boris trying to extract money from candidates for jobs in the incoming administration, including Scott Bessent, the future treasury secretary.

Solomon didn't publish his article for several more days, but his call to Trump's team had prompted an internal investigation headed up by David Warrington, the Trump campaign's top attorney and the future White House counsel. As Warrington began his probe, he wrote a confidential memo to President-elect Trump, which has been described to me in detail.

"You asked us to investigate reports of Boris Epshteyn using his proximity to you and your office for personal financial gain," the memo begins, giving a status update of the investigation. So far, Warrington wrote, his team had compiled sworn statements and conducted interviews with more than a half-dozen people "who have reported dealings with Epshteyn and with many more to interview." The memo goes on to detail two of those individuals "who were approached by Epshteyn for payments in exchange for his influence." One of those two was Scott Bessent.

The memo alleged that Boris first approached Bessent in February 2024 about paying him "a monthly stipend of $30-40k" to promote him around Mar-a-Lago. Bessent refused, according to Warrington, and later called his press consultant to say, "I can't believe this asshole just shook me down." The memo detailed a second incident, in which Boris allegedly tried to get Bessent to invest $10 million in a three-on-three basketball league.

According to the memo, Bessent had become convinced in the days after the election that, because he had not paid him off, Boris was "knifing" him and trying to destroy his prospects of becoming treasury secretary. At the suggestion of JD Vance's team, Bessent set up a call with Boris in an effort to confirm his suspicions, asking Trump's aide if he would help him become the president's choice for the role. Warrington's memo describes what allegedly happened next, with Boris telling Bessent "it was 'Too late today. You should have done this months ago' and 'you should have done what I told you' and that he was 'Boris Fucking Epshteyn.'"

Warrington's memo ended with a recommendation that Trump fire Boris and cease any contact with him:

> Over the course of the interviews a pattern of behavior has become clear. Epshteyn is using his proximity to President Trump for personal financial gain creating conflicts-of-interest. The mechanics of Epshteyn's scheme take the form of demands for payments for "consulting" in exchange for promoting individuals or businesses relying on Epshteyn's relationship with President Trump. Even if there were legitimate services being provided by Epshteyn, and we have yet to find any evidence of any bona-fide business services that he has provided to anyone, most of the activities would likely constitute illegal lobbying efforts.
>
> Epshteyn's conduct must be stopped and his employment and proximity to President Trump should be terminated. Otherwise, his conduct will likely lead to, at best a scandal involving the incoming Trump Administration, and at worst could lead to criminal indictments.

I didn't have any of these details when Boris and I finally sat down at the Four Seasons that day. He had nothing to say on the record other than to insist that he had done nothing wrong and that others in Trump's circle were lying about him. Despite all the turmoil, he seemed as confident as ever. A major effort to push him out of the president-elect's orbit was underway, but Boris had no intention of going voluntarily.

When John Solomon finally published his article a few days later, it included an interview with Trump himself, who said he was unaware that any staffer on his payroll was soliciting consulting fees from people seeking jobs in his administration and that he would not condone that kind of behavior. "I suppose every president has people around them who try to make money off them on the outside. It's a shame, but it happens," he told Solomon. "But no one working for me in any capacity should be looking to make money. They should only be here to Make America Great Again."[21]

"No one can promise any endorsement or nomination except me," Trump added. "I make these decisions on my own, period."

Solomon's article also included a firm denial from Boris, which had been forwarded to him by a spokesperson for the Trump transition. "I am honored to work for President Trump and with his team," it read. "These fake claims are false and defamatory and will not distract us from Making America Great Again."

After Solomon broke the news about the allegations against Boris, several other news organizations—including CNN and *The New York Times*—confirmed much of what Solomon had reported, leading Democratic Congressman Jamie Raskin to demand the Trump transition team turn over documents related to the allegations to the House Oversight Committee. Democratic Senators Dick Durbin and Sheldon Whitehouse also wrote to the Trump transition team demanding nominees turn over all communications they'd had with

Boris Epshteyn. The Trump team ignored the letters, and not a single senator asked a question about Boris during confirmation hearings for cabinet nominees.*

Boris had weathered the storm. Despite a monumental effort by his enemies to drive a wedge between him and the president-elect, he would remain by Trump's side.

When January 20 rolled around, Epshteyn didn't go work inside the Trump White House, opting instead for an arguably more valuable position on the outside as President Trump's all-purpose legal advisor.

It would be Boris, for example, who spearheaded Trump's lawsuits against media companies, including ABC, and the negotiations with the many law firms Trump targeted with his executive orders. These efforts were controversial, of course, but they were also incredibly lucrative, securing millions of dollars in settlements for Trump's political entities and the promise of hundreds of millions more in pro bono legal work for conservative causes.

Amid the frenzy of activity during Trump's first several months in office, Trump spoke to Boris virtually every day—and often several times a day. He was a regular visitor at the White House and the Department of Justice and was often spotted traveling with the president on Air Force One. Despite it all, he remained as important as ever to Donald Trump. As he had reminded Scott Bessent during the transition, he was "Boris Fucking Epshteyn."

---

*Democratic Senator Ron Wyden did, however, ask Scott Bessent about the alleged shakedown when he had a one-on-one meeting with him before his confirmation hearing to be Treasury secretary. According to Wyden, Bessent told him Boris "talked to him about payments for 'public relations'—a sleazy way of pitching an obvious quid-pro-quo." But later, in response to written questions from Wyden, Bessent revised his answer, saying nobody ever asked him about payments in exchange for an appointment.

CHAPTER SIXTEEN

WEAPONIZED

On January 3, 2025—just seventeen days before Donald Trump would be sworn in as president—his two top personal lawyers were summoned to an unmarked glass building behind Union Station in Washington, DC. The building, a generic-looking office complex, was located in a nondescript part of Washington about a dozen blocks from the US Capitol. Although there were no identifying signs outside, the building was a special annex of the Justice Department that housed the legal team conducting the most politically charged federal prosecution in American history.

Special counsel Jack Smith and his staff of more than three dozen prosecutors and FBI agents had been operating out of this annex for more than two years, conducting an investigation that might have landed Trump in prison had he not been elected president of the United States for a second time on November 5, 2024. Before the election, Smith's team had convinced grand juries in Florida and in

Washington to indict Donald Trump on serious charges that, if juries convicted, could have resulted in the former president spending the rest of his life in prison.

The lawyers—Todd Blanche and Emil Bove—had been summoned to the special counsel's offices to review Jack Smith's final report. Though Smith had secured four indictments of the former president, the election had effectively ended the special counsel's prosecution of Trump. Long-standing Justice Department policy forbids the prosecution of a sitting president. And even if it didn't, Trump had already declared his intention to fire Smith as soon as he took office.

Smith recognized this obvious reality and began winding down his cases hours after it became clear Trump had won the election.

But while Smith's prosecution was over, he still had one final act to play out. Like every special counsel had done before him, Smith planned to write a final report summarizing his investigation. The report was divided into two sections: one detailing evidence that Trump had illegally attempted to overturn the 2020 presidential election with a series of actions culminating in the attack on the Capitol on January 6, 2021, and the other detailing evidence Trump had illegally removed some of the nation's most sensitive national security secrets when he left the White House and defied legal orders to return them.

The special counsel had given Trump's lawyers one chance to review his final report—and to make comments—before it was to be delivered to outgoing Attorney General Merrick Garland, who would then deliver the report to Congress and likely release it to the public. The lawyers were told the only way they could see the report was to show up in person to the special counsel's unmarked office building at the appointed time to view the document in a secure conference room. Before entering the room, Bove and Blanche had to surrender their electronic devices and hand in some of the evidence they'd already reviewed, making it impossible to compare the report to the underlying source documents. A third Trump lawyer was having trouble making it up from Florida because of a snowstorm in Washington; he was told he would not be able to view the report unless he could get to the special counsel's office in person.

The Trump lawyers were taken aback by the treatment they were receiving from the special counsel's office. Why did they have to go through the indignity of checking their phones at the door? What did Jack Smith think they were going to do with their electronic devices? Why couldn't he just send an electronic copy of the report for them and their colleague stuck in Florida to read? More fundamentally, why was Smith rushing to release his report before Donald Trump's inauguration?

To Todd Blanche and Emil Bove, this was just the latest in a string of indignities they felt Smith had inflicted upon them and their client. Defendants often feel aggrieved and mistreated, but their client wasn't any defendant. He was about to become the president of the United States. And they weren't just any defense attorneys. Trump had recently announced his intention to appoint Blanche and Bove to two of the most powerful positions in the Justice Department.

In other words, these two men would soon be leaders of the same Department of Justice that wasn't trusting them to bring cell phones into a conference room to read a DOJ report.

Trump's team didn't understand why Smith felt compelled to write a report at all. Although the law governing the appointment of special counsels requires the submission of a final report, Trump's lawyers felt this one should be nothing more than a simple notice announcing the case was being closed, but, regardless of what was included in the report, they believed it should be turned over to the next attorney general to decide what to do with it. Why the rush to get it out? Trump's lawyers believed it was one last effort to embarrass the incoming president of the United States right before his inauguration.

"Rather than acknowledging, as he must, President Trump's complete exoneration, Smith now seeks to disseminate an extrajudicial 'Final Report' to perpetuate his false and discredited accusations," Bove and Blanche wrote in a letter to Garland on January 6, 2025, to implore him to stop the release of the report.

Todd Blanche had known Donald Trump for less than two years, but during that time he had become a near constant presence by his side as his lead defense counsel fending off prosecution in three different jurisdictions. A former federal prosecutor in the office of the US attorney for the Southern District of New York (SDNY), Blanche came to the Trump team in April 2023 with a solid reputation as a criminal defense attorney. He had successfully defended former Trump campaign chairman Paul Manafort against campaign finance charges brought by the Manhattan district attorney.

Some of Blanche's former colleagues believed Blanche was a Democrat and were surprised when he signed up to defend Trump. At first, it looked like a terrible career move. To take the job, he had to resign as a partner in one of New York's most respected law firms—Cadwalader, Wickersham & Taft—because the firm, like many other elite law firms, wanted nothing to do with Trump.

At first, Blanche took charge of Trump's defense in the Stormy

Daniels hush money case brought by the Manhattan district attorney, but soon he was taking a leading role in the federal cases brought by Jack Smith, too. The job quickly became a lifestyle for Blanche, flying up and down the Eastern Seaboard to hop among three courthouses where Trump was a defendant—in Manhattan, Washington, DC, and Fort Pierce, Florida. By the time his two-year run as Trump's defense attorney concluded, he had relocated his family to a house in Florida a short drive from Mar-a-Lago.

To deal with the monumental workload associated with defending a former president facing multiple prosecutions, Blanche added Emil Bove to the team. Bove was forty-two years old at the time, but he looked ten years older. A former college lacrosse player with a bone-dry sense of humor, Bove exuded intensity. He was almost never seen cracking a smile in public. Like Blanche, he had served in the office of the US attorney for the SDNY, where he had a reputation as a hard-working but temperamental prosecutor.

Bove's drive and attention to detail endeared him to many of the prosecutors in Manhattan's prestigious US attorney's office, but above all, he was known for his hot temper, something he seemed proud of. He publicly disparaged the work of colleagues that he believed was subpar and had a blowup with one fellow prosecutor that lasted so long he refused to make eye contact with him for years.[1] When a group of defense lawyers wrote a letter to Bove's bosses raising concerns about his antics—including his rudeness, recklessness, and need for "adult supervision"—Bove pinned the letter on a corkboard in his office. He told his colleagues that the email—which blocked him from getting a promotion to a management position—was a badge of honor.[2]

While Blanche was more social and outgoing than Bove, both

men were cut from similar cloth at the famously competitive office, where hotshot associates at law firms from the country's best law schools would cultivate their careers before making the jump to seven-figure partnerships at elite firms. The SDNY was a magnet for well-connected graduates of the top law schools in the country—a place where those with a newly minted law degree from Harvard, Yale, or Stanford could kick off a storied legal career.

Unlike most of their fellow assistant US attorneys in the Southern District of New York, though, neither man went to an Ivy League school; Blanche attended American University and Bove was a University at Albany graduate. They started out as paralegals, working long hours doing the grunt work—printing exhibits, producing discovery, making binders—needed to get a case to trial. On the Senate questionnaire Blanche filled out before his confirmation as deputy attorney general, he wrote that he'd worked on hundreds of investigations and testified at trial or before grand juries more than fifty times as a paralegal. Blanche eventually worked his way through Brooklyn Law School at night as he continued working as a paralegal, while Bove graduated from Georgetown University Law Center.

Both men came into the office with something to prove and generally thrived during their decade as prosecutors, with Blanche leaving the office as a well-liked supervisor and moving on to a top law firm in New York City. Bove had a rockier exit, to put it mildly.

Bove's workhorse reputation led him to one of the most prestigious jobs in SDNY, running the unit in charge of investigating and prosecuting acts of terrorism and international narcotics. But that job—which should have been the perfect off-ramp into a prestigious law firm partnership—ended in what was one of the most embarrassing periods for the famed office.

Already Bove had a challenging time as a supervisor. He was passed over for a promotion because of that letter he had pinned up in his office from defense lawyers raising serious concerns about his aggressive legal tactics. While he eventually got the promotion he wanted, his subordinates also raised concerns about morale and his "abusive" management style.

In early 2021, a team of lawyers overseen by Bove was prosecuting a businessman for violating US sanctions on Iran and discovered a batch of evidence that had never been turned over to the defense. In the middle of an intense trial, the prosecutors contemplated burying the evidence in a pile of largely irrelevant and unrelated documents.

While the team never actually carried out the plan to bury the documents, the fact that they considered it was a cardinal sin in the eyes of Judge Alison Nathan, a progressive judge with a deep skepticism of prosecutors. After learning about the evidence issue, the judge accused Bove's team of failing the justice system.

"The cost of such Government misconduct is high. With each misstep, the public faith in the criminal-justice system further erodes. With each document wrongfully withheld, an innocent person faces the chance of wrongful conviction," she wrote.

In addition to issuing the scathing opinion, Judge Nathan required every prosecutor in the Southern District of New York to swear they read the opinion—an attempt to ensure the error would never happen again.

Beyond being admonished by her, Bove and his entire team had to hand over their emails and texts to the judge, who combed through them for evidence of misconduct. In those texts, Bove and his co-chief Shawn Crowley—who would go on to represent E. Jean Carroll in her sexual assault and defamation cases against Trump—seemingly acknowledged that their team of prosecutors had told a "flat lie" when they tried to explain themselves to the defense team.

Bove himself acknowledged that his team had "done some pretty aggressive stuff here over the last few days" and boasted of how they would "smash" the defendant. Instead, they had to drop the case because of how the evidence was handled. Bove simultaneously faced demotion, allegations of violating his oath, and losing the case his team had spent years building. By the end of the year, Bove had left SDNY for private practice, an inglorious exit after a largely successful career in the country's most high-profile US attorney's office.

But just three years later, Bove would be back and in a much more powerful role at the highest ranks of the Department of Justice, poised to enact his retribution against his old colleagues in spectacular fashion.

Blanche and Bove had been beside Trump throughout the entirety of the New York hush money trial. While Blanche did the talking—making opening and closing statements and cross-examining witnesses—Bove wrote most of the briefs, often including acerbic and bitter criticism of the prosecutors and, occasionally, the court too.

After winning the election in November, Trump announced he would nominate Blanche to be deputy attorney general, a position that would require Senate confirmation and effectively put Blanche in charge of running the day-to-day operations of a Justice Department that had spent much of the past two years trying to put Donald Trump in prison.

"I continue to be frustrated," Blanche told the Senate Judiciary

Committee about the DOJ's treatment of his former client. "That's power, and that's power that's corrupted."

And Trump announced Bove would be the principal associate deputy attorney general, another one of the most powerful jobs at DOJ. Because Bove's job did not require Senate confirmation, he would go to work immediately after Trump became president on January 20—effectively running the entire department until the Senate confirmed Blanche and Trump's choice of attorney general, Pam Bondi.

Bove's reign over the DOJ began just hours after Trump was sworn in as the forty-seventh president. He immediately got to work as the leading edge of Trump's effort to fulfill his promise of exacting revenge on the people who'd gone after him. Bove wasted no time leading a reign of terror against Trump's perceived enemies. He used his first days in office to fire the top leadership of the FBI—all of them career agents who had served under Democratic and Republican presidents. He fired or forced the resignations of several of the top prosecutors at the Justice Department, targeting those who were assigned to work on the special counsel's cases against Trump. He further demanded the new acting director of the FBI give him a list of every FBI employee who worked on any of the 1,500-plus prosecutions of those who attacked the Capitol on January 6—a list that would include agents in every single FBI field office in the country. It was a political bloodbath far beyond the so-called Saturday Night Massacre during the darkest days of Watergate, when two senior officials resigned.

Bove's retribution campaign continued throughout the first weeks of the Trump administration, as he had virtually unchecked power in his role as the de facto leader of the Justice Department. On

February 10, 2024, he demanded federal prosecutors drop a criminal corruption case against New York Mayor Eric Adams, a Democrat who had attended Trump's inauguration and signaled his support of the administration's immigration policies.

In his letter ordering federal prosecutors in Manhattan to drop the case, Bove said his decision was made "without accessing the strength of the evidence or legal theories on which the case is based." Instead, he said the charges should be dropped based on an unprecedented political rationale. First, Bove said the criminal case embodied the "weaponization" of justice that Trump vowed to root out and that the upcoming trial of Adams—which was due to start in April—would interfere with the New York mayor's reelection campaign. Second, he said the ongoing prosecution would limit Adams's ability to cooperate with the Trump administration on immigration policy.

"The pending prosecution has unduly restricted Mayor Adams' ability to devote full attention and resources to the illegal immigration and violent crime that escalated under the policies of the prior Administration," Bove wrote.

Bove demanded the charges be dropped "without prejudice"—leaving open the possibility the case could be revived, giving the Trump administration personal leverage over Adams. If the mayor stopped cooperating with the Trump administration, the criminal charges could come back.

Bove's demand was so controversial, it led to the resignation of seven DOJ prosecutors in New York and Washington, none of whom wanted to sign the order dropping the charges against Adams.

Danielle Sassoon, the top prosecutor at SDNY—the office where Bove started his career and left under a cloud of controversy—resigned after she refused to carry out Bove's demand. Sassoon was a conservative who had clerked for the late Justice Antonin Scalia. In a letter to Attorney General Pam Bondi, she said Bove's demand was "inconsistent with my ability and duty to prosecute federal crimes without fear or favor and to advance good-faith arguments before the courts." The lead prosecutor on the Adams case, Hagan Scotten, wrote a blistering resignation letter, saying any attorney who would go along with Bove's demands would either be a "fool" or a "coward."

Scotten wasn't some liberal deep-state critic of Donald Trump. He was an Army combat veteran, twice awarded the Bronze Star for meritorious service during the Iraq War. He served as a law clerk for Justices John Roberts and Brett Kavanaugh and had worked to prepare Kavanaugh for his Senate confirmation hearing. He believed Bove's actions represented a threat to the rule of law—and his conservative principles.

"No system of ordered liberty can allow the Government to use the carrot of dismissing charges, or the stick of threatening to bring them again, to induce an elected official to support its policy objectives," Scotten wrote.[3]

After Sassoon, Scotten, and five other prosecutors resigned, Bove himself signed the order dropping the charges—a highly unusual move for a senior DOJ official who was not directly involved in the case.*

Bove's actions during the first weeks of the second Trump term surprised even Steve Bannon, who had been calling for retribution against Trump's enemies for years. He marveled at how fast Bove—a guy who had never been involved in politics and who had known

---

*President Trump looked glowingly on Bove's short tenure at the top of the Department of Justice and rewarded him in May 2025 by nominating him to be a judge on the US Third Circuit Court of Appeals.

Trump for less than two years—was acting to implement an extreme version of what Trump had talked about on the campaign trail. Bannon told me Bove was "separated at birth from Stephen Miller," Trump's hard-charging deputy chief of staff and architect of some of Trump's most extreme policy proposals.

"He's a Stephen Miller. You've given a tiny little guy power, and he's a fucking Himmler. He's crazy. Trump loves him," Bannon told me, comparing Bove to one of Adolf Hitler's most notorious enforcers after Bove carried out the firings at the FBI.

"You give these nerds a little power—they've been picked on and beat up their entire life—they get power, and they're out of fucking control," Bannon said with a laugh. "They're fucking out of control. I love it, because this is the way you deconstruct the administrative state."[4]

But before Bove could begin personally firing the attorneys he had spent the last two years fighting in court and redirect the Department of Justice to serve Donald Trump's personal and political interests, he and Blanche had to handle what they thought was the last legal hurdle Trump would face before his inauguration as the forty-seventh president. As Bove and Blanche entered the special counsel's office on January 3, he was operating as the defense counsel for the former president of the United States, not the soon-to-be enforcer for the future president.

Blanche and Bove arrived at the special counsel's office at about 9 a.m. on January 3. They dutifully put their phones aside and went into the room to review Smith's final report.

They didn't like what they saw. Smith was not going quietly. His report was a direct attack on the man about to be sworn in as president, making the case that he had committed serious crimes and abused his power as commander in chief. Smith outlined the evidence gathered in both investigations and declared it was strong enough to secure criminal convictions in both cases. The cases were being abruptly terminated solely because Trump had won the presidential election.

As harsh as the report was, it would have been far worse for Trump, of course, if the cases had gone to trial. In the January 6 case, Smith's investigators had gathered evidence that had eluded the January 6 Committee, including the testimony of those closest to Donald Trump about what he was doing as the Capitol came under attack.

Dan Scavino—a man so close to Trump that he was the only person authorized to control his Twitter account—described to investigators Trump's demeanor as he was watching the attack on the Capitol unfold. In vivid detail, Scavino told prosecutors that Trump sat in his dining area next to the Oval Office, his arms folded, transfixed by what he was seeing on the television.

Scavino, who had known and worked for Trump since he was fifteen years old, was as loyal an aide as Trump ever had. But under oath, he told investigators he found Trump's behavior during the attack on the Capitol unsettling and said that Trump was angry—but not angry that his supporters were smashing windows and beating up cops. Scavino said Trump was angry about the same thing fueling the rage of his rioting supporters, angry about the election he had lost. The president was cursing—ignoring the pleas of the people closest to him to do something to stop the violence. And staring at the television on the wall—his eyes homing in on live images of the escalating violence.

With the January 6 investigation over, the world will likely never hear Scavino tell that story. We will also likely never hear Scavino or Trump chief of staff Mark Meadows say what both told investigators: that they never saw any evidence that the 2020 election was rigged or stolen. A jury will never hear how Trump repeatedly rebuffed every attempt to convince him that he had lost the election. And no jury will see the handwritten notes taken by Trump's own vice president, Mike Pence, on January 6, detailing how Trump had browbeaten him repeatedly that morning, trying to pressure him to overturn the election.

Pence's notes from the morning of January 6—hastily scribbled on the vice president's day planner—were used by prosecutors to piece together a timeline of the final hours leading up to the violent attack on the Capitol. They were never presented in court or publicly disclosed, but you can see them in the photo section of this book.

In those notes, Pence writes how Trump berated him as a "wimp" and said he "made a big mistake 5 years ago" when he picked him to be his running mate because Pence was refusing to use his ceremonial role presiding over the certification of the election later that day to overturn the election.

"You're not protecting our country, you're supposed to support + defend our country," Pence wrote, summarizing what Trump had told him.

"I said we both [took] an oath to support + defend the Constitution," Pence said, according to his notes. "It doesn't take courage to break the law. It takes courage to uphold the law."

And Jack Smith would never have the opportunity to present the evidence he found when he was able to get access to the cell phone Donald Trump used on January 6. The device included a record of each time Trump locked and unlocked the device, providing investigators a second-by-second account of how Trump spent most of the afternoon—scrolling through Twitter—as his supporters attacked the Capitol.

The FBI found that Trump also used his phone to look at multiple images depicting the violence at the Capitol, including violent confrontations between officers and protesters, and photos of Ashli Babbitt, who was later pronounced dead at the hospital after being shot as she tried to break into the chamber of the House of Representatives. And they were able to see that at 7 p.m. on January 6—not long after he was suspended from Twitter—Trump's phone was used to visit a Twitter help page about locked accounts.

Another thing that would never be revealed at trial: the background image on the iPhone Trump used as president—an image of himself wearing a red MAGA hat and giving a big thumbs-up. Every time Trump looked at his own phone, he would see a close-up image of himself.

But as the Trump lawyers read through the special counsel's final report, it wasn't the section on the January 6 investigation that most concerned them; it was the section on Trump's alleged mishandling of classified documents—a criminal case his own lawyers believed posed the most serious legal threat to the former president.

According to sources familiar with it, the section of the special counsel's report on the classified documents investigation outlined the case in exhaustive and damning detail.

Had the case been presented to a jury, Smith would have argued that Trump endangered the country's national security secrets in the two years following his exit from the White House by bringing boxes of documents to his Florida social club that detailed the country's nuclear programs, attack plans, and defense vulnerabilities. Smith alleged that Trump hastily purloined the records from the White House—tossing classified records into dozens of boxes that carried everything from newspaper clippings to toiletries and undergarments—and stored them in unsecured locations at Mar-a-Lago including a bathroom, ballroom, and storage closet.

Some of the allegations detailed pure vanity—showing a book publisher an "attack plan" for Iran before remarking how the material was "highly confidential" and "still a secret"—while others were dangerously careless. My colleague Katherine Faulders in 2023 reported that Trump discussed potentially sensitive information about US nuclear submarines with a member of Mar-a-Lago—Australian billionaire Anthony Pratt. Pratt, who donated prolifically to Trump's campaign, allegedly shared the information with more than a dozen foreign officials, several of his own employees, and a handful of journalists.

When federal investigators attempted to retrieve Trump's classified White House keepsakes, he allegedly worked with two aides to ensure the FBI couldn't find the records. Trump allegedly lied to his own lawyer who did the first sweep for classified material—going so far as to change the locks on the door to a storage closet while his lawyer looked around Mar-a-Lago's basement—then pushed the lawyer to lie on his behalf.

"I don't want anybody looking, I don't want anybody looking through my boxes, I really don't, I don't want you looking through my boxes," Trump allegedly told his lawyer Evan Corcoran, according to notes Corcoran took of his conversations with Trump. "Look, I just don't want anybody going through these things."

While a federal judge was considering blocking the notes from being used as evidence, my colleagues Katherine Faulders and Peter Charalambous obtained and published the contents of the notes, detailing the deeply incriminating evidence that Smith planned to present that came from none other than Trump's own lawyer.

Corcoran wrote that he repeatedly warned Trump about the legal consequences of not complying with the subpoena.

"Well, what if we, what happens if we just don't respond at all or don't play ball with them?" Trump asked, according to the notes.

"Well, there's a prospect that they could go to a judge and get a search warrant and that they could arrive here and get a search warrant," Corcoran responded.

According to Corcoran, Trump repeatedly asked if it would be "better if we just told them we don't have anything here."

Of course, the search warrant was eventually issued, resulting in the FBI search of Mar-a-Lago in August 2022 and the discovery of hundreds of classified documents at the former president's home.

If the special counsel's final report on the classified documents case had been released, the public would have likely learned what Susie Wiles, who would go on to serve as Trump's White House chief of staff, told investigators. In his indictment of Trump, Smith described how the former president showed an unnamed campaign aide (described in court papers as a "PAC representative") a classified map while describing a military operation, telling her he "should not be showing the map" and warning her "not to get too close." As Katherine Faulders reported, that "PAC representative" was Susie Wiles.

And there's more that has not been previously reported.

Wiles also told investigators she was shocked when she found out how many classified documents Trump had taken from the White

House—and worried about how he was handling the situation. Wiles told them she had left it up to others—primarily Trump's lawyers at the time—to handle the situation because she didn't want to get involved, but in retrospect wished she had been more forceful in getting Trump to return the documents before the FBI decided to take the extraordinary step of searching Trump's Mar-a-Lago home. She said she was not proud of how she handled the situation—something the public may have seen in Smith's final report or in a courtroom if the case had ever gone to trial.

Of course, the classified documents case never got to trial, but Smith outlined the facts against Trump in his final report. He wouldn't get his conviction, but he wanted the world to know how much evidence he had gathered in his effort to prove Trump's guilt.

After reviewing the report for about six hours, the lawyers took a break and stepped outside the reviewing room, where they could again check their phones. It was shortly after 3 p.m. on what was supposed to be a slow Friday, the first of the new year.

But within a few minutes, their phones were inundated with news alerts of a story out of New York: an announcement from Judge Juan Merchan, who oversaw Donald Trump's hush money trial, that he would hold a hearing to impose his sentence in the case on January 10—just seven days away.

The announcement came as a shock—not just to Trump's legal team but also to reporters who had covered the case. "I didn't believe it when I first read it," my colleague Peter Charalambous, who had covered every day of the trial, told me. "I thought I might have been hallucinating."

Did a local judge in New York really think he had the power to impose a punishment on someone about to be sworn in as president of the United States? Not exactly. Even as Judge Merchan announced he would be moving forward with sentencing, he made it clear he would not be imposing any actual punishment. He wasn't going to try to put Trump in jail days before his inauguration, for God's sake.

Judge Merchan signaled that he would like to impose a sentence of "unconditional discharge"—which, in reality, is no sentence at all. It's the bare minimum allowed under New York state law. No prison time. No probation. No community service. Nothing.

And he wouldn't be dragging the president-elect up to that old New York courthouse again; instead, the judge would allow Trump to attend the hearing virtually from the comforts of Mar-a-Lago.

But Merchan felt it was important to go through with this last step of the trial to make Trump's felony convictions an official part of the record, while also preserving Trump's right to appeal the conviction. To forgo sentencing, Merchan reasoned, would be to vacate the jury's verdict that Trump had committed multiple felonies and force the case into an unprecedented legal limbo.

For the very same reason, Trump's lawyers were determined to do anything possible to stop the sentencing from going forward. Now they had another big battle to wage in the days before the inauguration.

The coming showdown over sentencing was about power, ego, and history. The judge wanted to be sure that "convicted felon" would forever be words used to describe Donald Trump, just as Trump wanted that verdict to be forever vacated and rendered so illegitimate that the proceedings were never truly finished.

Merchan's order announcing the sentencing hearing was a scathing critique of both Trump and his lawyers—the same lawyers who would soon be running the Department of Justice.

"Defendant's [Trump's] disdain for the Third Branch of government," Merchan declared, "is a matter of public record. Indeed, Defendant has gone to great lengths to broadcast on social media and other forums his lack of respect for judges, juries, grand juries and the justice system as a whole."

Merchan criticized Trump's lawyers for using rhetoric that "has no place in legal pleadings" and for repeatedly delaying the proceedings, which "led us down the path we are on."

Now Trump's lawyers had two urgent tasks to accomplish before taking their positions at the top of the Department of Justice. They wanted to try to stop Jack Smith from releasing his report and to prevent the spectacle of President-elect Trump getting sentenced in New York less than two weeks before his inauguration.

Over the course of the next six days, Trump's lawyers went to court four separate times pleading with judges to delay the New York sentencing. Each time, they argued that Trump should be immune from criminal cases as president-elect.

The first attempt was to ask Merchan for a delay. He rejected the request, telling Trump's lawyers that they had made claims that were "legally inapplicable" to the case.

Next, a mid-level appeal judge in New York dismissed the claim Trump should be immune as president-elect.

"I'm curious about that," Judge Ellen Gesmer said to Todd Blanche in court. "Do you have any support for the notion that presidential immunity extends to presidents-elect?"

"There has never been a case like this before, so no," Blanche said.

In their third attempt, Trump's team went to New York's highest court to appeal for a delay. That court took less than twenty-four hours to reject the request.

The power duo of Todd Blanche and Emil Bove had gone 0 for 3 in their efforts to stop the sentencing.

But Trump's team had one final long-shot play to make—going to the US Supreme Court with an emergency application asking the court to stop New York from moving forward with Trump's sentencing.

Like everything about the situation, it was a move without precedent.

Trump's lawyers quickly wrote their emergency application and briefed the president-elect on the argument they would be making to the Supreme Court. But before the application was sent to the justices, Trump had a call to make.

With the full knowledge that his lawyers were about to ask the Supreme Court to take an extraordinary action on his behalf, Trump placed a phone call to one of the justices who would be ruling on the matter: Justice Samuel Alito.

Both sides of the call later insisted it had nothing to do with the case. Trump had asked to talk to Alito about another matter entirely. One of Alito's former clerks had applied for a job in the administration and Trump wanted to see what Alito thought about him.

If that's all the call was about, it may have been the most high-level and awkwardly timed job reference in American history.

The former Alito clerk's name was William Levi. It had been more than a decade since he had clerked for Justice Alito, but Levi had solid credentials and was eminently qualified. He had actually worked in the previous Trump administration. But that was the problem. Levi had served as the chief of staff to Attorney General Bill Barr. Barr had refused to go along with Trump's efforts to overturn the election, something for which Trump would never forgive him.

Trump's call to Alito was yet another major story first reported by my colleague Katherine Faulders. When we asked the Supreme Court about it, we received back a written response from Alito, including a lengthy explanation of how he ended up on the phone with the president-elect just as his attorneys were asking the Supreme Court to intervene on Trump's behalf in New York.

"William Levi, one of my former law clerks, asked me to take a call from President-elect Trump regarding his qualifications to serve in a government position," Justice Alito told us in a written statement. "I agreed to discuss this matter with President-elect Trump, and he called me yesterday afternoon.

"We did not discuss the emergency application he filed today, and indeed, I was not even aware at the time of our conversation that such an application would be filed," Alito said. "We also did not discuss any other matter that is pending or might in the future come before the Supreme Court or any past Supreme Court decisions involving the President-elect."

We'll never know for sure the full contents of the call, but sources close to Trump also insist the two men did not discuss the emergency applications that had just been written by Trump's lawyers.

At any rate, at 7 p.m. the night before the scheduled sentencing hearing in New York, the Supreme Court rejected Trump's application with a short two-sentence notice explaining that "the burden that sentencing will impose on the President-Elect's responsibilities is relatively insubstantial in light of the trial court's stated intent to impose a sentence of 'unconditional discharge' after a brief virtual hearing."

The vote was 5–4 against. Alito, despite the appearance of a conflict of interest, did not recuse himself. Instead, he voted in favor of Trump's request.

President-elect Donald Trump was hosting a group of Republican governors in Mar-a-Lago when the Supreme Court posted its decision.

"I read it, and I thought it was a fair decision, actually," he calmly told reporters, less than twenty-four hours before Judge Merchan would cement Trump's reputation as a convicted criminal. "So I'll do my little thing tomorrow. They can have fun with their political opponent."

And so, on January 10, Donald Trump became the first former president sentenced for a criminal conviction.

Trump went into his sentencing knowing full well the punishment, or lack thereof, he was about to receive. Unlike the days of his criminal trial, when he had to suffer the indignity of coming to New York's grimy criminal courthouse on a daily basis, he attended the sentencing remotely from a gilded Mar-a-Lago meeting room.

Before Trump logged on for his 9:30 a.m. sentencing hearing, hundreds of reporters showed up in the early morning hours of January 10 and withstood the bone-chilling New York winter to find a courthouse that had been transformed since the trial six months earlier. The scaffolding that had enveloped the historic building was gone. The layers of security screening designed to protect the former president were gone, too. The courtroom itself was slightly refurbished with a shiny new linoleum floor. Trump would never see any of that; instead, from the comfort of Mar-a-Lago, he logged on to his criminal sentencing via Microsoft Teams. He stared into the low-resolution camera with Todd Blanche by his side.

Nearly every screen in the courtroom—in the jury box, console tables, and facing the gallery—displayed the future president and soon-to-be deputy attorney general as they quietly awaited Judge Merchan to commence the sentencing.

With his colleagues and Trump dialed in from Florida, Emil Bove—ramrod straight and with an American flag pinned on his lapel—quietly sat alone at the defense counsel table, the sole in-person representative of the former president. To his left, Blanche and Trump appeared on a massive flat-screen television that was wheeled into the courtroom and angled directly at Judge Merchan.

Judge Merchan took the bench at 9:35 a.m. and began by confirming whether Trump and his lawyers received and reviewed the report that a probation officer had prepared about Trump's conduct. Back in June 2024, Trump had to sit down with a probation officer for a virtual interview that mainly served to determine if the former president had any remorse for his conduct and to recommend a sentence for punishment.

That sentencing report has never become public, but Joshua Steinglass—a prosecutor with the Manhattan district attorney's office—described what the probation officer said about Trump: "He sees himself as above the law and won't accept responsibility for his actions."

"That's certainly consistent with everything else that we've seen," Steinglass told the court.

Over the course of nine minutes, Steinglass was able to do what few men have and will likely never be able to do again—harshly criticize Donald Trump without interruption while Trump was forced to sit and listen in silence.

"Instead of preserving, protecting, and defending our constitutionally established system of criminal justice, the defendant—the once and future president of the United States—has engaged in a coordinated campaign to undermine its legitimacy," Steinglass said. "Far from expressing any kind of remorse for his criminal conduct, the defendant has purposefully bred disdain for our judicial institutions and the rule of law."

In a speech that foreshadowed the first months of Trump's second administration, Steinglass warned of Trump's public threat to retaliate against prosecutors and delegitimize the courts.

"Such threats are designed to have a chilling effect, to intimidate those who have the responsibility to enforce our laws in the hopes that they will ignore the defendant's transgressions because they fear that he is simply too powerful to be subjected to the same rule of law as the rest of us," Steinglass said.

As Steinglass continued, Trump leaned back in his chair and shook his head.

"Put simply, this defendant has caused enduring damage to public perception of the criminal justice system and has placed officers of the court in harm's way," he added.

Despite Trump's conduct, his guilt, his lack of remorse, and his repeated attacks on the rule of law, the Manhattan district attorney recommended that he face no punishment at all.

"The American public has the right to a presidency unencumbered by pending court proceedings or ongoing sentence-related obligations, but imposing this sentence ensures that finality. Sentencing the defendant permits this court to enter judgment to cement the defendant's status as a convicted felon while he pursues whatever appeals he intends to pursue, and it gives full effect and respect to the jury's verdict while preserving the defendant's ability to govern," Steinglass concluded.

After some remarks from Blanche defending his client, it was Trump's turn to make a statement.

"This has been a very terrible experience. I think it's been a tremendous setback for New York and the New York court system," Trump calmly began his remarks before gradually escalating, eventually condemning the day's proceedings by invoking deadly wildfires that were then consuming Los Angeles.

"With all that's happening in our country today, with a city that's burning to the ground—one of our largest, most important cities burning to the ground—with wars that are uncontrollably going on, with all of the problems of inflation and attacks on countries, and all of the horrible things that are going on, I got indicted over calling a legal expense a legal expense. It's called a legal expense," Trump said, returning to the argument that he had been making since the earliest days of the trial.

Trump went on for several more minutes, revisiting some of the arguments his lawyers had made in the case and quoting several legal commentators who had criticized the prosecution. Finally, he concluded with what ended up being the most consequential issue, which ended up dictating the outcome of the entire trial—the election.

Despite the hours of embarrassing testimony, scathing jury addresses, and the jury's unanimous verdict, Trump's election in November was a political acquittal that effectively rendered the legal proceedings moot.

"The people of our country got to see this firsthand because they watched the case in your courtroom. They got to see this firsthand and then they voted, and I won and got the largest number of votes by far, of any Republican candidate in history and won, as you know, all seven swing states. Won conclusively, all seven swing states, and won the popular vote by millions and millions of votes, and they've been watching your trial, so they understood it," Trump said.

"I won the election and a massive landslide. And the people of this country understand what's gone on. This has been a weaponization of government. They call it lawfare. Never happened to any extent like this, but never happened in our country before, and I just like to explain that I was treated very, very unfairly,"

And with that, Trump leaned back in his chair and muted the microphone.

Judge Merchan concluded the hearing by laying out his rationale for the sentence, which he had deliberated for the last six months. There was a time when he had a weighty decision to make—potentially sentence Trump in the heat of a campaign and send him away to prison, or let him get off scot-free in spite of the jury's unanimous verdict. But by January 10, the decision was out of his hands, as he explained to Trump and those gathered in court.

"It is the Office of the President that bestows those far-reaching protections to the officeholder, and it was the citizenry of this nation that recently decided that you should once again receive the benefits of those protections, which include, among other things, the Supremacy Clause and presidential immunity. It is through that lens and that reality that this court must determine a lawful sentence," Merchan said before formally imposing Trump's sentence of an unconditional discharge.

Over the course of the trial, Trump had attacked Judge Merchan as "corrupt" and "totally compromised" and attacked his daughter as a "rabid Trump hater." Before he brought the gavel down to end the only criminal trial of a former or future president, Judge Merchan bid Trump a final farewell.

"Sir, I wish you Godspeed as you assume your second term in office."

CHAPTER SEVENTEEN

RAGING FIRE

Throughout the 2024 campaign, one of the key arguments made by the Democratic nominee—first Joe Biden, then Kamala Harris—was that a Donald Trump victory would be catastrophic for America. Biden had gravely declared that "democracy itself is on the ballot,"[1] and Harris made the case on national television that her opponent was a "fascist." While the Trump campaign held its October 27 rally inside Madison Square Garden, the Democratic National Committee projected a message in big, bold letters on the outside of the building:

TRUMP PRAISED HITLER.*

*The accusation was a reference to comments former White House chief of staff John Kelly had recently given to *The Atlantic*, in which he claimed Trump had once told him, "Hitler did some good things." The former president denied ever saying those words. (Jeffrey Goldberg, "Trump: 'I Need the Kind of Generals That Hitler Had,'" *The Atlantic*, October 22, 2024.)

But then he won.

The day after democracy rendered its verdict, Harris, who'd described Trump as a "predator who abused women," called her opponent and congratulated him on his victory. Biden, who'd said years earlier that he would have taken Trump "behind the gym and beat the hell out of him" if they went to high school together, did the same, inviting him to visit the White House and offering to do everything he could to ensure a smooth transition.[2]

Trump had not extended the same courtesy to Biden four years earlier. Instead, he had done everything in his power to undermine him, refusing to concede his loss and desperately seeking to overturn the results of the 2020 election. But now on the winning side once again, Trump eagerly accepted the invitation. His campaign putting out an uncharacteristically positive statement after Biden called him. "President Trump looks forward to the meeting [with Biden]," Trump spokesperson Steven Cheung said, "and very much appreciated the call."

When Trump arrived in Washington on November 13, 2024, his armored SUV was waved onto the driveway on the South Lawn of the White House, dropping him off precisely where he had left the building at the sad, violence-plagued conclusion of his first term. Joe and Jill Biden were there to welcome him as he returned to the place he had called home for four years, doing their part to carry on the traditional post-election White House meeting between an incoming and outgoing president.

Neither man acknowledged the glaring awkwardness of the moment: that Trump never acknowledged the legitimacy of Biden's presidency, that Biden's Justice Department had indicted Trump multiple times, that Trump had been impeached in 2019 for trying to extort an ally into digging up information on Biden and his son Hunter. In fact, Trump totally ignored it, instead turning on the charm. "You're a really beautiful couple," Trump said to Joe and Jill, according to two people who were there as Trump walked into the White House. "You're always so close. It's really nice to see you." The three of them, all smiles, posed for a photograph.

The closest Trump came to apologizing for his behavior was when he turned to Biden and, according to one of the people there with both presidents, said with a shrug, "Politics brings out the worst in people."

And with that, President Biden walked with President-elect Trump along the colonnade next to the Rose Garden and into the Oval Office, while Jill Biden returned to the White House residence. The First Lady had extended an invitation to Melania Trump to have tea at the White House—another longstanding tradition—but Melania had declined. She didn't offer any public explanation for being a no-show on her husband's first trip back to the White House, but people close to the Trumps said Melania was still upset about the FBI raid of Mar-a-Lago two years earlier. She had previously described the FBI's actions as "an invasion of privacy" that made her "angry," and she was particularly upset that FBI agents had searched her and her son Barron's living space and closets for classified documents that her husband had taken at the end of his first term.

The White House press pool was briefly invited into the Oval Office to witness the meeting of the forty-fifth, forty-sixth, and forty-seventh presidents. Both Biden and Trump have well-deserved reputations for speaking at length when cameras are present, but in this instance, their remarks were strikingly short. Sitting in front of the fireplace, Biden reached out to give Trump a hearty handshake.

"Mr. President-elect, and the former president, and Donald, congratulations and, uh, I'm looking forward to having a, like we said, a smooth transition," Biden said, the crackling of the raging fire behind him nearly as loud as his words. "I'll do everything we can to make sure you're accommodated, what you need. And we're going to get a chance to talk about some of that today. So, welcome. Welcome back."

"Thank you very much," Trump replied. "Politics is tough, and it's, in many cases, not a very nice world. But it is a nice world today, and I appreciate very much a transition that's so smooth, it'll be as smooth as you can get. And I very much appreciate that, Joe."

"You're welcome," Biden said, as the White House press pool was escorted out.

The public exchange lasted just thirty-eight seconds, but the meeting between Biden and Trump was just getting started. In fact, the two men sat there in those chairs in front of the fireplace for another two hours, joined only by Biden's chief of staff, Jeff Zients, and Susie Wiles, who would fill the same role for Trump. By all accounts, the meeting was remarkably friendly, as though all those vicious personal attacks on the Biden family—and dire warnings about the threat Trump posed to democracy—had never happened.

"We'd be great friends if it weren't for politics," Trump told Biden, according to a source familiar with what was said. "We'd be great friends, Joe."

Trump also mentioned during the meeting that he believed Biden would have been a tougher opponent than Kamala Harris, and that Democrats made a mistake when they forced him out of the race.* He

*Trump offered Barack Obama similar flattery during their Oval Office meeting following the 2016 election. In that instance, Trump told Obama that the two of them had

even tried to bond with his former opponent by bringing up the supposed evils of Biden's Justice Department, which had been prosecuting Trump, of course, and also Biden's son Hunter.

Shortly after the meeting was over, Trump continued to sing Biden's praises in public. "You know, it's been a long slog," he told the *New York Post* in a telephone interview shortly after the meeting ended. "It's been a lot of work on both sides, and he did a very good job with respect to campaigning and everything else. We really had a really good meeting."[3]

"We got to know each other again," Trump added, noting that they talked about the war in Ukraine and the situation in the Middle East, where the Biden administration was coordinating with the incoming Trump national security team to secure the release of hostages being held by Hamas. "I wanted to know his views on where we are and what he thinks. And he gave them to me, he was very gracious."

Trump's own graciousness toward Biden would, predictably, not last very long. When Biden announced in May 2025 that he had been diagnosed with stage 4 prostate cancer, Trump initially wished him well. Days later, however, he shared a post calling the forty-sixth president a "decrepit corpse," and said he did not feel sorry for Biden. "If you feel sorry for him, don't feel so sorry," Trump said in the Oval Office. "Because he's vicious."

As Biden grinned ear to ear with Donald Trump in front of the fireplace in the Oval Office during that November 2024 meeting, many

something in common: They both attracted much larger crowds at their political events than Hillary Clinton.

prominent Democrats began to question whether the leaders of their party truly meant what they had said about Trump during the campaign. "I'm glad it's a peaceful transition of power, but what happened to the 'threat of democracy' talk? What happened to the 'fascist' talk?" Lenard McKelvey, a popular radio host also known as Charlamagne tha God, said on his show the following day. "I'm just trying to figure out, how do you go from, 'He's an existential threat to democracy,' to, 'Welcome back'?"[4]

One week earlier, the day after the election, Charlamagne had argued very bluntly that Biden was to blame for Trump's return to the White House. "He should've let everyone know he was just a transitional president," he said. "Biden should've dropped out a year ago, or two years ago."[5]

He was far from alone in making that case. "This Is All Biden's Fault," blared a headline in *The New York Times* from writer Josh Barro, who had years earlier been one of the president's most outspoken supporters.[6] In *The Atlantic*, Tyler Austin Harper made the case that "nobody bears more responsibility" for Trump's victory than the sitting president. "If the worst comes to pass, if the next four years are as bad as Biden warned, if the country—teetering before the abyss—stumbles toward that last precipice," he wrote, "it will have been American democracy's self-styled savior who helped push it, tumbling end over end, into the dark."[7]

"Joe Biden cannot escape the fact that his four years in office paved the way for the return of Donald Trump," Franklin Foer, a journalist and author of a respectful biography of Biden, wrote two days after the election. "This is his legacy. Everything else is an asterisk."[8]

Biden's remaining loyalists pushed back on some of these claims, telling reporters that Harris's loss was her own fault. Some said she should have campaigned more with Biden, rather than exiled Republicans like Liz Cheney. Others argued that $1.5 billion should have been more than enough to defeat an unpopular convicted felon like Trump. But few of those operatives made those comments on the record.

Blaming Harris for blowing the election hardly absolved Biden of responsibility. If she were as flawed a candidate as these people said, why had Biden selected her as his running mate in 2020? Why did he compound that mistake by immediately endorsing her for the nomination after he dropped out?

Ultimately, it was Biden's decision to run for reelection—after implying that he wouldn't—that doomed his party's chances, forestalling a real primary process. "Had the president gotten out sooner, there may have been other candidates in the race," former House Speaker Nancy Pelosi said days after the election on a *New York Times* podcast with Lulu Garcia-Navarro. "The anticipation was that, if the president were to step aside, that there would be an open primary."*

"Kamala may have, I think she would have, done well in that and been stronger going forward," Pelosi added. "But we don't know that. That didn't happen. We live with what happened. And because the president endorsed Kamala Harris immediately, that really made it almost impossible to have a primary at that time. If it had been much earlier, it would have been different."[9]

Among Democratic political operatives, only members of Biden's inner circle strongly disagreed with this analysis. Their counterargument was that Democrats' panicky efforts to push Biden out of

*As noted earlier in this book, Pelosi and Obama had discussed the need for a competitive process to replace Biden even before he dropped out of the race.

the race after the debate were what did the party in, not Biden's decision to run for reelection in the first place. "Lots of people have terrible debates," Mike Donilon, one of Biden's most trusted advisors, said in an interview at the Harvard Institute of Politics in February 2025. "Usually, the party doesn't lose its mind. But that's what happened—it just melted down."[10]

Donilon was even more pointed in an interview with me after Biden left office, arguing that, despite all the questions about his age and mental acuity, Biden was a stronger candidate than Harris and would have fared better than she did if he had stayed in the race. There was little doubt Biden himself shared this view.

"I think I would've beaten Trump, could've beaten Trump," Biden told reporters at the White House shortly before leaving office. Then, perhaps realizing he was effectively condemning Harris and putting the blame on her for Trump's victory, he added, nonsensically, "And I think that Kamala could've beaten Trump, would've beaten Trump. It wasn't about—I thought it was important to unify the party."

Appearing on ABC's *The View* in May 2025, days before he would announce his dire prostate cancer diagnosis, Biden continued to insist he would have won the race had he stayed in, noting that Trump's victory "wasn't a slam dunk." When asked about Harris's loss, Biden both accepted some blame and chalked it up to factors beyond either his or her control.

"Look, I was in charge, and he won. So, you know, I take responsibility," he said. "I was disappointed [Harris lost], but not surprised. . . . I've never seen quite as successful and consistent campaign undercutting the notion that a woman couldn't lead the country, and a woman of mixed race."[11]

According to two people who spoke with her after the election,

Harris believed she lost in large part because she ran out of time. She only had 107 days to run against Trump, which, she told people, was just not enough time to execute a winning campaign.

One member of Biden's inner circle scoffed at that idea, telling me that the opposite was true—that Harris may have lost because she had *too much time.* The more voters saw of her as a presidential candidate, this advisor suggested, the less inclined they were to vote for her. Harsh, sure, but looking strictly at the polling, this person may have had a point. Harris's standing with voters peaked shortly after the Democratic National Convention in August and her debate with Trump in early September. If Election Day had been two months earlier, she very well could have won.

For all the finger-pointing between the Biden and Harris camps, there was one person virtually all Democrats in Washington agreed deserved a good deal of the blame for Donald Trump's comeback: Merrick Garland, Biden's attorney general. The president's closest advisors were particularly harsh in their assessment of the man Biden chose to run the Department of Justice, arguing he waited too long to investigate Donald Trump's alleged crimes, ensuring there would not be a federal trial of Trump before the 2024 election and making his comeback possible. If Garland had been more aggressive, more than a few senior Democrats suggested to me, Trump might have ended up in prison rather than back in the White House.

Making matters worse, in the view of Biden loyalists, Garland had appointed a special counsel to investigate—and ultimately prosecute—the president's son Hunter and another special counsel to investigate—and ultimately embarrass—the president himself related to his handling of classified documents. The way these Democrats saw it, Garland ultimately let Trump get away with his crimes while forcing President Biden and his son to pay a steep price for transgressions that were far less serious.

Under this theory, which has become conventional wisdom for some Democrats, Garland wasted more than a year before directing prosecutors at the Justice Department to start investigating Donald Trump. While the DOJ dedicated a massive amount of resources to identifying and prosecuting the people who stormed the Capitol on January 6, the theory goes, senior leadership waited too long to launch probes into the man who had sent them there.

There are valid criticisms of Garland's tenure, but the notion that he waited more than a year to begin looking into Trump's efforts to subvert the 2020 election is simply not true. In fact, Garland began quietly investigating Trump's actions related to January 6 within weeks of being sworn in as attorney general. He did not make any public announcements—as was appropriate—but Garland devoted significant resources to investigating whether Trump had any direct involvement with the people who had attacked the Capitol. The investigation started with a tip, the details of which have never been previously reported.

In the spring of 2021, the Department of Justice received what officials believed to be a credible information that Dan Scavino, Trump's deputy chief of staff and longest-serving advisor, had set up a meeting between Trump and leaders of the Proud Boys during a visit to Las Vegas on September 15, 2020, suggesting a direct link between Trump and the men who carried out much of the violence at the Capitol. The tip was taken seriously and seen as potentially explosive. If true, it might have led to evidence that Trump had coordinated with those who attacked the building.

DOJ officials investigated the Las Vegas tip and searched for any other evidence that Trump had prior contact with the Proud Boys or any other militant groups that spearheaded the January 6 attack. They found nothing; the tip about the meeting in Vegas was bogus. Trump may have inspired the rioters. He may have incited them. Many of them clearly believed they were carrying out Trump's wishes when they stormed the Capitol. But after more than a year of investigating, the DOJ could not find any evidence that Trump or anyone in his inner circle had direct contact with those who carried out the attack.

The Justice Department also looked into the "War Room" at the Willard Hotel, on Pennsylvania Avenue between the Capitol and the White House, where several Trump associates—including Rudy Giuliani, Steve Bannon, John Eastman, and Boris Epshteyn—reportedly gathered while the January 6 attack was underway. *The Washington Post* reported the so-called War Room at the Willard was a "command center" for "overturning the results of the 2020 election."[12] The Justice Department, according to two senior Biden DOJ officials familiar with the investigation, searched for any connections or communications between Trump's associates at the Willard Hotel and those who attacked the Capitol building and found nothing.

If those initial investigations had turned up evidence that Trump directed or organized the Proud Boys or the other militia groups, one of those senior Justice Department officials told me, he would have been indicted earlier. "There was no crime found there," the official said.

With no evidence of direct coordination between Trump and those who committed the violence on January 6, the Justice Department—led by special counsel Jack Smith—proceeded instead with a more far-reaching and complicated case against the former president related to his efforts to overturn the election. A grand jury indicted Trump on these charges on August 1, 2023, but the prosecution was further delayed when Trump's lawyers appealed the indictment, claiming Trump enjoyed immunity for any actions that occurred while he was president. The Supreme Court eventually took up the appeal, taking months to hear the case and make its ruling. The court's opinion, issued on July 1, 2024, found that presidents enjoy far-reaching, but not total, immunity from charges even remotely related to their official actions as president, forcing Smith to revise and narrow his indictment.

But even before the Supreme Court's lengthy deliberation and decision, Garland believed there was no chance Trump's 2020 election case would head to trial before the election. "This is not happening this year," he bluntly told his senior advisors in early January 2024.

A few days before the end of the Biden presidency, I met with one of Garland's top advisors at the Robert F. Kennedy Department of Justice building and asked him how quickly Trump's federal criminal trials would have started if Kamala Harris had been elected president. "We were probably at least a year away. Maybe two," this senior DOJ official told me. Trump would likely have been able to bring at least two more challenges to the Supreme Court: one reviewing whether Jack Smith's revised indictments included charges related to actions protected by presidential immunity; another regarding the constitutionality of Smith's appointment as special counsel in the first place. The Garland advisor believed Trump would have ultimately lost both cases, but his appeals would have significantly delayed the case.

In other words, Trump's two federal indictments may not have gone to trial before the 2024 election no matter how fast or aggressive Merrick Garland had been.

That's not, however, how most Democrats saw it. And Biden himself, like Trump before him, had grown increasingly bitter about his own Justice Department by the end of his presidency. After the election, *The Washington Post* reported that the president had told people he regretted selecting Garland as attorney general, citing the DOJ's "slowness under Garland in prosecuting Trump, and its aggressiveness in prosecuting Biden's son Hunter."[13]

During his final weeks in office, Biden couldn't do anything about how the Trump cases were handled, but while he was still president, he had the power to make the prosecution of his son go away. All he had to do was give him a pardon.

The problem, however, was that the elder Biden had repeatedly promised to respect the legal process as Hunter's criminal proceedings were underway, pledging that if his son was found guilty, he would not pardon him or commute his sentence. White House officials had repeated the promise on multiple occasions, and Biden himself left no room for ambiguity in an interview with ABC News's David Muir in June 2024.

"Will you accept the jury's outcome their verdict—no matter what it is?" Muir asked the president.

"Yes," Biden said, without hesitation.

"And have you ruled out a pardon for your son?"

"Yes."

Biden officially pardoned Hunter on December 1, 2024, after the Biden family had spent Thanksgiving together in Nantucket.

A lot had changed in the six months since Biden had vowed not to pardon his son. He had dropped out of the presidential race, his vice president had lost, and Trump was set to return to the White House, with a vengeance, in less than two months. Trump had been unabashed on the campaign trail in vowing to go after his political enemies, and none were higher on Trump's list than Biden's only remaining son.*

"This has to end," the president said to Hunter that weekend as he told him he would be issuing the pardon.

On one level, Biden's change of heart was entirely unsurprising. Hunter faced the very real possibility of going to prison for two years or more after pleading guilty to tax evasion from 2016 to 2019. The sentencing was scheduled for mid-December. It's hard to imagine he would have let his only son—a recovering addict—go to prison when he had the power to do something about it.

At 8 p.m. on that Sunday, Biden exercised that power, issuing Hunter a "full and unconditional pardon" that covered all federal offenses he "has committed or may have committed or taken part in during the period from January 1, 2014 through December 1, 2024." The pardon was one of the most sweeping ever issued by an American president, encompassing all the offenses for which Hunter had been prosecuted by special counsel David Weiss, but also anything the incoming Trump administration could possibly uncover. The move drew immediate comparisons to President Gerald Ford's pardon of Richard Nixon, which covered any crimes the disgraced former president "has committed or may have committed" during his time in office.

Biden issued a lengthy statement alongside the pardon, explaining

*Even when Hunter was first indicted, Trump attacked the prosecutor as a "coward" for not seeking more serious charges against Joe Biden's son. "He gave out a traffic ticket instead of a death sentence," he wrote on Truth Social in July 2023.

why he believed his son had been "selectively and unfairly prosecuted."

"No reasonable person who looks at the facts of Hunter's cases can reach any other conclusion than Hunter was singled out only because he is my son, and that is wrong," the statement read. "There has been an effort to break Hunter, who has been 5½ years sober, even in the face of unrelenting attacks and selective prosecution. In trying to break Hunter, they've tried to break me, and there's no reason to believe it will stop here. Enough is enough."

By condemning "selective prosecution," Joe Biden wasn't just pardoning his son. He was issuing a blistering attack on his own Department of Justice. The investigation into Hunter Biden had begun during the first Trump presidency, and the lead prosecutor, US Attorney for the State of Delaware David Weiss, was a Trump appointee. But it was Biden's Attorney General Merrick Garland who elevated Weiss to special counsel and approved Weiss's decision to move forward with the cases against Hunter.

"Here's the truth," Biden continued in his statement. "I believe in the justice system, but as I have wrestled with this, I also believe raw politics has infected this process and it led to a miscarriage of justice, and once I made this decision this weekend, there was no sense in delaying it further. I hope Americans will understand why a father and a President would come to this decision."

Biden's statement was released just two hours after Donald Trump had announced his intention to nominate Kash Patel as the director of the FBI. To President Biden, Trump's decision to put Patel in charge of the FBI only underscored the importance of pardoning Hunter—and making the pardon so broad. Patel was a hard-edged Trump loyalist who spoke about tracking down and prosecuting the president-elect's enemies, and it was hardly a stretch to think he would use the vast powers of the FBI to go after Hunter Biden.

Even so, many Democrats, already frustrated with the president's role in returning Trump to power, issued withering criticisms of the pardon. "A president's family and allies shouldn't get special treatment," Democratic Senator Gary Peters said in a statement. "This was an improper use of power, it erodes trust in our government, and it emboldens others to bend justice to suit their interests."[14] Fellow Democratic Senator Michael Bennet argued that Biden's pardon "put personal interest ahead of duty and further erodes Americans' faith that the justice system is fair and equal for all."[15]

Those whom Biden had appointed to run the Justice Department were frustrated by the pardon as well, but they were even more outraged by the president's justification for it. The president had the right and the power to pardon his son, they believed, but Hunter—represented by highly qualified and highly paid defense counsel—had been duly convicted by a jury on the gun charges and had pleaded guilty to the tax charges. Top DOJ officials felt betrayed that Biden was calling the result of that process a "miscarriage of justice." In their view, Biden was doing the same thing Trump had been doing for years: undermining the credibility of the justice system.

While Biden was dealing with the backlash to his pardon of Hunter, special counsel Jack Smith was spending his final weeks in office trying to wrap up what was left of his two investigations of Donald Trump.

Trump had vowed on the campaign trail to fire Smith within "two seconds" of being sworn into office, and Smith in the days immediately following Trump's victory signaled plans to resign. But before he could depart, Smith had had to deliver the final report on his investigations—the same report he had invited Trump's lawyers to review at the special counsel's office on January 3—to Attorney General Merrick Garland.

The final report presented Smith with an opportunity to lay out for the public all the evidence he and his team had collected, making the case for what would have happened if Trump had ever gone to trial. After two years of investigating and battling with Trump's lawyers in court, Smith reviewed the documents one final time on January 7, 2025, sealed a printed copy inside an envelope, and got into a car with one member of his team for the two-mile drive to the Department of Justice headquarters. He wanted to deliver his report to Garland in person.

Other than the indictments he drafted against Trump and the largely technical court filings that had come to define the cases' legal purgatory, Smith's final report would be the most detailed and public accounting of the allegations against Trump.

Trump's legal team successfully blocked the release of the report on the classified documents case thanks to a favorable ruling from Judge Aileen Cannon—Trump's favorite federal judge*—but the report on the election interference case was published shortly after midnight on January 14.

In it, Smith argued that Trump would have been convicted of

*In a speech he delivered at the Department of Justice in March 2025, Trump thanked Judge Aileen Cannon for all she had done to help him during his criminal case. "We had an amazing judge in Florida," Trump said. "Actually, she was brilliant. She moved quickly. She was the absolute model of what a judge should be. She was strong and tough." Hours after the public praise, lawyers within the Department of Justice filed a brief urging Judge Cannon to permanently seal the report in case a future attorney general "ever expresses an intention to release Volume II outside the Department of Justice."

multiple felonies for his actions following the 2020 election if voters had not decided to send him back to the White House in 2024, claiming that Trump used lies and deceit "as a weapon to defeat a federal government function foundational to the United States' democratic process." The decision to drop the case was fully driven by his reelection, Smith wrote, not because there was a lack of evidence.

"The Department's view that the Constitution prohibits the continued indictment and prosecution of a President is categorical and does not turn on the gravity of the crimes charged, the strength of the Government's proof, or the merits of the prosecution, which the Office stands fully behind," the report read. "Indeed, but for Mr. Trump's election and imminent return to the Presidency, the Office assessed that the admissible evidence was sufficient to obtain and sustain a conviction at trial."

And in a final rebuke of the man he had spent two years investigating and prosecuting, Smith wrote a letter to Garland in which he denounced Trump's constant attacks on him and his team of prosecutors.

"Throughout my service as Special Counsel, seeking to influence the election one way or the other, or seeking to interfere in its outcome, played no role in our work. My Office had one north star: to follow the facts and law wherever they led. Nothing more and nothing less," Smith wrote. "And to all who know me well, the claim from Mr. Trump that my decisions as a prosecutor were influenced or directed by the Biden administration or other political actors is, in a word, laughable."

After two years of operating mostly in silence, the letter was the most outspoken Smith had been about Trump's incessant criticism of the investigators. But Smith also knew there was a limit to how candid he could be about the man who, days later, would become the most powerful person in the United States. In the days before his report was publicly released, Smith discreetly approached Covington & Burling, a top law firm based in Washington, about obtaining a criminal defense attorney. He didn't believe he had committed any crime, but he had reason to believe Trump would do what he had promised and come after him.

Smith also resigned from the Justice Department in those final days of the Biden administration, but he didn't mark the end of his tenure in a news conference or even a press release. Instead, Jack Smith announced his departure in a footnote on the final page of a court filing in Trump's classified documents case: "The Special Counsel completed his work and submitted his final confidential report on January 7, 2025, and separated from the Department on January 10."

With a whimper, the historic and long-running federal investigation into the alleged crimes of Donald Trump had come to an end.

CHAPTER EIGHTEEN

COME RETRIBUTION

I WAS THE HUNTED, AND NOW I'M THE HUNTER.

—Donald J. Trump, June 18, 2025

The morning's events at 1600 Pennsylvania Avenue on January 20, 2025, were carefully choreographed and steeped in history. Joe and Jill Biden welcomed Donald and Melania Trump at the front door of the White House—the North Portico—and posed for pictures before walking inside for a small reception in the presidential residence. The festivities culminated with the incoming and outgoing presidents sharing a ride in the presidential limo from the White House to the US Capitol. The First Ladies—Jill and Melania—joined the motorcade, too, sharing a ride in another vehicle.

It was, in a word, *normal.*

For nearly two hundred years, just about every newly elected president has been welcomed to the White House by his predecessor on the morning of the inauguration and shared a ride up Pennsylvania Avenue for the swearing-in ceremony. The tradition began in 1837, with Andrew Jackson inviting Martin Van Buren, his vice president, to ride to the Capitol in his horse-drawn carriage made of wood from the USS *Constitution*.[1]

The early morning White House visit and shared ride are more than a common courtesy: This tradition sends a message to both the nation and the world about the United States' commitment to a peaceful transfer of power. The incoming and outgoing presidents may be bitter political foes—Herbert Hoover and Franklin Delano Roosevelt despised each other so much that they didn't speak at all on their joint ride to the Capitol and, after it was over, never met again—but by coming together on the morning of the inauguration, they demonstrated a shared respect for the will of the voters, and for American democracy.

But in 2025, the continuation of the tradition could not be taken for granted. Biden was, after all, welcoming a man back to the White House who did not recognize the legitimacy of his presidency. He was extending a courtesy to Trump that Trump himself had refused to extend four years earlier, when Trump left town before the inaugural ceremonies began. In 2021, Biden became the first newly elected president not invited to ride from the White House to the Capitol on his first day in office since the bitter and impeached Andrew Johnson snubbed Ulysses S. Grant in 1869. So by inviting Trump back, Biden was doing more than extending a courtesy to his successor. He was recommitting the American presidency to a tradition Trump had trashed on his way out of the White House.

But Biden also engaged in some norm-busting behavior himself before leaving office that day, deciding to issue last-minute, preemptive pardons to a number of individuals whom he believed could be unfairly targeted by the incoming Trump administration. Shortly after 7 a.m. on January 20, the president issued pardons for General Mark Milley, Dr. Anthony Fauci, former Representative Liz Cheney, and other members of the congressional committee that investigated January 6—as well as their staff. The police officers who testified before that committee about being assaulted by Trump's supporters also received pardons.

"I believe in the rule of law, and I am optimistic that the strength of our legal institutions will ultimately prevail over politics," Biden said in a statement announcing the moves. "But these are exceptional circumstances, and I cannot in good conscience do nothing. Baseless and politically motivated investigations wreak havoc on the lives, safety and financial security of targeted individuals and their families."

"Even when individuals have done nothing wrong—and in fact have done the right thing—and will ultimately be exonerated," he continued, "the mere fact of being investigated or prosecuted can irreparably damage reputations and finances."

None of these individuals had been charged with—or even credibly accused of—any crime, but they had come under relentless attack from Trump and his supporters during a campaign in which "retribution" had become a central theme.

Trump had repeatedly and baselessly accused Cheney and the rest of the January 6 Committee of destroying evidence that exonerated him and his supporters, and he had accused Milley, whom he had appointed chairman of the Joint Chiefs of Staff during his first term, of treason because he had called his Chinese military counterpart two days after the January 6 attacks to say the United States remained stable and would not be attacking China. And Milley, as first reported by Bob Woodward and Robert Costa, had also called his

Chinese counterpart shortly before the 2020 election to offer the same assurance, saying, "If we're going to attack, I'm going to call you ahead of time. It's not going to be a surprise."[2]

"In times gone by," Trump had declared about Milley during the campaign, "the punishment would have been DEATH!"[3]

Dr. Anthony Fauci, who had honorably served seven US presidents as a leading expert on infectious diseases, was constantly under attack by Trump's allies for his role in advising Trump during the COVID-19 pandemic and had been accused of misleading Congress about the National Institutes of Health's role in funding so-called gain-of-function research in China.

I called Fauci as soon as the White House announced the pardons. He had not yet heard the news and had mixed feelings when I told him what Biden had done for him. "Let me be perfectly clear, Jon," Fauci told me. "I have committed no crime, you know that, and there are no possible grounds for any allegation or threat of criminal investigation or prosecution of me."

Even so, Fauci said he appreciated the pardon, because he feared that the incoming Trump administration would come after him whether or not it had a legitimate reason to do so. Just the possibility of prosecution, he continued, "creates immeasurable and intolerable distress on me and my family."

Trump reacted to the pardons shortly after they were announced. "It is disgraceful," he texted Kristen Welker of NBC News. "Many are guilty of MAJOR CRIMES."[4] But when Biden greeted him on the front steps of the White House at 9:55 a.m., Trump didn't seem the least bit upset. In the twenty-five minutes he and his wife, Melania, spent at the White House that morning, he made no reference whatsoever to the pardons.

When Biden and Trump stepped back outside the White House at 10:37 a.m., Biden got into the limo first, sitting in the right rear seat. As he sat down, he noticed a phone sitting on the armrest to his left and grew alarmed. Biden had been using the presidential limo now for four years, and he had never seen a stray phone in the back seat before. How did it get there? Was it really a phone? Did someone sabotage the vehicle?

As Biden started to ask the Secret Service agents in the front of the car about the device, Trump walked over to the rear door on the driver's side and stepped into the presidential limo for the first time in four years. As he sat down next to Biden, Trump reached over and picked up the phone—it was his. An enterprising aide to the incoming president had been able to place the phone into Biden's limousine so that Trump would have access to it during his ride to the Capitol.

The next part of the scene played out on live television, almost like a silent movie. On the video feed being broadcast by all the television networks, Trump could be seen through the tinted rear window picking up the phone and, it seemed, either scrolling through his messages or sending a message while Biden sat next to him.

I later learned what had actually happened. Trump, sensing that Biden was a little startled to find an unfamiliar object in the presidential limo, tried to cut the tension. He grabbed the phone and said it was his, telling Biden, "Let's see what people are saying about you!" As the president-elect began to dramatically scroll through his notifications, he joked to Biden, "Oh look, they are all talking about what a great job you've done!"

The two men chatted for the remainder of the 2.1-mile ride up Pennsylvania Avenue, joined in the limousine by Democratic Senator Amy Klobuchar of Minnesota, who was there in her capacity as the co-chair of the Joint Congressional Committee on Inaugural Ceremonies. There was no mention of the pardons Biden had just issued, or the fact that Trump didn't give Biden a ride four years earlier. Klobuchar later said the three politicians discussed the NFL playoffs during the ride, as well as the weather. The temperature in Washington, DC, that day was only about 7 degrees with the wind chill—so brutally cold that officials had decided to move Trump's inaugural ceremony inside for the first time since Ronald Reagan took the oath of office inside the Capitol rotunda in January 1985.

That little trick of getting the president-elect's cell phone prepositioned in what was still Joe Biden's presidential limousine was a minor example of a crucial reality as Donald Trump started his second presidency: He was no longer a political novice. He had done it before. He and the people around him knew how to get things done. They knew how to make the rules work for them and to get around them—maybe even break them—if they didn't.

Trump was coming back to the White House more experienced, more powerful, and less restrained than he had been eight years earlier. He was empowered by his own experience. He was empowered by a Supreme Court that had set an new precedent for wide-ranging presidential immunity, which, rightly or wrongly, Trump interpreted as a green light to do whatever he wanted while in office without fear of ever being prosecuted again. Trump was also empowered by his control over the Republican Party. When he first became president, the Republican leaders in Congress—especially Senate Leader Mitch McConnell and House Speaker Paul Ryan—were people who felt no real loyalty to Trump and had initially not even supported his presidential campaign. It was Trump's party now. The leaders answered to him.

His cabinet and his White House this time would be led by people who had proved their loyalty to him.

The president-elect was ready to test the limits of his power—and whether there were any real limits at all.

As Trump made small talk with Biden about sports and weather on the way to the Capitol, his advisors were already making final preparations for the frenzy of activity that would begin shortly after he was sworn in. Stephen Miller, a speechwriter and policy advisor during Trump's first term, had founded an organization called America First Legal just months after Trump left the White House in 2021. In the years since, Miller prepared for Trump's return to power, drafting scores of potential executive orders and outlining a plan for reshaping the federal government that was more far-reaching and coherent than anything Trump had tried during his first go-round.

Russell Vought, Trump's incoming director of the Office of Management and Budget (OMB), would also need no time to settle into his job. He had held the same position at the end of Trump's first term and had been hard at work during the Biden presidency, helping craft the Heritage Foundation's "Project 2025," the policy blueprint put together to "prepare for a new conservative administration through policy, training, and personnel." Trump had distanced himself from the effort during the campaign when it came under fire from his Democratic opponents, claiming during the ABC News debate with Kamala Harris that he had "nothing to do with Project 2025" and that he "purposely" hadn't even read it. Now that the election was over, however, Vought was back in his position atop OMB, ready to put much of the plan into action, starting on day one.

Sergio Gor, a man whose low public profile belied his status as one of the most powerful men in Trump's Washington, was also ready to get to work the moment Trump was sworn in. Installed at the Presidential Personnel Office, Gor would pick up where Johnny McEntee left off four years earlier. As I documented in *Betrayal*, when McEntee held the position in 2020, he transformed what was essentially the executive branch's human resources department into a vehicle to root out any disloyalty within the administration. Now, Gor was using this position to ensure that only true Trump loyalists would be hired in the first place, scouring work histories, political activities, and social media accounts of prospective federal employees and their families for any sign of Trump dissent.

Because the cold weather had forced the inauguration to be moved indoors, fewer people could attend the ceremony. The Capitol rotunda, where Trump would take his oath of office and deliver his inaugural address, could only seat about six hundred people, forcing a number of VIPs who would have ordinarily had a spot on the inaugural platform to watch a video feed of the festivities from an overflow area, Emancipation Hall. Among those who didn't make the cut were several Republican governors—Ron DeSantis of Florida, Brian Kemp of Georgia, and Glenn Youngkin of Virginia—and some staunch Trump supporters like Kari Lake, who had lost a gubernatorial race and a US Senate race in Arizona in consecutive election cycles.

But there was one group that didn't have to worry about being banished to the cheap seats: tech industry titans. As Trump prepared to take the oath of office, sitting behind him would be Meta CEO Mark Zuckerberg, Amazon founder Jeff Bezos, Apple CEO Tim

Cook, Google CEO Sundar Pichai, TikTok CEO Shou Zi Chew, and, of course, the world's richest man, Elon Musk.

Their attendance marked the culmination of an astounding turn of events. Four years earlier, in the wake of the January 6 attacks, Trump had been banned from Facebook, Instagram, and Twitter. Around the same time, Amazon and Google's political action committees had announced they would not make donations to any politicians who voted, as Trump had demanded, to challenge the results of the 2020 presidential election. There was a deliberate and unambiguous effort on the part of tech industry leaders to ostracize Trump and his political allies.

Now, many of those same executives were sitting in the Capitol rotunda as President-elect Trump's special guests, with better seats than most members of his incoming cabinet.

The day before the inauguration, I interviewed Steve Bannon on ABC's *This Week* and asked him if he had any concern about Donald Trump inviting all these tech billionaires to his inauguration. After all, Bannon had recently gone after what he described as "oligarchs in Silicon Valley" who "take jobs from American citizens, give them to what become indentured servants from foreign countries, and then pay 'em less."[5]

To my surprise, Bannon told me he wasn't upset at all. The tech oligarchs had tried to defeat Trump, he said, and now they were coming to his inauguration to surrender to him. He compared their attendance at Trump's inauguration with the leadership of imperial Japan going aboard the USS *Missouri* to surrender to General Douglas MacArthur at the end of World War II.

"They're there as supplicants," Bannon told me. "President Trump broke the oligarchs. He broke them, and they surrendered."[6]

This surrender to Trump began well before he won the election. Amazon resumed donations to Republicans who objected to the 2020 election results in late 2022, just as Trump was preparing to run for president again.[7] Meta reinstated Trump's Facebook and Instagram accounts a few months later, in early 2023. Jeff Bezos's *Washington Post*—which had a particularly adversarial relationship with Trump during his first term, as exhibited by its slogan, "Democracy Dies in Darkness"—announced two weeks before the presidential election that the paper's editorial page would not endorse a presidential candidate[8] for the first time in thirty-six years—after the paper's editorial board had already drafted an endorsement of Kamala Harris.[9]

The morning after the election, Bezos offered Trump some words of encouragement. "Big congratulations to our 45th and 47th President on an extraordinary political comeback and decisive victory," he posted on X. "Wishing @realdonaldtrump all success in leading and uniting the America we all love."[10]

A few weeks later, the day before Thanksgiving, Zuckerberg made a pilgrimage to Mar-a-Lago to have dinner with Trump, delighting the president-elect with his willingness to fly all the way from Hawaii to Palm Beach for one meal. But Zuckerberg was willing to do it because he knew his relationship with Trump needed some work. Two months before the election, Trump had published a coffee table book titled *Save America*, which included a photograph of Trump and Zuckerberg—and an ominous warning. "[Zuckerberg] would come to the Oval Office to see me. He would bring his very nice wife to dinners, be as nice as anyone could be, while always plotting to install shameful Lock Boxes in a true PLOT AGAINST THE PRESIDENT," Trump wrote, referring to donations Zuckerberg and his wife, Priscilla Chan, made to support election infrastructure in 2020.

"We are watching him closely, and if he does anything illegal this time he will spend the rest of his life in prison—as will others who cheat in the 2024 Presidential Election."[11]

In addition to his efforts to curry favor with Trump at Mar-a-Lago, Zuckerberg also made substantive changes to how his company operated. In late August 2024, for example, he sent a letter to the Republican-led House Judiciary Committee in which he expressed "regret" for throttling the spread of stories related to Hunter Biden's laptop in the weeks before the 2020 election and for acquiescing to pressure from the Biden administration to censor posts related to certain topics.[12] Two weeks before Trump's inauguration, Meta announced that Dana White, the CEO of the Ultimate Fighting Championship and one of Trump's closest friends, would join the company's board of directors, and that the company would be winding down its fact-checking program. "The fact checkers have just been too politically biased and have destroyed more trust than they've created," Zuckerberg said in a video announcing the change.* Less than a month later, Meta would pay Trump $25 million to settle a lawsuit he had brought against the company in 2021 related to his ban from Facebook and Instagram.[13]

Zuckerberg's supplication may have been over-the-top, but he had good business reasons for courting Trump. The Federal Trade Commission (FTC) was engaged in a years-long antitrust lawsuit against Meta, and it was set to go to trial within months. If the government was successful, the company could be forced to sell off two of its most successful platforms, Instagram and WhatsApp, with devastating

*Erasing any doubt about whom he was courting with these changes to the company's fact-checking program, Zuckerberg had Joel Kaplan, a former Republican lobbyist and Meta's new global policy chief, announce them on *Fox & Friends*, one of Trump's favorite cable news programs.

effects to its bottom line. Trump himself could shape the outcome of the trial by urging his administration to reach a settlement before the lawsuit went to trial—if he wanted to.

The Meta CEO visited the White House three times during Trump's first one hundred days, making his company's case to the president directly. The White House visits were widely reported at the time and confirmed by Meta. But what was not reported at the time, or mentioned by Meta, was that Zuckerberg had visited the Department of Justice during one of his visits to Washington, before heading over to the White House. According to a source familiar with the meeting, Zuckerberg met with Attorney General Pam Bondi on March 12 and asked her for advice on how to effectively speak with Trump about Meta's concerns.

Zuckerberg's efforts, however, did not appear to pay off. On April 8, according to *The Wall Street Journal*, FTC Chairman Andrew Ferguson, Assistant Attorney General for Antitrust Abigail Slater, and White House Chief of Staff Susie Wiles met with Trump in the Oval Office to discuss the FTC's case, and Trump agreed to let it go to trial.[14] The proceedings began less than a week later, and Zuckerberg himself was forced to take the stand to defend his company's actions.

At 11:38 a.m., just twenty-two minutes before Trump would be sworn in, the White House announced Biden's final act as president. It was a big one—and one that even some of his own allies said would tarnish his legacy: He issued five pardons for members of his immediate family. The pardons of Biden's siblings James, Frank, and Valerie (as well as James's wife and Valerie's husband) were as sweeping as the one issued to Hunter weeks earlier, clearing them of "any nonviolent offense committed against the United States" that any of them "may have committed" since the beginning of 2014.

Republicans had long accused Biden's family members of leveraging their proximity to him to cash in—and federal investigators were reportedly looking into James's business dealings as recently as 2024[15]—but Biden said in a statement that the pardons were purely precautionary. "My family has been subjected to unrelenting attacks and threats, motivated solely by a desire to hurt me—the worst kind of partisan politics," the statement read. "Unfortunately, I have no reason to believe these attacks will end."

The pardons were announced at the exact moment Biden was walking into the Capitol rotunda to take his seat just five feet away from where Trump would be sitting during the inaugural ceremony. Biden hadn't decided until late the night before to issue them—a decision that surprised his senior White House staff. Several of his advisors—including White House counsel Ed Siskel—had recommended against doing it, arguing that the pardon power should be used narrowly and with discretion and that using it for family members would be a stain on Biden's legacy. Biden had deliberated over whether to issue the pardons for weeks; two of Biden's senior advisors told me they believed Biden had been convinced not to do it.

His late change of heart created a scramble in the nearly empty Biden White House on the morning of January 20. Most of the staff was already gone. The counsel's office didn't finish writing the pardons and the accompanying statement until about 11 a.m. Nervously watching the clock, the few staffers left in Biden's communications office were worried they would lose access to their White House computers before they could send out the announcement. When they were finally able to hit send on the press release—at 11:38 a.m.—they were relieved to find they could send outgoing emails from their government computers.

Trump and some of his Republican allies in Congress would later claim that because Biden's pardons had been signed using an autopen—a mechanical device that presidents have used for years* to imprint their signatures on documents using real ink—they were not binding. In a post on Truth Social in March 2025, Trump himself claimed the pardons were "hereby declared VOID, VACANT, AND OF NO FURTHER FORCE OF EFFECT, because of the fact that they were done by Autopen." Trump even alleged that the pardons were issued without Biden's knowledge.[16]

So, were the pardons signed with an autopen? Was Biden fully aware of what was being signed?

A senior Biden White House official later told me that, yes, the pardons Biden issued at the end of his presidency were, in fact, signed with an autopen. The official said this was a common practice in the Biden White House and was done for convenience, given the large number of documents that require a presidential signature on any given day. But the idea that important documents were being signed without Biden's knowledge, according to this official, is preposterous. "That whole thing is just garbage," the official told me. "Yes, he made the decisions. The autopen was used just because it was the convenient thing to do relative to everything that was going on." There was, however, one pardon Biden did not sign with the autopen. He personally signed, with his own hand, the pardon he issued for his son Hunter in December.

Whether issuing the pardons for his family members was the

*Even Thomas Jefferson had an early version of an autopen that allowed him to sign two documents at once.

right thing to do or not, two things are indisputable: (1) He had the constitutional power to pardon anybody he wanted to; and (2) the decision was clearly Biden's and it was made against the advice of at least some of his senior advisors. The notion that a rogue staffer was commandeering the autopen to make pardons against Biden's will is, indeed, preposterous.

Before the inaugural festivities began, Trump's aides had informed reporters that the president-elect's second inaugural address would strike a much more positive and uplifting tone than his first, which had come to be known as the "American Carnage" speech due to how darkly Trump spoke about the state of the country. Trump himself had told my ABC News colleague Rachel Scott days earlier that the three themes of his speech would be "unity, strength, and fairness."[17]

The description wasn't *entirely* off-base. "National unity is now returning to America, and confidence and pride is soaring like never before," Trump said toward the beginning of his approximately thirty-minute-long remarks. "In everything we do, my administration will be inspired by a strong pursuit of excellence and unrelenting success. We will not forget our country, we will not forget our Constitution, and we will not forget our God."

"My proudest legacy will be that of a peacemaker and unifier," he added. "That's what I want to be, a peacemaker and a unifier."

But for the most part, his second inaugural address echoed the themes of his first. It sounded a lot like "American Carnage 2.0."

"For many years, a radical and corrupt establishment has extracted power and wealth from our citizens while the pillars of our society lay broken and seemingly in complete disrepair," Trump said, with the four leading figures of that "radical and corrupt establishment"—Presidents Bill Clinton, George W. Bush, Barack Obama, and Joe Biden—sitting right there with him in the rotunda.

"We now have a government that cannot manage even a simple crisis at home while, at the same time, stumbling into a continuing catalogue of catastrophic events abroad. It fails to protect our magnificent, law-abiding American citizens but provides sanctuary and protection for dangerous criminals, many from prisons and mental institutions, that have illegally entered our country from all over the world. We have a government that has given unlimited funding to the defense of foreign borders but refuses to defend American borders or, more importantly, its own people."

"My recent election is a mandate to completely and totally reverse a horrible betrayal and all of these many betrayals that have taken place," Trump continued, "to give the people back their faith, their wealth, their democracy, and, indeed, their freedom. From this moment on, America's decline is over."

At the conclusion of his remarks, the newly sworn-in president and the first lady escorted Joe and Jill Biden out the east side of the Capitol building where the Marine helicopter was waiting to take the now former president and first lady on one final trip out of Washington. One of the people sitting inside the helicopter shot cell phone video as the Trumps and Bidens approached. I've viewed this remarkable piece of video. It shows Trump leaning into Biden to offer some parting words. "Stay in touch," Trump tells Biden. "Let me know if there is anything you need."

As I've personally experienced many times, Trump has a unique capacity to be savagely ruthless at one moment and exceedingly generous and complimentary the next. On several occasions, he brutally attacked me publicly and then talked to me days later—sometimes even minutes later—as though nothing had happened. He did it with Barack Obama eleven days earlier at the funeral service for Jimmy Carter, which was attended by every living president. Trump sat next to Obama at the Washington National Cathedral and could be seen smiling and laughing, frequently whispering to Obama as the memorial proceeded. I later learned that while the two of them sat there in the cathedral, Trump invited Obama to play golf with him. The golf date never happened; months later, Trump made a series of unfounded allegations against Obama and accused him of treason.

But even by Trump standards, the whiplash of his relationship with Biden was staggering. One moment, he was condemning the outgoing president in his inaugural address for betraying America; the next, he was telling him to "stay in touch." And Trump's attacks on Biden would soon become even harsher.

With the Bidens on the first leg of their journey home, Trump returned to the Capitol complex to speak to those who couldn't fit into the rotunda for the inaugural ceremony. In these unscripted remarks—"a better speech than the one I made upstairs," he claimed—Trump reverted entirely to form, bringing up the "totally rigged" 2020 election and boasting that the 2024 contest was "too big to rig," despite Democrats' best efforts.

To this overflow crowd, Trump explained that he had toned down his official inaugural address on the advice of his aides. "I was going to talk about the J6 hostages," he said, referring to the men and women sentenced to prison for their actions at the Capitol on January 6, 2021. "But you'll be happy because, you know, it's action, not words, that count. And you're going to see a lot of action on the J6 hostages."

He was correct.

Trump signed twenty-six executive orders and a couple dozen other official documents and memoranda on the first day of his second term, significantly more than he signed on day one in 2017 and a record for any US president on his first day in office.* Many of those executive actions were hugely consequential—establishing the Department of Government Efficiency; directing federal agencies to eliminate diversity, equity, and inclusion initiatives; designating drug cartels as foreign terrorist organizations—but Trump's sweeping pardons for those so-called J6 hostages stood above the rest.

Trump had long talked about pardoning January 6 prisoners on the campaign trail, but the assumption—among both people inside and outside Trump's inner circle—was always that those promises referred only to those who may have trespassed on Capitol grounds on that fateful day but didn't engage in any violence. In fact, JD Vance made that argument on national television one week before Trump's inauguration.

"If you protested peacefully on January 6, and you've had Merrick Garland's Department of Justice treat you like a gang member, you should be pardoned," Vance told Fox News's Shannon Bream. "If you committed violence on that day, obviously you shouldn't be pardoned, and there's a little bit of a gray area there, but we're very much committed to seeing the equal administration of law. And there are

*During his first term, Trump had signed only one executive order on his first day in office.

a lot of people, we think, in the wake of January 6, who were prosecuted unfairly. We need to rectify that."[18]

Vance's words sounded reasonable enough. Although all the protestors who went into the Capitol that day had committed a crime, surely many of the more than 1,500 people charged in connection with the riot had gotten swept up in the emotion of the day. If all they did was follow the crowd and wander around the Capitol, maybe they deserved a pardon. But those who attacked police officers or committed other acts of violence surely didn't.

But Vance received immediate and fierce blowback for his remarks—and not from the left. "Better rethink what you just said JD," a prominent MAGA account on X with more than three million followers warned menacingly.[19] The brothers behind the account, known as the Hodge twins, were not upset with Vance for floating pardons to nonviolent January 6 protesters. They were upset because he had ruled out pardons for the violent ones.

The blowback was so severe that Vance, only days away from being sworn in as vice president, was forced into full damage-control mode, scrambling to explain that he had been defending the J6 prisoners for years and that all he was advocating for was the president making pardon decisions on a case-by-case basis. "I assure you, we care about people unjustly locked up," Vance wrote in a bid to mollify his MAGA critics. "Yes, that includes people provoked and it includes people who got a garbage trial."[20]

Despite the walk-back, Vance continued to be attacked by members of the MAGA right who had made the J6 prisoners their main focus. Trump was fully aware of the heat Vance was taking, and on January 16—four days before his inauguration—he asked his personal assistant, Natalie Harp, to call Julie Kelly, a political pundit who had made herself the leading advocate of the J6 prisoners. Kelly was the author of *January 6: How Democrats Used the Capitol Protest to Launch a War on Terror Against the Political Right*, and she was the first person to record J6 prisoners singing the "Star-Spangled Banner" at a Washington, DC, jail—a later version of which would later be played at Trump's political rallies.

Kelly had spoken to Trump only once before, in August 2022. Back then, she had arranged a meeting with him to urge him to take on the cause of his supporters who were being prosecuted for their actions on January 6. It was not long after that meeting that Trump began saying the January 6 prisoners—whom he eventually started calling "J6 hostages"—were being mistreated.

When Kelly answered her phone on January 16, 2025, she suddenly found herself on a conference call with the president-elect and two of his top allies: Boris Epshteyn and Charlie Kirk. Over the course of the forty-minute conversation, Trump asked Kelly which January 6 prisoners she thought should be pardoned, and she advocated for virtually all of them—even those who had assaulted police officers. Even those who were charged for violent acts deserved clemency, she argued, because they had been provoked by the police.

By the end of the call, Trump made clear to Kelly that he was going to take her advice. "Julie, I'm going to pardon all these people. And I'm sorry, I'm going to put you out of work," he joked. "You're not going to have any more work. I'm going to put you out of a job." After all, Kelly had spent most of the last three years of her life trying to free these prisoners.

Trump kept his word. At 7:40 p.m. on the first day of his second term, he issued what amounted to a get-out-of-jail-free card for everyone charged in connection with the assault on the Capitol. All but fourteen of the convicts were issued full pardons, expunging the convictions from their records; the others—members of the Proud Boys and Oath Keepers militia groups who had been convicted of seditious conspiracy against the United States—had their sentences commuted instead, freeing them from prison while keeping their convictions on their records. Enrique Tarrio, unlike the other leaders of the Proud Boys who had been charged with sedition, was among those granted a full pardon.

And just like that, one of the largest and most far-reaching investigations in the history of the FBI was effectively erased. Before the night was over, people who had sought to disrupt the peaceful transfer of power four years earlier were released from prisons around the country.

The pardons were quickly condemned by the Fraternal Order of Police, the largest law enforcement union in the United States, which had endorsed Trump in all three of his campaigns. "Crimes against law enforcement are not just attacks on individuals or public safety—they are attacks on society and undermine the rule of law," the group said in a joint statement with the International Association of Chiefs of Police. "When perpetrators of crimes, especially serious crimes, are not held fully accountable, it sends a dangerous message that the consequences for attacking law enforcement are not severe, potentially emboldening others to commit similar acts of violence."[21]

In an interview on January 22, Fox News host Sean Hannity asked Trump about his decision to free those who had attacked police. Why did they get a pardon?

"They were in there for three and a half years, a long time, and many in solitary confinement, treated like nobody's ever been treated," Trump replied. "They were treated like the worst criminals in history, and you know what they were there for? They were protesting the vote, because they knew the election was rigged. And they were protesting the vote, and they should be allowed to protest the vote. You should be allowed to."

One of those people who traveled to Washington to "protest the vote" was Pamela Hemphill, a sixty-seven-year-old grandmother from Boise, Idaho. She had undergone breast cancer surgery when she decided to take the trip to attend Trump's January 6 rally. She had no intention to take part in any violence or break any laws, but she believed what Trump was saying about the election being stolen and wanted to support him. Outside the Capitol, Hemphill encountered a group of Proud Boys who had broken through police barricades; she shot video of her experience with her phone and livestreamed it on Facebook. She joined the crowd going into the building, continuing to shoot video with her phone. After she was prosecuted for illegally entering the building, several Trump allies, including Laura Loomer, urged her to fight the charges. But she knew she had broken the law and pleaded guilty. She was sentenced to two months in prison—serving her time at the notorious Dublin Federal Correctional Institution in Dublin, California—and three years of probation.

Among many of the loudest voices in Trump's movement, Hemphill had become known as the "MAGA Granny"—a symbol of what they said was a weaponized Justice Department punishing people because they supported Donald Trump. While she was in prison, she heard that Tucker Carlson was speaking about her on his Fox News show. "She's got breast cancer," Carlson said, expressing his disgust at those who had prosecuted her. "She's going to prison."

Donald Trump's pardon would have effectively eliminated the stigma of her criminal record. She could have touted it as an exoneration.

But she rejected it. The "MAGA Granny" wanted nothing to do with the effort to rewrite the history of January 6. "Accepting the pardon would be an insult to the Capitol Police officers, to the rule of law, to our nation," she told the *Idaho Statesman* the day after Trump's mass clemency. "The J6 criminals are trying to rewrite history by saying that it was not a riot; it wasn't an insurrection. I don't want to be a part of their trying to rewrite what happened that day."[22]

She later told me that she considered the Capitol Police officers her heroes who had tried to protect the Capitol—and tried to protect her, too. After she got inside the building, she said, she had found herself getting crushed by the crowd. A Capitol police officer reached out and pulled her back to safety. She believes that officer saved her from serious injury. "My dream is to meet him and hug him and let him know how sorry I am that I was ever there that day," she told me.

While Hemphill was adamant she would not be part of an effort to exonerate the January 6 mob, rejecting a presidential pardon is an extraordinarily rare thing to do. The first such instance occurred when a convicted postal robber named George Wilson, who had been sentenced to death, refused a pardon from President Andrew Jackson in 1830. Because the presidential pardon was considered absolute, the Supreme Court was asked to decide whether Wilson had a right to reject it. In an opinion written by Chief Justice John Marshall, the court held that Wilson could not be forced to accept a presidential act of forgiveness. "A pardon is an act of grace," Marshall wrote, "[but] delivery is not completed without acceptance. It may then be rejected by the person to whom it is tendered."

Wilson's reasons for rejecting President Jackson's "act of grace" have been lost to history. And while his Supreme Court case, *United States v. Wilson*, established a right to reject presidential clemency, the precedent hadn't been invoked by the recipient of a pardon for more than a century—until Pamela Hemphill stepped forward on the first full day of Trump's second term.

Rejecting the pardon turned out to be more difficult than she thought. Hemphill reached out to a university professor for advice. She contacted the Susan B. Anthony Museum, which had objected to a posthumous pardon Donald Trump had granted Susan B. Anthony in 2020 to expunge her conviction for illegally voting in 1872 (the suffragette had made it clear during her lifetime that she didn't want a pardon because she considered the conviction a badge of honor). Based on the advice she received, Hemphill wrote a letter on January 24 to the office of the pardon attorney at the Department of Justice, but she got no response. She kept at it. "There's no way I wanted that on my record—that I had accepted it. No. No. No."

"It's hard to explain," she told me. "It would have been such a disgrace that I couldn't sleep at night. I don't want to die with that in my life—that pardon from Trump, it's like having a spider on you and you can't get it off."

After being ignored by the Department of Justice's pardon attorney, Hemphill reached out to the office of Republican Senator Jim Risch for help. More than three months later, Risch's office received a response officially recognizing Hemphill's rejection of Trump's pardon and assuring her the pardon would not be mentioned on her criminal record.

Hemphill's refusal to accept Trump's pardon caught the attention of the person who enraged the mob on January 6 by refusing to use his position to overturn the 2020 election: former Vice President Mike Pence.

"I am writing to express my admiration for your decision to refuse a presidential pardon and accept responsibility for your actions on January 6," Pence wrote Hemphill in June 2025. "Your honorable decision speaks volumes about your commitment to the Rule of Law, and I wanted to pass along my genuine respect."

The so-called MAGA Granny had indeed made her mark on history—becoming one of the first people—if not the very first—to stand up to Donald Trump at the start of his second term.*

*Not long after Hemphill declared her intention to reject Trump's pardon, another January 6 convict did the same thing. Jason Riddle, who stole a book from a Senate office and drank a bottle of wine while he was with the mob in the Capitol, had been sentenced to three months in prison. He rejected the pardon saying, "Just because the guy who started the riot says it's okay, it means absolutely nothing."

POSTSCRIPT

THE NEW ERA

In June 2025, Donald Trump visited the Fort Bragg military base in North Carolina to kick off a series of events commemorating the 250th anniversary of the US Army. The setting was festive as the troops put on a public show for their president. Black Hawk helicopters and fighter jets flew overhead. Six hundred paratroopers jumped out of massive C-17 aircraft from the skies above. Soldiers rappelled down from dual-propeller MH-47G Chinook helicopters.

The scene was perfectly set for the commander in chief to mark a milestone for the fighting force that made America possible and to boost the morale of the troops. When Donald Trump took the stage, however, he didn't just pay tribute to the Army—he delivered an inflammatory speech filled with invective for his political foes. The remarks were indistinguishable from those Trump had given at political rallies for a decade; he lambasted his predecessor, attacked California's Democratic governor and the mayor of Los Angeles, and went after the reporters covering his speech. In all three instances, the military crowd, in perfectly pressed uniforms, booed right on cue.

Had this been a campaign rally, neither Trump's rhetoric nor the crowd's response would have been particularly noteworthy; such call and response has long been par for the course at the president's events. But Trump wasn't giving a campaign speech at some fairgrounds or hockey arena; he was speaking at one of America's largest and most significant military bases. A pop-up store was selling red "Make America Great Again" hats and other Trump campaign merchandise right on the base, and some troops and base employees were wearing it as the president spoke.

The appearance of a political sales booth on a military facility was jarring, as were the active-duty soldiers in uniform booing and cheering Trump's political attacks. After all, longstanding Department of Defense policy prohibits servicemembers from wearing political garb while in uniform.

As a reporter, I covered the Pentagon for several years during the wars in Iraq and Afghanistan. I traveled with our troops from Baghdad to Fallujah to Kandahar to the Sahara Desert. The men and women whom I got to know along the way—from the senior officers to the newly enlisted troops just out of basic training to families who endured unthinkable sacrifices—are some of the most impressive public servants I have ever encountered. I admired their selfless commitment to their country, which was never confused with a commitment to a political party or a political leader. Civilian control of the military is essential in our system of government—and so is the apolitical ethos of our troops. They serve the elected leaders—and follow all legal orders—without regard to political affiliation. Their allegiance is to the Constitution.

The day after Trump's speech, the news organization military.com reported that leaders within the Army's 82nd Airborne Division, which is based at Fort Bragg, worked to handpick the audience for Trump's speech based on political leanings. As an internal message sent to one of the units put it, "If soldiers have political views that are in opposition to the current administration, and they don't want to be in the audience then they need to speak with their leadership and get swapped out."[1]

The Army announced that it would review how political merchandise came to be sold on the base, and a spokesperson for Fort Bragg insisted it was an aberration, telling my ABC News colleague Anne Flaherty that "the Army remains committed to its core values and apolitical service to the nation."[2] An unnamed Fort Bragg commander went further, telling military.com, "This has been a bad week for the Army [and] for anyone who cares about us being a neutral institution. This was shameful. I don't expect anything to come out of it, but I hope maybe we can learn from it long term."[3]

What will come out of it? Was the scene at Fort Bragg an anomaly? Or was it symptomatic of the breakdown of an essential American value—that the military does not engage in politics? General Dan Caine, the new Trump-appointed chairman of the Joint Chiefs of Staff, told Congress the following day he had not seen the reports about what had happened there, but he said America demands an "apolitical, nonpartisan military."

At the start of the second Trump presidency, Donald Trump seemed to be demanding something much different.

The United States military may be the last institution in America that large majorities of Democrats and Republicans trust. It seemed impervious to political manipulation during Trump's first term. The retired generals he had put into positions of authority proved to be more loyal to the Constitution than to the president they served, and leaders in the Department of Defense—civilian and military alike—did not let the institution they led be leveraged in a partisan crusade to overturn an election. The military abided by its apolitical ethos throughout Trump's first four years in office—and he didn't like it.

At the beginning of his second term, Donald Trump sought firmer control of the armed services. His first move—coming just hours after he was sworn in—was entirely symbolic, ordering a portrait of General Mark Milley to be removed from the hallway of the E-Ring of the Pentagon, where it had been on display alongside portraits of all the other men who had served as chairman of the Joint Chiefs of Staff.

A second portrait of Milley—this one as a former Army chief of staff—was also taken down elsewhere at the Pentagon, another part of the effort to erase his storied career as a soldier and an officer. Although Trump had chosen General Milley to serve as America's highest-ranking military leader, he had grown to resent him for not supporting his effort to overturn the 2020 presidential election. "We don't take an oath to a wannabe dictator," Milley said in his farewell speech before retiring in 2023. "We take an oath to the Constitution, and we take an oath to the idea that is America—and we're willing to die to protect it."[4]

More portraits would soon come down. Trump's defense secretary fired several of the military's top leaders, including Joint Chief Chairman Charles Q. Brown and Admiral Lisa Franchetti, the first woman to serve as chief of Naval Operations. Leaders in such positions are intended to serve four-year terms that stretch across presidential administrations, but some of Trump's top advisors questioned

Brown's and Franchetti's personal loyalty to the new commander in chief, so they were purged. The top lawyers for the Air Force, Army, and Navy were also fired.

The spectacle surrounding Trump's speech at Fort Bragg was particularly unnerving to people who feared that Trump's return to power posed a threat to democracy, and that he could become America's first dictator. I have long believed—and still hope—that those fears are overblown. Trump has always seemed to me to be more interested in fame and glory and the love of the crowd than in absolute power. But even if he does care more, in the end, about public adulation than dictatorial power, Trump has set a series of precedents—and has provided a road map—for a future leader with more sinister ambitions. Trump may not topple American democracy, but he has shown how it can be done.

During the first six months of his second term, Trump was tearing apart American institutions and challenging long-held American values and norms on an almost daily basis.

He put his personal legal team in charge of the Justice Department, demolishing the longstanding policy that criminal justice should operate independently from politics.

He attacked the courts and judges and challenged their legitimacy, drawing a rare public rebuke from the Chief Justice of the Supreme Court.

He upended a half-century's worth of ethics and anti-corruption reforms by mixing family business deals with government business, going so far as to accept a $400 million luxury jumbo jet as a gift from Qatar—agreeing that it would be used as the new Air Force One but then transferred to his presidential library shortly before he was scheduled to leave office.

He used the power of the presidency to force changes on America's top law firms, punishing them financially for taking on clients or legal work he personally didn't like.

He issued a slew of executive orders challenging the policies, procedures, and curricula of America's private colleges and universities.

And with an assist from Elon Musk, he dismantled the US Agency for International Development over the course of a couple of days, thereby demolishing an instrument for projecting American influence and goodwill—so-called soft power—that had been broadly supported by leaders in both parties since the 1960s.

With his 2016 election victory, Trump had succeeded in taking power and becoming the most famous person on the planet. But despite his virtually limitless ability to shock and to command attention, Trump's impact on the world during his first term proved to be remarkably ephemeral; he spent more time playing to the cameras than working to fundamentally change America. As I wrote while he was still in office during his first term, "Donald Trump is the creator, chief publicist, executive producer, and star of The Trump Show."

He was still at it all these years later, playing to the crowds, obsessively tracking his ratings, and using the world stage to produce what he considered the greatest reality TV show on the planet. But the second Trump presidency is poised to be more consequential, more radical, and more lasting than his first.

Plenty of what Trump does during these four years will be undone by future presidents, and some will be unwound by the courts while he is still president. But undoing the damage Trump is doing to the psyche of the country will be much harder. Over the course of his campaigns—especially the 2024 campaign—Trump hammered home the message to his supporters that they were victims, that they had been screwed over by the elites, by immigrants, by Europe, by the courts, by the political leadership. He didn't just promise to make America great again; he promised to be the way people could get revenge—"I am your retribution"—on all of those they felt had wronged them. The message resonated to the point where it is now commonplace for Americans across the political spectrum to view those who disagree with them not just as political opponents but as enemies.

Consider the remarkable statement Donald Trump made on Memorial Day 2025. "HAPPY MEMORIAL DAY TO ALL, INCLUDING THE SCUM THAT SPENT THE LAST FOUR YEARS TRYING TO DESTROY OUR COUNTRY THROUGH WARPED RADICAL LEFT MINDS," he wrote in all-caps on his Truth Social media platform at 7:22 a.m., just as Americans were waking up to mark a day where they pay tribute to those who lost their lives defending our country. The statement went on for 171 words, denouncing "USA HATING JUDGES WHO SUFFER FROM AN IDEOLOGY THAT IS SICK, AND VERY DANGEROUS FOR OUR COUNTRY," calling them "MONSTERS WHO WANT OUR COUNTRY TO GO TO HELL."[5]

The rant was vile and hateful, but perhaps the most disturbing part about it was the reaction. There was almost none. No president had ever spoken that way about fellow Americans—public servants—let alone as a part of statement on Memorial Day. But if the post bothered the president's supporters, there was no public sign of it. Republican leaders didn't publicly condemn the words, and there's no indication any of them reached out privately to urge the president to tone down his rhetoric or to remind him the meaning of Memorial Day. America had changed to the point where a president of the

United States could call judges monsters who want the country to go to hell, and almost nobody seemed to care.

A series of events at the end of the first month of Trump's second term vividly demonstrated that this time around, he wasn't just clamoring for attention; he was changing America . . . and maybe the world, too.

At about 10:45 a.m. on February 24, 2025, President Trump convened a meeting with his top national security advisors in his personal dining room adjacent to the Oval Office. It was a big day at the start of a highly consequential week for the new Trump presidency. French President Emmanuel Macron had already visited the White House to join the president for a conference call with the leaders of the five other G7 countries, and Macron would return in less than two hours for another one-on-one meeting. British Prime Minister Kier Starmer would also be visiting a few days later. The European leaders were coming to Trump with an urgent sense of purpose: to discuss the US president's plans for peace talks between Russia and Ukraine and to plead with him to continue US military support for Ukraine and its president, Volodymyr Zelensky, who was tentatively planning to visit Washington to meet with Trump at the end of the week.

As President Trump sat at his dining table in the West Wing, he looked out at the most important and powerful officials in his administration—Treasury Secretary Scott Bessent, Secretary of State Marco Rubio, special envoy Steve Witkoff, National Security Advisor Mike Waltz, Defense Secretary Pete Hegseth, and Vice President JD Vance.

At Trump's instruction, his advisors had worked out an agreement with their Ukrainian counterparts whereby, in exchange for continued military support, Ukraine would promise the United States a share in the development of its natural resources, including its vast deposits of rare earth minerals. But as Trump reviewed the draft agreement, he didn't like what he saw, believing the terms were not favorable enough to the United States. He turned to National Security Advisor Mike Waltz and made an unusual request.

"Get Steve Bannon on the phone," Trump demanded.

Bannon had not served Donald Trump in any formal capacity in nearly eight years, but he had become one of the loudest voices in the activist wing of the MAGA movement, cementing his standing as a die-hard Trump loyalist by serving four months in prison on his behalf. He was undoubtedly a key figure in Trump's movement, but he had no role in the Trump administration, let alone a position on the National Security Council.

Bannon's phone rang as he was live on television, hosting *The War Room* podcast—the twice-daily dose of resentment, retribution, and populism for the most hard-core MAGA supporters. Bannon saw Waltz calling and sent him to voicemail with a text.

"The show is live. I'll call you at noon," he wrote.

With that, Bannon continued on with his show, which had just shown live video of the French president leaving the White House.

A few minutes later—at 10:58 a.m., to be precise—while Bannon was interviewing a former British Conservative Party official based in Rome named Ben Harnwell, his phone rang again. This time he could see it was President Trump calling from his personal cell phone. Bannon quickly went to commercial break, telling his producer to make it a long one.

"Yes, Mr. President."

"Hey, Steve, I've got the boys here," Trump said. "I'm going to put you on speaker[phone]."

And with that, Steve Bannon found himself talking to the president and his national security team through the little speaker on Trump's iPhone. Viewers of Bannon's podcast had no idea Bannon had just left the show to speak to the president, but they knew *something* had happened because after the commercial break, Bannon was gone and the guest he had just been interviewing was suddenly hosting the show from Rome.

"One of the beauties of live television is there are occasional unforeseen moments," Harnwell, the guest-turned-anchor, told the audience. "Steve stepped out for just a moment. He'll be back very shortly."

Not quite. For the next thirty minutes, Trump had Bannon tell his national security team why he didn't like the deal they had just negotiated with Zelensky and why he didn't trust the Ukrainian leader. As Trump knew, Bannon was a harsh critic of Zelensky and had long argued the United States should stop supporting Ukraine's efforts to repel the Russian invasion. He had also seen Bannon attacking the natural resources deal on his podcast.

"I hear you don't love this deal," Trump said to him.

"The Ukraine deal?"

"Yeah."

"I fucking hate it," Bannon said. "I hate everything to do with it. I understand you want to recoup the $350 billion [that Trump had calculated the US had spent on Ukraine]. But that's not the way it is being described to me."

"Yeah, it's not that," Trump said.

"I hate it," Bannon said. "It ties us to Ukraine, and they are going to want a security guarantee,"

Looking ahead to Zelensky's expected trip to Washington—which had not yet been announced—Bannon referred to the Ukrainian president as "that punk."

"If that punk comes here, he's going to want a security guarantee," Bannon said. "You can't trust him. You can't trust any of the Europeans. You can't trust Putin either, but these guys are really slippery."

After nearly thirty minutes, Bannon was dismissed and returned to anchor the rest of his show. Neither he nor anybody at the White House ever revealed that the podcaster and professional MAGA agitator had joined such a high-powered West Wing meeting just minutes after the French president left the White House—and just days before Zelensky and Trump would have an intense, public confrontation in the Oval Office.

There's little doubt that the tone of Bannon's advice to the president—calling Zelensky "that punk"—and the substance of what he said set the tone for the coming confrontation.

The proposed deal with Ukraine wasn't in trouble because of what Bannon said, but Trump's doubts about it—and Zelensky—were solidified. Three days later, Trump gathered with a slightly smaller group of advisors to go over, once again, the deal that was set to be signed when Zelensky visited the White House the following day. As they discussed the key points of the deal, one of the advisors in the room asked if the agreement had been through a legal review by the White House lawyers. It had not. Lawyers at the Treasury and State Departments had reviewed it, but National Security Advisor Mike Waltz had not shared it with White House Counsel Dave Warrington.

"I can have Usha take a look at it," Vice President Vance said, referring to his wife, who is an accomplished lawyer and graduate of Yale Law School.

And with that, the vice president asked the second lady of the United States—who, like Steve Bannon, had no role whatsoever on the National Security Council—to come over to the West Wing and review a bilateral agreement that was supposed to be signed the next day by Donald Trump and Volodymyr Zelensky.

The rest of the saga surrounding Zelensky's visit to Washington is an extraordinary piece of US history—the disintegration of US–Ukrainian relations, which was broadcast to the world. The nearly hour-long meeting between Trump and Zelensky on February 28, 2025, started to go off the rails when Vance accused Zelensky of being "disrespectful" and suggested the Ukrainian president should be *negotiating* with the Russians instead of fighting them. When Zelensky pointed out Vance had never bothered to visit Ukraine, Vance accused him of taking US officials on "propaganda tours" and attacking "the administration that is trying to prevent the destruction of your country."

Before long, Trump and Zelensky were shouting and speaking over each other.

"You're not in a good position," Trump told Zelensky, his voice rising. "You don't have the cards right now. With us, you start having cards."

"I'm not playing cards," Zelensky interrupted. "I'm very serious, Mr. President. I'm very serious."

"You're playing cards," Trump shot back. "You're gambling with the lives of millions of people. You're gambling with World War III."

"What are you speaking about?" Zelensky asked.

"You're gambling with World War III," Trump repeated. "And what you're doing is very disrespectful to the country, this country that's backed you far more than a lot of people said they should have."

"Have you said thank you once?" Vance interjected.

"A lot of times," Zelensky answered. "Even today."

The meeting was supposed to be immediately followed by a signing of the security agreement now reviewed by the second lady. The East Room of the White House had also been set up for a joint Trump–Zelensky press conference. None of that happened. Trump angrily dismissed Zelensky.

For nearly a century, America had helped to keep peace in Europe, standing shoulder-to-shoulder with our allies and against the aggressors. But there in the Oval Office, in front of the television cameras, Trump was doing more than berating an American ally; he was declaring to the world that America was no longer the country that, in John F. Kennedy's words, would "pay any price, bear any burden, meet any hardship, support any friend, oppose any foe to assure the survival and the success of liberty." Now, a US president was showing an ally the true meaning of America First.

Trump's final words before the cameras left the Oval Office made clear that, although he was angry, Trump was also enjoying himself. The implications of the meeting for the world and for America's place in it were hard to comprehend, but Trump knew he had accomplished at least one thing.

"All right, I think we've seen enough," Trump said to the reporters in the room, still in a state of shock because of what they had just witnessed.

"What do you think" he asked as the reporters started to leave. "This is going to be great television. I will say that."

ACKNOWLEDGMENTS

With this book, I set out to write a definitive account of the most fascinating and consequential election of our time—and the equally fascinating and consequential transition that followed. It's been the most ambitious and demanding project of my career, and through it all, Declan Garvey has been a true collaborator. We started working on this book days after the Biden–Trump debate in June 2024 and spoke regularly throughout the campaign. One afternoon shortly after the election, we stepped into a newly opened French bistro on Capitol Hill called Butterworth's, and, on one of those old-fashioned legal pads, we wrote the initial outline for this book. At the time, we had no idea Butterworth's would go on to become the go-to gathering place for Trump's MAGA supporters in Washington.

Declan joined me on some of the key interviews, and for most of the others, he listened to the audio recordings. Lots of audio—hundreds of hours of conversations with the central players in this book. I don't know if I could have done this book without Declan, but

I do know the book is much better because of his dedication to our project. Declan did it all while continuing his important work as the executive editor of *The Dispatch*. He's a true journalist, a thoughtful observer of our strange world and a first-rate editor. Thank you, Declan, and I'm sorry if all the work here distracted you from what looks to be a very good season for the Chicago Cubs (and also the awful season the Bears had over the course of the fall campaign and the presidential transition).

Sometime in early September 2024, my friend and ABC News colleague Katherine Faulders told me that the Trump transition was going to be one of the wildest and most important stories of our lifetime. I must confess that I had my doubts (mostly because I wasn't sure there would *be* a Trump transition), but nobody has better reporting instincts than Katherine and on this she was, once again, correct. Katherine is as deeply sourced and relentless as any reporter in Washington. She generously shared her reporting and her ideas—and her time, too.

At one of many points where I was having doubts about whether I would be able to finish this book, Peter Charalambous joined Declan and Katherine as part of the core team and helped me get it over the line. Peter may be the hardest-working person at ABC News—and possibly in any news organization. He helped me with research, editing, ideas, fact-checking, and more—all while being ABC's indispensable reporter on the courts and more.

No single person has been a bigger influence on my work as a writer and reporter or a better friend than Douglas Kennedy. As Douglas and I wrote in our first joint project more than thirty years ago, *most excellent*.

The second draft of every chapter in this book was read by Chris Donovan, Rick Klein, and Claire Brinberg—my great triumvirate of friends and ABC News colleagues who have provided a healthy mix of criticism and encouragement on all my books about the Trump era. As in the three previous books, Rick read my drafts and told me what to take out; Chris told me what more I needed to add; and Claire told me bluntly what was good and what needed to be better.

I am grateful to ABC News for supporting this project. Thank you to Bob Iger and Dana Walden for your unwavering support of me and my ABC colleagues during a time when fact-based reporting is both under assault and critically important. Thank you, Debra OConnell and Almin Karamehmedovic, for allowing me to pursue this project and understanding how it both builds on and supports my work at ABC. David Muir was with me for so many of the central moments in this book; I am grateful for our ongoing dialogue about what it all means and for David's enthusiasm for this project.

Thank you, Kerry Smith and Karen Leo, for taking the time to read through my drafts—something Kerry has now done on *four* of my books.

I am indebted to my talented colleagues at ABC News. Justin Fishel shared ideas and encouragement. Rachel Scott, Lalee Ibssa, and Ben Siegel shared with me their recollections of this incredible campaign, including the horrifying hours they spent in Butler, Pennsylvania, on July 13. At key points along the way, I relied on help from Hannah Demissie, Pat O'Gara, Jon Garcia, Allie Pecorin (a huge help on all four of my books!), Will Steakin, Alex Mallin, Patrick Reevell, George Sanchez, and John Parkinson. Anthony Perrone helped bring the audiobook book to life—just as he did with *Betrayal* and *Tired of Winning*—all while cheering on the New York Mets. And, once again, John Santucci was there when I needed him.

This book builds on the solid, straightforward journalism of many of my friends and colleagues at ABC News, including Mary Bruce, Martha Raddatz, Pierre Thomas, Aaron Katersky, Linsey Davis, Molly Nagle, Sarah Kolinovsky, Luis Martinez, and Anne Flaherty. I have been enormously fortunate to work with some of ABC's finest, including George Stephanopoulos, Marc Burstein, Jenn Metz, Emily Cohen, Tom Shine, and Maggy Patrick. And thank you to my hard-charging *This Week* team, including Quinn Scanlan, Julia Cherner, Mitch Alva, Imtiyaz Delawala, Brooke Brower, and Eric Fayeulle. They didn't even mind when an important meeting was interrupted by an incoming call from Donald Trump.

I have a group of talented friends who were willing to take the time to read early drafts of this book and give me both constructive criticism and encouragement, including Mike Allen, Scott Alexander, Don Rockwell, Mary Ann Gonser, Todd Harris, Mike Feldman, and Mark Montgomery. Franco Nuschese helped open many doors and has been as generous a friend as anybody has ever had. My many, many conversations with Yousef al-Otaiba have helped shaped the way I look at how our world is changing. Frank Luntz offered crucially important edits and pushed me to explore how the Trump era has changed the American people. Paul Freitas and Dave Almy have given me, and always will, the way-outside-the-Beltway perspective.

Alan Berger constantly pushed me to write more, and to write faster. He read early drafts of every chapter and was this project's biggest cheerleader. David Larabell is the one who encouraged me to write this book—just as he worked on me for years to write *Front Row at the Trump Show*.

It's been a joy once again to work with the team at Dutton, especially John Parsley, who has now edited four of my books. Are you sure you want to do a fifth, John?

ACKNOWLEDGMENTS

The real driving force behind this book has been my family. My father-in-law, Salvatore Catalano, with his wit, knowledge, and intolerance for mediocrity has been an inspiration. In fact, so has the entire Catalano family—Maryann, Sal Jr., Nancy, Sarah, and Louis.

And the Karls, too, of course. My brother Jim dispatched me to Washington College, his alma mater, to give a commencement speech that helped me formulate some of the ideas for this book. I hope nephew Aiden will read this and find encouragement for his future ventures.

Robert Karl Jr., offered me some key edits—and stopped me from making some big mistakes.

My brother Allan has been a monumental influence on my life. We have talked and intensely debated global affairs, politics, sports, travel, and, of course, wine. You might say it all started with a conversation about Joe Biden's 2008 commencement speech over a glass of Tannat from Uruguay.

Audrey Shaff, my sainted mother, read through and offered edits and suggestions on every draft of this book. As I've said before, she's the kindest woman on the planet.

The greatest blessings in my life are, without doubt, my daughters, Emily and Anna. They both contributed to this book in ways big and small—and gave me a reason to smile no matter how stressful things got.

And, finally, the single most important contributor to this book is my wife, Maria. As with virtually every major writing project since my senior year in college, Maria read my first, often incomprehensible, drafts and made them readable. More important, she put up with me as I worked obsessively for a year to complete this project. I love you, Maria.

NOTES

CHAPTER ONE: FELON AND FRONT-RUNNER

1. Elliot Smith, “Divide Between Political Elites and the Working Class Is a Major Risk, Allianz CEO Says,” CNBC, January 16, 2024.
2. Robert Downen and William Melhado, “Trump Vows Retribution at Waco Rally: ‘I Am Your Warrior, I Am Your Justice,’” *Texas Tribune*, March 25, 2023.
3. Aaron Katersky, Peter Charalambous, Olivia Rubin, Lucien Bruggeman, and Julia Reinstein, “Trump Trial: 1st Week of Testimony Ends with Testimony from Cohen’s Former Banker,” ABC News, April 26, 2024.
4. “Trump Launches \$399 Gold ‘Never Surrender’ Sneakers After Court Ruling,” *The Guardian*, February 17, 2024.
5. Jill Colvin, “Trump Is Selling ‘God Bless the USA’ Bibles for \$59.99 as He Faces Mounting Legal Bills,” Associated Press, March 26, 2024.
6. Michael Warren and Sarah Isgur, “How Trump’s New York Criminal Trial Might Play Out,” *The Dispatch*, April 18, 2024.
7. JD Vance (@JDVance), post on X, May 13, 2024.
8. Emily Jane Fox, “Michael Cohen Would Take a Bullet for Donald Trump,” *Vanity Fair*, September 6, 2017.
9. Alex Isenstadt, “Trump Attacks Daughter of Judge Overseeing Hush Money Case,” *Politico*, March 28, 2024.
10. Jennifer Jacobs and Nicole Sganga, “Sean Curran, ‘the Unknown’ Leading the Secret Service,” CBS News, February 26, 2025.
11. Sarah Fortinsky, “Trump Removes Truth Social Post Complaining About Next Hush Money Trial Witness,” *The Hill*, May 7, 2024.
12. Erica Orden, “Michael Cohen Is an Admitted Liar. He’s Still Going to Be the Star Witness Against Trump,” *Politico*, April 14, 2024.

NOTES

CHAPTER TWO: THE BRIDGE TO NOWHERE

1. Letter from Alexei Navalny to Evgeny Feldman, December 3, 2023, obtained and translated by Patrick Reevell, ABC News.
2. "Kremlin Critic Navalny Convicted of Extremism and Sentenced to 19 Years in Prison," Associated Press, August 4, 2023.
3. Anton Troianovski, "Inside Aleksei Navalny's Final Months, in His Own Words," *New York Times*, February 19, 2024.
4. Ekaterina Bodyagina and Anatoly Kurmanaev, "5 Convicts Familiar with Navalny's Prison Confirm Hellish Conditions," *New York Times*, February 29, 2024.
5. Ezra Klein, "Democrats Have a Better Option Than Biden," *New York Times*, February 16, 2024.
6. Meredith Deliso, "Overwhelming Majority of Americans Think Biden Is Too Old for Another Term: Poll," ABC News, February 11, 2024.
7. Tommy Christopher, "Here's What Biden Said Before and After 'If Trump Wasn't Running' Remark at Private Fundraiser," *Mediaite*, December 6, 2023.
8. "Michigan Poll: Gov. Whitmer Ten Points More Favorable Than President Biden in Michigan," Emerson College Polling, October 16, 2023.
9. Eric Bradner and Sarah Mucha, "Biden Says He's a 'Bridge' to New 'Generation of Leaders' While Campaigning with Harris, Booker, Whitmer," CNN, March 9, 2020.
10. Alex Thompson, Zach Montellaro, and Max Tani, "The Obama Path Biden Chose Not to Take," *Politico*, August 24, 2022.
11. Alexander Bolton, "Democratic Senators Say They Bungled Border Security in 2024," *The Hill*, November 29, 2024.
12. Price St. Clair, "The Allegations Against the Bidens, Explained," *The Dispatch*, August 17, 2023.
13. Hunter Biden, *Beautiful Things: A Memoir* (Gallery Books, 2021), pages 215–16.
14. Hunter Biden, interview with the author, January 28, 2025.
15. Marshall Cohen, "Hunter Biden Settles Arkansas Child Support Case," CNN, June 29, 2023.
16. Ryan Lizza, "Biden Signals to Aides That He Would Serve Only a Single Term," *Politico*, December 11, 2019.
17. Hunter Biden, interview with the author, October 10, 2024.
18. Mike Allen, "Inside Biden's Private Chat with Historians," *Axios*, March 25, 2021.
19. Joey Garrison, "Democratic Rep. Dean Phillips Says He Doesn't Want Biden to Run for Reelection in 2024," *USA Today*, July 29, 2022.
20. David Ignatius, "President Biden Should Not Run Again in 2024," *Washington Post*, September 12, 2023.
21. "Recorded Interview Between Special Counsel Robert Hur (SCO), Deputy Special Counsel Marc Krickbaum (SCO), Assistant Special Counsel [Redacted] (SCO), Supervisory Special Agent [Redacted] (FBI), Special Agent [Redacted] (FBI), Edward Siskel (WHC), Richard Sauber (WHC), Rachel Cotton (WHC), Robert Bauer (OC), David Laufman (PC), and President Joseph R. Biden, Jr.," Department of Justice, October 8, 2023.

22. Robert Hur, "Report on the Investigation into Unauthorized Removal, Retention, and Disclosure of Classified Documents Discovered at Locations Including the Penn Biden Center and the Delaware Private Residence of President Joseph R. Biden, Jr.," Department of Justice, February 2024.
23. Tom Emmer (@tomemmer), post on X, February 8, 2024.
24. Andrew Solender, "Special Counsel Report Sends Shockwaves Through Congress," *Axios*, February 8, 2024.

CHAPTER THREE: FREE ON WEDNESDAYS

1. Rebecca Shabad and Emma Barnett, "Trump Says He Wants to Debate Biden," NBC News, February 5, 2024.
2. Donald Trump (@realDonaldTrump), post on Truth Social, March 6, 2024.
3. Brooke Singman, "Trump Campaign Demands Biden Debate Him 'Much Earlier' and More Often," Fox News, April 11, 2024.
4. Peter Baker, "In-Your-Face Biden Takes on Trump and His Own Doubters," *New York Times*, March 8, 2024.
5. Zach Montellaro, "Trump Posts Running Commentary on Social Media," *Politico*, March 7, 2024.
6. Joe Biden (@JoeBiden), post on X, May 15, 2024.
7. Donald Trump (@realDonaldTrump), post on Truth Social, May 15, 2024.

CHAPTER FOUR: A TALE OF TWO JUNES

1. Seema Mehta, "'Not a Happy Election': Why This Star-Studded Hollywood Fundraiser Is So Crucial for Biden," *Los Angeles Times*, June 14, 2024.
2. Dan Diamond, Samuel Oakford, and Carol Leonnig, "Inside the Glitzy Fundraiser Where Biden Lost George Clooney," *Washington Post*, July 12, 2024.
3. Diamond, Oakford, and Leonnig, "Inside the Glitzy Fundraiser Where Biden Lost George Clooney."
4. "Remarks by President Biden and President Obama in a Moderated Conversation with Jimmy Kimmel at a Campaign Reception," Los Angeles, Biden White House Archives, June 15, 2024.
5. Associated Press, "George Clooney, Julia Roberts Help Biden Raise Record $30 Million-Plus at Star Studded Hollywood Gala," *New York Post*, June 16, 2024.
6. Chris Gardner (@chrissgardner), post on X, June 16, 2024.
7. Annie Linskey and Siobhan Hughes, "Behind Closed Doors, Biden Shows Signs of Slipping," *Wall Street Journal*, June 4, 2024.
8. Ben LaBolt (@WHCommsDir46), post on X, June 4, 2024.
9. Nancy Pelosi (@SpeakerPelosi), post on X, June 5, 2024.
10. Meredith Deliso, "Overwhelming Majority of Americans Think Biden Is Too Old for Another Term: Poll," ABC News, February 11, 2024.
11. Patrick Reilly and Ronny Reyes, "Biden Wanders Away at G7 Summit Before Being Pulled Back by Italian PM," *New York Post*, June 13, 2024.
12. Ben LaBolt (@WHCommsDir46), post on X, June 13, 2024.
13. Nick Catoggio, "When Democrats Cry 'Fake News,'" *The Dispatch*, June 18, 2024.

14. Rob Wile and Jason Abbruzzese, "Presidential Debate Drew 51.3 Million Viewers, Down from Recent Events," NBC News, June 28, 2024.
15. Eugene Daniels, "Biden Issues a Rare Statement on His Son's Criminal Trial," *Politico*, June 3, 2024.
16. Alex Gangitano, "Jill Biden Criss-Crosses Atlantic to Attend Day 5 of Hunter Biden Trial," *The Hill*, June 7, 2024.
17. Lucien Bruggeman, Olivia Rubin, Will Steakin, Chris Boccia, and Laura Romero, "Hunter Biden Trial: 'Politics Never Came Into Play,' Juror Says After Guilty Verdict," ABC News, June 11, 2024.
18. Bruggeman, Rubin, Steakin, Boccia, and Romero, "Hunter Biden Trial."
19. Meridith McGraw, Alex Isenstadt, and Jonathan Lemire, "Suddenly Trump's Got Nothing to Say About Hunter Biden," *Politico*, June 5, 2024.
20. "Remarks by President Trump in Press Briefing," Trump White House Archive, September 27, 2020.
21. Alex Isenstadt and Meridith McGraw, "Trump Ramps Up Debate Prep: 'Policy Discussions' Instead of Mock Debate," *Politico*, June 17, 2024.
22. Maggie Haberman and Jonathan Swan, "Trump Participates in His Form of Debate Prep, Readying to Face Biden," *New York Times*, June 14, 2024.
23. Kristen Holmes, Alayna Treene, Melanie Zanona, and Lauren Fox, "Donald Trump Back in Washington for Meetings with Vice Presidential Contenders, Congressional Allies and Former Foes," CNN, June 13, 2024.
24. Scott Wong, Sahil Kapur, Ali Vitali, and Julie Tsirkin, "Republicans Host 'Pep Rally' with Trump in His First Visit to Capitol Hill Since Jan. 6 Attack," NBC News, June 13, 2024.
25. Lisa Mascaro, "Cheers, Cake and a Fist-Bump from GOP as Trump Returns to Capitol Hill in a First Since Jan. 6 Riot," Associated Press, June 13, 2024.
26. Burgess Everett, Ursula Perano, and Katherine Tully-McManus, "Trump and McConnell Shake Hands, Thawing Icy Relationship," *Politico*, June 13, 2024.
27. Wong, Kapur, Vitali, and Tsirkin, "Republicans Host 'Pep Rally' with Trump."
28. MJ Lee, Alayna Treene, Kayla Tausche, and Kevin Liptak, "How Biden and Trump Are Preparing for Their First Presidential Debate," CNN, June 20, 2024.
29. Joe Biden (@JoeBiden), post on X, June 27, 2024.

CHAPTER FIVE: DEBATE DEBACLE

1. Ted Johnson, "Joe Biden Tells Guests at Hollywood Fundraiser, 'You're the Reason That Donald Trump Is a Former President,'" *Deadline*, December 8, 2023.
2. C. Todd Lopez, "3 U.S. Service Members Killed, Others Injured in Jordan Following Drone Attack," *DOD News*, January 29, 2024.

CHAPTER SIX: BIDEN DIGS IN

1. Thomas L. Friedman, "Joe Biden Is a Good Man and a Good President. He Must Bow Out of the Race," *New York Times*, June 28, 2024.
2. David Remnick, "The Reckoning of Joe Biden," *New Yorker*, June 29, 2024.
3. Barack Obama (@BarackObama), post on X, June 28, 2024.
4. Annie Karni and Maya C. Miller, "Leading Democrats Vouch for Biden, but Concede a 'Bad Night,'" *New York Times*, June 28, 2024.

5. Chris Whipple, *Uncharted: How Trump Beat Biden, Harris, and the Odds in the Wildest Campaign in History* (Harper Influence, April 2025).
6. Matthew Choi, "Democratic Congressman Lloyd Doggett Calls on Biden to Withdraw from Presidential Race," *Texas Tribune*, July 2, 2024.
7. Rebecca Shabad, "Nancy Pelosi: It's a 'Legitimate Question' Whether Biden's Debate Performance Was a 'Condition' or Just an 'Episode,'" NBC News, July 2, 2024.
8. "Congresswoman Gluesenkamp Perez Says 'Biden Is Going to Lose to Trump,'" KATU, July 2, 2024.
9. Victor Nava, "Kentucky Gov. Andy Beshear on Biden's Upcoming Meeting with Democratic Governors: 'We Want to Make Sure He's Doing OK,'" *New York Post*, July 2, 2024.
10. Reid Epstein and Maggie Haberman, "Biden Tells Governors He Needs More Sleep and Less Work at Night," *New York Times*, July 4, 2024.
11. "Governors Speak After Meeting with President Biden on Future of Candidacy," C-SPAN, July 3, 2024.
12. Jason Miller (@JasonMiller), post on X, July 5, 2024.
13. Joe Biden (@JoeBiden), post on X, July 5, 2024.
14. Libby Cathey, Gabriella Abdul-Hakim, and Lalee Ibssa, "Biden Argues Trump Is an Existential Threat to America; Trump Tries to Point Finger Back at Biden," ABC News, December 5, 2023.
15. Leigh Ann Caldwell and Liz Goodwin, "Sen. Mark Warner Works to Gather Senate Democrats to Ask Biden to Exit Race," *Washington Post*, July 5, 2024.
16. Alexander Bolton, "Tester Says Biden Must 'Prove' He's 'Up to the Job,'" *The Hill*, July 8, 2024.
17. Jamie Raskin letter to Joe Biden, Office of Representative Jamie Raskin, July 6, 2024.
18. Joe Biden, "Letter to the Democratic Party on Intention to Accept the Presidential Nomination," American Presidency Project, July 8, 2024.
19. Isabella Ramírez and Myah Ward, "Biden Slams Dem Critics as 'Elites' During Surprise 'Morning Joe' Interview," *Politico*, July 8, 2024.
20. "Nancy Pelosi: It's up to Biden to Decide if He's Going to Run. Whatever He Decides, We Go With," MSNBC News, July 10, 2024.
21. George Clooney, "I Love Joe Biden. But We Need a New Nominee," *New York Times*, July 10, 2024.

CHAPTER SEVEN: BUTLER

1. Interview [name redacted], Task Force on the Attempted Assassination of Donald J. Trump, U.S. House of Representatives, November 12, 2024, page 98.
2. JD Vance, interview by Joe Rogan, *The Joe Rogan Experience*, October 31, 2024.
3. Eric Freehling, "Pullman-Standard Closure Devastated County," *Butler Eagle*, October 7, 2024.
4. "1947 Butler Yankees," baseball-reference.com.
5. "Pullman-Standard Car Manufacturing Company of Butler PA Records," Pennsylvania State Archives, https://www.phmc.state.pa.us.
6. Freehling, "Pullman-Standard Closure Devastated County."

7. Task Force on the Attempted Assassination of Donald J. Trump, *Final Report of Findings and Recommendations*, United States House of Representatives (US Government Publishing Office, December 5, 2024), page 17.
8. Jaclyn Diaz, Dave Mistich, and Quil Lawrence, "What We Know About the Trump Shooter," NPR, updated July 18, 2024.
9. Michael Biesecker, Martha Bellisle, Jim Mustian, and Peter Smith, "Three Days After Attempted Assassination, Trump Shooter Remains an Elusive Enigma," Associated Press, July 17, 2024.
10. Katherine Faulders, Mike Levine, and Alexander Mallin, "FBI, in Private Meeting with Trump, Revealed New Details About His Would-Be Assassin: Sources," ABC News, August 9, 2024.
11. Nadine El-Bawab, Pierre Thomas, Jack Date, Luke Barr, Aaron Katersky, and Olivia Rubin, "Did Trump's Alleged Shooter Expect to Survive the Attack? What the Evidence Suggests So Far," ABC News, July 18, 2024.
12. Meredith Deliso, Aaron Katersky, Jared Kofsky, Mike Levine, and Juwon Funes, "Suspected Trump Rally Shooter Visited Gun Range Dozens of Times, Senator Says, as New Video Emerges," ABC News, August 9, 2024.
13. Nick Matoney, "'I Feel Him Guiding Me at Times': Wife and Daughters of Corey Comperatore Speak with '4 the Record,'" WTAE, August 25, 2024.
14. Matoney, "'I Feel Him Guiding Me at Times.'"
15. Task Force on the Attempted Assassination of Donald J. Trump, Final Report, page 166.
16. Task Force on the Attempted Assassination of Donald J. Trump, Final Report, page 23.
17. Sasha Pezenik, Jack Feeley, and Josh Margolin, "Local SWAT Team Blames Trump Assassination Attempt on Lack of Planning, Communication," ABC News, July 29, 2024.
18. Task Force on the Attempted Assassination of Donald J. Trump, Final Report, page 24.
19. Task Force on the Attempted Assassination of Donald J. Trump, Final Report, page 22.
20. Task Force on the Attempted Assassination of Donald J. Trump, interview with Butler ESU Op. 2, page 87.
21. Task Force on the Attempted Assassination of Donald J. Trump, interview with Butler ESU Op. 2, page 29.
22. Task Force on the Attempted Assassination of Donald J. Trump, interview with Beaver ESU Witness 3, page 108.
23. Ricky Sayer, "Marc Fogel's Mom Was Set to Take Stage with Trump at Butler Rally Before Shooting," KDKA News, July 19, 2024.
24. Task Force on the Attempted Assassination of Donald J. Trump, interview with Butler Township Police PD Witness 4, page 18.
25. Task Force on the Attempted Assassination of Donald J. Trump, interview with Butler Township Police PD Witness 4, page 18.
26. Task Force on the Attempted Assassination of Donald J. Trump, interview with Butler Township Police PD Witness 4, page 174.

27. Task Force on the Attempted Assassination of Donald J. Trump, interview with CS Sgt. Tech, page 37.
28. Task Force on the Attempted Assassination of Donald J. Trump, interview with ASAIC DTD, page 121.
29. Task Force on the Attempted Assassination of Donald J. Trump, interview with ASAIC DTD, page 101.
30. Jennifer Jacobs and Nicole Sganga, "Sean Curran, 'the Unknown' Leading the Secret Service," CBS News, February 26, 2025.
31. Task Force on the Attempted Assassination of Donald J. Trump, interview with ASAIC DTD, page 123.
32. Gustaf Kilander, "Trump Says He 'Sleeps with' and 'Kisses' Immigration Chart That He Flashed on TV Moments Before Getting Shot," *The Independent*, October 14, 2024.
33. Matoney, "'I Feel Him Guiding Me at Times.'"
34. Tom Llamas and Daniella Silva, "2 Men Who Were Wounded When a Gunman Opened Fire on Trump at Rally Say Secret Service Failed Them," NBC4 Los Angeles, October 14, 2024.
35. JD Vance (@JDVance), post on X, July 13, 2024.
36. JD Vance, *The Joe Rogan Experience*, October 31, 2024.
37. Elon Musk (@elonmusk), post on X, July 13, 2024.
38. David Wright and Alex Leeds-Matthews, "Elon Musk Spent More Than $290 Million on the 2024 Election, Year-End FEC Filings Show," CNN, February 1, 2025.
39. Robert Kennedy Jr. (@RobertKennedyJr), post on X, July 13, 2024.

CHAPTER EIGHT: "I HAD GOD ON MY SIDE"

1. Gabriella Abdul-Hakim, Fritz Farrow, and Will McDuffie, "After Trump Assassination Attempt, Biden Campaign Pauses Ads, Events, Attacks," ABC News, July 14, 2024.
2. Donald Trump (@realDonaldTrump), post on Truth Social, July 14, 2024.
3. JD Vance (@JDVance), post on X, July 13, 2024.
4. Donald Trump, phone conversation with the author, July 15, 2024.
5. Robert Costa and Melissa Quinn, "Sen. Ron Johnson Says He Read Wrong Version of Speech at Republican National Convention," CBS News, July 16, 2024.
6. Michael Warren, "The GOP's New Sunny Disposition," *The Dispatch*, July 17, 2024.
7. Tim Alberta, "Trump Is Planning for a Landslide Win," *The Atlantic*, July 10, 2024.
8. Ken Bensinger, "Iowa Pastors Say Video Depicting Trump as Godly Is 'Very Concerning,'" *New York Times*, January 11, 2024.
9. Ebony Davis, "Haley Offers Sharpest Criticism of Trump Yet, Saying He Is 'Toxic' and Lacks 'Moral Clarity,'" CNN, January 31, 2024.
10. Nikki Haley (@NikkiHaley), post on X, February 10, 2024.
11. J. D. Vance, "Why Trump's Antiwar Message Resonates with White America," *New York Times*, April 4, 2016.

12. Michael Warren, Em Steck, and Andrew Kaczynski, "Senate Hopeful J.D. Vance Apologizes for Criticizing Trump as 'Reprehensible' in Deleted Tweets," CNN, July 6, 2021.
13. J. D. Vance, "Opioid of the Masses," *The Atlantic*, July 4, 2016.
14. Cameron Joseph, "Trump-Endorsed Candidate JD Vance Once Said Trump Might Be 'America's Hitler,'" *Vice*, April 18, 2022.
15. Em Steck and Andrew Kaczynski, "JD Vance Repeatedly Indicated in 2016 That He Believed Donald Trump Had Committed Sexual Assault," CNN, July 23, 2024.
16. Ross Douthat, "What J.D. Vance Believes," *New York Times*, June 13, 2024.
17. Seung Min Kim and Connor O'Brien, "Graham: Choice Between Trump, Cruz like 'Being Shot or Poisoned,'" *Politico*, January 21, 2016.
18. Nolan McCaskill, "Graham: We Should Have Kicked Trump Out of the Party," *Politico*, March 7, 2016.
19. Editorial Board, "Trump's New Running Mate Imperative," *Wall Street Journal*, July 7, 2024.
20. Maggie Haberman and Jonathan Swan, "How Tucker Carlson Helped Sell J.D. Vance as Trump's Running Mate," *New York Times*, July 16, 2024.
21. Shawn McCreesh, "Vance's Mother Deals with Her Past and His Future," *New York Times*, September 26, 2024.
22. Alex Isenstadt, Meridith McGraw, Natalie Allison, and Lisa Kashinsky, "Trump Will Describe the Shooting in His RNC Speech. He Won't Mention Joe Biden," *Politico*, July 18, 2024.

CHAPTER NINE: LOCKED UP

1. Vivian Salama, "Steve Bannon Reports to Prison. He'll Still Have Influence in Trump World," *Wall Street Journal*, July 1, 2024.
2. Vaughn Hillyard, Dan Gallo, and Megan Lebowitz, "Steve Bannon Continues Sowing Doubts About the 2024 Election as He Heads to Prison," NBC News, July 1, 2024.
3. Ryan Bort, "Steve Bannon Said 'All Hell Going to Break Loose' After Talking to Trump on Jan. 5," *Rolling Stone*, July 12, 2022.
4. Salama, "Steve Bannon Reports to Prison."
5. Ken Bensinger, "Stephen Bannon Goes to Prison, but His Podcast Won't Stop," *New York Times*, July 1, 2024.
6. David Brooks, "My Unsettling Interview with Steve Bannon," *New York Times*, July 1, 2024.
7. Doug Specht, "El Salvador's Controversial Offer: Housing U.S. Criminals in Its Mega-Prison," SAIS Review of International Affairs, March 7, 2025.

CHAPTER TEN: BIDEN BOWS OUT

1. Noor Ibrahim, "Listen: Cops Scramble to Secure Hospital for Biden Health Scare," *Daily Beast*, August 9, 2024.
2. "ABC's George Stephanopoulos's Exclusive Interview with President Biden: Full Transcript," ABC News, July 5, 2024.

3. Eli Stokols, "Biden's 'Big Boy' Press Conference May Not Quiet the Doubters," *Politico*, July 11, 2024.
4. Bernie Sanders, "Joe Biden for President," *New York Times*, July 13, 2024.
5. Mark Halperin (@MarkHalperin), post on X, July 18, 2024.
6. Carol E. Lee and Monica Alba, "Biden Privately Remains Torn Between Defiance and Acceptance amid Calls to Step Aside," NBC News, July 3, 2024.
7. Joe Biden (@JoeBiden), post on X, July 21, 2024.
8. Joe Biden (@JoeBiden), post on X, July 21, 2024.
9. Donald Trump (@realDonaldTrump), post on Truth Social, July 22, 2024.

CHAPTER ELEVEN: KAMALA RISING

1. Nancy Pelosi (@TeamPelosi), post on X, July 22, 2024.
2. Josh Shapiro (@JoshShapiroPA), post on X, July 21, 2024.
3. Barack Obama, "My Statement on President Biden's Announcement," Medium, July 21, 2024.
4. Barack Obama, "Our Endorsement," Medium, July 25, 2024.
5. Jamie Gangel, "Biden Drops Out of the Race, Endorses Kamala Harris to Be Nominee," CNN, July 21, 2024.
6. April Rubin, "Harris Campaign Raises a Record $81 Million in 24 Hours," *Axios*, July 22, 2024.
7. Donald Trump (@realDonaldTrump), post on Truth Social, July 21, 2024.
8. Donald Trump (@realDonaldTrump), post on Truth Social, July 22, 2024.
9. Victor Nava, "Trump and Harris Locked in Tight Races in Four Key Swing States: Poll," *New York Post*, July 26, 2024.
10. Kipp Jones, "Trump Takes Victory Lap After 'Coup' Forces Biden Out: 'We Officially Defeated the Worst President,'" *Mediaite*, July 26, 2024.
11. Ed O'Keefe, "Biden Announces Running Mate Vetting Committee," CBS News, April 30, 2024.
12. Sarah Ferris, Nicholas Wu, Meredith Lee Hill, and Daniella Diaz, "Why Pelosi and Other House Dems Were Privately Pushing Walz," Politico, August 6, 2024.
13. Katie Glueck, "Inside the Obama-Shapiro Relationship," *New York Times*, August 4, 2024.
14. Josh Shapiro (@JoshShapiroPA), post on X, August 6, 2024.
15. Kamala Harris (@KamalaHarris), post on X, August 6, 2024.
16. Donald Trump (@realDonaldTrump), post on Truth Social, August 6, 2024.
17. Justin Engel, "'Fight for the Future': Kamala Harris Rallies Crowd of 15,000 in Michigan," *MLive*, August 8, 2024.
18. Donald Trump (@realDonaldTrump), post on Truth Social, August 8, 2024.
19. Donald Trump (@realDonaldTrump), post on Truth Social, August 11, 2024.
20. "Sen. Kamala Harris's 2019 Report Card," GovTrack, January 18, 2020.
21. Tim Balk, "'A Terrible President': 12 Times Robert F. Kennedy Jr. Criticized Trump," *New York Times*, August 28, 2024.
22. Meg Kinnard, "Trump Is Increasingly Directing Personal Attacks Against Independent Rival Robert F. Kennedy Jr.," Associated Press, May 11, 2024.

23. Donald Trump (@realDonaldTrump), post on Truth Social, April 28, 2024.
24. Mike Allen, "Obama Considers Stars for Cabinet," *Politico*, November 5, 2008.
25. Tim Balk, "'A Terrible President.'"

CHAPTER TWELVE: "THE WEAVE"

1. Donald Trump (@realDonaldTrump), post on Truth Social, August 23, 2024.
2. Donald Trump (@realDonaldTrump), post on Truth Social, August 25, 2024.
3. Donald Trump (@realDonaldTrump), post on Truth Social, August 25, 2024.
4. Stephen Collinson, "Trump's Fury over Harris' Switch with Biden Is Increasingly Driving His Campaign," CNN, August 16, 2024.
5. Nick Robertson, "Fox News Host Challenges JD Vance on 'Childless Cat Lady' Remarks," *The Hill*, July 29, 2024.
6. Patrick Marley, "Vance Once Advocated That Children Get Votes That Parents Could Cast," *Washington Post*, July 25, 2024.
7. Kevin Roberts, with a foreword by J.D. Vance, *Dawn's Early Light: Taking Back Washington to Save America* (Broadside Books, 2024).
8. Dave Portnoy (@stoolpresidente), post on X, July 26, 2024.
9. Ben Domenech, "Who Will Wish They Chose a Different Running Mate?," *The Spectator*, August 8, 2024.
10. Editorial Board, "Will Donald Trump Blow Another Election?," *Wall Street Journal*, August 7, 2024.
11. Brian Kemp (@BrianKempGA), post on X, August 3, 2024.
12. Beacon Research and Shaw & Company Research, Georgia Poll, Fox News, August 23–26, 2024.
13. Kellyanne Conway (@KellyannePolls), post on X, August 2, 2024.
14. Maggie Haberman and Jonathan Swan, "Inside the Worst Three Weeks of Donald Trump's 2024 Campaign," *New York Times*, August 10, 2024.
15. Chris McGreal, "Trump Rebrands His Ramblings as 'I Do the Weave'—But Is He Just Losing It?," *The Guardian*, September 7, 2024.

CHAPTER THIRTEEN: CATS AND DOGS

1. Isabella Murray and Oren Oppenheim, "Former Republican Vice President Dick Cheney Says He'll Vote for Harris," ABC News, September 6, 2024.
2. Kelly O'Donnell and Megan Lebowitz, "Former President George W. Bush Has No Plans to Endorse the Election," NBC News, September 7, 2024.
3. Jonathan Swan, Maggie Haberman, Katie Rogers, and Reid Epstein, "Inside the Trump-Harris Debate Prep: Method Acting, Insults, Tough Questions," *New York Times*, September 7, 2024.
4. Laura Loomer (@LauraLoomer), post on X, September 8, 2024.
5. Laura Loomer (@LauraLoomer), post on X, September 9, 2024.
6. JD Vance (@JDVance), post on X, September 9, 2024.
7. JD Vance (@JDVance), post on X, September 10, 2024.
8. Kyung Lah, Tami Luhby, and Gregory Krieg, "Kamala Harris Unveils 'Medicare for All' Plan That Preserves Role for Private Insurance," CNN, July 29, 2019.

9. Ronn Blitzer, "Kamala Harris Contradicts Herself on Illegal Immigration, in Latest Backtrack Since Debate," Fox News, July 29, 2019.
10. Trump's post-debate conversations with JD Vance and Marco Rubio were captured on video in the documentary series *The Art of the Surge: The Donald Trump Comeback*, produced by Justin Wells for Ashokan Studios, October 31, 2024.
11. Taylor Swift (@taylorswift), post on Instagram, September 10, 2024.
12. Laura Loomer (@LauraLoomer), post on X, June 24, 2023.
13. Laura Loomer (@LauraLoomer), post on X, September 11, 2024.
14. Jason Miller (@JasonMiller), post on X, September 11, 2024.
15. Jeff Cercone, "How an Unsubstantiated, Anonymous Affidavit About the ABC Presidential Debate Was Amplified Online," Poynter, September 20, 2024.
16. Elon Musk (@elonmusk), post on X, September 12, 2024.
17. Ted Cruz (@tedcruz), post on X, September 15, 2024.
18. Marjorie Taylor Greene (@mtgreenee), post on X, September 15, 2024.
19. Angie Orellana Hernandez, "Springfield, Ohio, Sues Neo-Nazis over Hate Campaign Against Haitians," *Washington Post*, February 8, 2025.
20. Bill Ackman (@billackman), post on X, September 15, 2024.
21. Bill Ackman (@billackman), post on X, October 16, 2024.
22. Robert Tait, "Giggling Elon Musk Revisits 'Joke' About Kamala Harris Assassination," *The Guardian*, October 8, 2024.

CHAPTER FOURTEEN: CLOSING ARGUMENT

1. Jonathan Karl, telephone interview with Donald Trump, October 26, 2024.
2. Michael Schmidt, "As Election Nears, Kelly Warns Trump Would Rule like a Dictator," *New York Times*, October 22, 2024.
3. Greg Jaffe, "Lt. Gen. John Kelly, Who Lost Son to War, Says U.S. Largely Unaware of Sacrifice," *Washington Post*, March 2, 2011.
4. Jonathan Karl telephone interview with Donald Trump, October 26, 2024.
5. Bob Woodward, *War* (Simon and Schuster, 2024), page 179.
6. Jeffrey Goldberg, "James Mattis Denounces President Trump, Describes Him as a Threat to the Constitution," *The Atlantic*, June 3, 2020.
7. Shane Goldmacher, Maggie Haberman, and Michael Gold, "Trump at the Garden: A Closing Carnival of Grievances, Misogyny and Racism," *New York Times*, October 27, 2024.
8. William Vaillancourt, "Joe Rogan Told Trump to Hire Racist Comedian to 'Write Bangers,'" *Daily Beast*, October 29, 2024.
9. Ashley Carnahan, "Trump Denies Knowing Comedian Who Told Crude Joke About Puerto Rico: 'I Have No Idea Who He Is,'" Fox News, October 28, 2024.
10. Sabrina Rodriguez, "Nicky Jam, Reggaeton Singer, Pulls Endorsement of Trump After Puerto Rico Insult," *Washington Post*, October 30, 2024.
11. Suzanne Gamboa, Nicole Acevedo, Daniella Silva, Carmen Sesin, and Deon J. Hampton, "Record Voter Gains Among Latinos for Trump Mainly Boiled Down to Their Top Issue—the Economy," NBC News, November 6, 2024.
12. Ed Komenda, "Kamala Harris in Las Vegas: 'Donald Trump Never Had a Fight on a Playground. Well, I Did,'" *Reno Gazette-Journal*, November 8, 2019.
13. Jonathan Karl, telephone interview with Donald Trump, October 19, 2024.

14. Kamala Harris (@KamalaHarris), post on X, October 15, 2024.
15. Mia McCarthy, "Trump: Military Could Be Used to Preserve Order on Election Day," *Politico*, October 13, 2024.
16. "Full Text: Trump Talks Abortion, IVF, Immigration and More on EWTN," *National Catholic Register*, October 17, 2024.
17. Jonathan Karl, telephone interview with Donald Trump, November 3, 2024.
18. Caitlin Yilek, "Trump Campaign Has Spent Millions on Anti-Trans Ads," CBS News, October 16, 2024.
19. Shane Goldmacher, Maggie Haberman, and Jonathan Swan, "How Trump Won, and How Harris Lost," *New York Times*, November 7, 2024.
20. Bridget Bowman, Ben Kamisar, and Joe Murphy, "How Harris' Campaign Spent $277 Million in the Final Weeks," NBC News, December 6, 2024.
21. Dana Mattioli, Emily Glazer, and Khadeeja Safdar, "Elon Musk Has Said He Is Committing Around $45 Million a Month to a New Pro-Trump Super PAC," *Wall Street Journal*, July 16, 2024.
22. Landon Milon, "Elon Musk Pushes Back on Reports That He's Donating $45M a Month to Super PAC Backing Trump," foxbusiness.com, July 24, 2024.
23. Elon Musk (@elonmusk), post on X, July 23, 2024.
24. Trisha Thadani, Clara Ence Morse, and Maeve Reston, "Elon Musk Donated $288 Million in 2024 Election, Final Tally Shows," *Washington Post*, January 31, 2025.
25. Joe Holden, Adam Fox, and Brad Nau, "Elon Musk's $1 Million Voter Sweepstakes May Continue, Pennsylvania Judge Rules," CBS News, November 4, 2024.
26. Theodore Schleifer, "Judge Refuses to Stop Musk's $1 Million Giveaway," *New York Times*, November 4, 2024.
27. Jake Lahut, "Workers Say They Were Tricked and Threatened as Part of Elon Musk's Get-Out-the-Vote Effort," *Wired*, October 30, 2024.
28. Caitlin Doornbos, "How Trump Won Pennsylvania's Amish Vote—with the Help of Missionaries and Elon Musk," *New York Post*, November 12, 2024.
29. Rebecca Falconer, "Musk Gave $20M to PAC That Used Late Justice RBG to Defend Trump on Abortion," *Axios*, December 5, 2024.
30. Shane Goldmacher, Theodore Schleifer, Maggie Haberman, and Jodi Kantor, "New 'RBG PAC' Spending $19 Million from Secret Donors to Aid Trump on Abortion," *New York Times*, October 25, 2024.
31. Jon King, "Musk-Connected PAC Behind Mailers Targeting Muslim and Jewish Voters in Michigan," *Michigan Advance*, October 16, 2024.
32. Hugh Tomlinson, "Musk-Funded Ads Tell Voters Kamala Harris Is Pro-Israel—and Anti-Israel," *The Times*, October 21, 2024.

CHAPTER FIFTEEN: MEET THE NEW BOSS

1. Jonathan Karl, interview with Enrique Tarrio, May 10, 2025.
2. Kai Trump (@kaitrump), post on X, November 10, 2024.
3. Elon Musk (@elonmusk), post on X, June 5, 2025.
4. Todd Gillespie, "Howard Lutnick Emerges as Trump's No. 1 Salesman on Wall Street," *Bloomberg*, September 5, 2024.

5. Jonathan Karl, telephone interview with Donald Trump, October 21, 2024.
6. Donald Trump (@realDonaldTrump), post on Truth Social, November 9, 2024.
7. Gabriel Sherman, "Trump's Defense Secretary Pick Pete Hegseth Said to Face Previous Sexual Misconduct Allegation," *Vanity Fair*, November 14, 2024.
8. Michael Kranish, Josh Dawsey, and Jonathan O'Connell, "Defense Pick Hegseth Paid Accuser but Denies Sexual Assault, Attorney Says," *Washington Post*, November 16, 2025.
9. Jane Mayer, "Pete Hegseth's Secret History," *New Yorker*, December 1, 2024.
10. Sharon LaFraniere and Julie Tate, "Pete Hegseth's Mother Accused Her Son of Mistreating Women for Years," *New York Times*, November 29, 2024.
11. LaFraniere and Tate, "Pete Hegseth's Mother Accused Her Son of Mistreating Women."
12. Jonathan Martin and Maggie Haberman, "How Kristi Noem, Mt. Rushmore and Trump Fueled Speculation About Pence's Job," *New York Times*, August 8, 2020.
13. Dominik Dausch, "'Solidarity': All 9 South Dakota Native American Tribes Endorse Kristi Noem's Banishment," *Argus Leader*, May 21, 2024.
14. Glen Moberg, "Duffy, Commentator Wife Analyze Trump's Campaign Surge," Wisconsin Public Radio, September 7, 2015.
15. Senator Markwayne Mullin, *Meet the Press*, NBC News, November 17, 2024.
16. Donald Trump (@realDonaldTrump), post on Truth Social, November 13, 2024.
17. Mike Davis (@mrddmia), post on X, November 6, 2024.
18. Eugene Daniels and Rachel Bade, "Playbook: Gaetz Pick Sends GOP into Panic," *Politico*, November 14, 2024.
19. Elon Musk (@elonmusk), post on X, November 19, 2024.
20. Donald Trump (@realDonaldTrump), post on Truth Social, November 21, 2024.
21. John Solomon, "Inquiry into Trump Lawyer's Consulting Push Risks Undercutting Signature 'Drain the Swamp' Pledge," *Just the News*, November 25, 2024.

CHAPTER SIXTEEN: WEAPONIZED

1. Erica Orden, "Before He Became Trump's Bulldog at DOJ, Emil Bove Was Nearly Demoted for Bellicose Management Style," *Politico*, February 23, 2025.
2. Joshua Goodman, Jim Mustian, and Eric Tucker, "Trump's Justice Department Enforcer Has Long Shrugged Off Criticism of Aggressive Style," Associated Press, February 24, 2025.
3. Jeremy Roebuck, Shayna Jacobs, Mark Berman, and Carol D. Leonnig, "Justice Officials Move to Drop Adams Case After 7 Lawyers Refuse, Resign in Protest," *Washington Post*, February 14, 2025.
4. Jonathan Karl, interview with Steve Bannon, February 2, 2025.

CHAPTER SEVENTEEN: RAGING FIRE

1. Joe Biden, "Speech Before the National Educational Association," September 23, 2024.

2. John Bat, "Biden: I Would Have 'Beat the Hell Out' of Trump for Comments About Women," CBS News, March 21, 2018.
3. Samuel Chamberlain and Diana Glebova, "Biden Congratulates Trump, Tells Him 'Welcome Back' to White House in Historic Meeting," *New York Post*, November 13, 2024.
4. Ahmad Austin Jr., "Charlamagne Stunned by Biden Welcoming Trump Back to White House: 'What Happened to the Fascist Talk?'" *Daily Beast*, November 14, 2024.
5. Mark Elibert, "Charlamagne tha God Blames Biden for Trump Re-Election," *Complex*, November 6, 2024.
6. Josh Barro, "This Is All Biden's Fault," *New York Times*, November 9, 2024.
7. Tyler Austin Harper, "Blame Biden," *The Atlantic*, November 6, 2024.
8. Franklin Foer, "Why Biden's Team Thinks Harris Lost," *The Atlantic*, November 7, 2024.
9. Lulu Garcia-Navarro, "The Interview: Nancy Pelosi Insists the Election Was Not a Rebuke of the Democrats," *New York Times*, November 9, 2024.
10. Elise A. Spenner, "Mike Donilon Says Democratic Party 'Melted Down' After Biden's June Debate at IOP," *Harvard Crimson*, February 15, 2025.
11. Alexandra Hutzler, Oren Oppenheim, and Brittany Shepherd, "Biden, on 'The View,' Takes Blame for Trump's Win and Rejects Reports of Cognitive Decline," ABC News, May 8, 2025.
12. Jacqueline Alemany, Emma Brown, Tom Hamburger, and Jon Swaine, "Ahead of Jan. 6, Willard Hotel in Downtown D.C. Was a Trump Team 'Command Center' for Effort to Deny Biden the Presidency," *Washington Post*, October 23, 2021.
13. Tyler Pager, "Joe Biden's Lonely Battle to Sell His Vision of American Democracy," *Washington Post*, December 28, 2024.
14. Maya C. Miller, "Democrats Sharply Criticize Biden's Pardon of His Son," *New York Times*, December 2, 2024.
15. Michael Bennet (@SenatorBennet), post on X, December 2, 2024.

CHAPTER EIGHTEEN: COME RETRIBUTION

1. "Procession to the Capitol," Joint Congressional Committee on Inaugural Ceremonies.
2. Bob Woodward and Robert Costa, *Peril* (Simon & Schuster, 2021), page 129.
3. Donald Trum(@realDonaldTrump), post on Truth Social, September 23, 2024.
4. Kristen Welcker (@kwelkernbc), post on X, January 20, 2025.
5. Hafiz Rashid, "Steve Bannon Joins War Against Elon Musk as MAGA Implodes," *New Republic*, December 27, 2024.
6. Jonathan Karl, interview with Steve Bannon, *This Week with George Stephanopoulos*, ABC News, January 19, 2025.
7. Kate Ackley, "Amazon, Other PACs Resume Donations to Electoral Objectors," *Roll Call*, November 3, 2022.
8. Will Lewis, "On Political Endorsement," *Washington Post*, October 25, 2024.
9. Manuel Roig-Franzia, "Post Owner Bezos Defends Endorsement Decision," *Washington Post*, October 28, 2024.

10. Jeff Bezos (@JeffBezos), post on X, November 6, 2024.
11. Donald Trump, *Save America* (Winning Team, 2024).
12. Lara Korte, "Zuckerberg Says He Regrets Caving to White House Pressure on Content," *Politico*, August 26, 2024.
13. Annie Linskey and Rebecca Ballhaus, "Meta to Pay $25 Million to Settle 2021 Trump Lawsuit," *Wall Street Journal*, January 29, 2024.
14. Dana Mattioli, Rebecca Ballhaus, and Josh Dawsey, "Inside Mark Zuckerberg's Failed Negotiations to End Antitrust Case," *Wall Street Journal*, April 15, 2024.
15. Ben Schreckinger, "DOJ Looked at Transactions Linked to Jim Biden as Part of Criminal Investigation," *Politico*, March 26, 2024.
16. Donald Trump (@realDonaldTrump), post on Truth Social, March 17, 2025.
17. Rachel Scott, "Trump to ABC's Rachel Scott: Inaugural Address Themes Will Be 'Unity, Strength and Fairness,'" ABC News, January 19, 2025.
18. Shannon Bream interview with JD Vance, *Fox News Sunday*, Fox News, January 12, 2025.
19. Keith and Kevin Hodge (@hodgetwins), post on X, January 12, 2025.
20. JD Vance (@JDVance), post on X, January 12, 2025.
21. International Association of the Chiefs of Police and the Fraternal Order of Police, Joint IACP-FOP Statement on the Recent Presidential Pardons, January 21, 2025.
22. Sally Krutzig, "'Trying to Rewrite History': Boise Woman Guilty in Capitol Riot Rejects Trump Pardon," *Idaho Statesman*, January 22, 2025.

POSTSCRIPT: THE NEW ERA

1. Konstantin Toropin and Steve Beynon, "Bragg Soldiers Who Cheered Trump's Political Attacks While in Uniform Were Checked for Allegiance, Appearance," military.com, June 11, 2025.
2. Anne Flaherty, "Trump Merchandise Sold at Fort Bragg for President's Speech Now Under Review," abcnews.com, June 12, 2025.
3. Konstantin Toropin and Steve Beynon, "Bragg Soldiers Who Cheered Trump's Political Attacks While in Uniform Were Checked for Allegiance, Appearance," military.com, June 11, 2025.
4. Ivan Saric, "Milley Appears to Call Trump 'Wannabe Dictator' in Exit Speech," *Axios*, September 29, 2021.
5. Donald Trump (@realdonaldtrump) on Truth Social, May 26, 2025.

INDEX

INDEX

INDEX

INDEX

INDEX

INDEX

INDEX

INDEX

INDEX

INDEX

INDEX

ABOUT THE AUTHOR

Jonathan Karl is the chief Washington correspondent for ABC News and co-anchor of *This Week*. Karl has asked questions of seven American president and covered every major beat in Washington, DC, including the White House, Capitol Hill, the Pentagon, and the State Department. A former president of the White House Correspondents' Association, Karl is the author of three *New York Times* bestsellers: *Front Row at the Trump Show*, *Betrayal*, and *Tired of Winning*.